本丛书出版得到广东省高水平大学重点学科建设项目支持

系统功能语言学文献丛书

丛书主编：彭宣维 黄国文

语篇·语法·认知

——话语分析面面观

DISCOURSE, GRAMMAR and COGNITION

Aspects of Discourse Analysis

任绍曾 ◉ 著

上海外语教育出版社
外教社 SHANGHAI FOREIGN LANGUAGE EDUCATION PRESS
www.sflep.com

图书在版编目（CIP）数据

语篇·语法·认知：话语分析面面观 / 任绍曾著.
—上海：上海外语教育出版社，2019（2022重印）
（系统功能语言学文献丛书）
ISBN 978-7-5446-6023-5

Ⅰ.①语… Ⅱ.①任… Ⅲ.①语言学－研究 Ⅳ.①H0

中国版本图书馆CIP数据核字（2019）第216961号

出版发行：上海外语教育出版社
（上海外国语大学内） 邮编：200083
电　　话：021-65425300（总机）
电子邮箱：bookinfo@sflep.com.cn
网　　址：http://www.sflep.com
责任编辑：李健儿

印　　刷：上海信老印刷厂
开　　本：635×965 1/16 印张 27 字数 428千字
版　　次：2020 年 4月第 1版　2022 年 7月第 2次印刷

书　　号：ISBN 978-7-5446-6023-5
定　　价：85.00 元

系统功能语言学文献丛书

编委会名单

总　序

彭宣维　黄国文

初学者对文献的重要性往往缺乏足够的认识，想写文章的时候绞尽脑汁却一筹莫展，勉强凑一个东西出来却不入流：缺乏研究背景，缺乏研究问题，缺乏研究方法，缺乏创新观点，缺乏学科用语，缺乏组织策略，也缺乏格式规范。

确定一个研究方向，可先从汉语文献中选择自己感兴趣的章节入手，再及英文著述，半年一年，便会有所心得；三年五载，自当独树一帜。实践表明，知识来源于文献，己见发端于文献，学科推进更是少不了文献。文献的重要性由此可见一斑。

为此，我们组织汇编了这套"系统功能语言学文献丛书"，方便后学查阅细读，揣摩审视。丛书中既有综述介绍，也有前沿研究；有独著，也有合作；作者之中，有德高望重的耄耋长者，有硕果累累的学派中坚，也有勤奋精进的青年才俊。我们想借此机会感谢各位师友积极配合。

本丛书的内容涉及系统功能语言学理论与应用的各个方面，既体现了各位学者在学术领域孜孜不倦的研究历程，也凝结了中国系统功能语言学团队的集体智慧，代表了中国学人在这一领域的研究水平。读者可以看到，其中有不少高水平的成果发表于国外知名期刊，走向了国际学科前沿；有理论开拓，也有应用尝试。

今后，除了国际化和理论探索，本土化与应用研究仍将是一个需要集体努力的基本方向。从理论上看，除了语篇语境、词汇研究和语音书写，研究者还需放眼其他学派和其他学科领域,协同求进,积极从议题上做超学科思考。我们希望,应用研究能够成为各位同仁的责任意识,在诸如翻译理论与操作框架、语言生态视角、外语教育学、汉语系统描写、辞书多元义项梳理、语言过程的计算表征、语言的生理神经机制、语言的脑成像实证研究、语言病理、国家话语等等领域,打开全新的研究局面,取得丰硕的研究成果。

我们衷心感谢上海外语教育出版社对本丛书出版的鼎力支持,感谢各位责编的精心付出。

目　　录

第二部分　叙事语篇分析

第三部分 语 法 与 语 篇

第四部分 语篇与认知

Table of Contents

Part Four Discourse and Cognition

图表目录

前　言

本书讨论语篇分析(Discourse Analysis)。语篇,也称为话语,是指实际使用的口头或书面的语言,属于索绪尔语言理论的言语。语言和言语是相互依存的。语言使用必须遵守语言系统提供的准绳,否则语言使用的双方相互不能理解。正因为如此,语篇分析必须以说明语言系统的语法理论为基础,否则不成其为语言学意义上的语篇分析。语篇分析的目的在于说明语篇是如何表达其实际表达的意义的。语篇是语义单位,其语义由词汇语法体现,而语篇又体现它所处的语境。

语篇分析主要关注语篇结构和语篇理解。语篇结构可以从语义维度上考察,也可以从结构层次上分析。第 1、第 2 章是对这两个问题的探讨。语篇分析中语篇单位的层次,信息单位的构成都是带根本性的问题。第 3、第 4 章根据切夫有关意识的理论提出了介乎段落与小句之间的基本主题,并将二分信息和三分信息从理论上加以阐释和协调,以期有助于语篇进展的分析。这些都是语篇分析的理论问题。

语篇之所以成为语篇是因为它体现了它所处的语境。就其内部而言,语篇必须衔接,而且在此基础上还必须连贯,从而获得组篇(texture)和结构(structure)。第 5 - 7 章就是以叙事小说《夜幕下的大军》为语料探讨这些问题。对具体语篇的理解,要依靠语境,而书面语篇往往会提供语境线索,借助这些线索可以准确了解语篇意义。语篇中语句结构的型式化可以表达深层意义,要了解语篇的主题,需要搜索和分析语篇中主要的型式化,这是分析和了解语篇主题的有效途径。第 8、第 9 章是对这些论题的讨论。这五章都涉及对叙事语篇的分析。

语篇是语义单位,而语篇的语义要由词汇语法体现。了解语篇语义,要分析语篇的语言特征;而作为语义单位的语篇又会对语法结构提出要求。不同语言的语篇对意义近似的结构会有自己的选择。第 10、第 11 两章讨论这两个问题。在体现语义时,语法的结构和语法范畴都起作用。小句由名词词组和动词词组构成。名词词组可用于指称,因而具有其语篇功能。动词时态的语义特征也赋予它相应的语篇功能。第 12、第 13 章是这方面的探讨。具有自身特征的语言单位,如辅句(minor clause)——Yes 和 No,也能体现语篇语义,具有独特的语篇功能。这是第 14、第 15 章试图解决的问题。这几章都涉及语法和语篇的关系。

在语言使用中,当人们谈论抽象概念时,就会借助隐喻。文学语篇的主题往往由隐喻表达。这种隐喻有时是显性的,有时是隐性的。通常隐喻的源域比较明显,而目的域需要在语篇人物的生活经历中寻找线索,通过细致的语言分析和认知分析才能发现两者的映射。隐喻是概念系统的成分,是对现实的一种识解,是表达意义的一种手段,所以语篇隐喻,特别是隐性语篇隐喻,要由语言系统的语篇加以体现,但隐喻又引导语篇进展,促进语篇连贯、表达语篇主题,两者相互作用,相互依存。最后五章的语料涉及小说、短篇小说、散文和诗歌,集中讨论语篇和认知的关系。

所选 20 篇论文大体上按时间顺序排列。前期的论文大多是从系统功能语言学视角出发的讨论。随着学术视野的拓展,我认识到语言使用涉及社会过程和个人过程,涉及客观因素和主观因素,因此要对语篇进行综合处理,也就是说除了用功能语言学理论分析语篇的社会功能外,还需要其他理论,比如认知语言学、评价理论等分析个人对客观现实的识解或评价,才能比较全面地说明语言是如何用以表达意义的。认知语言学就其性质而言也是功能的,因其与语用学、社会语言学一样,也是说明语言使用的,这一点上与功能语言学一致。所以,后期的论文皆是从认知功能视角的探讨。

这 20 篇论文都已发表,其中有 6 篇用英文撰写,第 10—11、第 19—20 这四篇是国际研讨会的发言,分别为 1994 年 Georgetown University Round Table on Language and Linguistics、1997 年澳门大学国际话语分析研讨会、2009 年上海外国语大学第一届国际文体学研讨会和 2011 年宁波大学第二届国际文体学研讨会上的发言;第 6、第 7 篇是有著名功能语言学家出席的早期话语分析研讨会和功能语言学研讨会上的发言,后收入各次研讨会的论文集,第 20 篇发表于《外国语》,现结集于此,是希望能有利于交流。顺便提一下,在 20 世纪七八十年代,话语分析的研究初期大家都用"话语";到了 90 年代中期,学者们经过讨论决定使用"语篇"。其实两者都指实际使用的语言。这里早期文章中的"话语"就不作更动了。

诚为抛砖引玉,切望方家指正。

任绍曾

2017 年 9 月 10 日

第一部分

语篇理论探索

Part One

EXPLORATIONS IN DISCOURSE THEORIES

1

语篇的多维分析*

1.1 引　言

语篇是多功能的构建体。语篇的多功能决定了语篇的多维特征。本章拟从语篇的多维性出发,探讨语篇的多维分析,即从语篇的不同维度对语篇做出系统的分析。

1.1.1 什么是语篇?

迈克尔·霍伊(Michael Hoey)有一个很朴实的解说:"不论什么人提了个问题,别人加以回答,他们就共同创建一个语篇。同样,不论什么人给别人写信或为一个研讨会撰写论文,他们也是在创造语篇,虽然直到收信人收到这封信,与会者听到论文报告,并加以解释时语篇才算完成"(Hoey 1991b: 65)。霍伊的这一解说首先表明不论是问话人还是听话人,写信人还是收信人,论文的撰写者还是研讨会的参与者都在使用语言。

* 本章原载《外国语》2003 年第 3 期第 35—42 页,列为本章时稍有改动。

他们使用语言创造语篇或者理解语篇。写信人提供信息,也可能索取信息;收信人接受信息,或准备提供信息。论文报告人与与会者分享研究中的发现;听报告者则获得了知识或信息。他们实际上是在从事一种语言行为(act),更确切地说,是在进行一种社会互动(interact),而语篇体现了互动的过程,又是互动的结果。霍伊说收信人收到了信,与会者听到了论文报告并作了解释,语篇的构建才算完成。他强调了语篇的社会互动性。语篇在参与者之间的互动未完成之前还不能算完全意义上的语篇。思雷戈尔德指出:作为思想体系和信念系统的意识形态无所不在。人们在使用语言交际时,总是通过语言传达某种信念,在某种社会互动的背后总有一种意识形态在起作用(Threadgold 1986:16)。范戴克明确指出语篇有三个主要维度,即语言使用、信念的传递(认知)和社会情景中的互动(van Dijk 1997:2)。这可以作为对霍伊关于语篇说明的理论概括。韩礼德说在正常的生活当中,我们每天,而且成天通过语言与别人互动,我们在两个方向上进行推理,即从情景到语篇和从语篇到情景的推理(Halliday & Hasan 1989:36)。这里韩礼德也提示了语篇的三个维度。"通过语言"当指语言使用维度;"进行互动"当指社会情景中的互动这一维度;"推理"则指语言使用过程中智力的参与,指认知过程。通过推理人们获得信息,了解信念。这涉及信念传递维度。

1.1.2 语篇分析关注意义

语篇分析所关注的是语篇的意义,是语篇如何表达意义,又为何这样表达意义。范戴克是这样说的:语言使用者和分析者都关注意义(van Dijk 1997:31)。在他们理解和分析的时候他们都要问诸如此类的问题:这是什么意思?在现在的语境中这如何才具有意义?语篇是语义单位,而语义总是由词汇语法体现的。因此,语篇分析必须结合词汇语法,必须结合语言体系,否则,所作的分析只能是兴致所至、随意的、零星的评述,不可能揭示语篇的本质特征,说明不了语篇是如何表达意义以及为何如此表达意义的。语篇的意义源于语篇在其中展开的语境,因此对语篇的分析,对语篇不同维度的分析必须结合语境。韩礼德区分两种语境,即情景语境和文化语境(Halliday & Hasan 1989:49)。情景语境指确定语域的语场、语旨和语式的配置;文化语境,有时他称作社会语境,指赋予语篇以价值和制约语篇理解的机构性和意识形态性的背景。这里韩礼德区分了机构性背景和意识形态性背景,由于这两种背景对语篇的作用不同,我们把机构性背景称为社会语景,意识形态性背景称为文化语景。马丁也把意识形态作为语境中的一个单独的层面(Martin 1992: 496)。与语境有辩证关系的语篇既然有三个维度,我们就可以对语篇作多维分析。语篇的三个维度反映了语篇生成和理解所涉及的三个方面——语言、社会和认知。对语篇的多维分析就是从这三个角度考察语篇。

1.2 语言使用

1.2.1 多功能的构建体

把语篇作为语言使用加以分析首先要把语篇看作多功能的构建体,也就是说是体现意念功能、人际功能和语篇功能的构建体,那就要考察体现这三种元功能的语法结构,即及物性结构、语气结构和主位结构。这三种结构在小句中重叠,是语篇语法的基础,是语篇分析的基础。如果语篇是由一个小句构成,那么结合语境分析这三种结构就足以了解语篇如何表达意义。然而,尽管语篇不是一个量的概念,小至一个词,大至多卷本的巨著,都可视为一个语篇,但在大多数情况下是超句的、易于操作的语言块。那么我们的任务就在于考察磋商(negotiation)、识辨(identification)、连接(conjunction)和意念(ideation)四个语篇系统(Martin 1992: 26)怎样与语篇的人际、语篇、逻辑以及经验元功能相结合,如何与语法的基本结构相互作用,从而了解语篇是如何编织起来的(texture)。我们还可以从语境和语篇关系的角度分析语言使用。语篇之所以是语篇是因为它有内在的连接性(internal relatedness),这就要求我们考察语篇中句与句、段与段之间是如何衔接的。语篇之所以是语篇更重要的是因为它具有外在的连接性(external relatedness)。这就要求我们考察语篇如何体现语境中语场、语旨和语式的配置，考察语篇的连贯，考察语篇的结构。衔接的手段有结构性的和非结构性的，但都跟语义有关。连贯是指语义的连贯，语篇结构是指语义结构，所以这些分析都离不开智力的参与，离不开推理。阿瑟等指出，推理有两种，即连篇推理和篇外推理（Arthur et al. 1997：309）。连篇推理明确两个或更多命题在理性认识上是如何连接的。篇外推理则调用世界知识或从世界知识中衍生出来的信息给情景模式充实细节。这说明在分析语篇的内在连接性，即衔接时，我们要做连篇推理，在分析语篇的外在连接性，即连贯时，我们要做篇外推理。这两种推理，特别是篇外推理必须结合语境，否则无从了解语篇是否连贯。可见在作语言使用的分析时还得结合语篇的社会和认知维度。

1.2.2 三层次意义

在分析语篇结构时，可供参考的理论有韩茹凯的语类结构潜势理论（Halliday & Hasan 1989）、范戴克关于语篇微观结构和宏观结构的理论（van Dijk 1977）、马蒂森和汤普森的修辞结构理论等等（Matthiessen & Thompson 1988）。马丁（Martin 1992）把韩礼德的已知信息-新信息结构思想应用于整个语篇，区分了小句主位、语段主位和宏观主位，同时区分小句新信息、语段新信息和宏观新信息（Halliday & Hasan 1989）；他指出这三个层次的新信息集中了逐渐积累的意义，以阐明语篇的语场（Martin 1992：456）。这说明这类结构分析只能引出语篇反映现实的经验意义，说明语篇反映了怎样的社会行为，有怎样的参加者参与其中。语篇分析往往仅对这一层面的意义作语言分析。事实上，语篇不仅具有明晰的经验意义，而且作为社会实践，语篇具有社会意义，还具有体现语篇意图的隐含意义，即主题。这两层语篇意义也有各自的语言体现。这当然也属于语言使用这一维度的分析内容。究竟有怎样的语言体现，该如何分析，下面再作交代。

1.2.3 超越三种基本结构的分析

语篇系统是指体现元功能意义的纵向系统，包含结构和非结构的资源,因而必然包括语法的基本结构;语篇结构的分析又总是以语法结构为基础。一个值得思考的问题是:就语言分析而言,对语篇中若干小句的及物性结构、语气结构和主位结构的分析是否足以揭示语篇的意义?从韩礼德对本·约翰逊(Ben Johnson)的"To Celia"的分析来看,答案基本上是肯定的。但是仔细琢磨韩礼德对这首诗的分析我们就会发现韩礼德并没有囿于这三种结构的分析。在分析及物性结构的基础上,韩礼德揭示了经验意义;接着他说,"很显然我们还必须对此加上若干成分,使我们进入一个想象的或者间接的表现经验的领域"(Halliday & Hasan 1989: 19)。这里他所说的"想象的或者间接的表现经验的领域"是指认知领域,实际是指对语法隐喻的分析,如对 kiss 一词隐喻性转化的分析。在"Or leave a kiss in the cup, I'll not ask for wine"这行诗中 kiss 作为名词已经是比喻性的,因为 kiss 是过程的名称,而不是物件的名称,但这已经成了英语固有的比喻性转化。既然名词通常是物件的名称,而物件是可以随意放置的,所以可以说"leave a kiss in the cup",kiss 这样又经历了第二步隐喻转化。又如他指出,表面的 request plus offer 应理解为"offer conditional on acceptance of offer",对人际隐喻作了分析。韩礼德虽然对两行诗作了三种结构的分析,但分析的内容表明他实际说明的是隐喻如何赋予这首诗以意义。值得注意的是,韩礼德并没有把隐喻句纳入三种结构的分析,而是作为结构分析基础上的进一步探讨。隐喻,包括语法隐喻,是俯拾皆是的重要语言资源,诗歌中更是如此。其实,这句诗中的 wine 也有其隐喻意义。我们借以思考和行动的一般概念系统从根本上说具有隐喻的性质(Lakoff & Johnson 1980: 3)。难怪此书的作者用"赖以生存"来修饰"隐喻"作为书名。韩礼德在分析中当然也不会忽略他称之为"别出心裁"的隐喻。马丁指出:语法隐喻涉及名词化,而名词化是现代英语中语法隐喻的主导语义流向(Martin 1992: 406)。鉴于名词从根本上说是经验语法的产物,这就使得一切意义向经验意义倾斜。把意义视为物意味着把语篇视为一个物质个体——作为社会现实的物质部分,与此同时,又在构建(意念意义)和介入(人际意义)。无论是从概念出发,把语言中的隐喻看成是具有隐喻性概念的体现,还是从语言出发,把语言看成是解释经验的符号体系,而隐喻是其中的一种工作机制,人们都认识到隐喻和语法隐喻在反映现实中的重要性和普遍性,把语篇作为语言使用分析时当然不容忽视。韩礼德分析中另一个令人注目的地方是他分析了句子型式 you do

(x) and I will do (y),而且注意到了这个句型的重复。此外,他还注意到了诗行之间语法、语义的对称。句型的重复和对称构成型式化(patterning),而型式化是表达语篇深层意义、实现语篇目的的一个重要手段。以上提到的隐喻分析和型式化的分析都已超出了三种基本结构的分析。所以,在我们将语篇作为语言使用分析时,也不能囿于三种基本结构,必须探讨贯穿整个语篇的其他语言特征,作为对语法结构分析的补充。

1.3 社会互动

1.3.1 语篇的互动性

人们使用语言交际时,语篇成了一种社会行为,或社会行为的一部分,实际上是在社会文化语境中的一种社会实践,因而具有互动性。不仅对话、书信往来是一种互动,即使是个人札记也具有互动性。在谈到个人札记时,叶斯柏森指出,"你是你自己,在你阅读自己的札记时,你同时又是另一个人"(Jespersen 1925:6)。札记如此,日记也是如此。今日的你和往日的你在交流。语篇既是社会互动,就有互动的双方,即社会互动的参与者。参与者说什么话,做什么事,就是什么样的人。街头巷尾吆喝商品的人是小贩,会议厅里宣布开会的是主持人。语篇形成了参与者的社会身份,实际上是社会活动,兜售商品和宣布开会的活动,确定了社会互动参与者的社会身份。上述互动的另一方分别是兜售对象,即路人——潜在的顾客和会议的参加者。社会活动总是制度化的(institutionalized)。参与者不仅作为个人参与社会活动,而且作为某个团体、机构或文化的一员参与活动。通过语篇互动双方在展现、确认或挑战更为广泛的社会结构和政治结构(Halliday & Hasan 1989:30)。在购物的情景中,顾客和店主的社会角色是由商品生产、销售这一社会过程以及产生商品销售的社会结构确定的,同时他们又在展现以商品经济为特点的社会结构。没有商品销售以及推动商品生产和销售的社会结构,就没有顾客和店主,也就没有他们之间的买卖关系。可见互动双方的社会角色以及他们之间的关系是社会活动的性质确定的,而这种社会角色及他们之间的关系又是社会结构的表现。我们把社会互动这一社会过程与社会结构联系起来加以考察,便可以了解语篇作为互动的社会意义。

1.3.2 人际关系

把语篇作为社会互动加以分析当然要考虑社会互动参与者之间的人际关系,这包括说话人和听话人、作者与读者等等之间的关系,也包括书面语篇中人物之间的人际关系。语篇的社会意义首先反映在这各种错综复杂的人际关系上,因此语言上首先由语气结构体现。但是语篇的社会意义并不能由语气结构充分体现。马丁指出,韩礼德对语气结构的分析不能涵盖由整个小句表现的否定态度,如这样的句子:That stupid bloody cretin is really giving me the bloody shits(Martin 1992)。作为主语的名词词组中修饰语 stupid、bloody 和名词 cretin 都带有贬义,剩余部分的隐喻性动词词组“giving ... the bloody shits”也带有贬义,所以全句表现了说话人的否定态度。马丁采用韵律分析的方法给韩礼德的语气分析增加了“否定态度”(Martin 1992:11)。

1.3.3 评价系统

在此,马丁关于评价系统的思考已略见端倪。评价系统是对韩礼德语篇语法系统的补充。评价系统的中心是“态度”,而“态度”的中心是“情感”。就语言体现而言,不仅名词、形容词、副词可用以评价,动词也可用以评价。试比较:She *rushed* into the middle of the ball-room and *shouted* ...和 She *went* into the middle of the ball-room and *spoke* ... 用 went 替代 rushed,spoke 替代 shouted,我们就会觉得少了一点意义,而这个意义增强了语势,但同时又是作者对 she 的迫不及待的心情的态度,是人际意义的一部分。这可以说明评价系统是体现人际意义的重要资源系统。詹姆斯·保罗·吉认为,社会语言有自己的语法,但必须区分两种语法,他称为“语法 1”和“语法 2”(Gee 2000:29)。语法 1 指学校语法,语法

2指名词、动词、短语、小句等语法单位构成的可以表明情景、身份和特定活动的型式(pattern),是语法单位搭配的型式,也与非语言因素相互协调。吉并没有展开,但从他的例句中可以看出他指的是什么:What an ass that guy was, you know, her boyfriend。ass和guy是非正式用语,that guy所指含糊,多少有些轻慢,you know是非正式的插入语,her boyfriend则是非正式的右脱位(right dislocation)。所有这些非正式的词语和语法手段相互搭配,共同说明这句话是非正式的社会语言,用意是表示交际双方关系密切。看来吉要说明的不仅是词(马丁主要关注词的评价),而且还有插入语、右脱位等语法结构可以表示语体特征,说明人际关系中的社会距离。如果我们把吉的语法1看成是表示基本意义的语法,语法2是表示附加意义的语法,那么我们可以把韩礼德的语篇语法视为语法1,由于评价系统可以表示褒贬、正反、好恶、亲疏、强弱等态度意义,可以和吉的语法2一并归入语法2。把语篇作为社会互动分析以研究这两种语法如何体现人际关系和社会意义。

体现人际关系的语言手段还不仅于此。特定语类的人际关系有其特定的语言体现。李战子2000年的研究表明在自传语类中,认知情态表达式、人称代词、特别是第二人称代词you、现在时、直接语篇和反身表达式是体现人际关系的主要手段。实际上从语言的功能看,人们使用语言不是为了报告什么,交代什么,而是为了满足社交的渴望。人们借助语言相互接触,语言是把人与人、思想与思想连接在一起的高尚工具(Jespersen 1960: 844)。人际功能是应用广泛、充满活力的功能。在社会交往中人际意义非常丰富,它随语境的变化、语篇目的变化而变化。把语篇作为社会互动分析,探究语篇的社会意义,这方面还有许多问题尚待探讨。

1.4 信念传递

1.4.1 认知语境

范戴克在“信念传递”后面附加了一个注释“认知”,说明信念传递与认知有关,实际上是一个认知过程。信念或信念体系是意识形态的一部分。在讨论如何将语篇作为信念传递分析之前让我们再看一下语境。第1.1 节已经交代,语境可分为情景语境、社会语境和文化语境。从另一个角度看,情景语境和社会语境构成实际语境,作为意识形态的文化语境则属于认知语境。然而实际语境在它和语篇相互作用的时候,起作用的并不是客观存在的语境,而是通过感知由映在人们脑子里的实际语境的图象形成的认知表征,是内在化、认知化的实际语境,即认知语境。对同一个实际语境,不同的人可能有不同的印象。同样的咖啡厅,有人认为灯光柔和,有人认为昏暗;对那种"重金属"电子摇滚乐有人认为非常刺激,有人则认为吵闹不堪。经验不同,知识结构不同,感受不同,信念不同,对实际语境的印象就不同,认知语境就不同。在语言使用中经常起作用的是认知语境。难怪范戴克对熊学亮说,"语境就在你的脑子里"(熊学亮 1999: 115)。对于书面语篇,韩礼德是这样说的:有些语篇——明显的实例是文学语篇——其中除了我们作为读者这外部情景外,没有其他情景,我们必须从语篇的阅读中建构内在情景(inner situation)(Halliday & Hasan 1989: 36)。这内在情景是从语篇中推导出来的。阿瑟等(Arthur et al. 1997: 293)认为,这推导过程是一个认知过程,包括从头脑中的词汇目录中检索词汇,激发长期记忆中的概念,搜索信息,比较工作记忆中可找到的结构,然后通过增删、重组和连接信息建立结构,从而建立认知表征。可见从语篇中推导出来的语境是我们依靠知识推导出来的认知语境。从语境到语篇的推导和从语篇到语境的推导都必须通过认知。范戴克(van Dijk 1997: 31)说,实际上在许多方面,认知是语篇和社会的界面。语篇传递信念,把语篇作为信念传递加以分析都涉及认知。分析信念传递实际是分析这一认知过程,所以必然涉及认知语境。

1.4.2 意识形态

在语言使用中,意识形态无所不在。吉说当我们说话或写话时,我们总是对"世界"采取一个特定的看法(Gee 2000: 2)。当语言使用成为一种社会行为或社会行为一部分的时候,意识形态也会有其表现。韩茹凯说,在鼓励顾客多购货物的背后是企业"自由经营"的意识形态(Halliday

& Hasan 1989：60）。我们不妨先看词。词的选择反映意识形态，反映信念。持一种信念的人认为是强盗的人，持另一种信念的人则认为是好汉，他们根据各自的信念选择“强盗”和“好汉”。命题也反映信念。例如，“这件事可以完结了”“这件事可以了结了”，显然后一句的说话人从自己的信念出发对这件事持否定的态度。从这个例子也可以看出，评价系统在评价词汇意义的同时也在评价词汇背后的意识形态。态度出自信念，信念系统是意识形态的一部分，而意识形态是认知语境的一部分。可见信念的传递是渗透在语言使用中的。

1.4.3 深层意义

语篇的必要条件之一是目的性（intentionality）（魏真道 2002：13）。语篇的目的往往是传达一个信念、一个寓意，通常称为主题。这是整个语篇所要传递的信息和信念。韩茹凯说，主题是语言艺术最深层的意义，它是从语篇的具体特征中抽象出来的，是语篇目的之所在。就其性质而言，近乎一种概括（Halliday & Hasan 1989：97）。韩茹凯还说，语言艺术有两个指号过程（semiosis）。第一个指号过程是使用作为符号系统的自然语言的结果；第二个指号过程是通过第一层次意义的前景化和型式化而建立的艺术系统的产物。韩茹凯所说的“具体语言特征”是指第一指号过程中使用的自然语言的个别成分，当其中的若干成分形成第二指号过程时，他们就和具体语境脱离，构成第二层次符号系统，赋予语篇以深层意义。在说明一个意大利年轻女子史地知识贫乏时，作者用了 the New World/a new world、was discovered/has been discovered、Christopher Columbus/a certain Christopher Columbus。其中 the/a、was/has been、zero/a certain 的对比构成型式化，作为第二层次符号系统。海明威在《士兵之家》（*Solder's Home*）中则用了“He did not want to get into the intrigue and the politics”“He did not want to have to do any courting”“He did not want to tell any more lies”“He did not want any consequences”“He did not want any consequences ever again”等。否定句的接二连三的反复使用构成了型式化，说明主人公战后意志消沉，从而传达了反战的主题。请注意，前一例主题的意义不是来自这些语言成分——new world、Christopher

Columbus、be discovered，而是来自有定和无定的对比，一般时和完成时的对比；后一例主题的意义不是来自这些否定句的命题意义，而是来自否定句的多次重复。对比和重复成了构成型式化、构成第二符号系统的重要手段。但是型式化并不限于结构的重复和对比，有时可以通过词汇的重复、概念的重复，甚至命题的重复构成型式化，体现主题。这时往往是利用隐喻传达语篇的主要信息和信息背后的某种信念，参见本书第9章。语篇有前景和背景部分。构成型式化的语篇部分是提示语篇意图的部分，因而是语篇前景化部分。

韩茹凯指出主题近乎一种概括。概括是一个推理过程，而推理过程需要依靠语境。从语篇中推导主题需要依靠认知语境，即依靠知识。宏观图式包括若干通用世界知识组件（packages），如人物定型（person stereotypes）、物体概念（object concepts）和草图（scripts）。其中草图可以提供足以启动推理的世界知识（Arthur et al. 1997：296）。但知识需要语篇的语言成分激发。在主题的语义层上，推理依赖型式化。可见前景化的型式化是推导主题的语言基础，认知语境提供的知识是推导的依据（任绍曾 2000）。就一般推理过程而言，为了理解，人们需要选择合适的语境，而这个选择部分是由演绎机制的记忆内容、普遍短期记忆内容以及百科知识的内容确定的。在这些因素决定的若干语境中选择某一特定的语境则是由关联决定的（Sperber & Wilson 1986：141）。可见，通过推理理解主题、了解信念是一个复杂的认知过程。概括地说，为了理解语篇，人们要利用语篇成分、语境知识和信仰因素形成认知表征，从而理解信念，并根据听话人自己的信念系统，接受信念，修改信念或建立新的信念。如果说情景语境决定语篇的经验意义，社会语境决定语篇的社会意义，即韩礼德说的"机构性背景赋予语篇以价值"（Halliday & Hasan 1989），那么，语篇的深层意义，即主题以及由主题体现的信念则受文化语境的制约，即韩礼德说的"意识形态性背景制约语篇的理解"（同上）。综上所述，信念传递是语言使用中的认知过程，是认知语境起作用的过程。信念渗透在语言使用中，整个语篇传递的信念有它特定的语言体现。把语篇作为语言使用分析也应包括对这一层次符号系统的分析。

1.5 结 语

语篇具有多维性,本章从语言、社会和认知的角度对语篇的三维分析作了初步探讨。语言使用的分析不仅包括基本语法结构的分析,而且还应包括隐喻的分析;不仅分析经验意义的语言体现,而且应分析社会意义和主题的语言体现。社会互动作为社会过程应结合社会结构加以考察,从而了解语篇的社会意义。社会意义体现在各种人际意义上,而对人际意义的分析不应局限于语气结构的分析,评价系统是必要的补充。信念传递是认知过程,经常起作用的是认知语境。了解语篇的深层意义,即体现信念的主题,需要推理,而推理的语言基础是型式化,推理的依据是从认知语境中提取的知识。然而,语篇的三个维度是相互联系、相互影响的。语言使用的背后必有信念,而信念又影响词的选择、结构的使用;社会互动的性质要求使用相应的语言,而语言使用又会影响社会交往;社会互动有其目的,因而必有某种信念,出自信念的态度在社会互动中也必有表现,等等。这三个维度之间的相互影响是一个很有意义的课题,尚待进一步研究,如语言使用究竟如何影响信念传递和社会互动,社会互动又怎样影响语言使用和信念传递,信念传递又如何影响语言使用和社会互动。另一方面,着重某一个维度的分析应该有其价值,但置另外两个维度于不顾,恐怕不大可行。

2

叙事语篇的多层次语义结构*

2.1 引　言

在话语分析的领域中不乏描写语篇结构的理论，如叙事结构（Labov 1972）、语类结构潜势（Halliday & Hasan 1989）、微观结构和宏观结构（van Dijk 1977）、修辞结构（Matthiessen & Thompson 1988）等。这些理论一般都着眼于语篇的经验意义，对语篇作线形的描述，提出语义结构。据此，词在不同的语境里有不同的含义；句子有句义和含义之分，叙事语篇在一定的语境里自然有显性的直义和潜性的含义。经验告诉我们，叙事语篇，特别是文学叙事语篇，不仅讲述故事，而且具有社会意义和主题（theme）。本章试图从功能理论出发，通过对实际叙事语篇的分析来验证叙事语篇意义的这三个层次，说明这三个意义层次如何体现整体语境中的不同层次，如何与语境配置中的三个因素相对应，又如何为词汇语法特征所体现。下面先交代一下本章的理论依据和应用的材料。

---

* 本章原载《外语研究》2003 年第 1 期第 1—12 页，个别词句已作改动。

2.1.1 语境与语篇

韩礼德认为,语境和语篇具有辩证关系(Halliday & Hasan 1989: 47)。语境创造语篇,同样语篇也创造语境。语篇体现语言的元功能,而语言的元功能又与语境的因素一一对应;另一方面,语篇作为语义单位又为词汇语法所体现。韩礼德区分情景语境和社会语境。他对"社会(social)"有两个解释:一个解释把社会定义为社会系统,与"文化"同义,是一个意义系统。另一个解释特别着眼于语言和社会结构的关系,把社会结构看成是社会系统的一部分(Halliday & Hasan 1989: 4)。对于社会结构,韩茹凯结合买卖的实际情景说:买卖双方的角色和二人组合关系(dyad)是由社会活动(social activity)决定的,因此这角色和关系也就是社会结构的表现(Halliday & Hasan 1989: 57)。可见社会结构决定社会活动,决定语境,特别是语境中的人际关系。韩礼德有时也用文化语境这一术语代替社会语境。他对文化语境有一个简明扼要的说明:赋予语篇以语义价值、制约语篇解释的机构性(institutional)和意识形态性(ideological)背景(Halliday & Hasan 1989: 49)。这说明文化语境有机构性的和意识形态性的两个方面,共同构成情景语境的背景。本文把体现社会结构的机构性语境称为社会语境,由意识形态或信仰系统构成的语境称为文化语境。马丁鉴于意识形态对语篇的不同作用,也把意识形态看成语境的一个单独的层面(Martin 1992: 496)。关于意识形态,思雷戈尔德指出,在社会科学和人文科学的文献中,ideology 这个词有两个非常不同的用法(Threadgold 1986: 16)。本文取其第一种用法,把意识形态看作社会构建的思想体系。伦克马也把意识形态看成是关于社会关系的准则和价值体系(Renkema 1993: 146)。我们虽将社会语境和文化语境作为两个层面加以区分,但这两者是密切联系和相互影响的,而且这两个语境层面又和情景语境密切联系,构成与语篇相对应的总体语境。区别社会语境和文化语境有两个理由:表现为社会语境的社会结构是指与语言联系的社会部分,由语篇直接体现,因而决定语篇意义,而文化语境作为信仰系统或思想体系只影响社会行为,通过社会行为在语篇中体现,因此只制约语篇语义,而不决定语篇意义。第二个理由是语境可以从另一个角度区分为具体(physical)语境和认知(cognitive)语境。情景语境和社会语境是语篇所处的实际存在的

(material)语境,属于具体语境,由语场、语旨和语式三个语境因素组合而成;而文化语境则是涉及信仰、价值观、世界知识、意识形态等认知范畴的抽象语境,当属认知语境。然而,实际语境也涉及认知,因为具体的语境也是通过人们的感知而形成的对环境的心理表征或知识状态,所以认知语境实际上也包括具体语境,它是经验中实际语境的内在化、认知化。韩礼德说每一个语篇就是它自身的语境(Halliday & Hasan 1989: 48)。除了语篇可以提供上文为理解下文作为背景这一层含义外,还有另一层含义。他指出,有的语篇,文学语篇就是明显的例子,在阅读时,除了我们作为读者这一外部语境外,没有其他语境,所以我们必须完全从阅读语篇中构建内在语境(Halliday & Hasan 1989: 36)。这个内在语境只能是由语篇的语言激活知识草图,形成心理图式,根据读者的经验、记忆、知识等等来恢复和构建真实世界的事件、行为、人物及其角色关系和所处的具体环境,因而必然是一种认知语境。区分文化语境和社会语境、具体语境和认知语境可以较好地探讨叙事语篇的多层次语义。情景语境、社会语境和文化语境可用右图表示。

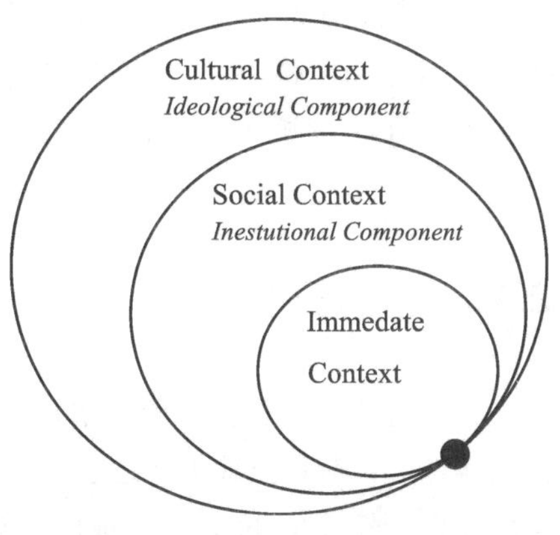

图 2-1　三层次语境示意图

这三个圆由小到大分别代表情景语境、社会语境和文化语境。三个圆切于一点,说明这三个语境构成一个整体语境作用于语篇。如图所示,情景语境的背后是社会语境,这两者的背后是文化语境。就对语篇的作用而言,情景语境最为直接,社会语境次之,使情景语境进一步语境化(recontextualizing),文化语境则作为背景,使具体语境进一步语境化。

2.1.2　叙事语篇

叙事的共同特征是描述事件从一个状态向另一个状态作时间上的推移(Ochs 1997: 189)。这是叙事语篇时间上的维度。叙事人之所以描述这个事件,是因为事件使他感到诧异、震惊、有趣,因而觉得值得叙述。叙事的另一方面是它的配置维度,即主题(mythos)或情节(plot),用以点明时间和感情如何交织成一个连贯的叙事。它把场景、人物、工具、行为和目的编织成一个连贯的图式,围绕一个非同一般、通常是令人不安的事件展开。它将一个问题置于一系列具有因果关系的事件及其环境之中,从而揭示这个问题。叙事有它的目的(point),常常是对一个事件、一个行为,或与若干事件有关的心理状态的道德评价(Ochs 1997: 193)。叙事是叙事人对过去的回忆,但他关心的是现在和将来(Ochs 1997: 191)。语篇之所以是语篇是因为除了衔接和连贯外,它还具有目的性(intentionality)和信息性(informativeness)(Renkema 1993: 34 – 40)。叙事语篇更是如此。我们在分析时将探索叙事语篇围绕怎样一个令人不安的事件展开,提出了怎样的问题,又作出怎样的道德评价。从语篇的角度,我们将探索语篇的内在联系和外在联系、语篇的目的和它要传达的信息。

2.1.3 话语分析

话语分析的任务在于研究语篇的意义。语篇既然是意义的单位,分析语篇当然应该分析语篇如何通过语言所提供的资源表达意义。马丁把他的话语分析著作 *English Text* 看成语篇语义学(Martin 1992: 1)。范戴克对话语分析的目的是这样说的,语言使用者和话语分析者都追求意义(van Dijk 1997: 31),在理解和分析时,他们会问这样一些问题:“这(她)在这儿是什么意思?”或者“在当前的语境中该怎样才能有意义?”“为什么这样说?为什么这样表达意义?”既然语篇有直义和含义,我们应当对不同层次的意义进行分析。至于如何分析,韩礼德说得很明确:未建立在语法上的话语分析根本不成其为话语分析,只不过是对语篇作流水账式的评述而已(Halliday 1994: xxi)。所以,对语篇的分析必须结合语言体系,结合词汇语法。

2.1.4 推　理

就语境和语篇的辩证关系而言,韩礼德指出,人们通过语言与人交往时,是在作双向推理,由语境推至语篇,由语篇推至语境(Halliday & Hasan

1989：36）。程雨民指出：语言的应用和理解，不论是直义的还是转义的，都需要智力的参与，也就是需要推理（1997：III）。在话语分析中，阿瑟等也指出，推理有两种，即连篇推理和篇外推理（Arthur et al. 1997：309）。连篇推理明确两个或更多的命题在概念上是如何连接的，篇外推理则调用世界知识或从世界知识中衍生出来的信息给情景模式充实细节。这说明直义和含义都需要推理。程雨民还指出，语言是用来指点信息的，也就是听话者从他的意义中推出当前语境下它所传达的信息（1997：3）。听话人结合情景，通过推理去领会那信息。如何推理？他说，语言知识给我们圈定了范围，世界知识给我们推理的前提，逻辑推理使我们得出必要的结论（程雨民 1997：35）。可见，推理须结合语境，借助世界知识，但也离不开语言材料，否则推理就没有依据，那就会产生任意性，推出来的结论也就难免武断，因而信息也不足信。在对叙事语篇进行分析时，基于语言材料上的推理是必不可少的。即使是篇外推理也离不开语言，也就是说，语篇每一个层次的意义都应该有具体的语言体现作为推理的基础。我们在分析中也将重视这一基本点。

2.1.5 材　料

本文仅对书面叙事语篇进行分析。所用的材料包括一篇用于快速阅读的短文"The New World"，以及海明威的中篇小说《士兵之家》（*Soldier's Home*）和诺曼·梅勒（Norman Mailer）的叙事小说《夜幕下的大军》（*The Armies of the Night*）。限于篇幅，我们主要对短文进行详细分析，说明叙事语篇三个意义层次，对于后两篇，我们着重于社会意义和主题的分析。现将短文按句编号如下：

[1] In the eighteenth century young ladies in Italy were taught reading, writing, music and arithmetic.

[2] But their knowledge of history and geography was very poor.

[3] Once the French Ambassador in Rome was giving a ball to which many important people were invited.

[4] The Italian Minister of Foreign Affairs came very late.

[5] A young lady, who was well acquainted with him, saw him enter the ball room and asked why he was so late.

[6] "You see," said the Minister, "there has been a little accident at the King's palace."

[7] The curious young lady asked the Minister to tell her what had happened at the King's palace.

[8] "Oh, nothing important," answered the Minister, "the Ambassador of Brazil, who was to be presented to the King, forgot to take his credentials with him and was obliged to go back to his hotel to bring them."

[9] If he had left them in Brazil we should have had to wait at least six months for them.

[10] "Is Brazil so far from Rome?" asked the lady.

[11] "It is in the New World," said the Minister.

[12] "In the New World?" repeated the lady in great astonishment.

[13] "Yes, in the New World," answered the Minister in a sarcastic tone, "which was discovered by Christopher Columbus."

[14] When the young lady heard this she rushed into the middle of the ball-room and shouted as loud as she could.

[15] "Ladies and Gentlemen, have you heard the latest news?

[16] A new world has been discovered by a certain Christopher Columbus."

2.2 三个意义层次

下面就这一短文作三个层次的意义分析。

2.2.1 轶 事

我们可以用本文开头提到的四种结构中的任何一种,或用韩礼德对

"To Celia"的分析方法,对语篇进行分析,即可了解语篇所叙述的社会事件(Halliday & Hasan 1989: 18-23)。作为多功能构建体(construct)的语篇,它的作用首先就是反映人们对客观世界的经验,也就是表述由若干过程构成的社会行为。语篇对客观世界的反映构成经验意义,我们简称为轶事(story)。对于这个短篇,我们可以逐句分析小句的及物性结构,从而了解语篇向我们叙述了什么社会事件。例如,句[1]含有物质过程 were taught,受益者(beneficiary)是 young ladies,中介物(medium)是几门课程。句[2]则含关系过程,将特征(attribute) poor 赋予 their knowledge of history and geography。这样我们了解到它们的命题意义或直义。但是要了解这两句对外部世界作了怎样的说明,我们还得推理。比如第一句中无动作者,但在瞬间即可完成的推理中我们可以推断出既有 were taught,当有教授者,无须交代。句[1]与句[2]有显性的逻辑关系,由 but 体现。但它们的意义联系还在于 their 回指 young ladies;句[1]所含的课程与句[2]不同,也形成对比。如果这样继续分析下去,我们便可了解语篇对客观世界作了怎样的反映。此外,我们还需要分析语气结构,以了解社会行为的参加者以及他们之间的关系,如分析 young lady 和 Minister 之间的对话。

从语篇创造语境的角度看,句[1]、句[2]为读者提供了实际语境:时间、地点和人物,可以称之为背景(setting)或指向(orientation)。阅读叙事语篇,读者总是要从语篇中推导出语境,即从语篇的语言所激发的图象、概念、结构等认知因素,依靠世界知识在脑子里形成认知语境。这是人们了解直接语境以外的事件、事态、行为的途径。从句[3]开始叙事人向读者提供情景语境:一次有许多要人参加的社交舞会,所发生的事件是一位意大利年轻女士(下简称为 YL)和意大利外交部长(下简称为 FM)的对话以及 YL 向与会者宣布"最新消息"。词汇是反映客观世界的重要手段。我们不妨汇总主要词汇现象集中分析。语篇有五个词汇链。它们是:(1) Young ladies — a young lady — the curious young lady — the lady — the lady — the young lady — she;(2) the Italian Minister of Foreign Affairs — him — the Minister — the Minister — the Minister — the minister;(3) asked — asked — asked — repeated — shouted;(4) said — answered — said — answered;(5) the New World — the New World — which — a new world。词汇链 1 体现主位连续,说明语篇的主人公是

YL。词汇链 3 和 4 表明语篇描述的是言语(verbal)过程,一问一答,过程的参加者是 YL 和 FM,前者提问,后者回答。YL 提问,说明她不知道新大陆在何方,FM 能回答,说明他具有这一地理知识。引语中的小句含关系过程,环境成分表示距离或地点,即新大陆,说明他们就此问答。语篇的最后,即句[13]至[15],通过物质过程(rushed)和言语过程(shouted)交代了 YL 如何向参加舞会的人士宣布有关 the New World 的"最新消息"。这也是语篇在结尾提供的宏观新信息。作者/叙事人用新大陆作为话题有其用意:一方面可以表明 YL 地理知识状况,另一方面,由于哥伦布是 1451 年出生的意大利人,后旅居西班牙,15 世纪 90 年代发现新大陆,身为意大利人的 YL 应该了解这一历史,所以用新大陆作话题还可以说明 YL 历史知识的状况。至此,语篇向我们提供了第一层意义:它告诉我们发生了怎样的社会行为,有些什么参加者,他们做了些什么,他们的关系如何。这是语篇的显性经验意义,就是轶事。

2.2.2 社会意义

语篇的社会意义(social significance)要从参与社会活动的重要的社会关系中寻求,因为这种社会关系反映了社会结构。在这个短篇中存在三对人际关系:作者/叙事人和读者、主要人物 YL 和 FM 以及 YL 和与会的先生和女士们之间的关系。通过对这三对人际关系的分析,我们可以了解语篇的社会意义。从第一对关系中我们可以看到作者的评价和态度。根据马丁的评价系统(王振华 2001),在"介入"一项中作者既有"自言"也有"借言",无论是"借言"还是"自言"都为了体现同一个令人不安的事件并向读者陈述同一个观点。在"态度"项下,体现"情感"的词语成分有 curious、repeated(试比较 continued)、rushed(试比较 went)和 shouted(试比较 spoke),用以评价作者眼中 YL 的急切心情;in great astonishment、the latest news、just 则说明 YL 的知识状况。在判断系统中,社会评判则是 YL 违反了行为规范性(normality)和真实可靠性(veracity),但作者并未用任何消极词语,只是暗示了社会评判。第二对人际关系是由几轮对话向读者交代的,语言上体现为语气结构。答方是外交部长,语篇中(句[3])用 him 和 he 指称,可见是男性。作为外交部长,他有很高的社会地位，当受过良好的教育，不仅知道巴西在何处，而且还知道在当时的情况下从罗马到巴西需时 6 个月。问方是年轻女士，与外交部长很熟，还能参加要人出席的舞会，当是名门闺秀，受过教育，但不知道新大陆，也不知道谁发现了新大陆。在 YL 和 FM 之间，FM 显然在政治地位、社会影响和知识水平上占主导地位，所以他在最后一轮用讥讽的口吻补充说："新大陆是 Christopher Columbus 发现的。"第三对人际关系是 YL 和舞会参加者的关系。从语篇的构成来说 YL 处于主动地位，与会者只能被动接受，无法参与。正因为作者/叙事人没有让他们作出反应，就使得 YL 宣布"最新消息"更加令人不安。在语言体现上，我们可以分析小句的语气结构。这儿我们仅分析两点。句[10]是 YL 的提问，从理论上讲，她可以有两个选择：Wh-问句或 Yes/No 问句。使用特殊疑问句如"Where is Brazil?"要求提问者具有一定的地理知识，即回答 where 的方位、地域、国度或洲作为提问的潜在参照点。YL 用她所处的 Rome 作为参照点，只能用一般疑问句"Is Brazil far from Rome?"，说明她对世界地理不甚了了。FM 对此句的回答并不是 Yes 或 No，似乎答非所问。其实，It 指上句的 Brazil，而且更重要的是，说话人认为对方知道新大陆在哪儿，也知道新大陆离罗马有多远，YL 应该能从答句中推断出她所想要了解的知识，所以 FM 还是回答了 YL 的问题，是与问句关联的。这句话说明无论从作者还是从说话人的角度看，有关新大陆的知识应该是普通的常识。如果对新大陆一无所知，这个答句就会显得不关联，所以 YL 就 the New World 提问。再看句[12]，这是一个省略了语气成分（mood ellipsis）的问句。假如我们恢复语气成分，那这个句子就成了句[12a]"It is in the New World?"请注意表示言语过程的动词是 repeated，所以不可能是以 Is it 的语气部分开始的问句。那么，句[12a]的意义是什么呢？它相当于 Is it true that it is in the New World？问句的焦点不是新大陆，而是整个 that 从句，问巴西是不是在新大陆，这与情景没有什么关联，当予以排除。另一方面，句[12]的语气省略并不是单纯为了与上句取得衔接，而是说明 YL 说话的出发点和问句的焦点都在 the New World，说明她对新大陆有兴趣。在一定的语境中社会行为创造社会角色。YL 在大庭广众宣布"最新消息"就使她成为一个文化水平极为有限的角色。作者/叙事人用创作/讲述故事的行为，FM 用回答问题的行为表现了他们知识阶层的角色。参与者不是作为个人参与社会活动，而是作为某个团体、机构或文化的一员参与活动。YL、FM 和作者/叙事人代表了他们各自所属的社会群体。叙事语篇有时是出于叙事人对某种情况的处理不满(Ochis 1997: 198),在这个语境里,作者/叙事人充当了鼓吹者、社会发言人的角色,表达了他们的不满;而 FM 与 YL 形成了男/女、知/不知、答/问、教育者/受教育者的角色关系。这种角色关系是社会结构的表现,而他们的互动反映出了意大利当时社会结构的缺陷,即教育制度中忽视女性普通教育的严重问题。这是语篇的社会意义之所在。

2.2.3 主 题

要了解主题(theme),应考察整个语篇是如何组篇的。实现组篇的衔接手段如指称、重复、省略、连词使用等都在这一语篇里得到了应用,使语篇衔接,成为一个整体。另一方面,语篇通过主位进展等手段获得了连贯。如 lady 链中的成员在句[1]、[5]、[7]、[10]、[12]、[14]的主位结构中都充当主位。这种主位连续不断、贯穿全文的使用体现了主位进展,集中表明了语篇旨在说明 YL。又如在句[11]、[12]、[13]中 the New World 都是述位,作为新信息加以陈述,在句[16]中虽然 a new world 处于句首,当是主位,但由于全句表示"新闻",短语又与不定冠词连用,所以也是新信息。可见 YL 是叙事的出发点,而 the New World 却是话题。就语篇语言使用的媒介渠道(channel)而言,语篇中既有书面语,也有口语,或口语的书面记录。语篇开始的三句是叙事人的叙述,句[5]应用间接引语(IQ)... asked why he was late。句[6]则是直接引语(DQ):"You see", said the Minister ...。句[7]又用 IQ,句[8]再用 DQ,结果形成 IQ—DQ/ID—DQ 的重复。这构成从叙事人的叙事到人物的对话的过渡,也是从主观叙事层面(subjective narrative plane)到客观叙事层面(objective narrative plane)的过渡,随后除句[14]外直至语篇结束便都是直接引语,是客观叙事层面。引语是一种投射,投射部分是客观的陈述,其内容不由叙事人负责,而由人物负责,因此就显得更为可信。这样,作者就用了叙事的书面语、作者的书面语和人物的口语(记录)合用和基本使用人物口语(记录)三种渠道来有效地组织语篇,为语篇目的服务。那么语篇的目的是什么呢? 这就涉及语篇的主题。我们从人物的对话,YL 的"新闻"发布中已经获得了这样的印象：YL 作为意大利年轻女士的代表（请比较句［1］的“young ladies in Italy”和句［5］的“a young lady”）史地知识贫乏。可是我们怎样证明我们的理解是对的？语篇中有什么语言证据？这就要求我们到语篇中寻找语言的型式化（patterning）。型式化是某一型式（pattern）或某一类同结构（parallel structure）通过重复而形成。正是型式化的意义或型式化之间的对比为我们探索主题提供了基础（任绍曾 2000）。型式化是语篇中凸显的部分，是语篇前景化的部分，用以突出语篇要传达的主要信息。在语篇展开的过程中，我们看到以对比为共同特征的三个型式化。它们是：

	A	B
（1）	the New World［11］	a new world［16］
（2）	was discovered［13］	has just been discovered［16］
（3）	Christopher Columbus［13］	a certain Christopher Columbus［16］

此处 A 栏内是 FM 的用语，B 栏内是 YL 的用语。第一项包含了两个对比，即 the 和 a 的对比，和大写的 New World 和小写的 new world 的对比。大写的 New World 是 FM 意识中的新大陆，是一个心理单位，是语言中的认可结构，是一个约定俗成的象征单位，是一个整体，体现一个意象；而小写的 new world 是两个象征单位的临时组合，是语言使用中的目的结构（target structure）。其中，the 和 a 的对比表明：the 说明对 FM 来说 the New World 是已知信息，是他知识结构的一部分；a 说明 new world 对 YL 来说是新信息，不构成她知识结构的一部分。不错，句［12］中 YL 的引语里用的是大写的 New World，但是我们必须看到她是在重复 FM 的话，作者不得不用与 FM 相同的形式，加上她正对此发问，所以不能说明她已了解新大陆。第二项包含时态的对比：FM 用了过去时“was discovered”，而 YL 则用了现在完成时“has just been discovered”。过去时的动词说明它表述的主语所进行的动作发生在过去，这里指 15 世纪 90 年代，有关的事件已经成为历史；现在完成时，特别由 just 加以修饰，表明动作刚刚完成，与现在有实际的联系或对现在有影响，这与事实不符。第三项含零位冠词与不定冠词的对比。Christopher Columbus 作为专有名词与所指的人特别是名人在一定的语境中有稳固的联系，所以有最高的可及性，说话人知道是谁，估计对方也知道指谁；而 a certain 用于人名之前相当于“someone by the name of”,说明说话人不认识此人,不知道这个专有名词指谁。我们注意到作者直到语篇结束时才暗示 YL 的知识状况。这是因为正如小句信息结构里的新信息一般处于结构的最后,语篇的新信息,马丁称为宏观新信息(Macro-New),也出现在语篇的末尾(Martin 1992: 456)。这也可说明句[16]中为什么用 by 短语。在句法层次上,被动句中的 by 短语可有可无,去掉这个短语,句子照样可以成立,但是在信息结构里,由于传达信息的需要,这个短语却不可省略。在小句信息结构里 by 短语引出了动作者,作为新信息,交代谁发现新大陆。在语篇里 by 短语传递宏观新信息的一部分,没有 by 短语就无法暗示 YL 不仅不知道新大陆而且也不知道哥伦布。这说明句法上可有可无的,由于语篇的需要却不可省去。

对比是语篇的一个资源,这儿对比的持续的重复使语言特征获得了前景化,构成了型式化。前景化的几个型式都具有语义指向的稳定性(stability of semantic direction),都指向同一个一般意义(Hasan 1989: 95)。上述三个语言特征的对比具有同一个意义指向,集中表现了知和不知的对比。韩礼德指出,一个突出的特征只有与整体意义有联系才能前景化,还说,前景化是有动因的突出(Halliday 1973: 104)。这种突出有助于表达作者的整体意义,常引导我们获得新的见解。实际上经过前景化而形成的型式化构成语言艺术的象征表达(symbolic articulation),成为语篇的次一层次(second order)的符号系统(Hasan 1989: 89),表示了语篇整体意义,也就是主题。韩茹凯指出:主题是语言艺术最深层的意义,它是从语篇的具体特征中抽象出来的,是语篇目的之所在(Hasan 1989: 97)。就其性质而言,它近乎一种概括。要抽象,要概括,就得推理,就得作篇外推理。语言知识为我们推理划定范围,而且有关的世界知识需要靠语言激活才能作为推理的前提,因此我们必须在语篇中寻找语言特征,特别是前景化的特征作为我们语篇推理的依据。从上面的分析可以看出,与情景相关、有共同语义指向的语言特征就是三个对比形成的型式化。我们的世界知识告诉我们,也正如 FM 的答话所表现的,哥伦布发现新大陆是人所共知的历史事件和地理常识。有意思的是作者以其所知暗示其无知。注意,作者在整个语篇中未用 ignorant 来点明她无知。语言是符号系统,作为语言使用的语篇也是符号系统,体现语言符号和信息意图的结合。由于语篇具有含义性(implicationality),因此,言语的显性意义和潜性含义共同构成符号系统的信息意图。语篇的潜性含义需要推理。如果我们应用"Premises：If P，then Q；P；Conclusion：Q"（Sperber & Wilson 1986：14）的语用推理规则，我们可以这样进行推理：如果她知道哥伦布发现新大陆是人所共知的历史事件，她就不会把它当作新闻宣布；她这样宣布了，说明她自己缺乏这一常识。这样，我们就为理解语篇找到了根据。从认知语用学的角度看，通过重复或对比而前景化的型式特征要求读者付出更大的努力以获得最佳关联，从而使重复激发出的语境效果得到增加，产生许多弱含义（weak implicatures），因而也就产生了诗境效果（poetic effect）（Sperber & Wilson 1986：222）。这种效果与语句的命题意义已相距甚远。所以我们可以说主题是前景化的型式化产生的弱含义。既然如此，主题就不可能是预知的，或是正确的或错误的，而是或然的或概率的。马丁把意识形态看成是通过语域和语类而体现的编码定向（coding orientation）（Martin 1992：581）。因为编码定向可以有各式各样的体现，所以意识形态不可能是孰此孰彼的问题，而是或多或少的问题。意识形态的性质如此，受制于意识形态的主题就不会是必然的。究竟主题是什么在很大程度上受制于读者的认知语境或意识形态。试设想如果我们作为读者不知新大陆在何处，哥伦布为何人，认为史地知识无关紧要，读了这篇短文，有可能得出 YL 无知的结论吗？可以想象在"女子无才便是德"的封建意识占主导地位的时代，这篇短文的主题可能就截然不同了。正因为主题是一种概括而且受到意识形态的左右，所以人们对同一语篇可以有不同的理解，传世的文学巨著得以跨越时空。

从上面的分析可以看出由意念功能体现的情景语境决定语篇的轶事，由人际功能体现的社会语境决定语篇的社会意义，而以意识形态形成的文化语境则制约了语篇的主题。韩礼德对文化语境的定义说明，其机构性部分给予语篇语义价值，而意识形态部分则制约（constrain）对语篇的理解。我们对语篇社会意义和主题的分析也证实了这一点。从另一个角度看，轶事体现意念功能，然而语篇是语言多种元功能的构建体，当然有人际功能的参与，也有语篇功能使意念功能和人际功能在语篇中得到具体体现，但从内容来看是回答"发生了什么事"这一问题，是对社会实际的反映，所以轶事这一层语义是以语场为中心的意义。马丁也指出拉波夫（William Labov）的叙事结构或语篇的"主位—述位"和"已知信息—新信息"结构只能将语篇积累的意义加以汇总，阐明语场（Martin 1992：456）。

语篇的第二层意义(即社会意义)体现人际功能,当然也离不开反映主客观经验的意念功能,也离不开组篇的语篇功能,但就其内容而言,是回答了"谁参与这一社会活动,各自起什么作用"这一问题,而且把社会成员的互动看成是社会结构的体现。语境中的语旨要求语篇体现各种人际关系,包括由人组成的集团、阶层、阶级之间的关系。这恰恰是社会意义之所系,因此社会意义是以语旨为中心的语义。语篇的第三层意义来自语篇功能。意念功能和人际功能是语篇功能的基础,主题当然也离不开这两个元功能。语篇区分背景部分和前景部分,文学叙事语篇通过重复和对比使若干语言特征型式化,成为表示主题的次一层符号,而这些正是语篇的谋篇策略,是语篇功能的重要方面,也正是这些语篇功能突出了主题,从这个意义上讲,可以说主题是以语式为中心的语义。轶事表示语篇的直义,社会意义是语篇的一般含义,而主题则是语篇的深层隐含。语篇的整体性使这三缕语义拧成一根绳,在揣摩语篇的信息时,我们不可以只顾一点,不及其他。叙事语篇不是为叙事而叙事,而是为了现在和将来。就拿这篇短文来说吧,我们概括出了主题,但主题这一潜性意义须以轶事这一显性意义为依托,结合社会意义才能了解整个语篇要传达的信息。一个年轻女士史地知识贫乏并不一定令人不安,但是当我们联系语篇的轶事和社会意义,就可以进一步了解到这是当时意大利教育制度的弊端所造成的可悲后果,从而使人们产生必须改革的评价。这应该是叙事语篇为现在和将来所要达到的目的。语境中的不同层次和语境配置中的不同因素对语篇三个层次意义的影响可用下图概括:

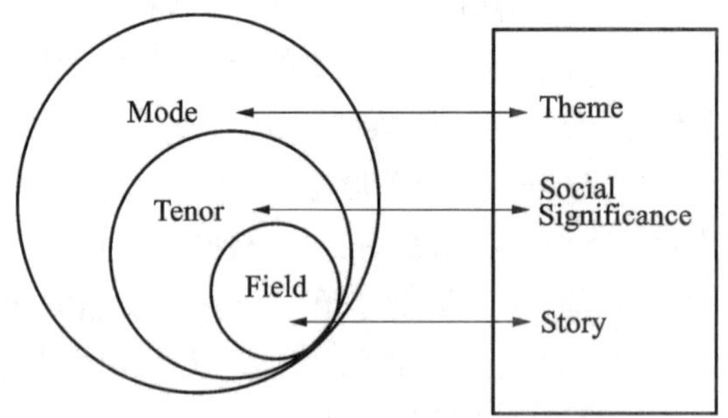

图 2-2　语篇意义和语境对应示意图

下面我们把这三层意义的分析应用于海明威的中篇小说《士兵之家》(*Soldier's Home*)。

2.3 中篇叙事小说的语义层次

从短篇叙事语篇中获得的三层次意义应该适用于中篇。

2.3.1 轶　事

《士兵之家》的轶事是描述主人公 Krebs 应召于 1917 年参加第一次世界大战,1919 年从德国战场回家后的精神状态。这通过与元功能对应的三种结构的分析(Halliday 1994),或通过主位、语段主位和宏观主位,以及新信息、语段新信息和宏观新信息的分析(Martin 1992：456)可以获得。特别明显的是语篇中 Krebs 和指称他的代词 He/he 是绝大多数小句的主位,形成贯穿全篇的主位连续,说明语篇是对他进行说明。另一方面,语篇中突出的过程是心理过程和言语过程。这集中说明叙事人着眼于主人公战后的精神世界。这是基于语篇提供的情景语境、以语场为中心的意义。

2.3.2 社会意义

至于社会意义我们可以考察叙事人语篇中的 Krebs。他对战争和讲述战争感到反感,对他在战争中经历的一切感到厌恶。对待女孩子他似乎无所谓。从人物对话中我们可以清楚地看到他对母亲缺乏起码的感情,对父亲全然冷漠,对妹妹只是敷衍。在语言上体现为他极为简短的应答。那么,这种人际关系又是怎样形成的呢？我们还是得从社会结构中寻找答案。战争是流血的政治,是特定社会制度下政治的继续,是体现这种政治的社会结构的产物。是这一社会结构把人送上战场,产生了退伍军人,Krebs 是其中之一。这是社会结构赋予他的社会身份(social identity)。当他回到家乡之后,他脑海中出现的人(女孩子)、他所接触的人(母亲、妹妹)都是没有经历过战争的普通人。在人际交往中,他的"政治"(Gee 2000: 70)是他的战争经历,这是他与别人不同之处。他作为退伍军人为一方,而其他没有战争经历的人为另一方,如此构成了语篇中的人际关系。他们的这种社会角色、他们的互动反映了社会现实的一个侧面。实际上,Krebs与这些常人并没有什么太多的互动,而且他也无心和他们往来。社会活动(social activities),包括言语交际活动,是社会身份,以及个人性格、心态的体现。他无心与人交往说明他的冷漠。这种冷漠使他与家庭、与社会格格不入。在这一叙事语篇中令人不安的事件是战争改变了Krebs,使得他失去了方向,无法再融入社会。这样,语篇就向人们诉说了战争对人的负面影响。这是语篇的社会意义,是以语旨为中心的语篇含义。

2.3.3 主 题

对于语篇的主题,我们可以从语篇的型式化入手。我们发现有三个通过重复形成的型式化:肯定式、转折式和否定式,其中否定式是主要型式化,前两种是铺垫和陪衬。对于Krebs对young girls的态度,语篇有这样集中的叙述:

> He liked to look at them from the front porch ...; He liked to watch them walking ...; He liked the Dutch collars above their sweaters; He liked their silk stockings and flat shoes; He liked their bobbed hair and the way they walked ... (Warren 1974: 309)

叙事人多次重复He liked无非是说明Krebs作为一个年轻人这方面仍有情致,然而即使在这自然不过的方面,他也感到厌倦。第二个表示转折的型式化让我们看到这一点。譬如:

> Krebs did not feel the energy or courage to break into it (the young girls' world). He liked to look at them, though./Now he would have liked a girl if she had come to him and not wanted to talk./He would like to have one of them. But it was not worth it./He did not want one badly enough. He liked to look at them, though; It was not worth it./Vaguely

he wanted a girl, but he did not want to work to get her./He would have liked to have a girl but he did not want to have to spend a long time getting her ... (Warren 1974: 309 - 310)

这些语句中 though、but、if 体现的转折，说明他的心态。虽然年轻，却无意追求情爱。第三个表示否定的型式化就反映了他对生活的态度。譬如：

He did not want to get into the intrigue and the politics; He did not want to have to do any courting; He did not want to tell any more lies; It was not worth it; He did not want any consequences; He did not want any consequences ever again; He wanted to live along without consequences; Besides he did not really need a girl ... (Warren 1974: 309)

这些否定结构的多次连续重复说明 Krebs 对生活的消极态度。对 girls 如此，对其他方面便可想而知。这是海明威对此不惜笔墨的原因所在。否定型式化还出现在对其他方面的叙述中。对于战争，语篇中有：

At first Krebs did not want to talk about the war at all./Krebs ... had a reaction against the war and against talking about it .../A distaste for everything that had happened to him in the war set in ...

对于回家，则有：He did not want to leave Germany; He did not want to come home。

在人物对话中，我们看到，Krebs 始终处于被动的应答地位。请看他与他妹妹的对话：

— Couldn't your brother really be your beau just because he's your brother?

— I don't know.

— Do you love me?

— Uh, huh.

他与他母亲的对话：

— Have you decided what you are going to do yet?

— No.

— Don't you think it's about time?

— I hadn't thought about it.

— God has some work for everyone to do. There can be no idle hands in His Kingdom.

— I'm not in His Kingdom …

— Don't you love your mother, dear boy?

— No, I don't love anybody.

最为前景化的否定型式化反映了主人公对一切的冷漠,对情爱、对亲情、对事业、对信仰都持否定的态度,而这极端消极的态度是他对战争的反感、厌恶造成的。他无法吐露战争中他的真实感受,他得编造、说谎(lies … lies … lies … lies … untruth or exaggeration),这使他感到恶心。这样:

All of the times … now **lost** their cool, valuable quality and then were **lost** themselves.

与他的谎言形成对比的是:

He had been badly, sickeningly frightened all the time. In this way he **lost** everything.

在追述战争经历中他认清了真实的自我,认识了战争的残酷,他对自己也完全失去了信心。难怪他母亲对他说: you have **lost** your ambition。这个 lost 词汇链让我们看到主人公失去了内心的宁静,失去了一切,也失去了生活目标。他愤怒,但他又不清楚对什么愤怒。涉及 Krebs 思想、感情各个方面,贯穿全文的否定型式化表明他对生活、对社会的态度,说明他迷惘、郁悒、消沉、心灰意懒、万念俱灰。这是基于否定型式化,经过推理而得到的语篇的主题。在推理过程中我们不禁会问,为什么叙事人不厌其烦地使用否定句式和否定词语。这种结构和语义上的一再重复促使我们思考,从而增加了语境效果,产生了含义。结合语篇提供的语境,可以找到最有关联的含义,也就是主题。在推理过程中我们得调用我们关于战争的世界知识。简单地说,我们知道战争的残酷,知道战争对人的创伤,对第一次世界大战也有了解。没有这些知识我们就无从得出上述主题。因此,主题是基于语篇的型式化,是从语篇中抽象出来的含义,但它受意识形态制约。

我们可以再进一步，将主题和轶事、社会意义结合起来考察，也就是将深层含义、一般含义和直义结合起来，以了解主题的社会根源，从而了解整个语篇的信息。Krebs 作为退伍军人，主宰他精神世界的因素是他的战争经历。即使在战争结束之后，他仍然生活在战争的阴影之中，是战争使他陷入了无法自拔的境地。叙事人展现战争对人的摧残，对主人公表示怜悯，对于这令人不安的事件他期望读者作出的道德评价是战争是残酷的，应该谴责战争、反对战争。这是语篇的信息。互文性(intertextuality)有助于我们对这一语篇的理解。参加过第一次世界大战并负过伤的海明威在《永别了，武器》(*Farewell to Arms*)中也表现了同一主题，表明了同一态度。

2.4 长篇叙事语篇的语义层次

现在我们将语义三层次的分析应用于梅勒的《夜幕下的大军》(*The Armies of the Night*)。这本书记述了 1967 年发生在美国首都华盛顿的一场声势浩大的反对越南战争的示威游行，同时叙述了作者梅勒作为参加者和见证人的经历和感受。

2.4.1 轶 事

对于长篇叙事小说难以用语类结构潜势、叙事结构或修辞结构加以分析。比较可行的是把握宏观结构，从而了解小说的直义。经过分析，我们发现这一叙事语篇的宏观结构包含以下几个宏观命题：梅勒参加了向五角大楼进军的反对越南战争的示威游行，被捕，获释；代表各种政治力量的游行示威者在安芭萨德剧院结集，游行从这里开始，以在五角大楼与军警对峙告终。这是对一系列事件按时间顺序的叙述，包括梅勒对亲身经历的记述和他对所见所闻的描写，实际是叙事语篇的梗概。这是轶事，是情景语境赋予语篇的直义。对此书的详细分析,请见本书第6、7两章。

2.4.2 社会意义

游行示威是一个政治事件。示威者反对当局推行的战争政策,反对越南战争。这就构成了对立,反映了社会结构中的矛盾。表现在对游行的态度上,当局竭力反对、阻止、限制,而示威一方则公开抗议,企图强占、破坏美国军事力量的象征五角大楼。语篇让我们看到了这显而易见的社会主要矛盾。但这还不是20世纪60年代美国政治图景的全貌。从反战的一方看,语篇告诉我们示威游行队伍中有各式各样的政治派别,代表不同的政治力量。在 Left 之中有 Old Left、New Left、White Left、Conservative Left,这些修饰语就显示了左派队伍四分五裂。Liberals 之中有 peace group Liberals、Black Liberals、Middle-class Liberals,由于肤色、阶级和目的不同又出现不同派别。Movement 又有 Negro Movement、Youth Movement、Peace Movement、Women Movement、Student Movement,各有各的纲领和目标。而且,同一个派别中还有分歧,如在1967年的中东战争问题上,the Old Left 分裂为两派,the New Left 也发生分裂。对示威游行,有的认为整个行动是错误的,有的甚至妄想用诅咒驱魔来结束越南战争。对这些政治派别之间的关系,语篇用动词链 severed from — never came together — was filled with bitter rifts — divided — did not like 来表现。他们的政治见解不一,目的不一,手段也不一。美国当时的社会现实是:一方面是各种政治势力与当局的严重对立,而另一方面这些反战派别之间的矛盾又无法调和,就连示威也都各行其是。这就勾勒出了当时美国政治上濒临分崩离析的困境(O'Neill 1980)。这是社会语境赋予语篇的社会意义。

2.4.3 主　题

长篇叙事小说的前景部分常常用通过重复某些命题来体现,而在语言上则通过词汇链来体现。词汇链,不论是同一词汇链,还是同义词汇链都能通过对同一个词或若干同义词或近义词的重复比较集中地传达某种意义。在这一叙事语篇里有几个引人注目的词汇链：分别以 schizophrenia、totalitarianism、apocalypse、existentialism 为中心词：

[17] ... for no American citizen likes to link arms at once with the two ends of his practical working-day good American *schizophrenia*. (p.107)

[18] The country had been living with a controlled, even fiercely controlled, *schizophrenia* which had been deepening with the years. (p.188)

[19] The love of the Mystery of Christ, however, and the love of no Mystery whatsoever, had brought the country to a state of suppressed *schizophrenia* so deep that the foul brutalities of the war in Vietnam were the only temporary cure possible for the condition. (p.188)

[20] ... since the expression of brutality offers a definite if temporary relief to the *schizophrenia*. (p.188)

[21] ... the small shift of opinions from day to day are the two nostrums of the apothecary where *schizophrenia* is treated. (p.189)

[22] They were men ... there down in the cellar of the hierarchies of *schizophrenic* ranch-house life in America. (p.197)

其他还有含同义词的：

[23] If one could find the irredeemable *madness* of America ... (p.151)

[24] Their country had always been *wild*. (p.152)

限于篇幅，其他词汇链就不一一列举了。仅从这个词汇链，我们便可以看出作者重复了一个重要命题：美国处于精神分裂状态。语言上各句中的 schizophrenia 都与 America 或 the country 有联系，都说明美国。作者突出这个词和这个命题是为了解释美国为什么要发动越南战争，这在句[19]、句[20]中实际上已经点明：越南战争的野蛮可以为美国的精神分裂症提供暂时的治疗。美国为什么会得精神分裂症？作者的解释是 the love of the Mystery of Christ and the love of no Mystery whatsoever，这玄而又玄的解释实际上不成其为理由。越南战争又如何缓解美国的病症作者也没有交代。作者自称是存在主义者(Mailer 1968：40)，承认在他的信念中有large parts of existentialism(Mailer 1968：23)。这也反映在他对时间、空间、思想情绪的看法上，如 existential edge(Ditto：24)、existential anxiety(Ditto：31)、existential promise(Ditto：29)、existential moment(Ditto：39)、existential situation(Ditto：39)。存在主义认为自在的存在是没有理由、没有原因、没有必然性的，它就是它现在所是的东西(许崇温 1984)。囿于 Mailer 的存在主义观点，他不能从社会结构中寻找问题的症结，而只能通过 schizophrenia、apocalypse、mystery 等词汇链用一种神秘主义的观点似是而非地作出解答。实际上，我们可以从上述词汇链看到作者试图对越南战争作出解释但又没有能解释，在这之中我们看到的是他以及他所代表的美国知识界的茫然、焦虑和不安。这是语篇的主题。这为语篇结尾的宏观新信息所证实。他写到书的最后还是觉得美国的前途未卜：他担心美国会沦为极权统治，但又希望美国成为新世界的婴儿。结合语篇的轶事和社会意义，我们可以看到越战时期的美国政治上矛盾重重，四分五裂，反战情绪高涨，民众焦虑不安。这是叙事语篇的信息。越南战争是个令人十分不安的事件，反对越战的队伍四分五裂也是令人不安的事件。Mailer 希望人们看到这一点。读者会根据自己的认识，自己的意识形态解释越战的起因和社会矛盾的根源。

2.5　结　语

2.5.1　话语分析的三个维度

范戴克指出语篇具有三个维度，即语言使用、信仰的传递(认知)和社会情景中的互动(van Dijk 1997：2)。我们对语篇三层次的分析反映了对语篇三个维度的考察。就语言使用而言，轶事出自对语言体系运用的分析，社会意义基于对语言和社会关系的分析，主题则是对语篇作认知分析的结果。轶事和社会意义的语言体现可以分别借用吉(Gee 2000：29)的语法 1 和语法 2 加以概括。语法 1 指语法基本结构,语法 2 指语气结构、评价系统和其他与人际关系有联系的语体特征。主题则由语法 3 提示。语法 3 的特点在于贯穿全文的语言特征的类型化,如短篇中的型式化(任绍曾 2000)和长篇中的命题链和词汇链(Ren 2001)。探索语篇的社会意义实际是考察社会情景中的互动。互动双方的关系是由社会结构决定的。人的活动、人际活动都受社会的制约(殷企平 2001: 206)。信仰传递中的信仰指人们的信仰系统,实际是指意识形态,指认知语境。语篇的构建和理解都受信仰系统的影响和制约,了解主题当然要依靠认知语境进行推理。可见我们对语篇第三层次语义的分析实际上考虑了语篇的语言、社会和认知三个维度。这三个维度是密切联系的。认知是语篇和社会的界面(van Dijk 1997: 3)。关于语篇的多维分析详见第 1 章。

2.5.2 语境、元功能、语义和词汇语法的对应关系

叙事语篇三层次——语义和语境、语境因素、语言元功能的关系以及这三层次语义如何为词汇、语法所体现,可用下表加以概括:

表 2-1 语境、元功能、语义和词汇语法对应关系一览表

语　境	语境因素	元功能	语篇意义	语用意义	词汇语法体现
情景语境(事件周围的物理环境)	语场	意念功能	以语场为中心的轶事	直义(直接反映社会现实的经验意义)	语篇结构(语法 1)
社会语境(社会结构)	语旨	人际功能	以语旨为中心的社会意义	一般含义(由社会语境赋予价值)	语气结构、评价系统以及体现人际关系的语体特征(语法 2)
文化语境(意识形态)	语式	语篇功能	以语式为中心的主题	深层含义(由意识形态制约)	语言型式化(语法 3)

以上分析说明,叙事语篇具有三层次构成的语义结构,而不是像本章开头提及的那些语篇结构理论所描述的那样,只有单一的线形结构。

3

关注中心和基本主题

——试析小句与段落之间的语篇单位*

3.1 引　言

在话语分析中话语究竟如何推进当是一个根本性问题。韩礼德(Halliday 1994)指出,英语话语是作为一系列不间断的具有旋律特征的单位推进的,这种单位称作语调组,每一个语调组体现一个信息单位。信息单位在无标记的情况下与小句重合。话语流以信息流作为基础,从根本上即使是书面话语也是以一个信息单位接一个信息单位逐一推进的。马丁和罗斯用波浪比喻信息流,将小句比喻为小浪,其中主位和新信息凸出;将段落比喻为大浪,超主题和超新信息凸出;将整个话语比喻为巨浪,宏观主位和宏观新信息凸出,这样就产生了大单位含小单位的周期性层次结构(Martin & Rose 2003)。在实际话语分析中,常出现这样的问题:在小浪与大浪之间,或者用非隐喻的话说,在小句和段落之间有没有中间单位。这就是本章试图探讨的问题。

* 本章原载《外语教学》2009 年第 4 期第 6—10 页,文字略有改动。

3.2 切夫的认知观

3.2.1 意　识

对于话语进展，切夫（Wallace Chafe）有另外一种看法，其出发点是意识在语言和语言使用中的作用。把韩礼德的信息单位称之为体现意识焦点的意义单位（idea unit）。切夫认为语言现象是基本认知过程的体现，不了解认知过程，就无法了解语言现象，而在认知过程中意识起中心作用，因为使用自然语言传达信息不仅涉及知识，而且涉及意识（Chafe 1980）。他指出人们如何使用语言很大程度上依靠他们在时间推移中意识到什么，依靠他们内在注意的焦点，同时关注听话人意识中的活动。意识的作用，我国古人早有论述，《礼记 · 大学》：心不在焉，视而不见，听而不闻，食而不知其味。就感知而言，意识不到，虽视却看不见，虽听却听不到，虽吃却觉不到。心不到，觉不到；觉不到，言不到，相应的词语不被激活，当然不会成为说话的内容。切夫认为思考涉及三个成分，即信息、自我和意识。信息指源于世界、记忆和情感的大量知识（Chafe 1980：11）。自我指对当前活动实施中心控制的执行者，意识指为自我服务将可获取的信息加以激活，因此，意识是自我利用信息的机制。

3.2.2 意识的特征

意识有若干特征，区分经常性特征和可变特征。前者包括：（1）意识有焦点，这意味着意识只是说话人经验或知识的一小部分被激活；（2）意识焦点处于边缘意识的包围之中，活性焦点周围的半活性信息为焦点提供语境；（3）意识是动态的，也就是意识由一个焦点向另一个意识焦点行进，持续不断，因而形成流程（flow），故而有信息流；（4）意识具有观点，说话人总是以自我为中心解释世界，对经验作出诠释；

(5) 意识需要自我所处的时间、空间、社会以及活动的背景取向。没有这些信息,自我就难以起作用(Chafe 1994)。其实最后两个特征与其说是意识的特征,不如说是在交际过程中自我的需要。另有几个可变特征,主要的是:有意识的经验源于感知、行为或情感;就与实际情景的关系而言,可以是直接的(immediate)或移位(displaced)的。对于信息,切夫提出了独到的见解。他区分三种信息(Chafe 1987:22),即(1) 活性信息,也就是被聚焦的信息;(2) 半活性信息,就是处于意识边缘区域的信息;(3) 非活性信息,也就是长期记忆中的信息。他认为新信息是在会话某一时间点上新激活的信息,已知信息是在会话某时间点上已经激活的信息。他还把从半活性状态中激活的信息称为可及信息(accessible information)(Chafe 1994:72)。

3.3 主题层次结构

3.3.1 关注中心和基本主题

上面说过,韩礼德的信息单位切夫称为意义单位,这可以从切夫识别意义单位的标准看出。这标准有三:一是语音上是一个语调单位,二是有停顿,三是句法上往往是一个小句。意义单位是意识焦点的语言体现,但是单个意义单位所包含的信息常常不足以充分地满足人们的需要。通常的情况是,足以满足说话人需要的信息量要溢过单个意识焦点的有限容量。这就需要允许几个焦点扫描这一信息,因此整个信息可以完整地加以表达和理解。这就构成切夫所说的关注中心(center of interest)。为了满足交际的需要,有必要将若干意识焦点连接起来,构成超意识焦点(super-focus),语言上也就是关注中心。若干意识焦点构成的关注中心与说话人的需要与目的紧密联系,意识焦点沿着焦点之间的语义联系所确定的路线行进,沿着超主题图式所确定的既定路线行进。

3.3.2 主题层次

切夫把语调、意义单位,还有体现语调特点与意义单位同义的“迸发”(spurts)笼统地叫作意识焦点的语言表现。我们认为有必要按认知、语言(即语义、语法、语音)和语篇的层次把各层次结构中的基本单位和操作单位加以定位。意识焦点是认知层面上的基本单位,它在相应的语音层面上的单位是语调,语法层面上的单位是小句,语义层面上的单位是意义单位(idea unit),语篇层面的基本单位就是准主题(sub-topic);而认知层面上的操作单位是超意识焦点(super-focus),其相应的语音单位是语调群,语法单位是扩展小句或句群,语义单位是关注中心,语篇层面上是基本主题(basic-level topic)。可以概括如下:

表 3-1 认知、语言和语篇基本单位及操作单位一览表

层　　次	基本单位	操作单位
1 认知活动	意识焦点→	超意识焦点→
2 激活状态	激活意识→	半激活意识
3 语音体现	语调组→	语调群→
4 语法体现	小句→	扩展小句,多个小句→
5 语义体现	意义单位→	关注中心→
6 语篇体现	准主题→	基本主题→

总的来说这里只有三个层次,即包括第 1、第 2 层的认知层次,包括第 3、第 4、第 5 层的语言层次,最后是语言使用的层次,即第 6 语篇层次。需要说明的是,并非单个意识焦点及其语言体现小句不能表达信息,在一定的语境里,肯定可以。当一个意识焦点一经激活立即就付诸言语,就更加明显。对话或独白中的语言使用就是如此,否则,小句也不可能成为体现信息、经验和对话的语法基本单位(Halliday 1985)。但是,在叙事过程中或叙事语篇中,通常需要意识激活几个焦点才能满足信息的传递。关注中心或基本主题有三点值得注意:(1) 是由若干意识焦点构成,是超意识焦点;(2) 既是焦点,所以表达的意义是相互联系而且相对完整的;(3) 通常出现在叙事语篇里。上述的操作单位是指在叙事语篇中相对充分表达

信息的单位。必须指出,意识焦点受制于人们的认知能力和生理局限,但超意识焦点或关注中心、基本主题不受人们认知和生理的局限。基本主题是为说话人当前的交际目的服务,主题充分表达后即告结束。意识焦点是活性信息,而关注中心是半活性信息,也就是意识边缘地区的信息。它的作用在于引导意识从一个焦点向另一个焦点转移。切夫(Chafe 1994：121)说：主题是可以处于半活性状态的大量信息,是以某种形式相互联系地存在于说话人边缘意识中的时间、方式和参与者的组合。在主题的层次结构中,有层次不同的大小主题,基本主题是相当于范畴化中的基本范畴。意识往往会在半活性意识区域,从一个基本主题往另一个基本主题行进,这样就构成超主题。超主题在语篇层次上往往是段落,是整个语篇图式的一部分,因而有总的取向而获得连贯,它支持若干基本主题,并由若干基本主题构成(Chafe 1994：138)。根据语篇目的,若干超主题构成整个语篇的宏观主题或总主题。我们拟用语义上的关注中心和语篇层次上的基本主题探讨介于小句与段落之间的语篇单位。

必须说明我们参照了切夫的理论,但是为了避免理论上的混乱,我们没有照搬他有关句子的说明。他说句子可视为超意识焦点,就其全面性而言介乎意识焦点和基本主题之间(1994：145)。句子可以一个小句构成,也可以几个小句构成。如果含一个小句,那它相应的认知单位是意识焦点,如果含几个小句,那就可能是超意识焦点,即关注中心和基本主题,不可一概而论。

3.4 基本主题

3.4.1 半活性的信息

主题是意识焦点加以扫描的半活性信息,被逐点加以激活,直至说话人认为主题已经充分表达为止(Chafe 1994：121)。值得用语言表达的主题必须具有要点(point)。与语篇目的相联系的图式为超主题提供指向,语篇段落作为语篇的一部分虽没有整体图式，却具有段落图式，所以可以为基本主题提供指向，使之获得连贯。图式为次语篇提供期待（expectations），使得基本主题获得要点（Chafe 1994：122）。所谓要点是指在一定语篇范围里的主题连接点（point of thematic integration），也就是与语篇主题有直接联系的内容。活性焦点周围的半活性信息为焦点提供语境，基本主题是半活性信息，是意识焦点的背景语境。一般认为有两种方式信息可以进入半活性状态。一是通过对先前的活性信息去激活化（deactivation）。一个概念如果不再次激活，不可能长久保持活性状态，然而，在去激活化之后，一个概念不会立即成为非活性信息，即进入长期记忆，而是在一段时间里处于半活性状态。另一个方式是通过与图式的联系。图式是一系列相互联系的期待的集合，当某个图式被唤起，所有的或部分期待即进入半活性状态，比之处于非活性状态时，这些被期待的概念更便于提取。因此在语篇推进中前言的内容对后语来说是处于半活性状态的信息，是后语的背景语境；在谈论奥运会时，有关奥运会的图式被激活，与这一图式有关的概念，如奥组委、运动员、金牌、赛场就进入半活性状态，处于说话人意识的边缘，成为半活性信息。基本主题就是处于半活性状态的信息。

3.4.2 实　例

人们在思考或说话时，单个意识焦点往往不能满足需要，所以需要体现超意识焦点的基本主题。切夫曾给过一个例子。他说在描述事件的背景时，就需要基本主题（Chafe 1980：27），如：

[1] The movie opened up on this nice scene,
it was in the country
it was oaks
it seemed like West Coast

这是有四个意识焦点组成的关注中心或基本主题，每一个意识焦点涉及背景的一个侧面，说话人在半活性意识中依次聚焦于一点，最后以降调结束，构成一个相对完整的心理意象（mental image），呈现一幅图景。就这一基本主题而言，它并没有图式结构，可是在叙事语篇中，它却是叙事结构成分取向的一部分,取向向它提供行进方向,也就是一个意识焦点向另一个意识焦点行进的路线。在书面语里,基本主题常由几个句子构成的序列体现,通常具有某种整体性(unity),表现同一"意象"的不同方面。例如,主人公 Mailer(见 Mailer 1968: 41)思忖着要质问 Lowell:

[2] What do you know of the dirt and the dark deliveries of the necessary? What do you know of the dignity hard achieved, dignity lost through innocence, and dignity lost by sacrifice for a cause one cannot name? What do you know about getting fat against your will and turning into a clown of an arriviste baron when you would rather be an eagle or a count or rarest of all some natural aristocrat from these damned democratic states. No, the only subject we share, you and I, is the species of perception which shows if we are not loyal to our unendurable and most exigeent inner light, then some day we may burn. How dare you condemn me!

"No"之前是三个问句体现八个意识焦点。三个问题实际上是同一个问题的三个方面,或者说三个疑问句共同体现一个问题,一个言语行为。这语义上的整体性使这多个意识焦点构成一个关注中心,或基本主题。意识焦点是活性信息,如说第一个 wh-问题时,它就是活性信息,是因为意识聚焦于此,第二、第三个问题这时就处于意识的边缘地区,是半活性信息。说整个关注中心是半活性信息,是因为意识在这个范围内激活一个又一个焦点。

3.5 语篇分析

3.5.1 基本主题和段落

基本主题是主题层次结构中的操作单位,它在语篇中的范围介于小句与段落之间，是段落的一部分。它与段落的区别有二：一是段落具有源于语篇图式结构的段落图式，而体现基本主题的语段则没有；二是段落通常有超主题和超新信息，而体现基本主题的语段通常没有。但是基本主题具有连贯性和整体性，并且从段落图式获得取向，所以构成段落的一部分。语义上的关注中心，如[1]的背景，[2]的质问就是语篇层次上的基本主题。两个基本主题之间的界限、语义上的联系强弱不一，取决于意识需要改变取向程度的大小。这界限往往有辅句、话语标记或附加语加以标识，当意识取向或意识起作用的方式改变，往往会引出新的关注中心或基本主题。

[3] You have your comptroller who is highly specialized. You have your treasurer who has to know finance ... You have manufacturing area. He has to be highly specialized in warehouse and in shipping. You have to know marketing, the studies, the effect of advertising. A world of specialists. The man at the top has to have a general knowledge. And he has to have the knack of finding the right man to head these divisions. That's the difficulty. (*Working* p.538)

在"A world of specialits"之前是一个由七个小句体现的关注中心，基本主题是不同业务范围的专业人才，辅句总结了基本主题的内容。由于意识取向从泛指的 you 转到具体的"The man at the top"，辅句引出了一个新的关注中心和基本主题。同样，在例[2]中，由质问"what do you know"转至共识"the only subject we share"，由归一性的否定转向肯定，"No"引出了新的关注中心和基本主题。辅句和接续语这儿标记了基本主题之间的界限。

3.5.2 比尔・盖茨的发言

下面我们来看从比尔・盖茨(Bill Gates)在达沃斯(Davos)经济论坛发言中选出的一个段落：

[4] *a.* Let me begin by expressing a view that some do not share: *The world is getting better; a lot better.* (HyperTheme) In significant and

far-reaching ways, the world is a better place to live than it has ever been.

b. Consider the status of women and minorities in society — virtually any society — compared to any time in the past.

c. Consider that life expectancy has nearly doubled during the last 100 years.

d. Consider governance, the number of people today who vote in elections, express their views and enjoy economic freedom compared to any time in the past.

e. In many crucial areas *the world is getting better*. (HyperNew) (Bill Gates' speech at World Economic Forum (Davos))

在这篇发言中,比尔·盖茨提出了"创造性资本主义"(creative capitalism)的思想,主张不仅要谋求个人利益,而且要关心他人,不仅要技术创新,而且要制度创新(system renovation)。我们的选段是他开始时对当今世界的评价。这是一个段落,共有五个基本主题。例[4a]包含了段落的超主位:The world is getting better, a lot better;[4b]的基本主题是 the status of women and minorities;[4c] life expectancy;[4d]是 governance and freedom;[4e]包含超新信息。可以看出,基本主题[4a]提出了超主位,[4b]、[4c]、[4d]虽然是三个祈使语气句,但实际上,比尔·盖茨把这三方面令人瞩目的进步作为事实提请听众考虑,加上语句重复,所以比直陈语气更为肯定。三个基本主题从三个不同的方面论证了超主位提出的命题,[4e]中的超新信息虽然内容上与超主位相同,但实际上是论证后的结论。从例[4]我们可以看到,五个基本主题构成超主题,语篇上为段落。超主题向基本主题提供了取向,所以意识可以为自我达到目的或部分目的起作用。每一个基本主题都有相对完整性,但没有自己的图式结构。基本主题的范围大小不一,这说明虽然意识焦点受认知和生理的局限,而超意识焦点,即基本主题,并不受此局限。它随说话人目的的变化而变化,可以体现为一个句子复合体,也可以体现为一个句子序列。

例[4b]、[4c]、[4d]是并列的基本主题,没有意识取向的变化,所以它们的边界没有任何标记。值得一提的是:它们与例[2]中的三个问题不尽相同,三个问句只涉及三个方面,语言上体现为三个宾语,并且比较含混,多少有点不知所云,其实 Mailer 因为解决"内急"有失检点,唯恐受人指责,所以寻思着质问 Lowell。句中,the necessary 指"内急",the dignity 指由"内急"涉及的"体面",getting fat 等等只是作者从想象中提取的比喻性说法,暗指生理特点无法自制,所以实际上是一个问题,构成一个基本主题。而本例中三个并列基本主题是明晰的三个方面,三个论据。而且,例[2]中凸出的是"What do you know",而并不是随后的宾语,而本例中凸出的是 Consider 后面的内容。此例还可以让我们看到在话语进展过程中信息是如何打包(packaged)的。

3.5.3 《时代周刊》对温家宝的简介

下面我们再来看一则篇幅适当的完整语篇。2006 年 5 月《时代周刊》(*Time*)特刊刊载了 100 位世界名人的简介,我们引用来加以讨论的是该刊关于我国国务院时任总理温家宝的介绍。

[5] **China's Mr. Pragmatic Gets to Work** *By ORVILLE SCHELL*

(*a*) LESS IRASCIBLE AND BLUNT THAN HIS HARD-DRVING PREDECESSOR ZHU RONGJI, Chinese Premier Wen Jiabo has earned his reputation of being a modest even-tempered and practical person capable of getting things done through consensus. (*b*) Along with President Hu Jintao, he is part of a leadership composed largely of technocrats rather than revolutionary military veterans. (*c*) As Premier Wen has guided China's tectonic economy, supporting continued economic reform and growth but also pointedly calling for greater emphasis on social equality for those who have been left out of the country's "economic miracle". (*d*) Indeed his expressions of concern for the plight of ordinary peasants and laborers whose disaffection has manifested itself in an alarming increase in social unrest have given him the image of something of a populist. (*e*) He has faced other political challenges: the AIDS crisis, SARS, China's worsening environmental problems.

(*f*) Wen has taken a relatively hard line on Beijing's claim to Taiwan saying, "We don't hope for foreign intervention but we are not afraid of it". (*g*) Yet he has also taken pains to emphasize that in foreign policy, "the path embarked on by China is one of peaceful development" which he described recently as "the natural choice for China". (*TIME*, Special Issue May 8, 2006)

这一简介的作者夏伟(Orville Schell),是一位曾出版9本关于中国的专著的"中国通"。他的观点未必正确,学者们自会判断是非。这里我们只是用作语料,以求说明基本主题在语篇中的作用。《时代周刊》杂志刊载的名人介绍篇幅都有限。关于温家宝的一段仅196个词,由7个基本主题构成。

让我们先看这则语篇的题目。根据功能语法理论,标题"China's Mr. Pragmatic Gets to Work"中China's Mr. Pragmatic是主位,由于温总理务实,因而以pragmatic作为他的基本特征,"Gets to Work"是新信息(Martin & Rose 2003: 185)。作为标题,对于段落而言,相当于超主位和超新信息。由于这一段落构成了整个语篇,所以也就相当于宏观主位和宏观新信息,也就共同构成了语篇的主题。我们有理由相信每一个基本主题都是构成语篇主题的一个组成部分。让我们仔细考察每一个基本主题究竟集中讲什么。

[5a] general remark on Wen Jiabao's personality and capability which amounts to a general evaluation telling the readers what kind of person Wen is
[5b] his official status and the kind of governing body he serves
[5c] the role he has played as premier
[5d] his concern for the people and his image as a populist
[5e] the challenges he has to face
[5f] his firm stand on the sovereign right on Taiwan
[5g] his stand on foreign policy for China's peaceful development

可以看出这七个基本主题每一个都体现一个关注中心,具有相对的完整性和明确的要点,集中说明温家宝这一意象的不同方面,共同体现语篇的主题;而温家宝这一专有名词提示的概念是主位连接点,也就是所有的叙述都与此有直接关联。语篇十分紧凑,这说明意识从一个意识焦点到另一个意识焦点,从一个基本主题到另一基本主题的行进,由于取向明确而非常顺畅。但是这语篇中存在意识取向的变化,因而需要语言手段加以标示,同时引出新的关注中心、基本主题。这七个基本主题中,有四个以语篇标记或附加语开始。第四个主题以 indeed 开始,这是因为意识从 Wen the Premier 转移到 his expression of concern。第七个基本主题以 yet 开始,这是因为意识从温家宝在台湾问题上的立场转移到外交政策,同时意识起作用的状态也发生了变化,即从移置状态转入直接状态,从作者引用他的话"We don't hope for foreign intervention but we are not afraid of it"到作者自己表述温总理强调的我国和平发展的外交政策。此外,第二个基本主题以附加语 along with President Hu Jintao 开始,因为这里意识取向从温家宝的个人特征转至包括他在内的领导集体。第三个基本主题以 As Premier 开始,尽管温家宝作为总理已不是新信息,这里还重提,原因就在于随后的新基本主题从上一个基本主题的领导集体转移到他作为总理的责任。这里还有一点需要关注。"温家宝"在第一个基本主题就已经激活,在第二个基本主题的范围里这个概念还处于活性状态,所以可以用代词 he,那为什么到第三个基本主题就要用他的姓 Wen 呢?这里若用代词也完全可以,之所以用过度明确的回指表达式(overspecified anaphoric expression)Wen 是为了引出新的基本主题。同样的分析也适用于以 Wen 引出的第六个基本主题。例[5]表明基本主题不仅可以作为段落的一个部分,如例[4],而且在需要的情况下可以直接构成语篇。

3.6 结　语

基本主题从根本上讲是个概念现象,它的构成需要知识处理(knowledge management)中的内容结构和关注处理(attention management)中对这知识的诠释。根据杜利的研究结果,知识处理的主要表现是语篇图式结构,关注处理中的重要认知现象包括意识、关注和兴趣(Dooley 2007)。基本主题需要知识处理,因为为了满足说话人在交际的某一时间点上的需要,基本主题必须包含足够的信息;基本主题需要关注处理,是为了便于受话人理解和实施基本主题的全部信息。

在认知层面上,主题是半活性信息,它的作用在于整合语篇或某一语段中的若干心理空间;在语篇层次上语篇或语段围绕主题构建。语篇主题是语篇所讲的内容(what the discourse is about),语段的主题,比如段落的主题,是该语段或段落所讲的内容。从以上的例子可以看出,语篇和段落的主题通常体现为命题,如例[4]的主题,实际是宏观主位和宏观新信息的整合,例[5]的主题由标题点明,这两个层次上的主题是杜利所说的命题主题(Dooley 2007)。至于基本主题,往往是以复杂概念加以体现,这点以上所有实例都可以证实。这是因为语篇都有目的,这一目的要求一定的图式来组织语篇,而图式结构的统领(head)就是主题(Dooley 2007)。具有图式结构的语篇和段落自然应该有明确的主题。基本主题只是段落的一部分,虽有取向,但没有图式结构,主题往往要从所讲内容中加以推断。小句的主题是小句所讲的内容,通常就是功能语法所指的主位。

话语以信息单位或意义单位逐一推进,但一个信息单位如何向另一个信息单位行进,就得考察处于半活性信息的段落和整个语篇如何向意识焦点提供取向,图式如何为意识焦点提供行径,因此在研究语篇如何进展时既得由下而上,也得由上而下进行双向考察。其次,是不是若干信息单位直接构成段落,值得探讨。本文的实例提示,在小句与段落之间往往存在一个体现基本主题的小段,而且常有形式标记。这个中间语篇单位便于知识结构的组织和对这知识结构的诠释。

4

信息单位与信息状态
——试析语言信息的二分说与三分说*

4.1 引　言

在话语分析过程中，人们往往会提出一个带根本性的问题：话语究竟是如何推进的？韩礼德和马蒂森指出英语话语的推进呈现为不间断的系列旋律单位，每个旋律单位称作一个语调组，而每个语调组构成一个信息单位（Halliday & Matthiessen 1994：59）。在无标记的情况下，信息单位与小句重合。韩礼德说明，信息单位是由两个功能成分构成的结构（Halliday & Matthiessen 1994：296）。他进一步指出，就结构而言，信息单位是由必要的新信息成分和可取舍的已知成分构成。可见韩礼德对信息结构采用了二分的方法。切夫认为，"已知信息"或"旧信息"、"新信息"容易被误解，但他还是保留了这两个术语，另外增加了"可及信息"，只不过他从意识的角度对这三种信息重新作了界定（Chafe 1987：21－22）。显然，切夫对信息采取了三分的方法。这就向我们提出了许多问题：韩礼德和切夫都关注语篇推进，也都关注语调，那么为什么前者主张二分，而

* 本章原载《外语教学与研究》2010 年第 3 期第 190—197 页。

后者却用了三分？这分歧从何而来？孰是孰非？抑或两者可以相容？是不是介于已知信息和新信息之间存在一种中间信息？这些就是本章拟探讨的问题。我们先看他们各自的观点，然后再从功能认知的角度加以分析和讨论，并提出解决分歧的思路。

4.2 信息单位：已知信息+新信息

让我们首先看韩礼德如何界定信息，处理信息单位，又如何以信息结构组织话语，推进信息流程。

4.2.1 信息结构

韩礼德从话语推进的角度考虑信息单位（Halliday & Matthiessen 1994：59）。他根据说话人希望听话人赋予具体信息以怎样的信息地位而把话语的信息单位分成两个部分。一部分是新闻，即说话人要听话人当作新信息的信息，或者是出乎意料的或具有重要意义的信息。另一部分是旧闻，即被当作听话人已知的内容加以陈述的信息。韩礼德用是否可以还原（recoverable）来界定已知信息和新信息。可还原的信息可能是已经提及的内容，也可能是存在于情境之中的，还可能是只能意会的，或者是说话人为了某种修辞目的权当已知的信息。不可还原的信息可能是未曾提及的内容，也可能是出乎听话人意料的内容（Halliday & Matthiessen 1994：298）。可以看出，首先，韩礼德始终把信息放在信息单位中讨论。其次，在界定已知信息时，韩礼德考虑了交际过程中的主客观因素。客观上，是在话语中已经出现过，或在语境中出现或者从话语或语境中可以推导出的信息；主观上，是说话人根据其交际目的的需要将某个信息作为已知信息陈述，并指望听话人给予它已知信息的地位。他借助语调重音或叫语调凸出来体现新信息，通常处于语调的末尾，落在最后一个重读音节上。其三，由语调体现的信息单位是一种结构，是由两个功能成分构成的信息结构。韩礼德指出信息单位是由两个功能成分构成的结构，即新信息和已知信息（Halliday & Matthiessen 1994：89）。说这两个成分是功能成分是因为它们可用于说明语言是如何使用的（*ibid.*：XI－XII），话语是如何推进的。

4.2.2 信息和信息生成

韩礼德认为，从严格的语法意义上讲，信息是已知或可以预期的信息与新的或无法预期的信息之间的张力（*ibid.*：XI－XII）。新信息与非新信息之间的相互作用产生了语言学意义上的信息。首先，这两种信息之间存在着相互界定的关系。已知信息就是非新信息，新信息就是非已知信息。新信息是对已知信息而言的新信息。看一个例句：

[1] I'll tell you what silver needs to have. It needs to have love.

例[1]中的第二个小句与信息单位重合，其中 love 是新信息；这是针对已知信息 It needs to have 而言的，而这已知信息的信息地位可以从前一小句的内容得到确立，即可以从前一小句的内容 what silver needs to have 加以还原。在信息交流中，我们需要把已经积累的已知信息作为出发点，然后加上些新的内容，所以信息结构需要两个成分构成。这两个成分之间的张力和相互作用还不仅限于相互界定。我们需要区分小句意义和使用小句所表达的信息。例[1]的新信息产生于 It needs to have something 这一命题，而这个命题由这一小句以及前一问句 what silver needs to have 引出，推理的结果是 that something is love，所以 love 是新信息。虽然小句有两个成分构成，但叶斯柏森指出新信息总是内在于两个成分的结合之中（Jespersen 1924：145）。例如：

[2] — Who said that?
— **Peter** said it.

在与小句重合的信息结构里 Peter 是新信息。这新信息产生于两个成分的结合或互动。问句和答句所引出的命题是 someone said it，由此引出的结论是 that someone is Peter。Peter 是新信息。新信息本由句末的重音凸出标记,这里 Peter 虽是语调核心所在,但却位于句首。已知信息本应作为出发点位于新信息之前,在例[2]中却位于新信息之后,所以与例[1]不同,例[2]是有标记的信息结构,是语义关系和情景因素影响线性排列的结果。**Peter** said it 也可能是对照性的信息结构。也就是语境提示 somebody said it,有包括 Peter 在内的若干人可能说这句话,而且确定是 Peter 说了这句话。这最后的选择是对照和对照信息结构的基础。根据切夫的观察,它与非对照性信息结构中的新信息的发音不一样(Chafe 1974: 118)。更为明显的事实是,小句中通常作为已知信息,如代词,甚至介词可以被对照凸出,如 *I* said it。因此信息结构有对照性和非对照性的对立,在非对照性信息结构中有无标记和有标记的对立。这就构成了信息系统。信息归根结蒂是意义,而这多种意义又是由语调体现的,所以我们需要探讨语调在语言系统中的地位。

4.2.3 信息单位——语法单位

韩礼德和马西森指出小句语法用结构手段安排话语流程(Halliday & Matthiessen 2004: 88)。这里有两个有联系的系统在起作用。一个是小句系统,也就是主位系统。从这个系统中产生主位结构,用主位和述位构成的资讯(message)解释小句;另一个系统是信息系统。信息系统不是小句系统,而是另一个单独的语法单位的系统,也就是信息单位的系统。信息单位与小句或与小句相同级阶的单位平行。在无标记的情况下信息单位与小句有相同的延伸范围。这里韩礼德和马蒂森明确交代信息单位是语法单位。语言是创造意义的系统,具有三个层次,即语义、词汇语法和语音。它们之间存在体现关系: 词汇语法体现语义,语音体现词汇语法。语法和语义之间的关系是"自然的",也就是说对语义而言,语法形式不是独立自主的,不是任意的;同时语法结构可用其功能加以解释,功能语法是用元功能加以解释的语法。韩礼德(Halliday 1963: 239)指出: 英语语调对立是语法性质的对立,它们为语言的语法所利用。以语调表现的系统和以其他手段表现的系统,如时态、数、语气是一样的语法系统。作为小句语法的一个部分,语调和以语调体现的信息结构具有人际功能和话语功能,因此也是语篇的资源。人际意义是与语气和情态相关的意义,体现在对语调的选择上,如降调与升调分别体现告知与询问,也就与语气系统中的陈述和疑问语气相联系。话语功能表现在将话语构成语调组或信息单位,以使话语可以按单位逐步推进;还表现在构成话语上:语调有指称(phoric)功能,或回指或预指(Halliday 1985c: 287),所以具有衔接语篇的功能。所有这一切都说明语调虽然就其实质而言是语音系统的,但就其表义的功能而言却是一个语法系统,以语调体现的信息单位是一个语法单位。人们往往笼统地说语音和词汇语法的关系是任意的,其实此话并不全面。韩礼德和马蒂森指出,语音系统可以分为两个部分,即发音部分(articulation)和韵律部分(prosody)(Halliday & Matthiessen 2004: 11)。原则上,与音位(元音或辅音)有联系的发音部分是任意的,音义之间没有系统的联系;与语调和节奏有联系的韵律部分作为体现语法对立的资源,和语义的关系是自然的,与意义系统地对应。信息结构本质上是"自然的",这表现在两个方面:新信息由语调凸出标示,已知信息通常位于新信息之前(Halliday & Matthiessen 1994: 296)。这种结构安排适应说话人传达信息的需要,所以信息结构可以其功能加以说明。

基于以上的讨论可以看出:(1)韩礼德着眼于话语如何推进,但立足于句子语法,在讨论信息流时,聚焦于信息结构。(2)信息结构由两个功能成分构成,它们在信息结构中有不同的信息地位:已知信息和新信息。(3)语调是一个表义的系统,是一个语法系统,也是组篇的资源。(4)以语调体现的信息单位与小句一样是语法单位,信息结构与小句(主位)结构一样都是语法结构。

4.3 信息状态:已知信息、新信息和可及信息

切夫认为已知信息、新信息等等语言现象都是认知过程的表现(Chafe 1980: 9)。人们如何使用语言在很大程度上取决于他们在时间的推移过程中意识到什么——取决于他们内在注意的焦点,同时关注听话

人意识中的活动。切夫认为意识应该被看成是有意识的人与环境之间关键性的界面(Chafe 1994：38,1996a：39)。这与韩礼德和马蒂森的观点相通：意义是出自意识与其所处环境之间的相互作用(Halliday & Matthiessen 1999：17)。因此在讨论信息的时候不能不考虑意识。切夫甚至认为不考虑意识就无法理解已知信息和新信息的区别(Chafe 1994：72)。

4.3.1 意识和意识特征

意识在很大程度上是由感知、行为和情感的经验构成的(Chafe 1994：31)。人们对周围的世界都会形成自己的意识模式,神志清醒的人可能动地聚焦于或者说激活其中极小的部分,意识就指这有限信息的激活(Chafe 1994：28)。切夫认为思考涉及三个要素：信息、自我和意识(Chafe 1980：11)。信息指来自三个来源的大量知识。这三个来源指对世界的感知、记忆和情感;自我指对当前活动实施中心控制的执行者;意识指为自我服务对现有信息的激活,所以,意识是自我利用信息的机制。对于意识的特征,切夫有详细的论述(Chafe 1980：11－12,1987：22,1994：28－34,1996a：38－39,2007：359)。概括地说,意识有五个经常性特征。其一,意识有焦点,容量有限,持续时间有限,也就是说在任何时刻只有极少量的信息能够被最大程度地激活,构成焦点。其二,意识有边缘区域。意识焦点被边缘意识区域的半活性意识所围绕。边缘意识是一个十分重要的理论构建,为切夫的信息分类理论提供了认知上的基础。其三,意识是动态的,由于生理和认知能力的局限,意识呈一浪推一浪的形式前进。每一次意识的迸发(spurt),就出现上面说的意识焦点,语言上体现为意念单位(idea unit)(Chafe 1980)或语调单位(Chafe 1994),也就是韩礼德所说的信息单位。意念单位有三个标准：语音上是一个语调单位,有停顿,句法上通常为一个小句。其四,意识有自己的观点,这是指自我对于周围世界有自己的模式。其五,意识需要有取向(orientation)才能起作用,包括意识所处环境中的时间、空间、事件、正在进行的活动和参与的人物。这五点中,后两点实际是自我完成交际目的需要,不应把意识和使用语言的主体人割裂开来。此外意识还有可变性特征,其中值得交代的是意识可以在三种方式中起作用：直接方式(immediate mode),指对所处环境直接感知的方式；转置方式（displaced mode），即意识脱离当时当地通过记忆或想象聚焦于以往意识中衍生出来的经验；通用方式（generic mode），即意识不聚焦于特定事件或人物的情况（Chafe 2001：677）。区分这三种方式对话语分析具有重要意义。

4.3.2 三种信息状态

对于信息状态，切夫的认识可以说经历了三个阶段。起初切夫根据信息是否在意识之中进行界定。他明确地说：说话人认为在说话那一刻已在听话人意识里的信息是已知信息，说话人认为在说话那一刻不在听话人意识里的信息是新信息（Chafe 1974：112）。这个定义看似比通用术语明确，却把已知信息和新信息之间的关系割裂了。这时切夫的界定没有考虑意识的动态特征和信息状态的变化。随后切夫认识到不应把意识看成是容纳信息的处所（place），应该把信息状态建立在激活（activation）的基础之上（Chafe 1994：53），所以他把已知信息界定为“已经是活性的信息”，意思是已经激活的信息，新信息界定为“原来是非活性信息”，即原来没有激活的信息。此时他增加了第三种信息：可及信息，即“原来是半活性的信息”（Chafe 1987：22）。这样，信息就可处于三种不同的激活状态：活性的、半活性的和非活性的。最后，到20世纪90年代，切夫考虑了意识的动态特征，在界定信息状态时引进了时间因素。这时他说新信息是在会话某一时间点上新激活的信息，已知信息是在会话某时间点上已经激活的信息。他还把从半活性状态中激活的信息称为可及信息（accessible information）（Chafe 1994：72）。为了说明激活状态更能表明特定信息的状态，他举了以下一个例子：

［3］I talked to **Larry** last night.

虽然听说双方都认识Larry，但却是新信息，因为Larry原来是非活性信息，即仅是在长期记忆里的信息，而此刻被激活了，所以具有语调凸出。在一个时间点上被激活的信息是否是新信息要看它原来的信息状态。这就要求我们设定不同的时间点。把说话前的停顿间隙称作T1，实际说话的时间为T2，如果在T1为活性信息，到T2激活后就为已知信息，即上面说的原来是活性信息；T1 为半活性信息，到 T2 激活后就是可及信息；T1 为非活性信息，到 T2 激活后就为活性信息，也就是上面说的原来是非活性信息，即新信息（Chafe 1987：73）。这三种信息所需的激活代价不同，新信息所需最大，可及信息次之，已知信息最小。激活前的状态不同，激活时激活代价不同，信息就处于不同的活性状态。这样，切夫就区分了三种激活状态，最终对信息作了三项区分。必须说明切夫所说的信息状态仅指某个概念在话语进展中所处的信息状态，详见 4.4.2 节。

4.3.3 可及信息

由于切夫区分了意识核心和边缘意识，所以信息不仅具有在不在听话人意识中的区别，而且还有存在于意识核心或边缘意识的区别，因而可区分三种信息状态。切夫的认知理论无法通过实验加以证实，只能借助心理学中的相关实验结果，如视觉有注意焦点和背景，来推断人脑的意识也有意识焦点和边缘意识。但更重要的是，交际是基于我们思考和行事的概念系统，所以语言是佐证概念系统的重要来源（Lakoff & Johnson 1980：3），为此，切夫也在语言和语境中寻找信息状态的依据（Chafe 1994：86）。在这三种状态中唯有可及状态最难以捉摸，在韵律特征方面重音的主次区别细微，难以确定，在词汇方面可及信息与新信息一样可以名词加以体现。为此切夫提出要确定一个信息是否可及信息可考虑以下三点：（1）是否在先前的话语中曾是活性信息；（2）是否与话语中的某个意念有联系或有过联系；（3）是否与会话的非语言环境有联系，因而具有边缘活性，但并不是焦点。举例如下：

［4］*a.* You'd look at **the sun**.

b. … **it** just looked red.

c. I mean you couldn't see **the sun**.（Chafe 2007：366）

例［4a］表达过去的视觉经验，用 look 表示动作，用 sun 表示目标；the sun 具有语调凸出，在话语中原是非活性信息，在说话此刻被激活，所以成了新信息。例［4b］用 it 回指 the sun，是因为说话人以为 it 所指的 the sun 已经是听话人的活性意识，所以是已知信息。例［4c］中没有用 it，而用 the sun，但没有赋予语调凸出,语调凸出落在 couldn't 之上,但 the sun 这个意念仍然在说话人和听话人的边缘意识里,所以是可及信息。之所以第二次用 the sun 是因为说话人感到自己前两句话没有说清楚,要重新陈述。再看一例:

[5] We checked **the picnic supplies**.
The beer was warm.

例[5]中 the beer 是新信息还是可及信息? 如果是新信息,那就违背了主语由信息量不太大的意念承担的制约。那么何以是可及信息? 显然因为 the beer 与 the picnic supplies 有联系。The picnic supplies 里很可能有 beer,由于这一联系 beer 这一概念可能已经在说话人和听话人的边缘意识里。

[6] Well the kid is asleep.

话语中未出现过 kid,但却有一个 kid 在说话人的怀里,所以 the kid 在会话过程中处于说话人和听话人的边缘意识里,因而是半活性信息,也就是可及信息。

从以上的讨论可以看出:(1) 切夫也关注话语如何推进,但着眼于意识的作用,在讨论信息流时,他也以语调单位或意念单位为基本单位,但他把语调看作意识焦点的体现。(2) 切夫对信息的界定建立在意识之上,是以信息本身的活性程度加以界定的,至于存在于已知信息和新信息之间的关系经他界定之后就不复存在了。(3) 切夫脱离信息单位讨论信息状态,在增加可及信息之后更是如此。(4) 信息状态对于切夫来说至关重要,因为是信息状态赋予意识焦点以活性信息,边缘意识以半活性信息,没有前者在后者范围内的行进,没有后者为前者提供取向(orientation),就根本无法解释话语如何进展,也无法说明意识是如何塑造(shape)语言的。

4.4 分析与讨论

上面是对韩礼德和切夫有关理论的扼要阐述与初步分析。可以看出他们有相同或相通之处,但他们的理论依据不同,切入点不同,侧重点也不同,现分述如下。

4.4.1 信息结构——韩礼德的研究对象

韩礼德以《功能语法导论》(Halliday & Matthiessen 1994, 2004)为代表的功能语法是以小句作为基本单位(Halliday & Matthiessen 2004: 16)的小句语法,其范围不超过小句复合体,但其核心还是在小句。由于语法自身是体现语义的系统,功能小句语法是为了说明语义的,虽然语法止于小句,但语义却不止于此(Halliday & Matthiessen 2004: 87)。语义的单位是话语,小句语法是为了说明话语是如何表达它所表达的意义的。韩礼德把信息结构看作是与主位结构平行的结构。他成功地证实了体现信息结构的语调是创造意义的系统,是和主位系统一样的语法系统,是话语的重要资源(Halliday 1963,1985c;Halliday & Matthiessen 2004: 11－16,87－93)。这说明韩礼德是把信息结构作为小句语法的一个部分加以阐述。他讨论的对象是作为小句语法一个部分的信息结构以及构成信息结构的功能成分——已知信息和新信息。

4.4.2 信息状态——切夫的关注焦点

20 世纪 70 年代以来,切夫一直研究意识对语言和语言使用的作用,关注体现意识焦点的语调单位或意念单位如何组织话语、推动话语进展。话语是随着意识焦点的推移,按语调单位或意念单位向前推进的。他说语调是认知和语言的加工单位,凭借回声记忆(echoic memory),即较图像记忆持续时间稍长的声音记忆,语调单位可以作为整体加工(Chafe 1994: 55)。他的假设是每一个语调单位体现说话人说话时刻脑子里的活性信息,是那一刻说话人的意识焦点(Chafe 1994: 63)。在谈到具体的语调时,他说在某种意义上语调单位在话语里表示了新信息,但另一方面他又说新信息和已知信息可以独立地应用于语调单位中的所指个体(referent)(Chafe 1994: 71)。"独立地"也就是新信息和已知信息互不联系。这就告诉我们切夫把语调单位作为整体体现新信息，不去考察语调单位如何构成，其构成成分之间的关系如何；另一方面确定语调单位内意念的激活状态也无需考虑这语调单位。切夫在提出可及信息时，没有说明可及信息在信息单位中有什么位置，甚至没有交代附加可及信息的理由（Chafe 1987）。这样，他在理论上和分析实践上就把自己提出的三种信息状态置于信息单位之外，也就没有赋予这三种信息以话语功能。他还说，三种激活状态不适用于由语调单位体现的大块信息，只适用于存在于这些信息块中的个别意念（Chafe 1994：25）。意念指所指个体、事件和特征或状态，也叫概念（concept）（Chafe 1994：25），分别由名词、动词、形容词表示。由于事件和状态的意念在话语中作为新信息出现都极为短暂，在随后的语调单位中即被取代，而退至半活性状态，但是所指个体的意念至少可以在几个语调单位里持续处于活性状态，为此切夫的三种激活状态几乎仅适用于所指个体的意念，即表示人、物或抽象概念的意念（Chafe 1974：79，1996a：41）。因此他对信息状态的研究不在信息单位而在话语中的个别意念，特别是名词表达的概念。

4.4.3 二分或三分？

就句法而言，语言学家们都把小句看成是二分的：参考语法把句子分为主语和谓语，如（Quirk et al. 1972：49）。结构主义的直接成分分析法首次切分也是将小句分成主语和谓语（Herndon 1970：108），短语结构语法的第一条规则是 S→NP+VP（Herndon 1970：138）。认知语法将小句分析为小句图形（clausal figure）和小句背景（clausal ground）（Ungerer & Schmid 1996：173），或者将语法核心分为主语和动词短语（Radden & Dirven 2007：48），因此兰布雷希特说，从严格的语法或音系观点看，只有二分法才是合理的（Lambrecht 1994：100）。切夫并非一开始就提出三分的见解。切夫不仅用于不在听话人意识里界定已知信息和新信息，而且指出了这两种信息的关系（Chafe 1974）。他说，已在意识里的信息要先传达，在新信息和已知信息的关系建立之后，再把新信息加上去。每个句子都是已知信息和新信息的混合（Chafe 1974：112）。不仅如此，他还批评菲尔巴斯的交际动态程度（degrees of communicative dynamism）说（Firbas

1992)。菲尔巴斯的交际动态程度是指句子中一个语言成分对推动交际所作贡献的程度。其实,菲尔巴斯也实行二分:先将小句切分为主位+非主位,再将非主位切分为过渡+述位(Firbas 1992: 89)。切夫本是二分说的维护者。他认为已知信息和新信息不是程度的问题,而是二分的问题。他说语言上还没有证据说明已知信息和新信息不是明确二分的(Chafe 1976: 33);说话人对于听话人意识状态的假设除了基于二分之外,看不出还可能有其他区分(Chafe 1974: 119)。

然而,自从他区分意识焦点和边缘意识以后,他就开始对信息作三项分析,在已知信息和新信息以外增加了"可及"或"原来是半活性的"的信息,也就是他说的"在某种意义上介乎已知信息和新信息之间的信息"(Chafe 1987: 22)。这样,他似乎就背离了自己坚持的二分观点。怎么解释切夫的这一转变?这要从切夫学术思想的演变中找答案。为了说明话语如何推进,切夫提出了由若干意识焦点构成的关注中心(center of interest)的设想,并试图用单一意象(single image)(Chafe 1980: 27)和全盘记忆(entire memory)(Chafe 1980: 23)加以解释,但这偏离他理论上的出发点——意识的作用,难以自圆其说。于是他又转向意识并区分出意识焦点和边缘意识。边缘意识是处于意识焦点周围的意识,可以说明说话人的意识聚焦于某一点时,同时还朦胧地意识到这背景信息。边缘意识中的半活性信息构成焦点意识的语境,为它提供指向,使意识焦点在边缘意识的范围里一个接一个地行进,从而构成关注中心,语言上则是基本主题。切夫说,语言上语调单位体现活性意识,基本主题体现半活性意识(Chafe 1994: 140)。他还说语言用语调单位反映活性信息的焦点,用有层次结构的主题和次主题表示连贯的语段或半活性信息的边缘区域。处于意识边缘的半活性意识,可以从视觉实验得到间接的证实,也与我们的内省经验相符,语言上也有所体现,所以我们不能否认它的存在(Chafe 2007: 359)。

兰布雷希特在批评切夫的三分信息主张之后说,在已知信息和新信息之间设定可及信息的范畴并非没有语法根据(Lambrecht 1994: 100)。可见,兰布雷希特也无法全盘否定切夫的三分说。由于意识有焦点和边缘区域之分,所以存在最大程度的激活和不同程度的轻度激活(Chafe 1980: 12)。实际上切夫认为信息不止三种信息状态。他说值得注意"三"这个数字可能太小(Chafe 1994: 54),应该容许三个或更多的界限模糊的激活状态(Chafe 1994: 55)。而且,交际中判断听话人意识中概念的信息状态归根结底要看话语,要看这一概念在话语中是否已经提到过,要看它的所指性(referentiality),而所指性或可识别性(identifiability)是一个有不同程度的问题(Lambrecht 1994: 84),因此意念可以处于不同的信息状态。这样看,韩礼德基于信息结构功能的二分法和切夫基于意识激活状态的三分法都有各自的理由成立。

4.4.4 症结所在

韩礼德和切夫都关注话语的推进,都以语调组作为话语推进的基本单位,但是从语言功能出发的韩礼德始终在关注语言使用;切夫用意识说明语言和语言使用,这就涉及认知和语言两个层面,而他往往是停留在认知层面上,没有在语言使用的层面上考察语言现象。他对三种信息状态的界定,对个别概念的关注,对意识焦点的推进都是认知层面上的阐释。在他提出三分信息之后没有关注意念单位中的不同信息对推动话语起什么作用,它们之间有什么联系,前一个意念单位对后一个意念单位有什么影响。而这些正是话语推进中不可回避的语言使用问题。然而,切夫毕竟是一位注意观察的语言学家,因此即使在增加了可及信息之后,他还是把已知信息和新信息的区别作为分析语句的基本框架(Chafe 1994: 71)。他指出当一个意识焦点取代另一个意识焦点时,所指个体、事件或状态的意念或者保留活性状态或转入活性状态。这就是通常所说的已知信息和新信息区别的基础(Chafe 1994: 81,1996c: 42)。这话表明切夫的意识中仍然存在二分结构。显然,他是试图用信息状态的变化来说明话语推进,但这里他进入了语言使用的层面。"保留活性状态"说明"原来就是活性状态",表明这意念是已知信息;"转入活性状态"说明"原来处于非活性状态",经激活后进入活性状态,说明这意念是新信息。注意:切夫此处只提了两种信息。当一个意识焦点取代另一个意识焦点时,话语就在推进之中,语言就在实际使用之中,这时切夫实际上承认了体现意识焦点的意念单位中有已知信息和新信息,这样,他又回到二分的立场上。

这就告诉我们,切夫在涉及意念单位的构成时并没有抛弃二分的看法。然而在只能二分的意念单位里,他无法找到可及信息的位置,这样他就只能脱离信息单位探讨意念的信息状态。话语是按意念单位逐一推进的，那么就出现了一个无法回避的问题：难道有游离于意念单位之外的意念吗？当然不可能。那么可及信息在意念单位中有什么位置呢？

4.4.5 初步设想

信息单位涉及两个问题：一是信息单位中成分的排列，二是每个信息成分以什么语言成分体现。对无标记情况下信息的排列，切夫最初的认识和韩礼德没有分歧；谈到语言体现时，切夫指出已知信息在英语中以轻读的代词作为语言体现，新信息和可及信息以重读名词作为语言体现（Chafe 1994：81），而小句的出发点可以是已知信息或可及信息（Chafe 1994：86）。另一方面，代词和名词或名词词组可以体现信息单位的起点。从 4.3.3 节的实例看，可及信息也可以是已知信息或新信息的一部分。作为已知信息，可及信息可以成为信息单位的出发点，体现为名词，如例[4]的 beer、例[5]的 kid，只不过认知状态不及相应的代词高。可及信息也可以出现在谓语部分作为宾语，也体现为名词，如[4c]中的 sun。这是一个有标记的信息单位，其中 you 是已知信息，couldn't see the sun 是新信息。其中 see 由于与[4a]中的 look 有语义上的联系，see 也是可及信息，语调凸出在 couldn't 上，see 只有重音或次重音，所以只是新信息的一部分。切夫说起点可以是已知信息或可及信息，那么是什么因素决定选择不同信息作为出发点呢？从 4.3.3 的实例看，是语境起作用。可及信息是边缘意识中的信息，边缘意识是切夫对语境的认知解释而可及信息的应用也离不开语言使用中语境的作用。例[4]提供显性的语言语境，例[5]是以语言知识为基础，结合世界知识经过推理而获得的语境知识，例[6]是交际时的直接情景语境。在这些语境的作用下，听说双方的认知状况允许可及信息用作已知信息并由名词体现。可及信息作为小句的出发点，这只是在一定语境条件下可供选择的一种体现。

其实，韩礼德也看到这点，他说已知信息就是你听话人已经知道的信息或对你是可及的信息（Halliday & Matthiessen 1994：299）。新信息中作为可及信息的名词也是一种体现的选择。至于新信息中非语调凸出的动词，“可及信息”这个术语倒可利用。新信息的中心（locus）是谓语，可以是谓语动词、动词的补语、宾语或状语（Chafe 1994：108）。新信息中心就是语调凸出，中心以外的信息也就是新信息的一部分。韩礼德承认信息结构中新信息的结尾由语调凸出标记，但从什么地方开始却没有标记，这造成结构中的不定性（indeterminacy）（Halliday & Matthiessen 1994：296）。这不能不说是信息二分的一个缺陷。

参考菲尔巴斯关于"过渡"（transition）的论述（Firbas 2007：70－73），考虑动词特别是动词范畴特征在连接已知信息和新信息中的作用，把非语调核心的动词作为新信息的起点，称它为可及信息，这样可以避免信息结构的不定性。参考菲尔巴斯的二分法：信息单位→已知信息+新信息；新信息→可及信息+语调凸出。举个简单的例子：Silver needs to have love.其中，Silver是可及信息，用作已知信息，needs to have love是新信息；needs是新信息的起点，叫可及信息，love是新信息终点，有语调凸出。这样就在二分的线性排列中给可及信息一个位置，也赋予它以结构功能。然而，可及信息主要是体现层次上的现象。在信息单位中可及信息可以是已知信息或新信息的一部分，具有相应的功能，但这只是语境允许的一种体现选择，切夫的贡献在于对这种选择的动因作了认知解释。这仅是一种思路，尚待进一步探索。

4.5 结　语

韩礼德从功能的角度出发，以信息单位为研究对象，阐明信息和信息单位的构成以及信息单位作为信息结构如何将话语组织成已知信息和新信息，从而推动话语的进展。韩礼德重视信息单位的结构和结构成分的信息状态，也就是功能。但是，韩礼德对信息结构之间如何联系，如何构成话语单位，没有作明确的交代，而是留给以主位结构为基础的主位进展（thematic progression）作出说明。切夫从认知的角度出发，也就是从意识的角度出发，以信息状态为中心，根据激活状态，确定交际过程中听说双方意识中信息的三种状态，并以意识焦点为基本单位，通过意识焦点在边缘意识中的行进,说明话语如何推进。切夫把信息单位作为整体对待,不关心它的内在结构,并脱离信息单位确定话语中单个意念的信息状态。

韩礼德的目的在于说明信息结构和主位结构一样是小句语法的一个部分,作为创造语义的资源信息结构怎样在话语中体现语义。切夫的目的在于说明意识如何塑造语言,以怎样的手段影响语言,并力求在这些手段中找出常规。在切夫(Chafe 1976: 44)看来,意识是一种机制,激活状态的改变是信息打包的手段。这是切夫始终停留在认知层面上,专注于信息状态的原因。

韩礼德始终抓住语言的语义,这是他的功能观决定的。切夫似乎更关注形式,然而形式和内容无法分开。后来切夫也说,在正常情况下,我们既意识到形式也意识到意义(Chafe 1996b: 185)。为了应答杰肯道夫(Ray Jackendoff)的批评,他力求证明人们所意识到的是意义。随后,他在意识特征中增加了"内容(content)有限"(Chafe 2007: 359),代替以往他提出的"容量(capacity)有限"(Chafe 1980: 11),显然已改变了最初偏重形式的倾向。假如切夫把意义作为首要因素考虑,那他就会把语言使用置于考察的中心。

某一概念的信息状态,特别是已知信息和可及信息主要依靠该概念在话语中是否出现过,所以切夫对话语中的指称十分关注。他的研究报告中有突出的实例:一本小说中的一个名词在与它第一次出现相隔 105 页之后,仍可以是有定的已知信息(参见 Chafe 1976: 40)。这说明他关心话语的纵向鉴别系统(Martin & Rose 2003)。他在信息焦点的基础上为话语的进展设定了认知层面上的不同单位,并拟定了相应的语音、语法单位和相应的语义单位。在语篇层次上他提出了包含"次主题→基本主题→超主题"的层次结构。虽然他并没有明确区分语言的几个层次,对主题的层次也没有充分展开,但对话语结构的研究却有帮助。对于话语中单位之间的连接手段,他论述颇多(如 Chafe 1980: 12;1994: 122;1996c: 45, 2001: 675-683)。如果说韩礼德以信息单位为主的论述属于小句语法,那么,切夫基于信息状态的论述涉及话语结构、话语连接以及成分识别等等内容,可视为以认知为基础的语篇语法的一部分。

第二部分

叙事语篇分析

Part Two

ANALYSIS OF NARRATIVE DISCOURSE

5

语境在叙事语篇中的语言体现*

5.1 引　言

本章拟用韩礼德的功能语法理论对美国当代名著《夜幕下的大军》(*The Armies of the Night*)作一分析,以探讨语境和语篇的关系。

1967 年美国首都华盛顿发生了一场声势浩大的向五角大楼进军的反对越南战争的示威游行,前后持续了四天。小说记述了这一场四五万人参加的反战行动,同时也叙述了作为参加者和见证人的作者诺曼·梅勒本人在这四天中的经历和感受,以及触景生情而发的议论。此书 1968 年获美国非虚构小说普利策奖。

5.1.1 叙事文的特征

叙事文应具备以下四个特征:(1) 记述过去的真实或虚构的一系列

* 本章原载《外国语》1992 年第 2 期第 15—20+9 页,在此小标题有所改动。

行动或事件;(2)这些行动或事件应有曲折、异乎寻常而且适宜于报道的情节;(3)叙事人是行动或事件的参加者;(4)有一定的形式特征,包括以语言体现的叙事宏观结构(Gülich & Quasthoff 1985)。

用这个标准来衡量《夜幕下的大军》,就会发现这是一本以事实为基础的叙事小说。

5.1.2 语 境

言语活动总是在一定的语言环境中进行的。语言环境不外乎是指时间、空间、语言交际参加者的关系和在语言活动中的目的、语言作用等等,通常简称为语境(context of situation)。语境决定语篇的内容,也只有在语境中才能对语篇加以解释。语言的交际功能使得语篇依附于语境,体现语境,又作为语境的一个部分。所以我们说语境决定语篇的组篇(texture)和结构(structure)。这既适用于经过剪辑的短文,也适用于篇幅相当长的小说。不论是短文还是小说在韩礼德看来都是话语(text)。语境由语场(field)、语旨(tenor)和语式(mode)组成。本文将从语境的这三个范畴出发,探讨《夜幕下的大军》是以怎样的语言特征来体现语境的。

5.1.3 取 样

对一本小说进行话语分析,人们无法从头至尾逐页研究,所以不得不取样,通过对样章的详细分析,求得对整个语篇的语言特征有一个总体的了解。本文采用了随意取样(random sampling)和原则取样(principled sampling)相结合的办法。所谓随意取样,顾名思义就是避免先入之见的影响或从印象出发寻找语言材料加以佐证,而是随意挑选一节或一段进行分析。但是为了使取样具有代表性,足以以部分说明整体,那就必须要有选择的原则。在叙事小说中,全书的开头,一章的开头或结尾往往交代事件的时间、地点、人物或某一具体场景的实际环境和出场的人物,因此所用的语言具有叙事文的典型特征。

本文采用了第一卷第三部分第一章的第一段(全文附后),选择这一段而不选择第二章或第四章的第一段,体现了随意取样,选择第一章的第一段而不是第二段或别的段落,则是根据上述的基本认识确定的。

5.2 话语和语境之间的辩证关系

人们可以从语境出发通过推理了解到话语的语言特征、组篇和结构,也可以从话语出发推测出语境的总体特征。对这样一本小说进行分析,我们首先得确定其语境的主要组成成分的内容,然后探讨语境怎样决定话语,或者说,探讨话语如何体现这一语境,如何体现语场、语旨和语式。

5.2.1 语　场

语场——指发生了什么事。这本小说描写的是 20 世纪 60 年代美国社会的政治图景,在读者面前展现了一系列的行动——示威、群众集会、向五角大楼进军的游行,其目的是表示人们反对越南战争。成千上万的美国人卷入了这一系列行动,代表了形形色色的政治派别和政治力量。作者诺曼·梅勒参加了这次游行示威,被捕后经过一番周折又具结获释回家。这一语境特征明显地反映在用以说明示威过程和示威参加者的词汇上,反映在以 Norman Mailer、march、participate、support、Pentagon 为中心标记的一系列语义链(semantic chain)上。

5.2.2 语　旨

语旨——指谁参与了活动,参加者的地位和作用。叙事者向读者记述了这一事件,同时又向读者倾诉了他本人在这一事件中的经历。他从自己的视角出发陈述事件、表明态度、确定叙述的重点,从这个意义上讲,在语言交际过程中他支配着读者。

语言的人际功能反映在代词 we 和 us 的使用上,同时也反映在语言功能的选择上。比如作者常用祈使语气,表示敦促与请求,如"Rush to the locks""Deliver us from our curses"。值得一提的是本书使用 Norman Mailer 为主人公的名字。陈述政治事件必须客观,诉述个人经历又必须是谈切身的感受。这本书兼有客观事实的记录和个人感受的吐诉,这样就出现了矛盾。使用 Norman Mailer 作为主人公的名字,不用 I 而以代词 he 指代,暗示了作者置身于事件之外,在一旁作客观的叙述;而另一方面,读者都知道 Norman Mailer 就是作者本人,这就使他对自己经历的叙述产生一种身临其境、耳闻目睹的效果,从而解决了客观性与主观性之间的矛盾。

5.2.3 语　式

语式——指语言在起什么作用。在本书中,语言无疑起着构成作用,因为语言活动参加者之间的交往完全是通过语言来实现的。这里要略谈一下话语语式中的两个概念:渠道和媒介。渠道是指信息传递的不同方式,是通过声波还是通过刻印的形象传递。前者称作语音渠道,后者称作文字渠道。媒介是指遣词造句的型式化,例如语法的复杂程度,词汇密度的大小。这两个概念虽有联系,但含义不同。在本书中,由于作者采用的是文字渠道,所以,不存在语言活动参加者共同创造话语的过程。读者所接触到的是业已完成的作品,即经过精密构思、潜心创造而产生的书,媒介因而是英语的书面语。然而,当作者在记叙他的经历和他参与的事件的时候,他的脑子里始终呈现出他的"谈话"对象,犹如与读者促膝谈心,在叙述中他不断使用包括"听话人"在内的 we、us 或者称呼对方为 reader。因此他又有意识地使用口语媒介。这本书使读者阅读时仿佛在听作者娓娓而谈。

话语语式作为语境的特征之一,反映在含有篇章意义的语言特征之中。

5.3 三种结构的总体分析

语境的这三个主要特征是与语言的三大元功能相联系的，而这三大元功能，即意念(ideational)功能、人际(interpersonal)功能和语篇(textual)功能，又分别体现为及物性(transitivity)、情态(mood)和主位(theme)结构。现在让我们首先从这三个结构出发分析这一选段。

5.3.1 及物性

及物性表明语言中的不同过程即语义关系，以及用以表示这些关系的结构。本段共 32 个小句，经过逐句分析，发现各种过程的比例如下：

物质 12=37.5%
言语 3=9.3%
心理 2=6.2%
关系 10=31.2%
存在 5=15.6%

这一比例分布表明，在这一叙事段落中，表示动作(doing)的物质过程以及表示"是"(being)的关系过程是主要的过程类型。语境中的语场要求作者关注谁做了些什么，发生了什么事情以及人物和事物处于什么状态，所以物质过程和关系过程占了 68.7%，反过来说，及物性的分析结果也反映了语言活动所处的语境。

5.3.2 情　态

从情态上说，一个完整的小句不是直陈语气就是祈使语气。若是直陈语气,它不是陈述句就是疑问句,这一段的句子皆为直陈语气的陈述句,这表示语言功能适应了叙事的需要。

5.3.3 主　位

主位是小句的第一个成分,是信息的出发点,是小句加以说明的部分(Halliday 1985a),某一篇章中,若干小句的主位可以体现语篇展开的方式,表示作者叙述的目的和意图。我们分析的这一段中,主位由表示时间、地点、人物、事物、气氛和存在的词语体现,其数目分别为 2、5、9、4、7、5,其中表示时间、地点、人物的占总数的二分之一。值得一提的是,在以表示人物的词为主位的 9 句中,有 4 句以 Mailer、the novelist 或代词 he 为主位,其余 5 句体现主位的词皆是非特指代词 everybody、one,或泛指的名词短语如 some of the Under-Thirties。Mailer 在这一段的第一句的述位中出现,在第 8 句中作为意念主位,到第 13、15 句就成了无标记主位,体现了他中心人物的地位。从上面的分析看,作者交代了事件的时间(Next morning)、地点(the City, the Capital)、具体场所(in the lobby, the streets of downtown Washington);而叙述场景的气氛(the atmosphere, this mood, the air),即使作为主位的事物名称,如 they(指 motor cycles)、funky redolence of gasoline,也是为烘托出环境的气氛。这样看来这一段确实具有叙事文的典型特征和结构,体现了语言的语篇功能和语境的主要范畴。

现在让我们进一步分析这一小段,看一看究竟有哪些体现语境的具体语言特征。

5.4 句与小句的具体分析

这一段共 488 个词,组成 32 个小句。按照话语分析的一般做法,定语从句如“saying hello to people they had not seen in years”“echo of voices a block away which promised violence”作为名词词组的修饰成分不作小句计算。不用作名词修饰语的非限定性动词词组却作为小句考虑,因为这些词组表示了过程。本段中小句的平均长度为 15.2 个词。

5.4.1 句　式

全段共 18 句,9 句为简单句,另 9 句为小句复合句,其中 6 句为并列,占 66.6%,仅有 3 句为主从,占 33.3%。

5.4.2 词　序

就词序而言,5 个小句为 SV 型,占 15.6%,18 个小句为 SVO 型,占 56.25%,6 个小句为 SVC 型,占 18.75%,3 个小句为“there be”型,占 9.3%,所有这些小句皆为正常词序,即使“there be”引导出的存在句,我们也没有必要看作倒装。

5.4.3 词　汇

除了 prevail、promise、predict 之外,所有的动词都是单音节词,如 meet、say、see、do、think、hold、wait、go、come 等。单音节词与双音节词的比例为 10∶1,而且几乎所有单音节词都源于古英语,都属常用积极词汇。

5.4.4 语　态

这 32 个小句中,仅 1 句为被动语态(that funky redolence … was not derived from nothing),其余皆为主动语态。

5.4.5 时　体

就时体而言,几乎所有的小句的动词都为过去时,5 个动词为过去完成时,因为它们所表示的动作发生在过去某参照点之前,1 个动词为过去进行时,这是为了说明它所表示的动作在过去某一时刻尚在持续。然而这一段中却有 4 个动词为现在时,它们都用于具有插入语性质的小句之中,置于破折号之后,用以表示叙事人在叙述过程中所作的评述或补充。例如:

— one waits for them to explode, but they never do. ... there is nothing like the search ...

过去时与现在时在一段中并用,说明作者在记述过去事实的时候,不时地用作者讲话时的观点审时度势,发表议论,提供解释。这在本书中到处可见,也许可以看作长篇叙事小说的语言特征之一,与单一用过去时的短小叙事篇章很不相同。

5.4.6 媒　介

上面提到过这一段句子的平均长度为 15.2 个词。这意味着句子长度适中,属于正常范围。但是全段 18 个句子的长度参差不齐。如果我们把 30 个词以上的句子称为长句,5 个或 5 个词以下的句子为短句(Cheng 1989),我们就会发现令人深思的结果:短句为 2 个(如果我们把短句标准限在 10 个词,那么我们就有 4 个短句),但有 5 个长句,各自的词数为 56、43、67、57 和 31,五句的总词数为 249,超过全段总词数的一半。不仅如此,这五句连贯而下,一句接着一句,构成了选段的后半部分。若不对这前后两个部分作一分析,就难以看出这一语篇的总体特征。前半部分有若干非正式用语,如"say hello to each other"(比较 exchange greetings)和"gunning up and down"(比较 speeding up and down, tearing up and down)。同时还有一些省略用法(Cheng 1989),如"the thousand days of John Kennedy",通常应该说 the thousand days of Kennedy Administration,

或者 the thousand days of the Presidency of John Kennedy。又如 Under-Thirties，意思是 30 岁以下的左派，正常的英语当为"the leftists under thirty years of age"，而在后半部分，我们发现有 10 个名词化的词组，如"excrement of putrefactions""torsion of lust""the search of a clear figure of speech"等，语法结构的紧凑，使得后半部分的叙述十分紧凑。此外还有若干相当正式的用语，如 redolence、excerbation 和 gyroscopic intensity 等。这些事实说明尽管作为叙事小说其渠道自然是文字，但本段前半部分却使用了口语媒介，而后半部则用了书面媒介。但情况并不如此简单。在前半部分并不乏正式用语，如"sartorial sense"和"subtle concomitants of power"，也出现了名词化的词组如"that same offering of fever"。而后半部分也具有非正式的色彩，这不仅表现在用 funky 这样的便语，而且更为突出地表现在小句的开头或中间不止一次加进了 no、yes，甚至具有口语特征的 yeah，用以表示肯定或者加强前面或后面的内容，或者表示说话人在叙述过程中的停顿。在连贯的书面语中通常不会出现这种情况，所以 no、yeah 等的使用体现了口语媒介。我们有理由说，这些口语媒介中含有书面成分、而书面媒介中又含有口语成分，两者交融互补，这不能不说是由语境决定的叙事语篇的特征。由于有这样的特征，这段话语在语场方面交代了场景和人物，在语旨方面作者向读者进行了描述，而在语式方面书面语听起来又似口语。

5.4.7 长　句

分析起来，上述长句的使用还有两个因素。一是叙述者讲述节奏的需要。一节开始，作者引出主题，逐步展开，场景从小到大，由内而外，由客厅到城市，由场景到人物，由人物对现场的反应到广泛的跨越时空的联想。叙述者为了进一步加深读者的印象，使用大量并列短语与小句，节奏不断加快，欲罢不能，所以出现了长句。最为突出的例子，当数这本书的第三部分第四节的一个长句。这个长句含 48 个限定性小句，8 个非限定性小句，总共 621 个词。这里作者在写游行拥挤受阻中停止不前的景象，同时又触景生情产生了许多联想，以 as if 引出许多表示比喻的小句。为了始终抓住"听者"的注意力，避免语调降至最低点，并加快节奏，一泻而下,以至出现罕见的长句。从结构上说,这个长句显然不像书面语那样严谨紧凑,句子中间也出现了 no、yes 以及用以补充、说明、修正的插入语,因此也反映了叙事者在书面语中两种媒介的混合使用。这也体现了语境的要求和特点。

本段使用长句的另一个原因是作者在本段前半部分介绍环境,而从第八句开始转向本书的主人公 Mailer,作者以外部观点描述主人公的内在思想活动,因而难以作十分肯定的叙述,于是出现了诸如"if not for tonight, then for another ..." "If the novelist had never heard ... he would still have predicted ..."含条件从句的说明。同时对主人公的思索,作出种种猜测,所以出现了"Mailer had no idea whether ... whether ... or if"等包含三个并列宾语从句的长句。

5.4.8 口头叙事

在上述分析的过程中,我们已经看出了语境在叙事语篇中的某些语言体现。上述另一些语言特征还告诉我们:66.6%的并列小句复合句说明叙事语篇按事件发生的顺序,平铺直叙,这些句子中的小句,对于传递信息来说具有同等重要性。在叙事中作者陈述事实,无需特别强调句子的任何部分,所以所有小句都属正常词序,而且绝大多数为主动语态。英语单音节动词的大量使用说明作者意识到在对读者"说话",读来具有非正式的口语色彩等。这些语言特征清楚地反映了叙事的要求和语境的需要。

5.5 体现语境的其他语言特征

除了这一选段显示的语言特征外,在小说的其他部分也有许多体现语境,特别是体现语旨和语式的语言特征,现略述如下。

5.5.1 正字法

作者在书面语中引进口语媒介，也表现在正字法上，如书中不止一次出现 Wo-eeeeee！Woo-eeeeee！这不仅表示了语音，语音变化，而且还表示发音持续时间。另一个典型的例子是：You must Fight ... fight ... fight, fite, ite ...作者用不同的字体，不同的拼法暗示了有力的呼喊逐渐减弱，直到辅音消失，最后整个词完全在空中消失。这说明作者始终意识到自己在对"听众""讲话"，所以对于语音十分关注。

5.5.2 并列系列句

一连串的句子成分，用 and 或 or 并列，或用逗号分开，这是叙事语篇的一个重要特点。它给人的印象是作者兴之所至随便说来，同时又以重复达到了渐次加强语气的目的。例如：

[1] ... and here the reason became *so many and so curious and so vague*, *so political and so primitive*, so that there was no need, or perhaps no possibility to talk about it yet ...

[2] ... they had had their minds *jabbed and pocked and twitched and probed and finally galvanized* into surrealistic modes of response ...

[3] So they came up one by one ... each breaking *the shield or the fence or the mode or the home or even the construct* of his own security.

叶斯柏森在论及类似结构时指出，当说话人开始列举的时候，他并不清楚他究竟要举出多少项目，显然这种结构适用于日常的谈话(Jespersen 1924)。实际上说话人在到达列举过程中某一点时，他甚至不清楚下面讲什么，只是边想边说，所有的项目皆用降调，随时可以停止。如果词语在脑际出现，说话还可以继续。下面一句是 10 个词紧贴着排列：

[4] *The middle class plus one hippie surrealistic symbolic absolutely insane* March on the Pentagon, bless us all.

这里用 4 个修饰语说明 march 的性质。叙述人并没有考虑对这些修饰语应如何作合乎逻辑的安排,也不加停顿,而是把它们串连在一起,这体现了即席讲话的语言特点。

如果说句[4]还有一点书面语的意味的话,那么句[5]就很难说有书面语的痕迹了。这显然是口语媒介的体现:

[5] Still he made no effort to *win the audience*, *seduce them*, *dominate them*, *bully them*, *amuse them*, no, they were there for him; to please him.

5.5.3 排比小句

上面讨论的这些多项并列结构几乎每页都有,下面看一看排比小句。

[6] One *worked* for the Revolution twenty-four hours a day, *one proselyted*, *one organized*, *one explained*, *one instructed*, *one inspired*, *one worked*.

这是一个小句复合句,包括 7 个小句,除了第一个小句外,其余皆由两个词组成。同样在最后一个小句之前没有 and,似乎作者还有意继续说下去。one 的一再重复,小句短得不能再短,这都是口语媒介的体现。

当然,我们也发现了许多主从复合句。例如:

[7] He *felt* his own age, forty-four, *felt* it *as if* he were finally one age, not seven, *felt as if* he were solid embodiment of bone, muscle, flesh, and vested substance, rather than the will, heart, mind, and sentiment to be a man, *as if* he had arrived, *as if* this picayune arrest had been his Rubicon.

这个句子中有 7 个小句,无论是 3 个主句,还是第二个主句引出的 3 个 as if 从句都是通过紧接排列体现并列关系。这又多少带有口头语的特点。

5.6 结　语

以上这些具体的语言特征体现了作者叙述往事和个人经历的需要,

体现了语境三个范畴的需要。我们分析这一段以求说明语境和话语之间的辩证关系。即使在这短短的一个段落中,我们看到了语言以怎样丰富的手段来展示小说主人公在特定的场合的心理状态,示威游行前华盛顿的气氛,人们之间的共同意志和相互分歧,这些语言特征也体现了作者通过两种媒介并用,向"听众"作绘声绘色的描述。

在这一叙事语篇中,语境固然体现在若干语言特征上,但作为一本著作,自然还应体现在全书的黏合(cohesion)和连贯(coherence)上,体现在宏观命题(macro-proposition)的展开以及作为其语言表现的叙事宏观结构上。限于篇幅,本章不再讲述,另见随后两章。

附录:本章所分析的样本

Next morning, Macdonald and Lowell met Mailer in the dining room of the Hay-Adams for breakfast. There was a crowd about now. In the lobby, a mood prevailed of well-dressed people come together for a collective celebration — a homecoming game or civic testimonial, or class reunion. Everybody was saying hello to people they had not seen in years, and everybody looked good. The thousand days of John Kennedy had done much to change the style of America; nowhere perhaps more than to the sartorial sense of the liberals and Left Wing intellectuals now gathering for breakfast — some drabness had quit them since the fifties, some sense of power had touched them with subtle concomitants of power — a hint of elegance. The city was awake. On the way to the hotel last night, somewhat after midnight, Mailer thought the streets of downtown Washington held a hint of Times Square in early morning hours, that same offering of fevers not abated, echo of voices a block away which promised violence — if not for tonight, then, for another. The whores were out: not a common sight in Washington. The Capital was usually about as lively at 1 A.M. as the center of Cincinnati late at night, but now there were motorcycles gunning up and down the avenues with their whine of constant climax looping into the new whine of higher climax — one waits for them to explode, they never do, they go gunning for the night. The air was violent, yet full of amusement; out of focus. Mailer had no idea whether this atmosphere was actually now typical of Washington on Friday night (as lately of more than one other quiet American city) or whether this mood came in with the weekend migrants from New York; or if indeed some of the Under-Thirties in Washington were warming up to repel the invasion. There was a hint of hurricane calm, then wind-bursts, gut-roars from the hogs. If the novelist had never heard of Hell's Angels, or motorcycle gangs, he would still have predicted, no, rather invented motorcycle orgies, because the orgy and technology seemed to come together in the sound of 1200 cc's on two wheels, that exacerbation of flesh, torsion of lust, rhythm in the pistons, stink of gasoline, yeah, oil as the last excrement of putrefactions buried a million years in Mother Earth, yes indeed, that funky redolence of gasoline was not derived from nothing, no, doubtless it was the stench of the river Styx (a punning metaphor appropriate to John Updike no doubt) but Mailer weak in Greek, had nonetheless some passing cloudy unresolved image now of man as Charon on that river of gasoline Styx wandering between earth and the holy mills of the machine. Like most cloudy metaphors, this served to get him home — there is nothing like the search for a clear figure of speech to induce gyroscopic intensity sufficient for the compass to work.

6

The Texture of *The Armies of the Night*[*]

6.1 Cohesion

6.1.1 Texture and cohesion

Texture is a matter of meaning relations, and semantic relations are the basis of cohesion (Halliday & Hasan 1989). To study the internal texture, it is necessary first of all to study cohesion. Cohesion means the linking together of different parts of a text through the use of words and grammatical constructions which depend on other parts of the text for their interpretation (Fries 1991a). What we must do is to find such cohesive ties between parts of a text, and it is these ties that help create cohesion of the text. In the case of a full-length novel, cohesion is expected to manifest itself between paragraphs of each chapter, between chapters of each part and between parts of a book. This means that we assume that each paragraph is a cohesive unit

---

* 本章原载《外语论丛》1991 年第 1—34 页。

Table 6－1 Summary of Cohesive Devices and Ties of Chapter II of Book I

(∗ =Substitution & Ellipsis)

Cohesive devices / Cohesive ties / Paragraph	Grammatical devices					Lexical device	Organic Relations			
	Reference				*					
	Pro-nominal	Demon-strative	Def. Article	Com-parison		Repetition	Adver-sative	Conces-sion	Transi-tion	Result
2						Norman Mailer		still		
3	he							Now that however		
4		such								
5	he	this				(he) lost his bet				
6	he								No	
7						Mailer	In fact			
8	us it					Mailer	In fact			
9	one									
10	here					Mailer				therefore
11			the							therefore

(Continued on page 85)

Cohesive devices / Cohesive ties / Paragraph	Grammatical devices					Lexical device	Organic Relations			
	Reference				*					
	Pro-nominal	**Demon-strative**	**Def. Article**	**Com-parison**		**Repetition**	**Adver-sative**	**Conces-sion**	**Transi-tion**	**Result**
12	I					Mailer circulars				
13	one	this							Well	
14		such				Mailer				
15	he	this								
16						Goodman				
17		this								
18	other		the			Goodman				
19						Mailer				
20				later						
21		that								
Total	11	7	2	1	0	11	2	3	2	2
Percentage	26.8%	17.1%	4.9%	2.4%	0	26.8%	4.9%	7.3%	4.9%	4.9%

Table 6 – 2 Summary of Cohesive Devices and Ties of Chapter II of Book II

(* =Substitution & Ellipsis)

Cohesive devices / Cohesive ties / Paragraph	Grammatical devices					Lexical device	Organic Relations					Meaning association
	Reference				*							
	Pronominal	Demonstrative	Def. article	Comparison		Repetition	Adversative	Concession	Transition	Result	Replacement	
2		this							Now			
3		these										
4										so		
5			the				But					
6									Then			
7		these				March				therefore		
8			the									
9						Congress						
10												ensued
11						Visionary	however					
12				later		Rubin						
13		such										

(Continued on page 87)

Cohesive devices / Cohesive ties / Paragraph	Grammatical devices					Lexical device	Organic Relations					Meaning association
	Reference				*							
	Prono-minal	Demon-strative	Def. article	Com-parison		Repeti-tion	Adver-sative	Conces-sion	Transi-tion	Result	Replace-ment	
14			the the									
15		these					none-theless					
16		this										
17	they						none-theless					
18			the			South Parking Area, the Pentagon						
19						the South Parking					on the other hand	
20						the north wall				so		
21			the									
Total	1	6	6	1		8	4	0	2	3	1	1
Percentage	3.0%	18.2%	18.2%	3.0%	0	24.2%	12.1%	0	6.1%	9.1%	3.0%	3.0%

and so we start at the paragraph level, and proceed to identify cohesive ties between paragraphs, those between chapters, and ultimately between the two books of the novel. Samples will be studied. They are Chapter II of each book, and also Part IV of Book I, which consists of as many as 11 chapters. Now let us look at the devices and ties found in Chapter II of Book I summarized in Table 6 – 1 (see pages 84 – 85).

Explicit cohesive ties are identified in each of the twenty-one paragraphs in this chapter. It is worthy of note that we invariably find a cohesive tie or ties linking the first sentence of a paragraph with the last sentence of the preceding one. This makes for easy transition from paragraph to paragraph and might be regarded as a characteristic feature of narration. Although semantic relations are the basis of cohesion, we have not found a single case in which two paragraphs hang together through association of sheer meaning. Besides, substitution and ellipsis as grammatical cohesive ties do not seem to apply across paragraphs, for they require immediate adjacency and often parallelism. As Table 6 – 1 demonstrates reference and repetition are the two major devices by which paragraphs are related. However, no exorphoric reference is found, for no immediate situation grants its use. Besides, the proper noun "Mailer" (7 occurrences) appears more often than the pronoun "he" (4 occurrences) that refers to it. The noun is repeated to achieve explicitness in a new paragraph. The reader will readily know who is being talked about. "He" appears in such short clauses as *He lost his bet* and *he growled* in one-sentence paragraphs, which will not pose any problem as to the identity of the theme.

6.1.2 Cohesion between paragraphs

Now let us turn to the second chapter of Book II, to see how the paragraphs cohere.

In comparison with Table 6–1, Table 6–2 (see pages 86–87) demonstrates the following features:

1) Logical connecters are used more often here than in Chapter II of Book I.

2) In a number of paragraphs the first sentence contains one end of a cohesive tie that does not find the other end of the tie in the last sentence of the previous paragraph, but in the middle of the paragraph.

3) Only one pronoun "they" is found as a tie.

4) Seven different words are repeated instead of two in Table 6 – 1.

These features reflect the difference in field between the two. Chapter II of Book I centers on the protagonist Norman Mailer, whereas Chapter II of Book II discusses what form the demonstration would take and which would be chosen as the target, Congress or the Pentagon. So different views were aired and argued, and possibilities explored. This may account for the repetition of different words and the use of a number of conjunctives.

Again, no instance of substitution, ellipsis or exorphoric reference is found as a device of cohesion. But we need to modify the observation we made about the cohesive ties found between paragraphs in Chapter II of Book I by saying that the cohesion of two paragraphs achieved through the linking of the first sentence of a paragraph to the last of the previous one by a cohesive tie might be regarded as a characteristic feature of long narration of personal experience. We must also note that repetition is still the major device in achieving cohesion between paragraphs.

In studying the cohesion of the two chapters we concentrate on the first sentence of each paragraph to see if there is any word or phrase that refers back to an item in the preceding paragraph, especially in the last sentence of the preceding paragraph, to form a cohesive tie between the two paragraphs. A question naturally presents itself to us: Does the cohesive tie thus identified mean that the two paragraphs cohere? To answer the question we need to take a quick look at the paragraph as a unit of written language. A paragraph is in itself a text, and therefore has its internal structure. The English paragraph is generally composed of Claim and Elaboration, usually centering round one theme or dealing with a particular point of it. Generally the first sentence that marks the beginning of the generation of the paragraph is the topic sentence.

As the term suggests, it sets out the topic or the theme of the paragraph. The English paragraph is generally deductively organized, so the last sentence of the paragraph, which may be the end of an elaboration, generally refers back to the theme. As a paragraph only forms part of a chapter, the theme of a paragraph is often the theme of the chapter, or a theme that is shared by more than one paragraph: a new paragraph often takes up the same theme and expands on it. These experiential meaning relations call for cohesive ties across paragraphs. On the other hand the logical meaning relations between paragraphs find expression in logical connectors. Furthermore, both meaning relations require the ties and connectors to appear in the first sentence of a paragraph. All this serves to justify our concentration on the beginning sentence of a paragraph.

6.1.3 Cohesion between chapters

With this explanation done, we will move on to Part IV of Book I to see how the chapters are brought together to form an even larger cohesive unit, for by the same token the first sentence of each chapter should contain cohesive ties and logical connectors that are the indications of cohesion of the whole part.

Table 6 - 3 Summary of the Cohesive Ties and Cohesive Devices of Part IV of Book I

Chapters	A Cohesive ties	B Cohesive ties	Cohesive device	Logical connectors
1 - 2	the *soldiers and Marshals* standing about had a cold professional studied indifference ...	*They* put him the rear seat of a Volkswagen camper ...	Reference	
2 - 3	Then the *truck* began to move	There was not much to see through the Canvas arch of the *vehicle*	Reference Meronymy	

(Continued on the next page)

Chapters	A Cohesive ties	B Cohesive ties	Cohesive device	Logical connectors
3 – 4	From when he sat in *the bus*, he could see …	*In fact the bus* is getting ready to leave the Pentagon.	Reference Repetition	Adversative
4 – 5	It was the *U.S. post office* in Alexandria	They … walked … through the empty downstairs floor of *the post office*	Reference Repetition	
5 – 6	It was getting near to ten o'clock on Saturday *night* …	*That night* at Occoguan, Mailer had a long revery about the war in Vietnam	Reference Repetition	
6 – 7	*The argument* in the brain can be submitted to the reader in the following pages …	He knew *the arguments* for the war, and against the war	Reference Repetition	
7 – 8	Mailer slept.	His suit was in poor shape by morning	Association of meaning	
8 – 9	*You lawyer* is wearing sneakers.	It was *de Grazia.*	Lexical, association	
9 – 10	"All right" he said quietly, "pending appeal we will then release the Defendant on his recognizance."	Five minutes *later* was a scene of congratulation …	Reference through comparison	
10 – 11	It was obvious *the good novelist Norman Mailer* had much to learn about newspapers, reporters, and salience.	Still *he* was not injured unduly	Reference	Adversative

In Column A are listed sentences containing lexical ties near the end of a chapter and in Column B are listed the first sentence of each of the subsequent chapters containing words that refer back to those in Column A, thus forming cohesive ties. It is interesting to note that all the cohesive ties found in Column A are found in the last paragraph of each chapter. In fact out of the ten sentences listed five are the first sentences of the paragraphs, two of them are also the last, since the paragraphs consist each of a single sentence. Two others are the second sentences. They are virtually a continuation of the first sentences. For instance, *It was the U.S. Post Office* follows *Now they reached their prison* stating the fact that the prison was in fact a post office.

On the other hand, all these words in the ties are referred back to or repeated by words in the very first sentence of each chapter. This seems to confirm what we claimed in 6.1.1. We also find that reference and repetition are still the more favored cohesive devices. There is one instance of cohesion through association of meaning. *His suit was in poor shape by morning* coheres with *Mailer slept* in the preceding chapter through the inference from the world knowledge that one takes off his suit when he goes to bed at night and that one gets up and dresses in the morning.

So far we have shown how paragraphs and chapters hang together through the use of cohesive ties between the end of one part and the beginning of the next. Needless to say there are far more ties than we have identified, but the three tables are indicative enough of the cohesion of the novel except that between the two books.

6.1.4 Cohesion between the two Books

The novel consists of two books, the first being self-contained and published in Haper's in 1968 and the second being added on when the novel came out in book form the same year. The subtitles of the two books suggest that they are related: *History as a Novel* and *the Novel as History*. The definite article "the" in the subtitle of the second book refers anaphorically to "a novel" in that of the first, thus establishing a relation of co-referentiality between them. The same entity is referred to but assumes a different form.

In the very last sentence of Book I, we find "*he ... found himself ready at last to write a most concise Short History ... some Novel of History ...*" This is taken up in the very first sentence of Book II: "*The Novelist in passing his baton to the Historian has a happy smile.*" As "historian" is associated with "history" and "novelist" with "novel" in meaning and formation, the end of the first book is related to the beginning of the second, thus signaling the hanging together of the two books. There are too many cohesive ties to list here, and what is more, one wonders if the repetition of a word or phrase can be counted as a cohesive tie when one deals with a lengthy text. If it does not establish semantic relation of co-referentiality, co-relation or coextension, the two items are not related as a tie. Distance is also a factor one needs to take into consideration. However, if we can identify salient cohesive ties, ties that depend solely on each other for their interpretation, distance does not seem to be a problem. Two examples will be enough. Near the end of Book II, we find "*So the weekend in Washington which had begun with a phone call from Mitchill Goodman gave promise of ending in Harrisbary or Leavenworth*". Here "the weekend" refers to the weekend when the March on the Pentagon took place and "the phone call from Mitchill Goodman" refers back to the beginning of Book I where we find "the phone rang ..." a call from Goodman urging him to participate in the rally and demonstration over "the weekend." This semantic relation enables one to understand why the weekend "gave promise of ending in" prison. One more salient example is a line of a poem in Book I repeated near the end of Book I: *the chinook salmon nosing up the impossible*. It is all but impossible to explicate the line until we get to where its repetition occurs. In spite of the mixed metaphors there, we are given to understand who "the chinook salmon" stands for, and what "nosing up the impossible" means. So since the interpretation of one depends on the meaning of the other, the repetition makes a cohesive tie that contributes to the cohesion of the two major parts of the book.

6.2 Macro-propositions

6.2.1 Semantic chains

In the texts we have examined we find a large number of cases of grammatical cohesion through reference and of lexical coherence through repetition. There are other meaning relations that underlie cohesive ties such as synonymy, antonymy, hyponymy and meronymy. Words and phrases are found to string together on the basis of such meaning relations, thus forming a chain that runs through the text. To examine the cohesion of a book it is necessary to identify semantic chains in the text. In such a book of nearly three hundred pages there are bound to be quite a number of semantic chains. What we can do is to identify those that are relevant to the intertextual thematic formation (Lemke 1995). Two points need to be made here. First, as a semantic chain is a semantic group, what counts as an item in the chain is determined by the thematic formation, which in turn is determined by the context of situation and the "socially meaningful doings" (Lemke 1995) in the larger context of culture. The word "speak" can only be grouped together with "support" in such a thematic formation as a demonstration in the U.S. To speak at a mass rally implies support on the part of the speaker. Secondly, a semantic chain may be composed of lexical items as well as recurrent propositions realized in clauses or clause complexes. Working carefully through the book we have found the following major semantic chains.

As the contextual configurations of the field indicate, Norman Mailer as a participant in the demonstration and the March on the Pentagon are what the book is concerned with. "Norman Mailer" or simply "Mailer" keeps recurring throughout the book. To count its frequency of occurrence does not seem to be necessary. So the chain consists of various ways of naming him: the protagonist — Norman Mailer — Mailer — the Novelist — the Beast — the

Historian — the author — the minor poet — the slumpering Beast — the Yere dwarf alter ego — our Participant — the Ruminant — the Existentialist — the ex-revolutionary.

The second chain consists of a group of words that are related in meaning as an action: demonstration — march — parade — protest — move (as in move on Washington) — mass manifestation — resistance — speeches — sit-in — teach-in — civil disobedience.

The third chain is a grouping of words denoting participants in the March: army — armies — old American armies — citizen — troops — protesters — demonstrators — participants — resisters — students — draft-resisters — student leaders — middle class liberals — pacifists — academics — flower children — hippies — fugs — negroes — sympathizers — black militants — new leftists — Under-thirties — old leftists.

A related chain, the fourth one, includes a number of names of influential personages: Dwight Mcdonald-Paul — Goodman-Ed de Grazia — Robert Lowell — Dr. Spock — Sidny Peck — Jurry Rubin — Noam Chomsky — Mitchill Goodman — David Dellinger — William Sloane Coffin, Jr.

The fifth is a semantic chain of names of organizations: the National Mobilization to End the War in Vietnam — the National Mobilization — the Mobilization — SANE — Women Strike for Peace — CORE — Southern Christen Leadership Conference — Students for a Democratic Society — SNCC — Jewish Peace Fellowship — National Lawyers' Guild.

The sixth consists of people related with the government: the President — Lyndon Johnson — LBJ — Dean Rusk — McNamara — Attorney General — U. S. Marshals — MPS — American Soldiers — police — corporate executives — lawyers — state troops.

The seventh cohesive chain groups together a number of nouns denoting the country, government bodies and a few semantically related words: the United States, metaphorically referred to as the beauty, the dowager and the bitch — the country — Washington — the Capital — the Capitol — the Pentagon — Johnson Administration — the Administration — Department of

Justice — technology Land — Corporation Land — the authority — the Authorities — social machine — Great Society — Social Program — Great Society's Super-machine — the military — industrial complex — workhouse — prison — Occoquan — Plainfield.

The eighth chain is made up of words denoting an action: demonstrate — participate — take part — take the action — oppose — resist — attack — invade (the corridor of the Pentagon) — invest (the Pentagon) — walk into (the Department of Justice) — turn in (draft cards) — march — protest — detest — sign (the protest) — hate — dislike.

Another group of verbs form the ninth cohesive chain: support — back-counsel — aid — abet — write a form letter — speak — make speeches — respect (their action) — to be behind — to be for.

Still another group makes up the tenth: explain — argue — arrive at the conclusion — approve — discuss — decide — say.

The eleventh semantic chain is one composed of names of places: the Ambassador theater — Department of Justice — Lincoln Memorial — the Pentagon — the North Parking area — Virginia — Arlington Memorial Bridge.

The twelfth cohesive chain consists of a few reccurring members: war in Vietnam — Vietnam War — Venture in Vietnam — conflict — battle — war — Vietnam.

6.2.2 How chains interact

There are a few more that are made up of words and propositions, which we shall come back to in the course of our discussion. The twelve cohesive chains are homogeneous semantic groupings of words denoting either participants, processes, goals or circumstances. The first, third, fourth and fifth chains are recurrently found to be the actors engaged in the processes denoted by members of the eighth, ninth and tenth chains. It is significant to note that members of the sixth and seventh chains never appear in clauses as actors of the actions expressed by words in the eighth and ninth chains. The only verb that they are found to be the subject of is "control" with words in the second chain as its object. The eleventh chain is a chain of words denoting circumstances, and the twelfth represents the issue that divided the country. This brief discussion leads us to the question how these semantic chains interact syntagmatically with one another (Fries 1991a). Before we answer the question we have to return to cohesion, which is our main concern for the moment.

Since cohesive ties are instrumental in achieving cohesion by establishing what might be called the "contact point" between two portions of the text, and semantic chains are based on semantic relations, which are the basis of cohesion, the cohesive ties and cohesive chains we have identified may testify to the cohesion of the book. However, cohesion refers to surface ties showing relationships obtaining between two parts of the text. As a text is a semantic unit, it is necessary to examine the coherence of the discourse, which refers to "underlying organizing structure making the words and sentences into a unified discourse that has cultural significance for those who create or comprehend it" (Tennen 1984). Cohesion contributes to coherence but does not guarantee it. There is more to coherence than the establishment of relations between parts of a text by lexicogrammatical means. We need to examine the propositions of the discourse, both the micro-propositions of the parts of a discourse and the macro-propositions of the discourse as a whole, for a proposition is a combination of semantic, logical and pragmatic representation. Also, if we perceive the book as the product of a macro speech act, there must be an illocutionary force of the act, which will suggest the message the writer intends to get across to the reader and the reader may derive from the meaning of the novel through inference on the basis of his knowledge of the world.

6.2.3 Chain interactions

Now we will return to semantic chains. Hasan also points out: "...

cohesion is the foundation on which the edifice of coherence is built. Like all foundations, it is necessary but not sufficient by themselves." "Although the chains go a long way towards building the foundation for coherence, they are not sufficient," for the notion of identity or similarity of chains should be extended to the content of the message as message rather than being limited to the components of it, which are what the chains by themselves represent. So we need to look into chain interaction, by which Hasan means "relations that bring together members of two (or more) chains." "The relations that lead to chain interaction are the very ones that exist between the constituents of a clause." The recurrence of a relation between two chains is indicative of "the semantic similarity that unites at least pairs of members from two chains" (Halliday & Hasan 1989). Now let us look at the chains and the interactions they enter into.

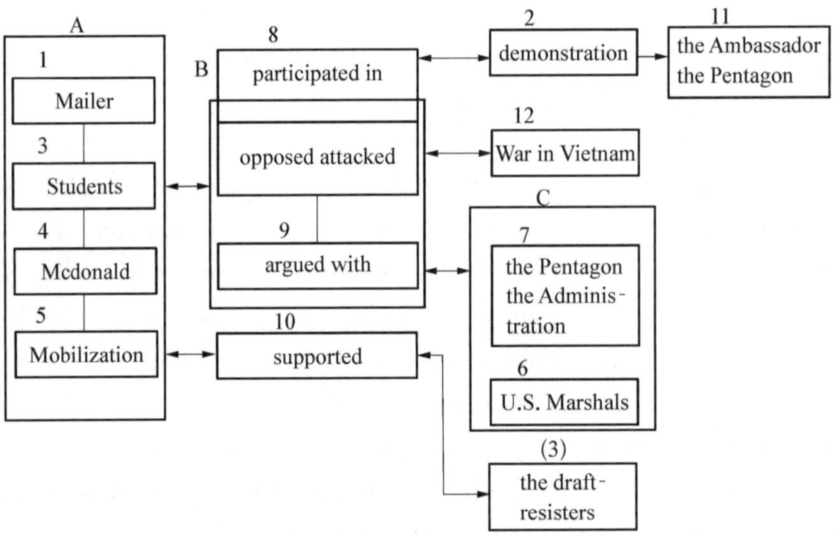

Figure 6-1 Basic interactions in the book

In the figure each rectangle represents a chain rather than a member of a chain and the central token is given to suggest the basic meaning of the chain. The chains that are capable of interacting with other chains in the same way are boxed together. Thus the four chains in box *A* can all interact with the chains in box *B* and the tenth chain. The eighth chain consists of two subgroups: one represented by "participated" that interacts with the second chain, and the other by "opposed" that interacts with chains in box *C*. The eleventh chain represents location.

The following are worth noting:

1) There is no break in the picture. All the interacting chains are related. This points to high degree of coherence.

2) The recurrent relation that brings together members of different chains is the process type of the clause as representation: actor — process — goal — location.

3) Each interaction between members from two or three or four chains in this makes up a clause and therefore represents a micro-proposition. In sorting out the chains, which are all of them focal chains, we have left out the lexical items that might form peripheral chains, so the interactions thus established represent the very basic fabric of the text.

6.2.4 Macro-propositions found

It is not difficult to list such micro-propositions as follows: *Mailer participated in the mass rally at the Ambassador theater*; *Mailer took part in the demonstration at the Department of Justice*; *Mailer spoke at the mass rally at the Lincoln Memorial*; *Mailer participated in the March on the Pentagon*. If we substitute members of the third, fourth and fifth chains for "Mailer", we will have many more clauses of the same process type and other interactions will give even more, but that would be tedious to list them. By applying the macro-rules of generalization and integration put forward by van Dijk (1977), we may arrive at the macro-proposition: *Mailer participated in the March on the Pentagon*, for other actions may be viewed as steps that can be subsumed under the general proposition. By the same token, instead of listing the members in the three chains, we may generalize the micro-propositions by saying *People of different political affiliations participated in the March* as another macro-theme. Here we need to introduce one more cohesive chain into the picture, the central members of which are "took place" and "happened". This chain interacts on the one hand with the second chain and on the other with the eleventh. The syntagmatic interaction thus established will give a large number of such clauses as *The demonstration took place at the Department of Justice*. Micro propositions represented by these clauses may be combined into a third macro-proposition: *The March began with a rally at the Ambassador theater and ended in confrontation at the Pentagon* by applying the macro-rule of integration. These macro-propositions as combinations of semantic, logical and pragmatic representation may be regarded as indexes of coherence.

6.2.5 Chains of propositions

Now we may do well to list the major cohesive chains of propositions we have found in the book so that we can pursue further our study at the propositional level. As we have just shown, a cohesive chain may be made up of propositions instead of lexical items. Let us look at the following:

[1] ... Mailer was perky enough to get himself arrested ... (p.4)

[2] ... the three men had argued they would ... seek to get arrested ... (p.79)

[3] ... the way they could best serve the occasion. "If the three of us are arrested ..." (p.84)

[4] ... they agreed again that they would be arrested early. (p.118)

[5] ... Mailer said, "Let's get arrested now." (p.128)

[6] "Why were you arrested, Mr. Mailer?" (p.137)

[7] "I was arrested for transgressing a police line." (p.137)

[8] "No. The arrest was correct." (p.138)

[9] Actually he had seen the protagonist get arrested ... (p.154)

[10] ... why anyone their age would wish for the purpose to get arrested ... (p.156)

[11] ... the point had been to get arrested. (p.194)

[12] ... he had actually believed he would be arrested and released ... (p.207)

This chain keeps telling the fact that Mailer and other two participants intended to get themselves arrested as the best way to serve the demonstration. This is linguistically borne out by the use of "get" in six of the clauses and can only be understood in the context of culture: *Mailer was arrested and later released*. This has to be added to the macro-proposition about Mailer.

We also find a chain consisting of the following:

[13] ... he had first come to love America, not the America of course of the flag ... he had come to love what editorial writers were fond of calling the democratic principle ... (p.47)

[14] What a mysterious country ... Awfully deadening programmatic inhuman dowager of a nation, corporation, and press — tender mysterious bitch whom no one would ever know, not even her future unfeeling communist doctors if she died of the disease of her dowager, deadly pompous dowager who had trapped the sweet bitch. (p.114)

[15] Once American faces were beautiful to me but now they look cruel and as if they had narrow thoughts ... (p.35)

[16] Nuclear warfare was dividing the country ... (p.154)

[17] ... the two halves of America were not coming together, and when they failed to touch all of history might be lost in the divide. (p.157)

[18] Or was it simply impossible ... had the two worlds of America drifted irretrievably apart? (p.158)

All these passages contain the word "America" or "the country" that forms an identity chain showing what is being talked about: the United States. We find contrasts: "the America of the flag" v. s. the America "with the democratic principle" in [13] "awfully deadening programmatic inhuman dowager" v.s. "tender mysterious bitch", both metaphorically referring to America in [14] and "beautiful" v.s. "cruel" in [15]. They speak of two sides of the country. In the other three we find the idea that the country was divided and there were "two halves" that would not come together. What was the result of the division and what state the country was in? The answer to these questions can be found in the following semantic chain:

[19] ... for no American citizen likes to link arms at once with the two ends of his practical working-day good American *schizophrenia*. (p.107)

[20] If one could find the irredeemable *madness* of America it was in those late afternoon race track faces. (p.151)

[21] ... the *fevers* of America go livid in the hum of the night. (p.151)

[22] Their country had always been *wild*. (p.152)

[23] ... it had always had a *fever*. (p.152)

[24] ... the *fever* to travel was in the American blood, but now the *fever* had left the blood. (p.152)

[25] ... the cells were as *insane* as Grandma with orange hair. (p.152)

[26] ... who knows which *fevers* were forged in such communion ... (p.152)

[27] ... one had to find it [fever] now where *fever*, force, and machine could come together ... (p.153)

[28] They were men ... there down in the cellar of the hierarchies of *schizophrenic* ranch-house life in America. (p.197)

[29] The country had been living with a controlled, even fiercely controlled, *schizophrenia* which had been deepening with the years. (p.188)

[30] ... since the expression of brutality offers a definite if temporary relief to the *schizophrenic*. (p.188)

Here we have a string of words like "schizophrenia", "madness", "wild", "fever", "insane", "schizophrenic", which all refer to the country. This prompts us to arrive at a fourth macro-proposition: *the country was living with schizophrenia.*

6.2.6 Macro-propositions revisited

Now we can reword the macro propositions we have found. The first one is: ***Mailer participated in the March on the Pentagon, got arrested and released***. The second, which was the third in the previous discussion, is: ***The March began with a mass rally at the Ambassador Theater and ended in confrontation at the Pentagon***. The third is: ***The March brought out the disunity of the political forces***. The rewording is necessary, for, as we shall show in the next chapter, it is the difference of opinion among the political factions rather than their participation in the march that is more relevant. The fourth is ***America was living with schizophrenia***. These macro-propositions can be formalized as follows:

[1] a = Norman Mailer p_1 = participated in the March

p_2 = got arrested P_3 = (got) released

$p_1(a) \wedge p_2(a) \wedge p_3(a)$

[2] a = the March p_1 = began with a mass rally

p_2 = ended in confrontation

$p_1(a) \wedge p_2(a)$

[3] a = the March b = the disunity of the political forces

p = brought out

p (a, b)

[4] a = America p = was living with schizophrenia

p (a)

As the four macro-propositions are semantically interrelated, they constitute the global proposition of the book. To see how they are related to achieve coherence we need to look into the structure of the book as a text.

6.3 Conclusion

To sum up what we have discussed above, we may make the following observations:

1) The study of cohesion of a long narration is based on the identification of cohesive ties between parts of a text and cohesive chains that run through the text. To identify cohesive ties focus is placed on the link between the beginning of a sub-text and the end of the previous one. Only focal chains are investigated, with such chains as might be formed with adjectives and adverbs omitted so that the central ideas are probed.

2) Cohesion contributes to coherence but is not sufficient. To see if a text is coherent it is necessary to look at its propositions, which, as our study has shown, can be studied on the basis of syntagmatic interactions of semantic chains.

7

The Narrative Structure of *The Armies of the Night**

7.1 Introduction

7.1.1 Four macro-propositions

This paper attempts to make an analysis of the narrative structure of the book *The Armies of the Night* (Mailer 1968) from a functional perspective. Text and context are in a dialectical relation. It is the context of situation that determines the texture and structure of a discourse, and the text reflects the context lexico-grammatically. On the basis of a careful study of the cohesion and coherence of the book we find the basic interactions of the semantic chains running through the novel, which in fact represent its four macro propositions.

The first one is: *Mailer participated in the March on the Pentagon, got arrested and released*. The second is: *The March began with a mass rally at*

* 本章原载《语言·语篇·语境》1993 年 3 月第 225—240 页,语言上已作个别订正。

the Ambassador Theater and ended in confrontation at the Pentagon. The third is: The March brought out the disunity of the political forces. As we shall show, it is the difference of opinion among the political factions rather than their participation in the march that is more relevant. The fourth is: *America was living with schizophrenia*.

These macropropositions can be formalized as follows:

[1] a = Norman Mailer p_1 = participated in the March

p_2 = got arrested p_3 = (got) released

$p_1(a) \wedge p_2(a) \wedge p_3(a)$

[2] a = the March P_1 = began with a mass rally

P_2 = ended in confrontation

$p_1(a) \wedge p_2(a)$

[3] a = the March b = the disunity of the political forces

p = brought out

p (a, b)

[4] a = America p = was living with schizophrenia

p (a)

As the four macro-propositions are semantically interrelated, they constitute the global proposition of the book. To see how they are related to achieve coherence we need to look into the structure of the book as a text.

7.2 A Structural Analysis of the Novel

7.2.1 Themes, elements and levels

The four macropropositions listed above are in fact four themes, each with its thematic formation based on the syntagmatic interactions of members from two or more semantic chains.The themes may briefly be stated as Mailer the protagonist as a *character*, March on the Pentagon as a political *event*, the difference of opinion among participating social groups as the *political scene* and finally the United States *the country*. As the book presents, among other things, a narration of a past event mixed with an account of personal experience in the event, it is natural to presume that it is hierachically structured consisting of more than one level. The structure of a text has its elements determined by the contextual configurations. It then follows that it takes elements to form each of the levels if the text has a multi-level structure. So what we need do is to give linguistic evidence for the levels of the structure.

7.2.2 The first level, the level about Mailer

A thematic analysis of the quoted passage at the beginning of the book will reveal that the author intends to narrate his past experience with Norman Mailer as the protagonist. It is a quotation from Time magazine, which is intended to bring to the reader news of the protagonist as a participant in the March and which may also serve as an "abstract", what Labov describes as the first component of a narrative structure. Let us first of all break the quotation down into clauses and then make a thematic study of each of them. We find out of the total of twenty-six clauses, including non-finite ones, thirteen have "Mailer", or "he" that refers to "Mailer" as the theme. This highlights the fact that Norman Mailer is what the book is about. As a matter of fact, the very first paragraph, a short text in itself, makes this quite clear if we look into the thematic relations between the three clauses it consists of. The rheme in the first clause, that is "demonstration" becomes part of the theme in the second since it is referred back to by "its", and the rheme of the second clause "Norman Mailer" becomes the theme in the third as it is what the relative pronoun "who" stands for. So we have

T1——R1
　　|
　　T2 (= R1)——R2
　　　　　　　|
　　　　　　　T3 (= R2)——R3

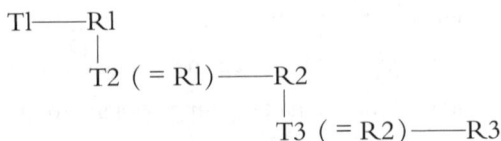

In terms of rhetorical structure theory the first clause provides the background for the second, which is the nucleus, while the third elaborates it, so the text can be represented as

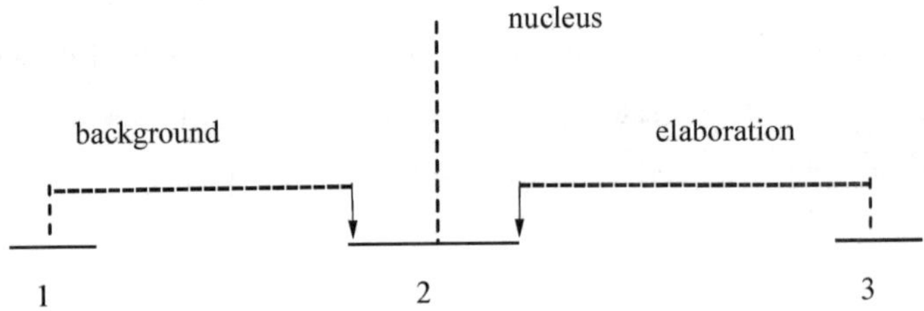

The fact that Norman Mailer is a central figure in the narration is reinforced by the numerous occurrences of the name, or "he", or other ways of naming him throughout Book I.

This first level is concerned with the character and composed of the following elements: abstraction, which includes orientation, sequences of actions he took part in and the attitude he expressed towards them, and finis, which is his arrest and release.

The author makes it explicit that he "makes our comic hero the narrative vehicle for the March on the Pentagon". Compare the following statements and we shall find some correspondence between the man and the action:

[1] No, let us leave it to *history* whether he lost his bet or eventually won it.

[2] The March ... whose essential value or absurdity may not be established for *ten or twenty years or indeed*, *ever.*

Statement [1] refers to Mailer's participation in the March. It is obvious that an uncertainty is expressed whether he should take part in the March. [2] refers to the march showing that its value was doubtful. One statement can be regarded as the paraphrase of the other.

[3] The March ... was an *ambiguous* event.

[4] An eyewitness ... must be *ambiguous* in his own proportions.

[5] The *arrest* of the notables would be in his [Rubin's] mind a superior aim.

[6] "Let's get *arrested* now."

The word "ambiguous" occurs in both [3] and [4] as predicative. So the eyewitness must be ambiguous as the March is ambiguous. Both [5] and [6] make reference to *arrest*, which shows Mailer's intention suits the aim of the organizer. All this may be regarded as links between the level concerning the character and the level about the March.

7.2.3 The second level, the level about the March

Mailer is not an adequate narrative vehicle, for what had happened before he took part in the demonstration and how the battle at the Pentagon came to an end after he was arrested cannot be covered in the narration. This makes it necessary for the author to write Book II. If he were content to recount Mailer's experience only, Book I would be good enough as it is. But the author also had in mind the March.

As we have said, "Mailer" has very high frequency of occurrence. But this is only true of Book One. In Book Two we only find ten occurrences of the name, and these occur only in the latter part of it. From the subtitles of the two books we know Book Two is a sequel to Book One: *The Steps of the Pentagon* and *The Battle of the Pentagon*. It adds on the planning and end of the March, skipping over the actions already recounted in Book I.

The second level is made up of the following elements: organizing and planning, execution of the plan, and the end of the action.

7.2.4 The third level, the level about disunity

Unlike the first and second levels, where the elements spread over the chapters of the book, the third level does not stretch out continuously from cover to cover, but contains elements made up of sub-texts that are interspersed in the narration. However, there is definite linguistic evidence to justify our recognition of this level.

There are a number of political organizations and groups of different affiliations or of different backgrounds. The identifying modifiers may give us some idea of the disintegration of the Left ranks: *Old* Left, *New* Left, *Black* Left, *White* Left and *Conservative* Left. With liberals we have *peace group* liberals, *Black* liberals and *Middle-class* liberals. They may be overlapping but viewed from different perspectives involving purpose, color and class. With movement we find *Negro* movement, *Youth* movement, *Peace* movement, *Women* movement and *Student* movement, each with its own program and objective. Besides, there were fugs, hippies, Diggers and Under-thirties.

The following words and phrases, which in fact form a similarity chain that interacts with words mentioned above, possibly as members of another semantic chain, are also suggestive of the division of the ranks: severed from — never came together — was filled with bitter rifts — divided — did not like.

The differences among these political groups caused much difficulty in the formation of a coalition and caused the demonstration to be "two-pronged" to attract the leftists and Middle-class liberals, the practical West and the visionary East.

The differences find expression also in the emphasis of the narration. Book II generally passes over what is already described in Book I, but there is a conspicuous exception. In Book I an account was given of an attack made on the Pentagon by a group consisting in fact of two groups, the students for a Democratic Society and the Revolutionary Contigent. In the vanguard of the charge was a man named Walter Teague, whom Mailer met in the Volkswagon he was put into after his arrest. Teague belonged to the Revolutionary Contigent. The author devotes much space to the description of the man, his mood in prison and, above all, his political views expressed in the speeches he made in the cell to fellow-prisoners. He was critical of the whole action, saying "the entire assembly, rally, March and the attempted investiture of the Pentagon has been wrong." The author shared his view, stating "There was much in what Teague said. It would probably not be far from his summary."

What is significant to us is the *repetition* in Book II of the attack, retreat and separation of the two groups because of their difference of opinion, which might be regarded as a footnote to Teague's speeches. The repetition and the high frequency of occurrence of "Teague" speak of the author's emphasis on Teague as representative of the revolutionaries, and their attitude towards the March.

The detailed account of the Fugs' exorcism on the North Parking lot is indicative of another aspect of the political scene. The Fugs would encircle the Pentagon with twelve hundred people to form a ring of exorcism sufficiently powerful to raise the Pentagon three hundred feet. Then all evil emissions would flee the levitation and the War in Vietnam would end. The repetition of the meaningless chanting of meaningless sounds in the description like *hari hari*, *hari rama*, *rama ram*, *krishna* ... serves to bring to light the absurdity of the ceremony, thus showing us that Fugs like Diggers and hippies were ready to do anything their whims and fancies took them to.

7.2.5 The fourth level, the level about the country

Now we come to the fourth level, a level concerning the War in Vietnam and America. The question is raised at the very first chapter: Why are we in Vietnam? Several attempts are made to answer the question, but only metaphorically. The book shows the country was living with schizophrenia — the macro-proposition that the fourth level will give structural representation to.

The fourth level finds linguistic expression in the use of argumentation as against narration and use of the present tense in the last chapter as against the usual past indefinite tense in narration.

To answer the question the author has to argue and this calls for argumentative style of writing. There is a chapter entitled "Why Are We in Vietnam", in which the author provides his answer to the question: "The love of Mystery of Christ, however, and the love of no Mystery whatsoever, had brought the country to a state of suppressed schizophrenia so deep that the foul brutalities of the war in Vietnam were the only temporary cure possible for the condition — since the expression of brutality offers a definite if temporary relief to the schizophrenic."

Now let us analyse the paragraph in which this conclusion occurs (See page 288 of the novel published by The New American Library). The paragraph, 421 words long, has eighteen sentences consisting of thirty-six clauses. The percentage of process types is as follows.

Material	Mental	Relational
50%	25%	25%

Of the eight clause complexes 5 are hypotactic, amounting to 62.5%.

While we find no colloquialism in the passage we do have quite a number of nominalized phrases: *the ... conclusion of them all*, *detestation of mystery*, *worship of technology*, *love of mystery*, *expression of brutality*, *temporary to* the schizophrenic, *shift of opinions*, etc.

Besides, we find the following logical connectors: *for ... for ... so ... since ... or* (=otherwise) and also *Yes and No*, *I and O*, all of which are instrumental in bringing to the fore the logical meaning of the text. These and the higher percentage of mental process type and hypotactic clause complexes as compared with the paragraph on page 81 of the novel (for its analysis see chapter 5) may indicate the opposition of argumentation versus narration. The difference in style of writing points to the need of an element of the fourth level: explanation. The last element of the level is Coda, which presents the prospect of the country. As it is in fact the end of the book, and therefore is more important, we will examine it in a separate section. Before we move on to that let us summarize the structure of the book. We have found the text is hierarchically structured, consisting of four levels. Each level is made up of elements, which may be grouped under the cover terms: Beginning, Middle and End. So we have the following table (Table 7 - 1).

Table 7 - 1 Summary of the structure of the book

Level	Elements		
	Beginning	**Middle**	**End**
I	Abstract	Sequence of Actions	Finis
II	Planning	Execution	End
III	Problem	Attitudes	Criticism
IV	Question	Explanation	Coda

As has been shown above the four levels are interrelated. As the country is broader in meaning than the political situation in a certain period of its history, and the March is only an event that took place against this background, and Mailer is only a participant in the action, so their logical relation may be represented as L1 ⊂ L2 ⊂ L3 ⊂ L4.

7.2.6 Final message analysed

Now we come to the Coda, which is made up of two paragraphs (see Appendix). Let us first look at the first paragraph, which consists of 8 sentences. A survey of the semantic chains will bring out the basic meaning relations.

Table 7 - 2 Summary of the Basic Meaning Relations

crisis	America	God	locks	the will of people
death	America	man	locks	the will of God
	the land	compassion		
	the country	power	locks	the will of Devil
	the military heroes			
	the unarmed saints			

The two items "military heroes" and "unarmed saints" are listed in the *America* chain on the basis of the meaning relation of meronymy; "compassion" and "power" are in instantial relation (Fries, 1982) with "God" and "man".

In the paragraph we find the following contrasts: 1) between "the military heroes" and "the unarmed saints", 2) between "the will of the people" and "the will of God", and 3) between "the will of God" and "the will of the Devil". The first contrast suggests the crisis the country is in, and a fourth contrast, one between what is expressed in the two it-clauses, one being affirmative, the other negative, makes the relations between man, God and the Devil dependent on the conditions, thus showing uncertainty. The interrogative sentence, (who by now could know where was what?) which contains three interrogative words: *who*, *where*, and *what* turns the uncertainty almost into an absolute lack of confidence, while the present tense in the sentence "The death of America rides in on the smog" suggests the reality of the situation. The key turn of expression "the locks of their life" savors of mystery, which adds to the uncertainty as to whose will will prevail, man's, that is God's, or the Devil's.

Now we will examine the last paragraph of the whole book. An analysis will show that "the country" and its synonyms, and the pronoun that stands for it are used as theme in nine out of twenty-three clauses, amounting to 39%. This may indicate what this chapter is about. However, to discover its macroproposition we need to sort out the semantic chains that appear in the passage.

We find here an identity chain based on co-referentiality indicating the country, consisting of as many as fifteen items, and a similarity chain with nine members semantically related about *child-birth*. These are focal chains, which are interrelated, and also related with a third chain, consisting of two members: "totalitarianism" and "baby". Then we have discovered the chains interact syntagmatically with one another. The meaning relations may be represented in the following two interactions:

Table 7 - 3 The Results of Transitivity Analysis

	Identified	Process (intensive)	Identifier
I	she	is	America
	she	is	a beauty
	she	is (attributive)	a beauty
	she	is (possessive)	heavy with child
	she	is having	her fearsome labor
	she	is not having	false labor
II	Actor	Process	Goal
	she	will give birth to	totalitarianism
	she	will deliver	a baby of a new world

These two interactions are in fact two micropropositions that go to make up the macroproposition of the paragraph. The contrast between a "beauty of magnificence unparalleled" and "a beauty with leprous skin", together with the contrast between "then" and "now" presents a gloomy picture of the present state of the country. A third contrast, one between "totalitarianism" and "a baby of a new world" speaks of the possible prospect of the country. We also find five imperative sentences, which are the manifestation of the interpersonal function of language. The narrator urges the reader to ponder over the country or ponder over the existential situation and apocalyptic future of the country, as the narrator sees it, and urges the reader to action. What action? *Rush to the locks*. The repetition of this sentence and the parallel structure bring about a relation between "God" and "us" as implied in "our curse". Rush to the locks and both God and "We" will be delivered. Then what does "locks" really mean? Since "liars controlled the locks", what can "we" do? The ambiguous meaning of the last sentence does not provide an answer, but speaks of the narrator's apprehensions. Three lexical chains with "existentialism", "apocalypse" and "totalitarianism" as central tokens that repeat themselves frequently in the book lead naturally to this conclusion: America is facing an apocalyptic situation, which is linguistically realized in the elliptical question: "to what?" and the alternative question connected by the conjunction "or".

One cannot fail to notice an important grammatical fact that all the verbs in the paragraph are in the present tense (*is*, *is*, *knows*, *languishes*, *begin*, *exists*, *is known*, *is not likely* ...), which indicates what is said here is true in the present or in the future. This aggravates the apocalyptic sense of the situation. As the final element in a clause normally carries the new information, so the last chapter carries the message the narrator wants to convey to the reader beyond the mere factual account of the event. The imperative and interrogative questions seem to be the linguistic data from which we may infer that the narrator tries to predict what seems to be unpredictable.

7.3 Conclusion

Now, we are in a position to conclude that a long narration like the one we have analysed is hierachically structured, consisting of several levels, each representing a macro-proposition of the text, and consisting of a number of elements. Besides, the end of the narration suggests the message that can be derived from the account the narrator gives of the past event and his personal experience.

Appendix

Text

The Metaphor Delivered

Whole crisis of Christianity in America that the military heroes were on one side, and the unnamed saints on the other! Let the bugle blow. The death of America rides in on the smog. America — the land where a new kind of man was born from the idea that God was present in every man not only as compassion but as power, and so the country belonged to the people; for the will of the people — if the locks of their life could be given the art to turn — was then the will of God. Great and dangerous idea! If the locks did not turn, then the will of the people was the will of the Devil. Who by now could know where was what? Liars controlled the locks.

Brood on that country who expresses our will. She is America, once a beauty of magnificence unparalleled, now a beauty with a leprous skin. She is heavy with child — on one knows if legitimate — and languishes in a dungeon whose walls are never seen. Now the first contractions of her fearsome labor begin — it will go on: no doctor exists to tell the hour. It is only known that false labor is not likely on her now, no, she will probably give birth, and to what? — the most fearsome totalitarianism the world has ever known? Or can she, poor giant, tormented lovely girl, deliver a babe of a new world brave and tender, artful and wild? Rush to the locks. God writhes in his bonds. Rush to the locks. Deliver us from our curse. For we must end on the road to that mystery where courage, death, and the dream of love give promise of sleep.

8

词汇语境线索与语篇理解*

8.1 引 言

本章从功能语言学理论出发,考察语篇和语境辨证关系中的一个重要方面,即从语篇推断语境时词汇如何作为语境线索,激活认知语境中的图式,经过推理,获得另一个词或几个词的情景意义,从而达到理解语篇的目的。本章着重考察体现为单句的书面语篇。所用材料出自英美人的著作、报刊等。

8.1.1 语 境

任何语言使用都有语境(Halliday & Hasan 1989),有语篇必有语境。语篇理解离不开语境,离不开作为一种资源的经验(Malinowski 1923; Halliday & Matthiessen 1999)。书面语篇没有任何外部语境,所以必须在阅读过程中创造内在的语境(Halliday & Hasan 1989)。这种内在语境实

---

* 本章原载《外语教学与研究》2003 年第 4 期第 253—259 页。

际上是从语篇通过推理而获得的认知语境,即基于经验的概念化、图式化的知识。由于语篇必须是衔接和连贯的,词汇之间存在多种语义关系,因此可以作由此及彼的推理。从语篇推导语境需以上下文中的词汇作为推理依据,并以此激活图式。韩礼德和韩茹凯指出,"句子或小句的组成部分同在一个结构之中,因此显然是黏合的,从而也具有语篇性(texture)"(Halliday & Hasan 1976: 6)。这为我们在单句语篇中确定词汇语境线索提供了依据。程雨民(1990: 7)指出:"逻辑推理在语言的使用中不仅在超句层次而且在句内也时刻都起着作用。"这说明单句语篇的理解不仅可以推理,而且必须推理。我们之所以把单句语篇作为研究对象,是因为如果词汇语境线索在单句语篇的推理中有效,能解决理解问题,那它在有上下文的语篇中就更加可以应用。

8.1.2 线 索

语言学家们在语言体系和语言使用两个方面的研究中都利用线索(cues)作为推理的依据。在语言体系方面,结构主义利用线索,或称标记(markers)、记号(signals),作为依据推测语法意义,如-s、-ed、a,并试图说明无需词汇意义即可了解句子"意义"(如 Fries 1952; Goodman et al. 1986)。在语言使用研究方面,社会语言学家首先提出了语境线索(contextualization cues)的概念。甘柏兹指出:"粗略地说,语境线索是语言形式的任何特征,它有助于标示语境预设"(Gumperz 1982: 131)。席弗林解释说:"可以把甘柏兹的语境线索看成框架手段(framing device),为解释话语指明框架(譬如是严肃的、诙谐的、认真的、闲聊的)"(Schiffrin 1994: 103)。可见社会语言学中的语境线索所提示的意义不是信息内容,而是说话人的态度或意图,是人际意义的内容。社会语言学家不是没有看到词汇的重要,比如甘柏兹就指出,"实际使用的词汇及重音处理的方式对激活常规框架至为重要"(Gumperz 1982: 5),但由于他们的注意力集中于附加在信息内容之上的语篇策略,所以不关注语篇内容,没有利用词汇作为语境线索。然而了解语篇的经验意义、信息内容离不开词汇。甚至了解人际意义也离不开词汇。马丁的评价系统理论就是系统地论述词汇对人际意义的影响(Martin 2003)。词汇的基本功能是命名,指客观世界的人或物及其属性、行为的过程、事件的状态或时空概念，而这些都是体现语境中语场的成分，因此从语篇推导语境就不得不重视词汇。其次，“词汇意义对语句结构的解释起着积极作用”(程雨民 1990)。叶斯柏森的例子很说明问题(Jespersen 1933b：49)：“She made him a good husband”与“She made him a good wife”以及“He promised her to go”与“He allowed her to go”都只有一字之差，但句子结构就完全不同。可见词汇对理解语篇起着如何重要的作用。

8.2 词汇语境线索的特征

既然词汇如此重要，那么什么情况下词汇可以用作语境线索？什么情况下无需语境线索？语境线索如何起作用？有些什么特征？

8.2.1 语境线索——词或词组

语境线索是语篇中的一个词或词组。它可以激活相应的语境，借以确定另一个词或几个词的情景意义。吉在论述情景意义时举了下面的例子(Gee 2000)：

[1] The coffee spilled, get a *mop*.
The coffee spilled, get a *broom*.

他解释说，第一句由 mop 激活，第二句由 broom 激活，加上对这类事情的经验，即可获得 coffee 的不同情景意义。第一句中 coffee 指“咖啡茶”，第二句中指“咖啡豆”。这个理解当然是对的，但 mop 激活了什么他未交代。其原文是：In the first case, triggered by the word “mop” and your experience of such matters, you assemble a situated meaning ... (Gee 2000：48)。人们会问：What is triggered？文中未提。从句法看，只可能是 you，

但 trigger 的宾语一般是某种动作或状态。那么 mop 起什么作用也就没有交代清楚。事实上 mop 激活了 your experience of such matters,激活了我们脑子里有关打扫卫生的图式,在这个图式里,作为图式成分的拖把和溢(泼、洒、流)出的残汤、水、茶、咖啡茶等液体联系着,扫帚和固体垃圾联系着。在语言里则体现为搭配(collocation)。这里说的搭配是一种语义关系,并不局限于动宾、补足、修饰、并列等句法关系,但常常潜在地有这种关系。韩礼德称作"共现趋势"(cooccurrence tendency)(Halliday 1994: 333)。例[1]中的 coffee 和 mop, broom 也是一种共现。其中 mop 和 broom 是语境线索,是这个语境线索激活了有关图式,根据图式中 mop、broom 和 coffee 的不同联系,决定了 coffee 两个不同的情景意义,从而了解了语篇的意义。

再来看一个汉语例子:

[2] *烟酒切勿登楼。*

这是写在宁波著名的藏书楼"天一阁"楼梯口一块牌子上的话,意思似乎清楚,但仔细一想又觉得有矛盾:烟酒如何登楼?"登"字成了语境线索。它激活的图式中"登"的动作只能与人联系,不能与无生命的东西,如不能与烟酒联系。这样就出现了在语境中无联系的成分,其相应的两个词在语言中却被放在一个搭配之中。这时联系直接语境进行推理受到阻碍,于是得联系我们的世界知识进行推理。世界知识告诉我们登楼的必是人,这里是以物代人的转喻。这符合我们的语言知识:有时人们由于某种原因可以用隐喻语言以物代人,如以"红帽子"代替车站上的搬运工。这里就是如此。"烟酒"首先指"抽烟喝酒"的动作,进而指抽烟喝酒的人。但并非抽烟喝酒的人都不能登楼。句中"登楼"限制了动作的特定场合,所以并非笼统指代一般抽烟喝酒的人。如平时抽烟喝酒的人登楼时不抽烟喝酒,按理还是允许上楼的。所以这句话隐含"不得将烟酒带上楼",进而可理解为"不得在楼上抽烟喝酒"。用"烟酒"而不正面提人是出于礼貌需要。这里"登"字作为语境线索确定了"烟酒"的情景意义。

8.2.2 何时需要语境线索

并非任何语篇都需要语境线索。在语篇意义一目了然的情况下就无需这种线索。所谓一目了然事实上是指单句语篇的语法关系清楚，词汇可以共同激活一个图式，并在图式中找到各自的对应成分，与有关的典型语境吻合，也就是语篇取得了外部联系。如：

[3] The rain showed no sign of stopping. (*Rain* p.312)

人们一看就懂，无需太多推理就可与经验联系起来而得到解释。甚至对

[4] Oil is going to turn into liquid gold. (*Master of the Game* p.286)

这样的句子，人们也无需语境线索激活语境才能理解。人们也许需要推理，如石油比作液体金子，保留了石油的状态特征，所以，石油还是石油。人们知道金子贵重，说石油变成液体金子，无非是比喻其贵重。人们可以根据石油变不了金子的世界知识推导出这一结论。这时的推理过程实际上是"自动而无意识的，在一瞬间内即可完成"(Arthur et al. 1997：293)。这种情况下我们不需要语境线索。相反，如果语篇中出现一词多义，如例[1]中的coffee，或者出现不合常规的搭配，如例[2]中的"烟酒"和"登楼"，这时我们就需要有语境线索，进行有意识的推理。又如：

[5] She was the *assistant* cook in the house. (*Word Formation* p.11)[2]

字面意义似乎清楚，但我们的世界知识告诉我们，一般的住宅人家即使有厨师也不大会有助理厨师，这就和我们的经验不符，和assistant cook激活的语境不符。身居豪宅的大户人家可能有不止一个厨师，但那就应该是in the mansion，而不是in the house。assistant cook在它激活的图式中与餐馆有联系。而我们的语言知识告诉我们house可作"餐馆""饭店""小吃店""小酒店""酒吧"解，如steak house，或coffee house。餐馆里饮料之类免费供应叫On the house。这样，assistant cook作为语境线索赋予了house合乎情景的意义。这种情况下我们需要词汇作为语境线索。然而，语境线索是从语篇推导语境的一种途径，由于知识状况、经验及语言水平等的不同，甲需要语境线索而乙可能未必需要。

8.2.3 推　理

语境线索赋予的情景意义是通过推理得到的。席弗林(Schiffrin

1994：371）指出："推理是置于情景之中的。有两种情况：置于当时当地的具体情景之中，或依靠我们对于社会情景的一般知识。"先看一个实例。2002 年 8 月波士顿动物园的一只猴子逃跑了。当地报纸 *Boston Metro* 报道中说：

［6］The monkey is a *family* man.

这一单句语篇和程雨民所引的一例"The prime minister is an old woman."（Cheng 1991：128）相像。The prime minister 指 William Gladstone，是个男人，怎么会是女人？字面的理解受阻。听话人在推理过程中，拒绝了把 old woman 看成是 old 修饰 woman 的名词组合，并进一步推理，把 old woman 看成一个符号，从而获得了"唠叨、关注琐事"的意义。这样表面的矛盾就解决了。同样，猴子不是 man，结合"当时当地的具体情景"的字面理解受阻，但结合世界知识可以知道 family man 是作为一个认知单元储藏在记忆里的，语言里是一个符号，意思是"有妻小的人"。把人的"有家小"的概念用于最接近人类的同属灵长目哺乳类的猴子是很自然的，再加上西方文化对动物的态度，这样说明这只猴子有配对、有猴崽是可接受的。所以猴子可以是 family man。这个推理过程引导读者理解了语篇。再看下例：

［7］Then I went through the bathroom and lastly the *bed-sitting room*.（*Linking Words* p.71）

这一句子看上去理解似乎不应有什么问题，是讲"我"穿过了两个房间，但是仔细一看 bed-sitting room 激活的图式是一个一室公寓房（studio），除了文中提到的浴室和卧室兼起居室外还有一个小厨房。有关的图式也提供了这种一室房的布局。通常不需要穿过这两间房才能到厨房，而且文中并未提到"进厨房"（into the kitchen）。作"通过两个房间"理解，作者意图不清楚，也没有什么信息可言，因而解释受阻。说话人当另有所述。昂格雷尔和施密德指出我们对世界的共同经验也储藏在我们日常的语言里，所以从我们表达思想的方式中也能有所发现（Ungerer & Schmid 1996：XII）。为了开发这一资源，我们必须超越小句型式的"逻辑"，探究比喻语言，特别是隐喻。在结合"当时当地具体情景"推理受阻的时候，我们必须考虑 went through 是否用于其隐喻意义，作"检查""察看"解，因为这个解释可与图式中的其他成分相容。我们的语言知识又肯定了这个推断，look through 可以作"examine, inspect carefully and successively"解。这样 bed-sitting room 就成了语境线索,根据所激活的语境,否定了联系认知语境中的直接语境而获得的字面理解,在结合世界知识的进一步推理中,得出了动词的比喻意义,这也就是动词的情景意义。

8.2.4 动态图式

词汇语境线索激活的图式应该是动态的,在阅读书面语篇的过程中,人们用从世界知识衍生出来的信息给情景模式补充细节,在有关图式中嵌进新的成分。

[8] The 50 strong medical team at UCLA's Mattel Children's Hospital cheered and whooped with joy at the end of marathon operation in which doctors successfully *separated* the brains, skulls, and skin of the 1-year-old girls. (*Boston Metro* 8/2002)

文中 medical team、hospital、operation、doctors 共同激活了医院手术的图式,但为什么叫 marathon operation? 为什么要 cheered and whooped with joy? 词汇 separated 和 brains、skulls、girls 中表示名词复数的-s 共同起了语境线索的作用,赋予了 operation 以情景意义。Operation 是单数,按常规应是给一个病人做手术,但这里 girls 是复数,而且 brains、skulls 也是复数, separated 就点明了怎样的手术。推理的结果是分离一对头部相连的连体女婴。这就回答了上面提的问题。图式起了利用先前知识接纳新事实的框架作用,同时给手术图式里增加了"分离""连体女婴"和医生在成功后的兴奋状态这些成分。这意味着人们增加了新知识。

8.3 词汇语境线索的具体功能

词汇语境线索在理解书面语篇时究竟有哪些具体功能? 根据现有材

料我们发现,词汇语境线索在解决歧义、表面搭配不当、词的临时组合、词义笼统、新词词义等方面有助于理解。下面分别说明。

8.3.1 解释歧义

上面例[1]中的 coffee 和例[5]中的 house 都因为是一词多义给理解造成困难,语境线索在激活语境之后确定了这两个词的情景意义,同时排除了另一意义。可以说我们对语篇的理解建立在语境线索解歧的基础之上。这是语境线索的一个重要功能。再看下面的例子:

[9] That was an act to *legalize* abortion. (*Word Formation* p.105)

[10] I was going to take the plane to Chicago, but it was too *heavy*. (*Experimental Psycholinguistics* p.87)

[11] She failed for the first time in her life to *turn up* for a 7:00 call. (*Linking Words* p.49)

例[9]中的 legalize 作为语境线索,激活了议会程序图式,赋予 act“法案”的情景意义,排除了其“行动”之意。这就解决了产生歧义的可能。例[10]中的前小句中 take the plane to Chicago 人们自然会理解为“乘飞机到芝加哥”。但格卢克斯堡等指出当读者读了后一小句后就会把 plane 理解为“刨子”了(Glucksberg 1975: 87)。为什么会这样理解,作者没有交代。事实上,heavy 起了语境线索的作用。太重不好随身携带,那么,如果不太重就可以携带了,可见是个可携带的物品。这就排除了“飞机”的意义,因为飞机再轻,也不能携带。但必须指出并非是后一个小句,而是 heavy 作为词汇语境线索起了解歧的作用。试看“The plane was too heavy to take to Chicago”中 heavy 还是照样赋予 plane 情景意义,达到解歧的作用。例[11]有人把其中的 call 理解为“一次电话”,但这与 turn up 不能搭配。turn up 是“make one's appearance”“arrive”的意思,打电话无需“露面”“到场”。在否定这一意义之后 turn up 就赋予了 call 一个与 turn up 词义相容的意义,也即在图式中有联系,在语言中可以共现的意义。我们的语言知识告诉我们 call 可作 short visit 解。这样,这句的意思就是“她平生第一次没有能应约七时到访”。很有可能是医生应约探望病人。

8.3.2 区分直义喻义

上面例[2]存在表面搭配不当,但语境线索提供了解释,从而使语篇意义清楚。例[7]的情况大体相同。表面搭配不当是因为某个词如例[2]中的"烟酒",例[7]中的 went through,被用于比喻意义。一个词究竟是用于本义还是比喻意义,语境线索可以帮助确定。例如:

[12] The climate was just right for *growing sugar*. (*Linking Words* p.58)

在人们的经验中,糖不能种植,但文中的 growing 激活了"种植"的图式,其中只有植物可作为图式成分,因此在否定 sugar 字面理解的同时,确定了 sugar 作 sugar-cane、sugar-beet 的意义,sugar 比喻性地替代了从中提取 sugar 的植物。这样就解决了表面不搭配的问题。

8.3.3 理解临时组合

有些临时组合,特别是名词作定语与另一名词的组合常常令人费解。这种情况下语境线索往往可赋予这种组合一情景意义,从而使语篇意义明了。请看下例:

[13] Please *sit in* the apple juice *seat*. (*Metaphors We Live By* p.12)

雷考夫和约翰逊在引用这句话时说:"孤零零地看这个句子根本没有意义,因为 apple juice seat 不是一个常规表达任何事物的方式。但在这句话出现的上下文里就完全有意义"(Lakoff & Johnson 1980: 12)。此话当然有道理,强调了上下文的重要。但是,我们想说明借助词汇语境线索,即使没有上下文也能理解这个语句。首先,"Please sit in ... the seat"为我们提供了一个明显的图式:主人请客人就座或主人为客人安排座位。请人坐下通常说"Sit down, please""Take a seat, please""Won't you take a seat?""Be seated, please"。很明显,在这些常用的表达式中,用了 sit 就不用 seat,用了 seat 就不用 sit。只有在给客人指定座位时才两词并用,please 可说明主人对客人礼貌。对家里人就无需说 please。我们的世界知识告诉我们,一般是在入座就餐时主人才分派座位。话语里的 apple juice 似乎也验证了这一点，可能是佐餐的饮料。至此我们可以看出，sit ... in the seat 作为语境线索已为我们激活了说话的情景。但是理解的症结似乎还在 apple juice seat。辛克莱指出："要使有关人或事的信息更加具体，可使用名词作为另一名词的前置修饰语"（Sinclair 1990：100）。这虽不一定算是一条规则，但名词，包括复合名词，做名词定语是英语中常见的现象，所以用 apple juice 修饰 seat 也是符合英语用法的。再看具体的词。表食品的名词可以做名词定语，如叶斯柏森例证中的"a prosperous, hot-sausage-and-meshed-potato shop"（Jespersen 1942：156）。这样 5 个词组成的复合词可以做定语，apple-juice 当然也可以。可能有人会想，叶斯柏森的例子中的复合词是修饰 shop，意思清楚。那么我们来看 seat 是不是可以有名词修饰语。乘过飞机的人都知道，在领登机牌的时候，可以选择座位。人们通常说 window seat 或 aisle seat，而且这个说法已经相当固定，意思是"靠近窗口的座位"、"靠近过道的座位"。可见名词修饰 seat 的时候，表示"靠近"。那么把靠近 apple-juice 的 seat 像"window seat""aisle seat"一样称作 apple-juice seat，看来也是可以的。这样，我们就靠 sit ... in the seat 激活的图式，再根据我们的世界知识和语言知识，就可以把这句话理解为"请在摆了苹果汁的位置上就座"。再看一句：

[14] He is a *coffee* after person.

这是一位美国教授在说她丈夫。看起来比上一句更加不合常规。理解的困难在于 coffee after，然而，恰恰是 coffee 为我们提供了理解的语境线索，激活了一个喝咖啡的图式。咖啡虽然任何时候都可以喝，但大多数美国人早晨都要喝咖啡。这样的话是常可听到的：You get up in the morning and go online before getting your coffee。coffee after 什么？通常 coffee 是早餐时喝，coffee after 当指 coffee after breakfast。用 coffee after 修饰 person，说明此人经常如此，已成习惯。所以，这句话的意思是"他总是早饭后喝咖啡"。对于临时性组合，词汇语境线索可激活有关图式，经过推理，帮助理解。

8.3.4 明确泛义

英语中有些意义很泛的形容词，如 good、sound、great，在语言使用中人们很难把握其确切意义，因此特别受语义分析家的重视。齐夫举了一个很说明问题的例子：This is a good strawberry. This is a good lemon.（Ziff 1960：202）他解释说，草莓取其甜，good strawberry 应该甜；柠檬取其酸，good lemon 应该酸。这里 good 的意义取决于它所修饰的词，因而获得两个完全不同的意义。如何理解 good 成了理解语篇的一个难点。

[15] When they took the *baby* from me to clean her up, she let out a couple of good screams.（*Linking Words* p.13）

这句中的 good 该如何理解？我们仍然要找词汇语境线索。这里 baby 能起这个作用。齐夫对理解 good 提出一个假说（Ziff 1960：212），大意是为 good 所修饰的话语成分必须对符合某种兴趣的事物作特征性说明，也就是要符合人们对某事物的期盼。从这个语句看，并不一定是 good 所修饰的词能确定 good 的意义；screams 不能说明 good 应该如何理解，而要靠 screams 的主体 baby，在语篇内这两个词还是共现关系。婴儿的叫声怎样才能符合人们的期待才算好？我们的世界知识告诉我们应该是"放声大叫"，所以有"响亮"并延伸出"健康"的意思。试想成人 scream 能用 good 修饰吗？这是 baby 赋予 good 的情景意义。再看一例。有位美国朋友曾向笔者谈他年轻时打工的经历。一次，工长对他讲：

[16] Why don't you hit that stake one more good *lick* with your hammer?

意思是要他再给桩敲一锤。他听后就使劲敲了一锤，结果把桩给砸到土里了。问题出在他没理解 good。其实，如果他想一想 lick，就不会用那么大力气了。毕竟，lick 是"舔"的意思，暗示无需用大力气；lick 作为语境线索，给了 good"力量适度"的情景意义。工长后来纠正他说，I said "hit it a good lick", not "beat the shit out of it"。

8.3.5 理解新词

在以上的讨论中，我们的前提是这些语句里的词语读者都认识。但以上例子说明，即便如此，理解语篇有时还会有困难。如果有不认识的新词，理解当然就更困难了。请看：

[17] The dot-coms *were floundering*, but some were still making the mark.（*Boston Globe* 9/11/2002）

句中 dot-com 是在口头介绍网址时要说的，书写是.com，是网址的最后部分。这里在 dot-com 之后有名词复数标记-s，在小句中作主语，据此我们可以推测这是个用作名词的新词。那么它的意思是什么？让我们看与它搭配的动词：flounder，其意义是"have many problems and may fail completely"。作为网址的末尾，不可能有什么困难，也不可能完全失败。我们知道很多网址是以 dot-com 结尾的，我们以此推断它是网址的缩写。然而，网址也没有什么困难或失败可言。网址有困难，实际是指使用这个网址的单位有困难。dot-com 中的 com 指 commercial，当指商业网址，区别于 dot-net、dot-edu 等。我们的世界知识告诉我们，有些公司就是以网络服务为业务的。这些公司的生存完全依赖网络。语言知识和有关的世界知识使我们把 dot-coms 所代表的实体限于这类网络公司。这类公司面临困难甚至濒临倒闭，看来是符合美国经济不景气的现实的，后一个小句说明其中"有的仍然获得成功"也符合事实。这说明这一理解通得过社会语境的检验。在上面解歧、解决表面搭配不当的推理中，我们是从两个或多个意义中选择一个，这里借助语境线索确定新词的词义还必须通过其他语篇的检验。我们看到有这样的语句：... we are fortunate that our programs are diverse and broad enough to withstand ... the recent downturn in dot-coms and information technology (*Boston Metro* 24/8). The rally also spilled over to other Chinese dot-coms. 后一句说明"搜狐"股票反弹带动了其他中国网络公司。有时 dot-com 写成一个词，并用于所有格，如 Analyze the reason for Dotcoms's hard situation（杨永林 2002：148）。还有作定语的，如 dot-com industry、dot-com company、dot-com layoffs。这说明我们对 dot-com 的理解是正确的。Flounder 作为语境线索为我们推理提供了依据，理解了新词 dot-com"网络公司"的意义，从而获得了语篇的信息。

8.4 结　语

从单句语篇推导语境往往要依靠词汇作为语境线索。词汇不仅影响语法结构,语法结构也体现在词汇上。在语篇层次上,无论是衔接还是连贯也都离不开词汇,所以理解语篇的信息内容离不开词汇。当语篇由于某个词难以理解时,我们可以在语篇中寻找一个意义相对明确、与疑难词之间存在某种搭配或共现关系的词作为语境线索。当语境线索在不同程度上激活图式之后,就要在作为框架的图式中寻找这两个词或几个词的对应成分及它们之间相互制约的关系,再赋予疑难词以适合于语境的意义,从而理解语篇。所以整个过程是从语篇推导到语境,然后再从语境回到语篇,达到对语篇的理解。

单句书面语篇既无上下文又无外部语境,所以推理的结果是语篇的直义,而其中的逻辑推理时常是概率性的。"由于调用的前提不同或对前提有不同的理解,结论可能不同"(程雨民 1997:167)。如例[10],如果出自儿童之口,那赖以推理的图式就不一样,plane 可能就是"玩具飞机",而不是"刨子"。隐喻的应用是造成理解困难的另一个因素,但最常用的是借喻,如例[2]、[12]。由于这种比喻用法常常是人们,包括作者和读者的共同知识,这是因为人们的概念系统是隐喻性的(Lakoff & Johnson 1980:6),所以推理的结论基本上是肯定的。

虽然语境线索可以使泛义词 good 意义具体化,但这类词有价值评价的意味,所以理解上常受文化语境或意识形态的左右。如对"8888 is a good number"这句话,中国人和英美人都能接受,但理解不同。中国人认为这个数字吉利,英美人则认为便于记忆。文化背景不同,所赋予的意义也就不同。

词汇语境线索可应用于翻译,也可应用于外语教学。外语教学中常常提到根据上下文了解词义的策略,但如何利用,语焉不详。如果学生在碰到难以理解的词或句时,引导他们寻找词汇语境线索,根据其激活的图式,进行推理,理解语篇,也许会更为奏效。

9

语篇中语言型式化的意义
——探索语篇主题的一种途径*

9.1 引　言

叙事语篇，特别是小说，往往具有三个不同层面的意义，分别称作本义(literary meaning)、社会意义和主题(theme)。本义取决于直接语境，即与事件发生过程以及过程参与者有直接关联的情景。韩礼德指出，"是实际的直接语境产生语篇"(Halliday & Hasan 1989：46)。同时，叙事语篇又是一定社会条件下的产物，其社会意义则由事件的社会语境即社会结构和社会制度所决定。主题则是叙事语篇的深层意义。韩茹凯指出，主题是"从语篇的具体特征中分离出来的。它是语篇目的之所在。就其性质而言，它近乎一种概括"(Hasan 1989：97)。既然主题是从语篇中概括出来的，也就是说是从语篇的个别的具体语言材料中分离出来的，那就必定有一个推理过程。我们面临的问题是：一方面主题已分离于具体的语言材料，而另一方面为了把握主题我们又必须为推理提供确切的语言依据。本章即试图在这方面作一探讨。

---

*　本章原载于《外语教学与研究》2000 年第 2 期 110—116 页。

9.2 语篇中的型式化

9.2.1 型式化

什么叫型式化(patterning)? 在语言学和语言教学中,人们常用型式这一术语,最普通的当是句型,当然也有短语型式、词组型式。型式是句法上的概念,它所体现的语法意义,可以是陈述、补足、修饰、并列或从属,通常指从具体句子或词组中概括出来的一种组合关系。型式化是某一型式或某一类同结构(parallel structure)的重复。通过重复某一型式的型式化具有与个别型式完全不同的意义。正是型式化的意义或型式化之间的对比意义为我们探索主题提供了基础。

9.2.2 短篇小说 *The Luncheon*

下面用毛姆(W. Somerset Maugham)的短篇小说 *The Luncheon* 来分析型式化的意义,并在此基础上了解语篇的主题。

The Luncheon 描写作家的一个女读者为了有机会与他探讨文艺,要求请她在 Foyot's 吃午饭。作家对她并不熟悉,而且收入甚菲,生活拮据,但还是同意了她的要求,请她在这家高级餐馆与他共进午餐。席间,这位女士反复强调"I don't eat anything for luncheon,""I don't eat more than one thing for luncheon",却不断点当令的菜或名贵的菜,而作家只吃了价格最低的一块羊排。结果,付款之后,他赖以应付当月生计的 80 法郎所剩无几,用作小费也显得寒碜。然而,作家自我解嘲,以为已进行了报复,因为女读者体重为 21 英石!

9.2.3 三层意义

这篇短篇小说有三层意义。结合直接语境中的三要素,即语场

(field)、语旨(tenor)和语式(mode)便可了解语篇的本意：作家应一个女读者的要求请她共进午餐，而这一事件中最为重要的过程是“吃”。当我们把语境扩大到整个社会，便可了解到当时英国社会作家与读者关系的一个侧面。在其他社会语境中作家与读者之间未必会有这样一种关系。至于主题，得从语篇的总体上加以考察，即从纵的方向考察贯穿整个语篇的规律性现象，主要是同一型式反复出现的现象以及这些现象出现的动因。

9.3 型式化探讨

那么，这一语篇中有哪些型式化？它们之间形成了怎样的对比？表达了什么意义？经过仔细阅读，我们发现了12个型式化了的型式。

9.3.1 否定加肯定：言行不一

首先让我们看一看型式化的第1式和第2式。

1 (1) I never eat anything for luncheon. (34)
(2) I never eat more than one thing. (36)
(3) No, I never eat more than one thing. (42)
(4) I never drink anything for luncheon. (51)
(5) I *am* only going to eat one thing. (69)
(6) No, no, I never eat anything for luncheon. (72)
(7) I never want more than that, ... (72)
(8) I couldn't possibly eat anything more. (74)
(9) ... I don't eat luncheon. (113)
(10) ... I never eat more than one thing for luncheon. (114－115)

2 She ate the caviar and she ate the salmon. (63)

I watched the abandoned woman thrust them [asparagus] down her throat in large voluptuous mouthfuls. (101–102)

At last, she finished. (104)

括号中的数字表示在短篇小说中出现的行次。全文共137行。第1式由以eat为动词的否定句重复几次而型式化。在这10句中,有七句含有斩钉截铁的否定词never,两句含否定词not。第5句虽以肯定形式出现,但only使句意成为否定,涵义与第2句相同。第2式是以ate、thrust ... down和finished三个同义词串联而成的型式化。三句皆为肯定句。从语法上讲,动词是句子的核心。第1式的核心成分是never eat,而第二式的核心是ate。值得注意的是第1式中句子的主语皆为I,第2式的主语或意念主语为she,同指作家的客人。此外,第1式句子的时态为现在时;第2式句子的时态为过去时。一般现在时实际上不指任何时间,以此说明句子所表示的命题是适用于任何时间的。过去时是指动作时间点先于参照时间点和说话时间点,以此说明动作已经在说话之前发生。这种人称和时态的差别集中反映了两种不同语篇的差别,即叙事人语篇和人物语篇。"I never eat"出自客人之口;"She ate"则是叙事人的陈述。这就形成了言与行的对照,否定与肯定的对照。这种矛盾说明客人言行不一。但是如果仅此而已,那这篇短篇小说也就失之肤浅了。为弄清其意义,让我们再来看第3式:

3 (1) "I never eat anything for luncheon." (34)

(2) "I never eat more than one thing ... A little fish, perhaps." (36–37)

(3) "No, I never eat more than one thing. *Unless* you had a little caviar." (42–43)

(4) "I never drink anything for luncheon," she said. (51)

"Neither do I," I answered promptly. (52)

"*Except* white wine," she proceeded as though I had not spoken. (53)

(5) "I *am* only going to eat one thing." (69)

(6) "NO, no, I never eat anything for luncheon. Just a bite." (72)

(7) "... I never want more than that, and I eat that more as an excuse for conversation than anything else." (72－74)

(8) "... I couldn't possibly eat anything more — unless they had some of those giant asparagus." (74－75)

(9) "I'm not in the least hungry," my guest sighed, "but if you insist I don't mind having some asparagus." (82－83)

(10) "... I don't eat luncheon." (113)

(11) "... but I never eat more than one thing for luncheon ..." (114－115)

9.3.2 迂回表述：装腔作势

第 3 式是第 1 式的扩展，其中有七句在含 eat 的否定句之后有后续说明，以句子或小句的形式出现。首先我们发现在第 3、第 4 句中，unless 和 except 首字母大写，置于小句句首引出独立的句子。unless 是连词，except 是介词，通常引出从句和介词短语，对前面的陈述加以限制。except 短语表示前面的陈述在什么情况下不适用；unless 从句则说明主句所表示的内容在什么情况下不会发生。两者不论从结构上还是从语义上讲都从属于主句。在第 3、第 4 句中，unless 和 except 的用法则与此形成对照。从信息结构的角度看，第 3 句 unless 之前的句子含两个语调组。语调核心，也就是新信息的焦点分别落在 no 和 one 上，为降调，说明信息已经完整。unless 引出的句子为一个独立的语调组，构成另一个信息单位，语调核心，即新信息的焦点落在 caviar 上。同样的分析也适用于第 4 句。Except white wine 为一个独立的语调组，新信息的焦点落在 wine 上。第 8 句中 unless 之前为破折号，表示较长的停顿，因而也使得 unless 从句成为单独的语调组，构成独立的信息单位。以上分析说明 unless 和 except 引出的成分并不是前面否定句的修饰语。这就使得否定陈述更为肯定，女客人说话似乎是当真的。否定句以句号结束，体现说话时一个较长的蓄意的停顿，而随后的独立信息单位传达完整的信息，因而也就否定了前面的否定。这一句式的型式化在这一语境中只能说明女读者装腔作势、故作姿态。其次我们还发现，另四句即第 1、第 5、第 10、第 11 句随后都没有跟

except 或 unless,以引出附加说明。这又与另七句形成对比。这四句是不是表示女客人当真不想吃东西?并非如此。结合语境观察一下说这几句话的时机,就不难发现说话人的用心。第 1 句说在点菜之前。作家看到菜单上的价格如此之高而感到吃惊。客人说这句话无非是让主人宽心。第 5 句是在她点鱼和白葡萄酒之后。虽然她挥手叫侍者走开,但还是叫了芦笋。所以实际上是第 8 句前半部分的前奏,后续的仍是 unless 从句。值得注意的是最后一句。酒足饭饱之后,她已无需再迂回曲折,所以又再次重复 never eat 的句式。请注意她仍用一般现在时陈述。如果说一般现在时可以表示习惯性或真实性的动作或状态,这儿却使得说话内容成了随时可说、不用兑现的空话。第 1、第 2 式的对比只是告诉我们这位女读者言不由衷,第 3 式则让我们看到她在玩弄伎俩。与前一式有联系的型式化是与吃有关的一条词链,包括 salmon、caviar、asparagus、champagne、ice cream and coffee 和 peach。这些词虽各不相同,但它们又都指在餐厅里可以点叫的酒、菜、甜点,因此也有共性。这词链只能说明客人并非没有吃,也并非仅吃了一样,而是吃了六样,从海鲜到水果皆吃到了。但是更说明问题的是下列型式化了的词组。

4 *a little* luncheon (16)
a little fish, perhaps (36)
a little caviar (43)
just a bite (72)
more as an excuse for conversation than anything else
(=*just* as an excuse) (73-74)

前三个词组中含 a little,第四个词组含 just,第五个词组意义上含 just,所以是相同及相似词组的重复。客人在用 except 和 unless 否定陈述之后,用 just 和 a little 表示她只能品尝少许食物或她的食量非常有限,借以表示她温文尔雅、素有教养。

9.3.3 否定说明:生活拮据

作者通过以上 4 个型式化刻画这位女士,同时也用了类似的手段表现了做东的作家。让我们来看一看下面几个型式化。

5 （1）I had a *tiny* apartment … overlooking a cemetery. （9）

（2）I was earning *barely enough* money to keep body and soul together. （10）

（3）… it was so far *beyond my means*. （18）

（4）… if I *cut off* coffee for the next two weeks I could manage well enough. （23）

（5）… the prices were a great deal *higher* than I had expected. （32）

（6）For myself I chose *the cheapest* dish on the menu … （46）

第5式由一组语句组成,它们都含有一个带否定意味的词或词组。tiny的意思是"very small",隐含"far from big";barely enough意为"not really enough";beyond my means意为"more than I can afford"或"I can't afford";cut off coffee意为"not drink coffee"。可见这儿反复出现的是这一否定含义。而这六句中除第3句含my外,其余五句皆含I而且都用作主位,可见被否定的是I,即作家,借以说明他的窘境。情况既然如此,在午餐过程中他又经历了些什么呢?请看第6式:

6 （1）… it was so far beyond my means that I had never even thought of going there. *But* I was flattered and I was too young to have learned to say no to a woman. （17－19）

（2）She was talkative, *but* since she seemed inclined to talk about me I was prepared to be an attentive listener. （30－31）

（3）Well, it was early in the year for salmon and it was not on the bill of fare, *but* I asked the waiter if there was any. （38－39）

（4）I could not afford caviar, *but* I could not very well tell her. （44－45）

（5）"Madame wants to know if you have any of those giant asparagus," I asked the waiter. （*But*） I tried with all my might to will him to say no. （57－59）

（6）She ate the caviar and she ate the salmon. … *But* I

wondered what the bill would come to. (63 - 64)

(7) I watched the abandoned woman thrust them down her throat in large voluptuous mouthfuls *and* in my polite way I discoursed on the condition of the drama in the Balkans. (101 - 103)

这是通过重复而形成的类同结构的型式化。这七个复合句中都含有 but (第 7 句中 and 可用 but 替代),表示转折。but 前的小句表示就作家的境遇或本性而言是不如意或不应该出现的情况,而 but 之后则表达意义相悖的内容。这 but 前后的对比,经一再重复,说明了主位 I,即作家的无可奈何的心态。这种心态和不安与焦虑交织在一起,从惊讶、沮丧、麻木不仁到产生报复心理。

9.3.4 第一人称自述:心态变化

7 (1) I *was startled* when the bill of fare was brought. (32)

(2) *My heart sank a little*. I knew I could not afford caviar. (44)

(3) *I fancy I turned a trifle pale*. I ordered half a bottle. (59)

(4) We waited for the asparagus to be cooked. *Panic seized me*. (89)

(5) "Yes, just an ice cream and coffee," she answered. *I was past caring now*. (107)

(6) I *have had my revenge* at last. (135)

第 7 式揭示作家的真实自我。这一式各句中都含有表示心理反应的词组和小句,表现了作家对眼前发生的一切所作出的自然反应。他的这种反感以至厌恶还反映在下面三个型式化的结构中:

8 (1) I answered *generously*. (35)

(2) I told the waiter *by all means* to bring caviar. (45)

(3) I asked, *hospitable still*, *but not exactly effusive*. (56)

(4) I order *half* a bottle. (59)

(5) I ordered them (no adverbial). (84)

(6) I ordered *coffee for myself and an ice cream and coffee for her.* (107)

第 8 式含一系列与 order 有关的状语和修饰语。从“generously”“by all means”到“hospitable still, but not exactly effusive”已显作家热情减退；到叫香槟时只要了 half a bottle。第 5 句的 ordered 无状语修饰，说明作家已在应付。最后他不再光为客人也为自己点咖啡，显然已不再专心款待客人了。更为明显的是作家对客人的称呼。

9 (1) I answered that I would meet *my friend* — by correspondence — at Foyot's on Thursday at half past twelve. (24)

(2) She was in fact *a woman of forty*. (26 – 27)

(3) "I'm not in the least hungry," *my guest* sighed, ... (82)

(4) It would be mortifying to find myself ten francs short and be obliged to borrow from *my guest*. (91 – 92)

(5) I watched *the abandoned woman* thrust them down her throat ... (101 – 102)

在见面之前，作家称她为 my friend，见面之后发现她是 a woman of forty，继而称她为 my guest，客人可亲可疏，一般不及朋友亲近。当不满、反感发展成为厌恶之后，作家则将她说成了 the abandoned woman。

10 (1) She gave me the impression of having *more teeth*, *white and large and even*, *than were necessary* for any practical purpose. (28 – 29)

(2) She gave me a bright and amicable flash of *her white teeth*. (57)

(3) I watched the abandoned woman thrust them down her throat in *large voluptuous mouthfuls*. (101 – 102)

在短篇小说中一般对人物的外貌会有所描写。第 10 式表明作者不描写客人的面庞、身材，而只集中于牙齿。她那多于任何实际需要，又白又大又均匀的牙齿显然不是作为美貌的一部分，而是作为吃的实际工具来描写的。这为读者了解她的吃相作了准备。

如果说第 6 式表现了作家扭曲了的自我，第 7 至 10 式则反映了作家的真实自我。那么这一对比又说明什么？是什么驱使作家勉为其难地邀请这个读者，又违心地款待她呢？那只能是作家虑及体面以及读者恭维所给予他的满足。简单地说是作家的虚荣心。

9.3.5 *A mutton chop* 重复:聊作午餐

现在让我们来看看这顿午餐东道主吃了点什么。

11 (1) For myself I chose the cheapest dish on the menu and that was *a mutton chop*. (45 – 46)

(2) When *my mutton chop* arrived she took me quite seriously to task. (64 – 65)

(3) "You've filled your stomach with a lot of meat" — *my one miserable little chop* — ... (123 – 124)

这三句中 mutton chop 或 mutton 之前的限定词值得注意。第 1 句用了 a,表示类别,意思是"羊排"而不是别的什么菜;第 2 句用了 my,意思是 the mutton chop I ordered for myself,即"为自己点的羊排";而第 3 句中则在 my 之后用了限定词 one,表示"仅一块而已"。这与客人吃高档菜、时鲜菜等等形成鲜明对比。

9.3.6 否定词语:无端指摘

然而,即使作家只吃了一块羊排,也遭到了女读者的再三指摘。请看第 12 式。

12 (1) "I think you're *unwise* to eat meat," she said. "I don't know how you can expect to work after eating heavy things like chops. I don't believe in overloading my stomach." (47 – 49)

(2) "I see that you're in the habit of eating a heavy luncheon. I'm sure it's *a mistake*. Why don't you follow my example and just eat one thing?" (66 – 67)

(3) "I know there are people who don't like them

[asparagus]. The fact is, you *ruin* your palate by all the meat you eat." (87 – 88)

(4) "You see, you've filled your stomach with a lot of meat" — my one miserable little chop — "and you *can't* eat any more. But I've just had a snack and I shall enjoy a peach." (123 – 125)

(5) Follow my example, "... and *never* eat more than one thing for luncheon." (131 – 132)

第1、第2句中含 unwise 和 mistake,其中 un-和 mis-皆为否定前缀;第3句含 ruin 意思是 cause not to function,有否定含义;第4、第5句则分别含 can't 和 never,它们皆为否定词。可见在各句中重复的是否定成分。这一语言上的特征表现了女读者所持的态度。

以上12式从内容上看可分三组:第1至4式指客人在午餐时的所言所行;第5至10式则指作为东道主的作家的生活背景、矛盾心理、自发的反应以及他对客人态度上的变化;第11、12式则指主人的午餐内容和客人对他的指摘。从结构上讲可分为两类:第一,某一单位跨越语句和跨越语段的重复。由于重复的单位或结构不同可分为下列几种:(1)简单句,如第1式;(2)一组单句,如第3式;(3)短语,如第4式;(4)意义相同或相近的词,如第5式。第二,类同结构跨越语段的重复,如第6式。有时语篇目的要求在同一句里对同一结构或词语进行重复。例如:

(1) ... She gave me the impression of having more teeth, *white and large and even*, than were necessary for any practical purpose. (28 – 29)

(2) She ate the caviar and she ate the salmon. She talked gaily of *art and literature and music*. (63 – 64)

(3) ... he assured me that they had some *so large*, *so splendid*, *so tender*, that it was a marvel. (80 – 81)

(4) I had made up my mind that I would *put my hand in my pocket*, *and with a dramatic cry start up and say it had been picked*. (94 – 95)

在较为正式的英语语篇中,若干同类成分在句中并列时,往往用逗号将它们分开,直到最后一个成分之前才加 and 与其前面的成分相连,可是第1

句在三个形容词之间皆用 and 连接,用以突出客人露齿的特征;第 2 句中 art and literature and music 也用了同样的方法连接,以示客人滔滔不绝、高谈阔论。有意思的是 She ate the caviar and she ate the salmon。这儿并没有遵循经济原则,采用通常的 She ate the caviar and the salmon,而将 she ate 重复一次,以显示女客人连续不断、吃了又吃的情景。第 3 句 so 的重复强调了芦笋的质量。第 4 句中 and 的重复则表示了一连串的快速动作。虽然句内的重复算不上型式化,但这一手段在语篇中的反复使用也可看作一种型式化。

9.4 型式化的主次和意义

有许多句子通过词汇手段,如词汇重复或同义词,而相互联系起来。霍伊(Hoey 1991a)指出,阅读这些相互联系的句子可以获得新的认识。韩茹凯(Hasan 1989: 15)也指出语篇是由句式的型式化的总体手段形成的。语言单位的型式化可以起到强调的作用,因而产生了与具体语言型式不同的新含义,而若干型式化汇总起来就可以体现语篇的深层含义。

9.4.1 型式化的作用

型式化是语篇手段,可以表达语篇的意义。从衔接的角度看,型式化体现了最为重要的衔接手段——重复。型式化构成贯穿语篇的经线,使语篇的不同部分有机地联系起来,从而加强了语篇性。从连贯的角度看,上述 12 个型式化交代了主客双方,客人点菜,主人对应;客人在午餐过程中的种种表现,主人不断变化的反应;主人如何克己,客人如何指责,因而交代了这一社会交往的过程,勾勒了这一语篇的结构,实际上,这些型式包含了这一语境所产生的语类应具有的结构成分。这也就使得语篇获得外在联系,即与语境的密切联系,因而也就集中体现了语篇的连贯性。更为重要的是,因为型式化具有与具体型式不同的较为抽象的意义,若干型式所体现的意义既不同于具体型式的意义,又与具体型式有密切的联系。这就为从语篇中概括出主题提供了可靠的依据。

9.4.2 型式化的主次

但是在形成语篇时,并不是所有的型式化都具有同等的重要性,因此要区分主次。区分的标准有三:

其一,重复频率的大小,也就是某一型式或单位在语篇中重复次数的多少。频率越高重要性就越大。

其二,关联程度,也就是型式化语句的内容与产生语篇的语境的关联程度,与语境中的语场、语旨和语式之间的关联程度,也可以说与语篇所激发的图式的关联程度。关联程度越高,重要性就越大。

其三,结构复杂程度。在其他条件相同的情况下,句子的型式化当比小句重要,小句比短语重要,短语比词组重要。理由是:句子和小句可以表示命题,陈述相对完整的经验,提供相对完整的信息,而短语只能表示复杂概念,而词语一般只能与简单概念相联系。然而这三项标准的运用并非总是如此简单,频率异常高的词语,特别是在不同语言环境中的大量重复有时可以提示主题,如 *All the King's Men* 中的 twitch(Ren 2001)。所以三项标准必须联系起来加以考虑。

现在让我们看一看这一语篇中的主要型式化和次要型式化。语篇的语境是一位作家邀请一位读者在一家高级餐馆共进午餐。语境中的语场要问"发生了什么事?",回答是"吃饭"。因此最为重要的过程是 eat。含 eat 的型式化有第 1、2、3 式和第 11 式。第 1 式的否定意义为第 2 式的事实所否定;第 3 式的前半部分虽仍是否定,但为 except, unless 引导的句子所否定。也就是说人物语篇中的否定为叙事人语篇的肯定所否定;人物语篇中的否定又为人物语篇的转折所否定,所以结果仍是肯定:吃。这与语境是密切相关的。其次第 1 式重复 9 次,第 3 式重复 10 次,第 2 式重复 2 次。三式皆为句子或一组句子,传达相对完整的信息,因此这三式当为主要型式化。值得注意的是在作家与读者之间谈话的内容当是文学艺术,而这正是这位读者要求作家请客的理由。可是在人物语篇中没有一句是涉及文艺的,只是在叙事人语篇中轻描淡写地提到过两次。一次是叙述读者如何滔滔不绝;另一处是作家见到客人狼吞虎咽,勉强说说巴尔干的戏剧。作者的意图在写午餐本身,所以这三个型式化就显得更为重要。第 11 式虽含 eat,但仅重复两次,加之语境是请客吃饭,就语旨而言作者当写主客双方,但在这特定的情况下作者侧重对客人的叙述,因此第 11 式算不上主要型式化。第 6 式重复 6 次之多,但这一式所含句子的内容与语境无直接关联,所以也不能作为主要型式化。

主要型式化以异乎寻常的重复频率为其特征,集中体现语境,又往往以句子的形式出现,对表达整个语篇的意义有重要作用,因而在语篇中自然成了前景化的成分,而次要型式化和非型式化部分则程度不等地成为衬托,为主要型式化提供背景,为其服务。韩礼德认为前景化是有动因的突出(Halliday 1973: 104)。这种突出对表达作者的整体意义有贡献,常引导我们获得新的见解。也就是说前景化是表达语篇整体意义的手段。他又说,"一个突出的特征只有与整体意义有联系才能前景化"(同上)。可见前景化了的主要型式化的作用在于体现作者或语篇的整体意义。整体意义即使不等于主题,也至少包括主题。那么,型式化就可以成为了解主题、进行推理的语言依据。

现在让我们回到 *The Luncheon*,看一看其中 12 个型式化,特别是三个主要型式化究竟向我们提供了怎样的深层意义。我们可以问为什么作者在第 1 式中让客人反复说明她午餐并不进食或进食极少? 又为什么在第 2 式中交代了客人吃了一样又一样? 是说明客人故意言行不一吗? 看来不是。作者又为什么用第 3 式让客人反复先说"不吃",而后又话锋一转点这点那? 是说明她有意自相矛盾? 看来也不是。世界知识告诉我们,在这样的社交场合没有一个头脑清醒的人会故意自相矛盾。对这言行不一和前后不一的矛盾的解释只能是客人故作姿态;表面假装温文尔雅(第 4 式),实际极为贪食,因而狼吞虎咽(第 9 式),这也只能用客人的虚伪做作加以解释;作家节约的苦衷(第 11 式),她故意不加理会,反而无端指摘,这也只能说明她冷酷无情。在型式化的基础上通过推理我们可以看到短篇小说向人们描述了这位女读者如何利用作家的虚荣心堂而皇之地占他的便宜,从而揭示了她的狡黠,一种并非大害又令人啼笑皆非的狡黠。这也是通过仔细查寻和分析这一语篇中的型式化所能获得的新见解,也就是主题。

9.5 结　语

话语分析的任务是结合语言系统的特征分析具体的话语或语篇。语篇是语义单位,因此话语分析的任务在于了解语篇的意义。主题是语篇的深层含义,是从语篇的具体语言特征中分离出来的。要避免理解上的任意性,应该为推理过程寻找语言依据。具体语言特征的型式化是语篇的表义手段,可以作为推理的语言依据。

区分主要和次要型式化有助于了解主题。符合本文所提三项标准的主要型式化当是与语篇的整体意义有关的前景化部分。次要型式化构成连续体,作为背景具有程度不同的重要性。

为获得深层意义所进行的推理必须结合语境,包括文化语境。推理的结果受到文化语境的制约。

韩礼德认为仔细阅读可以发现语篇中带规律的现象,获得新的见解。仔细阅读应该包括查寻贯穿语篇的型式化以了解作者表述的重点所在。这可能也可供阅读教学参考。

本章用短篇小说作为分析材料说明一种分析方法。这一方法可能也适用于其他文学语篇,如诗歌、小说。至于是否适用于某些非文学语篇,尚待进一步研究。

第三部分

语法与语篇

Part Three

GRAMMAR AND DISCOURSE

10

Discourse and Choice of Structure*

10.1 Introduction

In English as well as in Chinese (putonghua) there are two ways of expressing the same proposition that can be logically represented as F(x). For instance, the proposition "Rose (red)" can be represented as "The rose is red" and "a red rose" in English and as *meigui shi hongde* ("rose be red") and *hong meigui* ("red rose") in Chinese. Grammarians have tried to account for the relationship between the two structures from different perspectives: Noam Chomsky (1957: 72) in terms of transformation, H. A. Gleason, Jr. (1965: 128) in terms of agnation, and M. A. K. Halliday (1985a: 327) in terms of grammatical metaphor. Otto Jespersen (1924) approaches this phenomenon in his own way, regarding the two structures as two different ways of joining a primary to a secondary, and using the

* 本章原载 *Georgetown University Roundtable on Languages and Linguistics* 1994 年第 150—172 页,编入此书略有删节。

terminology "junction" and "nexus". What he calls a junction is in fact a noun phrase consisting of a head plus a modifier, and the grammatical function underlying this structure is modification. On the other hand a nexus is usually a clause consisting of a subject and a predicate, which in the case of English, is made up of a copula and a subject complement. The grammatical function underlying a nexus is complementation.

10.1.1 The difference

The difference between the two can perhaps be appreciated by Jespersen's comparisons:

- "A junction is like a picture, a nexus is like a drama or process." (1933a: 95)
- "Junction is static, nexus dynamic." (1937: 121)
- "A junction serves to make what we are talking about more definite or precise, while a nexus tells us something by placing two (or more) definite ideas in relation to each other." (1937: 121)
- "In a nexus something new is added to the conception contained in the primary." (1933a: 95) or "to what has already been named" (1933a: 96).

In spite of the differences, the fact remains that both structures may express the same propositional meaning. The term nexus also has a wider application, for it can be used to refer to what he calls inner structure such as "him happy" in "The baby made him happy."

10.1.2 The two structures

As modification and complementation are two of the major

syntactic functions in language, they naturally find expression in the two languages under investigation in this article, English and Chinese. In English, alongside "a pretty girl" we find "The girl is pretty." Their corresponding equivalents in Chinese are *haokande nühai* ("pretty girl") and *nühai hen haokan* ("girl very pretty"). Examples abound of the two kinds of structure: in English, we have "the tall man" and "The man is tall"; in Chinese *gaoger*, *gaogezi* ("tall height") and *zhege nanren hen gao* ("this man height tall"). In both languages one finds a junction and its related nexus. However, even here we see the difference in the usage of these structures. For instance in Chinese *nuhai hen haoken* we find the emphasizer *hen* ("very"), which is almost indispensable, especially when the predicative adjective is a monosyllabic word and there is no link verb in the Chinese nexus as normally expected in English. However, the internal differences in the structures between the two languages will not prevent us from seeing the fact that both languages share the two structures. The question presents itself: Do the two structures function in the same way in the flow of information or structuring of information in the two languages? This involves issues such as how does each of the two languages make the textual choice? What structural resources are available in the two languages that facilitate the choice. This paper aims to examine the differences in the use of the two structures between English and Chinese from a discourse perspective. A functional approach is adopted, and Jespersen's terms "junction" and "nexus" are used for the two structures for want of better ones. Data for the study were taken from English novels such as *The Armies of the Night* (Mailer 1968), *The Master of the Game* (Sheldon 1982), *Rich Man, Poor Man* (Shaw 1969) and *The Joy Luck Club* (Tan 1989), and Chinese novels such as *A Dream of Red Mansions* (Cao 1982), *The Song of Youth* (Yang 1958), and *Selected Essays by Yang Shuo* (Yang 1978). A number of examples were also taken from newspapers.

10.2 Differences

10.2.1 Each favors its structure

The following contrastive pairs may point to the fact that where English favors a junction, Chinese shows a marked inclination for a nexus:

English	Chinese
wet paint	*youqi wei gan*
	"paint not dry"
wet floor	*diban chaoshi*
	"floor wet"
small world	*shijie hen xiao*
	"world very small"

The point will become clearer when we contrast the following examples:

1E I have got a flat tire/My car got a flat tire.

1C *wo chetai bie le*

("I car tire flat")

As a message the sentence "I have got a flat tire" consists of a theme, which is what the message is concerned with or the starting point of the message (Halliday 1985) used to orient the hearer to the information he is about to process (Fries 1993) — realized in this sentence as "I" — and a rheme, which is the remainder of the message or the part in which the theme is developed (Halliday 1985a) — realized in this sentence as "had a flat tire". In terms of information structure, the sentence begins with what is given information and proceeds to what is new information. There seems to be a general correlation between the rhematic status and the culmination of the new information marked by the location of tonic prominence. In 1E what the speaker wants to draw the hearer's attention to is the junction "flat tire", which is presented as new information bearing the tonic prominence. This is how English presents the message. In 1C *wo* ("I") is made the starting point of the message, that is the first theme. Then comes the second theme *chetai* ("car tire"), which serves to narrow down what is being talked about. The speaker prepares the hearer for the information that he is going to give about *chetai*. The rheme that carries the new information is realized as *bie le* ("flat"), where the end focus is placed. *Le* is an aspectual particle, but it is a well known fact that it is difficult to tell adjectives from verbs in Chinese. *Bie le* could mean "deflated" or "flat". Grammarians call this kind of adjective an "adjectival verb" (Li & Thompson 1981: 142). Whichever way we choose to treat the word *le*, we still have a nexus. This is how Chinese presents the same message.

Now let us contrast another pair of sentences:

2E Poverty in the developing countries has been ascribed to low productivity, inappropriate domestic policies and inadequate national effort.

2C *Fazhanzhong guojia de pinkun shi yinwei shengchanli di, guonei zhengce bu dang, zishen nuli bugou.*
("Developing country PARTICLE poverty be because productivity low, national policy not appropriate, self effort not adequate")

Here the three junctions after the preposition "to" are turned into nexuses in Chinese, which are more natural and free-flowing to the Chinese ear than junctions would be.

Now let us look at two more examples. The first set (3C, 3E) is a rendering from Chinese (*A Dream of Red Mansions*) into English where we find a series of nexuses translated into junctions in English. We find the order of the two components in each of the nexuses reversed, turning them into junctions in English. The second set (4E, 4C) is a sentence translated from English (*Vanity Fair*) into Chinese:

3C ... *jun ren chen liang fu ci zi xiao.*

("princes benevolent ministers good father kind son filial")

3E ... benevolent princes, good ministers, kind father and filial son.

4E She had such a kindly, smiling, tender, gentle, generous heart of her own.

4C *Ta xindi houdao xingge wenrou keteng, qiliang you da weiren you leguan.* ("She moral nature honest kind character gentle tender tolerance also great disposition also optimistic")

The English junction with five premodifiers is rendered into a series of nexuses in Chinese. It is not impossible to use a junction with a number of premodifiers, but the nexuses are definitely more in tune with the Chinese language.

10.2.2 Cause of the difference

The difference in the choice of the structures is in fact a difference in signaling and using the information structure and the thematic structure, a difference in structuring the clause as a message; more specifically, it is a difference in choosing what to start the message with and in telling the hearer what is important in the message.

10.3 Structural Resources

The difference in the use of the two structures between English and Chinese is due to the choice each of the two languages makes of the textual function of language. Making the choice imposes the structure on the language. As a matter of fact, each of the two languages has developed a number of structural resources that make the choice possible.

10.3.1 Structural resources in English

In English, quite a number of resources are available that facilitate the choice of a junction. To use a junction as a subject complement, it is necessary to have some devices that can initiate the clause as a message. This leads to the question: What element is usually chosen as theme in such an English clause?

The following examples show the variety of choices commonly found in the data.

Impersonal "it" is most often used as the theme in English, usually followed by an inflected form of "be":

5E It's a hell of a long trip to Japan.

5C *Dao riben de lucheng chang de yaoming.*

("to Japan PARTICLE journey long PARTICLE terrible")

6E It was a cold clear day.

6C *Tianqi hanleng qinglang.*

("weather cold clear")

Since there is no such pronoun as impersonal "it" in Chinese, it is necessary to begin the Chinese sentence with *lu cheng* ("journey") in 5C and *tian qi* ("weather") in 6C. This is how the English junctions are rendered into Chinese nexuses.

Personal pronouns followed by a form of "be" are also often used as the theme in such clauses:

7E You're a hopeless case.

7C *Ni bukejiuyao.*

("you hopeless")

In 7E the personal pronoun "you" is used. Here again the English junction is rendered into a Chinese nexus.

Personal pronouns used as the theme take "have" as the main verb:

8E She had uncommon features, bright eyes and graceful eyebrows.

8C *Ta sheng de yirong busu meimu qingming.*

("she grow PARTICLE features uncommon eyebrows eyes graceful bright")

Here the junction in English ascribes some permanent features to the theme. This use of "have" is even more common when its object is a noun derived from a verb such as "walk", "laugh", or "smile". I shall discuss this more when I discuss structural compensation. The junction in 8E is rendered into a nexus as usually done by native speakers of Chinese when they express similar ideas.

"There" as an introductory word is also used to introduce a junction in English:

9E There was an awful predicament.

9C *Qingkuang zhen zaogao.*

("situation real awful")

This introductory "there" has no counterpart in Chinese, making it necessary to use a noun as the theme in Chinese.

In their nominal function, possessive pronouns such as "mine" and "ours" may also be used to introduce a junction:

10E Ours is a happy family.

10C *Women jiating hen xingfu.*

("we family very happy")

In 10E "ours" is used to avoid the repetition of the word "family" from a previous sentence, and at the same time maintains the tendency to use a junction as the complement. However, a nexus is used in Chinese, which also makes it possible to avoid the repetition of *jiating* ("family").

The use of a cognate object is still another way of introducing a junction:

11E Artie smiled her sad, beautiful smile.

11C *Artie xiao de qichu dongren.*

("Artie smile PARTICLE sad beautiful")

In 11E we have a cognate object, with two adjectives premodifying it, thus forming a junction, which refers to Artie's smiling being sad and beautiful. (For a detailed analysis of such a structure, see Li & Thompson 1981: 625.)

From a brief survey of the major structural means by which a junction is introduced, I now turn to the formation of junctions. For example, "one" is often used after an adjective in the predicative position:

12E You are a fine one to talk about Christian charity.

12C *Tan jidu cishan ni zhen gou hao le.*

("talk Christian charity you real enough good PARTICLE")

Without "one" the irony would be lost in English. However, the Chinese nexus retains the irony.

In English there are a number of nouns that are frequently used to form junctions. Most of them are vague in meaning, for instance "thing", "business", "story", "affair", and "situation".

13E Love is a tiresome, childish business.

13C *Aiqing lingren yanjuan, youzhi kexiao.*

("Love tiresome childish")

F. T. Wood (1981: 269) has called "thing" an overused word. Is this not perhaps dictated by the tendency to use a junction?

10.3.2 Structural resources in Chinese

On the other hand Chinese accommodates a number of structural resources that contribute to the employment of a nexus to express what is encoded as a junction in English. In English, messages usually start with something that is known to the hearer or that can be inferred from the context. This calls for an entity that is linguistically definite. However, as Chinese lacks a formal distinction between the definite and the indefinite, it is possible to make the theme be whatever the speaker is concerned with at the moment of speaking. This may account for the use of *lucheng* ("journey") and *tianqi* ("weather") as the point of departure in presenting the message in 5C and 6C. In terms of functional grammar, 5C and 6C belong to the relational process in which an attribute is ascribed to an entity. Since Chinese finds it necessary to choose words like *lucheng* and *tianqi* as the carrier, the attribute naturally will come after, thus forming nexuses.

Chinese adjectives can serve as subject complements without a copula as shown in all the Chinese sentences discussed above. In *jun ren chen liang* (3C), ("princes benevolent ministers good"), the adjectives come immediately after the nouns to which they attribute a moral quality.

Alongside the nexus *diban chaoshi* ("floor wet") used in the first examples, Chinese has an alternative construction with *shi* (a copula) and *de* (a particle), *diban shi chaoshi de* ("floor be wet PARTICLE"). Although the two constructions, with *shi* and without *shi*, are somewhat different — the former gives a description, the latter a comment — the fact remains that we have a nexus in each, realizing a relational process. This also contributes to the frequent use of nexuses.

Unlike English, Chinese is capable of having a nexus as the predicate of a clause. For instance, structurally in 1C *wo* ("I") is the subject and *chetai biele* ("tire flat") is the predicate. In this predicate, *chetai* is the subject, *biele* the predicate. "As the notion of subject is not structurally well defined in the grammar of Mandarin" (Li & Thompson 1981: 19), I will approach this structure from a functional perspective and use "theme" to refer to the first element in the clause, as it is relevant to discourse and reflects the syntax of Chinese. For the element like *chetai* I will use the term "second theme". Themes are ordinally numbered because there may even be a third theme in a Chinese clause, as shown later in this paper. For the rest of the clause I will use the term "rheme". Whichever way the structure is analyzed, there is a nexus within the clause. Chinese abounds with such sentences, and *zhege nanren gezi gao* ("this man height tall") and *xiangbizi chang* ("elephant nose long") are examples. The same analysis may also apply to

4C, 8C, and 10C.

Both English and Chinese have a number of structural resources that facilitate the choice of one of the two structures. But how do they function? What determines the choice in either case? The answers to both of these questions are found at the discourse level, and I shall examine the context in which the structure is chosen.

10.4 Discourse Determined

Functional grammar is designed to account for how language is used. Its two important features are its orientation to meaning and its orientation to text. To understand why English and Chinese differ in the choice of the two structures it is necessary to see how each organizes its text and how each encodes meaning.

10.4.1 Textually determined

The choice of one or the other structure is textually determined. It is the discourse organization that calls for the choice in either language. Examine the following text examples:

Text 1

Q: Why did you come to school by bus?
A: I had a flat tire.

Text 2

Q: Could you lend me your car?

A: Oh, sorry. It has got a flat tire.

To achieve cohesion and coherence in Text 1, "I" is used as the theme to set up a cohesive tie with "you" in the preceding sentence. In Text 2, "it" is used to refer anaphorically to "your car", part of the rheme in the preceding sentence. The theme is chosen to ensure that the text is coherently organized. Since "I" and "it" are used as themes, it is impossible to start the sentence with "the tire". This makes it necessary to use a junction "flat tire" as the rheme showing what the speaker sees as the important information for the hearer to pay attention to. If the question in Text 1 is asked in Chinese the answer is usually:

wo chetai biele

("I car tire flat PARTICLE")

or *chetai biele*

("car tire flat PARTICLE")

or *tai biele.*

("tire flat PARTICLE")

The answer to the question in Text 2 must be:

chetai biele

("car tire flat PARTICLE")

Or *tai biele*

("tire flat PARTICLE")

Wo ("I") is used to relate to *ni* ("you") in the question, but the personal pronoun is optional in everyday conversational Chinese. It is more often than not omitted and the answer will be like the second with *chetai* as the theme. An even simpler answer is possible using *tai* ("tire") instead of *chetai* ("car tire"), for *che* ("car") is understood from the context. In the answer to the second question no pronoun is used, for Chinese makes a sparing use of *ta* ("it") which, when used, sounds more or less foreign. Thus *chetai* is placed at the initial position as the theme. Here *che*, which occurs in the question, is repeated to make the answer relevant, but since it is made the theme or second theme in the Chinese translation of Text 1, the adjective *bie* can only occur in the rheme to show the state the *chetai* is in. The result is a nexus.

10.4.2 Thematic development

Thematic development correlates with the structure of a text. The following texts conform to the major patterns of theme-rheme (T-R) progression in English. (Parts I wish to emphasize appear in bold print.)

Text 3

Six months later he had a heart attack. It was a **mild one**.

The thematic development of Text 3 may be presented as T1 – R1 for the first sentence and T2 (= R1) – R2 for the second sentence. "It" in the second sentence refers back to "a heart attack" as part of the rheme in the preceding sentence, and yet "one" also stands for the same noun phrase and therefore has to be preceded by a modifier to present what is important in the message. This results in the use of a junction in which the attributive adjective "mild" bears the focal stress with "one" weakly stressed.

The counterpart of Text 3 in Chinese is something like *Liu ge yue hou ta xinzangbing fazuo, bijiao qing* ("six month after he heart trouble attack comparative mild"). The Chinese translation of the second English sentence is a nexus with a zero pronoun as the theme, so what is explicitly expressed is the adjective *qing* modified by *bijiao* ("comparatively") which, like emphasizer *hen*, is inserted to make the sentence flow more smoothly. As mentioned above, Chinese rarely uses *ta* ("it"). The nexus is added to the previous statement as part of the sentence. By parataxis the two nexuses are related, clarifying what the predicative adjective refers to.

To this we may add the following similar examples:

Text 4

On his desk there was a letter. **It was a short one**.

Text 5

And for the first time Jordan laughed. **He had a great laugh**. It washed away the remoteness and coldness you always felt coming off him.

Text 4 displays the same pattern of thematic progression as Text 3. In Text 5, however, the pattern is T1 – R1, T2 (=T1) – R2 (=R1), T3 (=R2) – R3. In Text 5, "laugh" in the second sentence needs a premodifier to make the rheme newsworthy.

For the junction in the parts of Text 4 and Text 5 in bold print, the Chinese translations would have a similar rendering into a nexus with a zero pronoun — *hen kailang* ("very cheerful"), *hen duan* ("very short") — as part of the sentence, just as the Chinese translation of Text 3. Thematic progression in the structure of the text calls for the choice of junction in English and of nexus in Chinese.

In English, "there is a feeling that the predicate of a clause should where possible be longer than the subject, thus a principle of structural compensation comes into force" (Quirk et al. 1985: 1401). For "He smoked", English prefers "He had a smoke". Text 5 shows that such a syntactic process is a valuable resource for textual structure. But in many cases the noun is a repetition of its corresponding verb in the preceding sentence, which makes it necessary to modify the action noun to make the rheme newsworthy. Sentences like "She has a fine laugh" is frequently used in spoken and written texts. This is in fact one of the means by which a text can be given added unity and coherence. It is also conducive to the employment of junctions in English.

10.4.3 Local discourse organization

Another aspect of discourse structure is local discourse organization. Text often consists of subtexts, each having its local structure that contributes to the macrostructure of the text. The kind of local organization that is relevant to this discussion contains a number of sentences or clauses, all of which maintain a unified orientation. This particular local organization is further constrained in that it forms a segment of the theme of the paragraph in which it occurs. It usually consists of three elements that are successively ordered: 1) Initiation, which is usually realized as an objective account or description, or a statement of fact; 2) continuation, which takes the form of further elaboration or description, or states the consequence; and 3) conclusion which, referring back to the previous statements, offers a subjective comment, generalization, or summary.

Text 6

Early this morning he had put his name on the list for the telephone, and so had been able to make a call to his wife just a little while ago. **It had been a merry call**.

The first clause is a statement of fact — what happened, or what "he" did "early this morning". As the first element it serves to initiate the local organization. Then comes the second element, introduced by "and so" but with the subject ellipted, which states the consequence of the previous action. Finally comes the conclusion, which begins with "it", referring back to "a call" in the second clause. Then in the rheme the word "call" is repeated, which would convey no information unless it is modified. It is the modifier that carries the focus and gives new information. This form of local organization calls for the use of a junction. As a segment it serves to develop the central theme of showing how Norman Mailer was anxious to get out of jail.

A few more examples will show that this kind of local discourse organization is fairly systematic:

Text 7

The solution, then, was television. Here the candidate could address the electorate effectively, but at a safe remove; **it was a costly procedure, but a prudent one**.

Text 8

I wanted to be honorable because I felt more comfortable telling the truth than lying. I felt more at ease innocent than guilty. I had thought it out. **It was a pragmatic desire, not a romantic one**.

The third element in each of the two texts serves to offer a judgment. The pronoun "it" refers back to the previous statements, and the nouns "procedure" and "desire" serve to sum up what is said in the previous clauses. The focus falls on the adjectives in the junctions. "One" is used as a prop word to present a contrast in either case.

However, in many cases the second element is optional, as can be seen in the following texts:

Text 9

The orchestra leader ... signaled for "Chinatown, My Chinatown."
It was a well-intentioned but entirely superfluous gesture.

Text 10

They had to stop twice because Billy got car-sick, but aside for that the trip was **a pleasant one**.

The subjective conclusion comes immediately after the objective statement of fact. This kind of local discourse organization is possible partly because English has a fairly large number of nouns — such as "account", "charge", "criticism", "excuse", "question", "reference", and "warning" — which can be used to refer back in a general way to what has already been said. They refer to whole sections of spoken or written text (Sinclair 1990: 389). Observe the following:

Text 11

"I must go. I've taken a leave of absence at school."
"For how long?" **It was a nervous question**.

Sometimes we find minor sentences, which are just junctions, used as the third element:

Text 12

Malomar had the rest of the day and evening scheduled for the cutting room. **His greatest pleasure**.

Text 13

"Your father's blood," his mother said. **Dreadful charge**.

As "it is" or "it was" has low information value, their deletion will not affect comprehension on the part of the hearer or reader.

10.4.4 Change to nexus in Chinese

This kind of English discourse segment can be transplanted into Chinese, for the elements are logically arranged. But in Chinese the third element will in most cases take the form of a nexus. A few examples will make the point clear. The final clause in Text 6 is likely to be translated as:

Dianhua shang liao de hen kaixin.

("telephone on talk PARTICLE very delightful")

Our talk on the phone was delightful.

The last clause in Text 7 finds its Chinese counterpart like this:

zheyang zuo huaqian hen duo dan bijiao jinshen.

("this way do cost very much but relatively prudent")

It costs much but it is prudent to do like this.

The change in structure is necessary because a similar local discourse organization in Chinese usually ends with a nexus:

Text 14

Ta zai yinian zhinei dapo liangci shijie jilu shifen nande.

("he in one year within break twice world record very rare")

He's broken a world record twice in one year. It's a rare feat.

The first part of the sentence states a fact and the last gives a comment, using a nexus with a zero pronoun.

10.4.5 Subtle semantic difference

So far I have shown the difference between English and Chinese in the choice of the two structures: Where English favors a junction, Chinese favors a nexus. But this does not mean that English does not employ a nexus in which an adjective is used predicatively, nor that Chinese avoids the use of a junction in which an adjective is used attributively. Alongside "She is a pretty woman", English has "She is pretty". But there is a subtle semantic difference between the two constructions. While the junction puts an entity into a specific class giving it some kind of permanent feature, the nexus usually has a temporary reference. This difference can be tested by adding an adverb of time like "today" to the two sentences. It would be acceptable to say "She is pretty today", but people are not likely to make such a remark as "She is a pretty woman today". This test brings out the distinction between the temporary and the permanent. The same is true of the semantic difference between "He is skeptical" and "He is a skeptical man". The former may imply that he is skeptical about something specific, while the latter ascribes a permanent feature to "he" to mean "He is generally skeptical about things". Similarly "a courteous man" is a man who is courteous normally, not merely at this moment. This permanent feature of an English junction may justify the use of a junction in the third element of the discourse segments discussed above. Some kind of stable quality is compatible with the function of the element of conclusion.

A subtle semantic distinction between a junction and a nexus is also found in Chinese, but it is of a different kind. While a nexus is a straightforward statement in Chinese, a junction may admit of more than one interpretation. Compare the following:

Zhe ben shu hen hao.
("this QUANTIFIER book very good")
This book is good.

Zhe shi ben hao shu.

("this is QUANITIFER good book")

This is a good book.

The first sentence simply means that the book is well written or informative. The junction *hao shu* may have the same meaning, but it may also mean a book free from filth and pornography. Compare also:

Ta hen congming.

("he very clever")

He is very clever.

Ta shi ge congming ren.

("he is QUANITIFIER clever man")

He is a clever man.

The first sentence has only one reading. But in the second sentence, *congming ren* may imply — often in a derogatory way — that *ta* is one that has common sense and knows what to do for his own good. Because of its clarity of meaning, the Chinese nexus lends itself to frequent use in discourse.

It must be noted that English also makes use of nexus with an adjective as the subject complement. The choice is made because of the temporary sense of the predicative adjective and is determined by discourse organization.

Text 15

Suddenly Cleo starts laughing and points ... Tessa is staring too, **only her eyes are big**, her mouth dropping open.

The part in bold print is a clause in which "her eyes" is used as the theme, because the word is semantically associated with "staring" in the previous clause. Thus the two clauses cohere through an association of lexical meaning. The nexus presents a temporary state: While "Tessa is staring", she keeps her eyes wide open. If "she" became the theme, there would be a junction, like "She has big eyes", suggesting a permanent feature that is somewhat out of place in this context.

Chinese sometimes uses junction with an adjective as a premodifier.

Text 16

Na ge guniang sheng de gao biliang, da yanjing, shencai gaogao de, zhuangjian de hen.

("that girl grow PARTICLE high nose ridge big eyes height tall PARTICLE healthy PARTICLE very")

The girl has a long-bridged nose and big eyes. She is tall and healthy.

Here the subject complement consists of two junctions that run parallel, followed by two parallel nexuses. It would sound unnatural if only one junction were used. Most Chinese would consider the sentence incomplete if it ended with the second junction. One would expect the description to go on until one reaches a nexus. This has much to do with the information structure in Chinese, discussed in the next section.

10.5 Typological Differences

There are typological differences between English and Chinese in how a message is presented and how information is structured. Each clause has a thematic structure, which assigns the functions theme and rheme. Thematic status is signaled in English by initial position in the clause. This is also assumed to be the case in Chinese. Information structure is not directly determined by the clause, but by the information unit. Information units are signaled in the spoken language as tone groups. Each tone group contains information which is presented as given and information which is presented as new (For a detailed discussion see Fries 1993). The theme is the point of departure for the clause as a message. The speaker has, within certain limits, the option of selecting any element in the clause as theme.

10.5.1 Difference in the choice of Theme

In the English language data presented in this paper, the theme is in most cases realized as a pronoun — most often "it", a personal pronoun, or the existential "there". This conforms to Halliday's observations, which order themes as follows: The item most often functioning as an unmarked theme in a declarative clause is the first person pronoun "I"; after that comes the other personal pronouns — "you", "we", "he", "she", "it", and "they" — and the impersonal pronouns — "it" and "there"; then come other nominal groups (Halliday 1985a: 45). In English the theme in a clause is justifiably referred to as a peg on which the message is hung. It is not the peg that really counts; it is the message that hangs on it that really matters. Thus the theme in an English clause has low information value. Conversely in Chinese, theme is not just a peg or a starting point for the information, but rather it is the basis on which the information is built. In Chinese the theme assumes a more important role than it does in English. Two facts testify to this:

1) Theme in Chinese is more often realized as noun phrases — as in 5C, 6C, and 9C — rather than pronominal substitutes.

2) Even when the clause begins with a pronoun, it is often followed by a second theme to specify what is being talked about — as in 1C, 4C, 8C, and 12C.

Sometimes there is a third theme in the clause:

Text 17

Jiali renren shenti jiankang.

("family everyone body health")

Everybody in the family is in good health.

Here *jiali* ("family") and *renren* ("everyone") stand in a part-whole relationship in which the first theme is the whole of which the second theme is a part. The second theme is possessed by the first. Similarly the third theme, *jiankang* ("health") is possessed by the second. The sense of the clause is made progressively more and more specific. It is the third theme that specifies what is really being talked about. In contrast to the English clause, in which the principle of end weight leads to a structural compensation that requires the predicate to be longer than the subject, the Chinese clause tends to be top-heavy, giving the theme more weight. Thus the rheme in English tends to be more complicated than the rheme in Chinese. This difference entails the difference in the choice of the two structures. In English information structure, given information is always realized by an element that is linguistically definite or generic. In Chinese, however, there is no overt distinction between generic and specific, definite and indefinite. It is the initial position in the clause that makes an element definite or generic. This gives Chinese more freedom in thematic choice. In the above example *jiali* is made definite by its initial position, referring to a family that the speaker expects the hearer to know. In English, the principle of end focus reserves the end position of the clause for new information. "Flat tire" in "I have got a flat tire" bears focal prominence. The same tendency obtains in Chinese in *wo chetai biele*, where *biele* bears the nucleus. End focus usually highlights new information, but in Chinese the tendency is more pronounced than in English:

Text 18

Xue yingyu de ren yuelaiyueduo.
("study English PARTICLE people more and more")
More and more people are studying English.

In the English translation of Text 18, the focus is on "more and more". But in its Chinese counterpart, *yuelaiyueduo* still comes at the end of the clause. The tendency to place end focus on the new information in Chinese may account for the use of a nexus to end a discourse segment, for the predicative adjective unmistakably has focal prominence.

10.5.2 Typological difference

The difference in the choice of the two structures also sheds light on the typological difference between English and Chinese. The thematic choice in the languages points to the fact that English is a subject prominent language while Chinese is a theme prominent language. The frequent use in English of pronominal substitutes as unmarked themes — i. e. both as theme and subject — is the result of making the clauses conform to the syntactic pattern embodying the subject-predicate relation. However in Chinese, the use of noun phrases as theme/subjects, and the reinforcement of the theme by a second or even third theme, testify to the fact that Chinese is a language in which theme is prominent. This typological difference has direct bearing on the ordering of elements in the thematic structure. English orders its elements in the clause by consideration of grammatical functions, whereas in Chinese "the order is governed to a large extent by consideration of meaning" (Li & Thompson 1981: 20). As has been stated, Chinese has more freedom to choose any element for the theme in a clause. For instance it is common in Chinese to say:

Text 19

Zhege xiaoxi zhidao de ren bu duo.

("this news know PARTICLE people not many")

There are few people who know this news.

In Chinese *zhege xiaoxi* ("this news") is made the theme. But in English, it is hardly possible to make "this news" the theme and say "This news there are few people who know". Text 19 shows that a Chinese speaker may place what is uppermost in his mind at the moment in the initial position without regard to the grammatical relation between the theme and the verb. This is especially true when the first element is followed by a nexus in which another noun phrase serves to set the frame for the presentation of the theme. Neither the notion of subject nor the subject-predicate relation in English totally applies to Chinese.

Subject and theme are concepts that belong to different levels of linguistic structure. The subject is a syntactic element that is related to grammar, whereas the theme is a discourse element that is related to the organization of meaning. In light of this it may be sensible to regard English as a sentence-oriented language and Chinese as a discourse-oriented language. An example taken from a Chinese newspaper will make the point:

Text 20

Shi zhi shen qiu, tianqi jian han, zouye wencha da, zheduanshijian xiaohai kesou fabinglü gao, shijian chang, quanyu man.

("time happen deep autumn weather gradual cold day and night temperature difference big, this period child cough incidence high, time long, recover slow")

> It was late autumn. It is getting cold with a great difference in temperature between day and night. During this period children are liable to have a bad cough. It lasts long and recovery is slow.

The single Chinese sentence consists of six nexuses, each with its own theme and rheme in thematic structure, but the English translation has four sentences, of which three have "it" as the theme. The Chinese sentence is in fact a subtext. In terms of rhetorical structure, the first three nexuses combine to provide the background, the fourth is the nucleus, and the last two perform the function of elaboration. They are so related semantically that they are logically sequenced together to serve the communicative goal of the speaker. They constitute a semantic unit, which is what grammarians call "text". Halliday (1975: 23) defines "text" as a semantic unit, realized as lexicogrammatical units. Furthermore, the six clauses cannot be made sentences, although there are no overt connecters between them. It is meaning that binds them together. To separate them would damage the coherent flow of the language. Text 20 thus indicates that Chinese is a text-or discourse-oriented language.

10.6 Cultural Impact

How is it that English and Chinese function the way they do? The factors that shape the languages can be found in their cultures.

10.6.1 Language as a semiotic system in a culture

Halliday defines semiotics as the study of sign systems — in other words, as the study of meaning in its most general sense. Linguistics, then, is a kind of semiotics. It is an aspect of the study of meaning. Language is the most important way of conveying meaning. But there are many other modes to convey meaning in any culture, which are outside the realm of language. These will include both art forms — such as painting, sculpture, music, dance, etc. — and other modes of cultural behavior such as modes of exchange, structures of the family, among others. All of these things bear meaning in a culture. Indeed we can define a culture as a set of semiotic systems — a set of systems of meaning, all of which interrelate (Halliday & Hasan 1989: 4). It then follows that a language, whether Chinese or English, is interrelated with other kinds of semiotic systems and shaped by the culture in which it is used.

10.6.2 Dynamism

China has a long cultural heritage. Insofar as this cultural heritage bears on the Chinese language, two features stand out prominently. One feature is its **dynamism**. In Chinese philosophy, "change" is the word. Traditionally, Chinese philosophy makes a distinction between "the formal" and the "formless". The two notions were interpreted in different ways by different schools of thought, but it was a consensus view among ancient Chinese philosophers that the formal and the formless represent two stages in the flow of *qi*, that is *yin* and *yang*. This means that one can change into the other. There are sayings that embody such a philosophical idea of change in Chinese:

- "Running water is never stale and a door-hinge never gets worm-eaten".
- "As there is no definite shape for water, so there is no fixed strategy for the military".

Thus things are viewed as constantly moving and changing. In Chinese painting, painters usually take a nonfocal perspective when they work on landscape. The scenery is presented as if it were viewed by the painter moving from place to place. It is a dynamic way of creating an aesthetic effect and conveying some kind of meaning. In Chinese calligraphy, the essential point is to be natural. To be natural, the calligrapher does not follow any conventional type of arrangement but aims to achieve overall harmony, as in group dancing. For instance what is called "regular script" is characterized by its abstract aesthetic value which can be appreciated without regard to the characters themselves, for each dot or stroke is usually suggestive of something in the outside world and shaped by following the dictates of the mind or will of the calligrapher. He works with facility, making sure to use the right size of characters and to vary the thickness of strokes so that he gives expression to vigor or delicacy as he sees fit. In calligraphy as in the language, what is important varies in the presentation. We need not look into other realms to see that Chinese culture is characterized by a dynamism that manifests itself in change and variation to achieve a natural, aesthetic value. This feature of Chinese culture has its impact on the Chinese language, making it fluid, pliable, or flexible in comparison with English. Chinese orders the elements in the clause according to the needs of meaning or communication. The elements in the sentence

Tushuguan you mei you zheben shu ("library have not have this book") can be flexibly ordered in six different ways, but in English the same idea can only be expressed in two ways, "I don't know whether the book is available at the library" or "Whether the book is available at the library, I don't know". As has been shown above in many cases, the Chinese sentence is not a sentence in the sense in which it is used in English. For one thing, Chinese sentences are not well defined. If you leave out all the punctuation marks in a Chinese passage, and ask some people to punctuate it, it is not likely that they will do it in exactly the same way. This means that the same passage may be regarded as consisting of different numbers of sentences to different people. For another, many Chinese sentences defy analysis in terms of a subject-predicate relation. Take 4C for instance:

4C *Ta xindi houdao xingge wenrou keteng, qiliang you da weiren you leguan.* ("She moral nature honest kind character gentle tender tolerance also great disposition also optimistic")

The theme/subject is followed by four nexuses, each ascribing a feature to one aspect of the theme. Having four nexuses as a predicate does not conform to Western grammar, but the use of a series of nexuses in Chinese makes the language flow naturally.

10.6.3 Form

In Western philosophy, "form" means the structure, pattern, organization, or essential nature of anything. **Form** is thus regarded as the deciding factor. In Western painting, the usual practice is to take a focal perspective with a figure and a background in the picture. There is some kind of form underlying the work of art. In language it is the form of a sentence that determines the construction of utterances. The subject and the predicate are of fundamental importance:

Any doubts concerning their legitimacy or even their mere usefulness

> therefore betray a crisis of grammatical thought, a new departure in grammatical thinking. They affect the whole system of grammar and not merely part of it. (Sandman 1954: 1)

Thus, English sentences are well defined. It is true that they permit variation, but not to the extent that they deviate from the subject-predicate pattern. This explains why English is sentence-oriented and makes frequent use of pronominal substitutes as the theme/subject that only perform a structural role, making utterances conform to the form of the sentence. This may also account for its preference for junction.

10.6.4 Explicitness

The other feature of Chinese culture that is related to the Chinese language is **explicitness**. Another important word in ancient Chinese philosophy — especially in moral philosophy — is *ren* ("benevolence"). *Ren* stands for the most important principle for social behavior and family relations. Of interest in language is *ren*'s application to people who hold different positions in social institutions and the family structure. In 3C we have four adjectives — ren ("benevolent"), *liang* ("good"), *ci* ("kind"), and *xiao* ("filial") — *each* denoting a moral code for people in different positions. Encoded in different words, *ren* is made quite explicit. In addition to the general word *ai* ("love"), Chinese has *ci* ("paternal/maternal affection"), *xiao* ("filial piety"), and *ti* ("brotherly love") to specify different kinds of love between family members. An even more revealing example is the various terms for different relatives for which English has a single word, "uncle": *bo* ("father's elder brother"), *shu* ("father's younger brother"), *jiu* ("mother's brother"), *gufu* ("husband of father's sister"), and *yifu* ("husband of mother's sister"). Here a distinction is made between the maternal side and paternal side, and an even finer distinction is made between the younger and the elder brother of one's father.

Explicitness is not limited to vocabulary, but is also reflected in clause structure. The theme, as has been noted above, may be followed by a second or even a third theme. The tendency is to move from the general to the specific, progressively narrowing down what is being talked about, thus achieving explicitness. On the other hand, the choice of a nexus with a predicative adjective probably owes to the effort to avoid the ambiguity that may arise in its corresponding junction containing a premodifier. Furthermore, in translation, Chinese tends to employ a higher-level linguistic unit for the English structure, that is use a phrase for a word, a clause for a phrase, or a sentence for a clause. For instance in "Yet, on these thoughts, he took a drink of water" the prepositional phrase "on these thoughts" must be expanded into a clause in Chinese. Such structural expansion contributes to explicitness in Chinese.

It seems that universal love, which is encouraged in Western culture, makes it unnecessary to specify different kinds of love among people and to distinguish between relatives on the maternal or the paternal side. But at the syntactic level English has its own way achieving explicitness. In complex noun phrases English usually starts with the specific and proceeds to the general. For *jialiren renren shenti jiankang* ("family everyone body health") in Text 17, English moves the other way round, saying "everybody in the family" or even "the health of everybody in the family". While the elements are linearly sequenced in Chinese, they are hierarchically structured in English with the help of prepositions. But when it comes to the sentence structure, English tends to use hypotaxis, whereas Chinese usually uses parataxis. With the connecters, English sentences are well-knit. In contrast, parataxis renders Chinese sentences loosely structured.

Nexus is dynamic, as pointed out by Jespersen, and is more explicit than junction in meaning. It appears that the preference of nexus in Chinese may be ascribed to the impact of Chinese culture. However, how culture shapes language is a subject that calls for a separate, careful study. What I have been trying to do in this section is to examine briefly the impact of culture on language, which may result in some general features — for instance dynamism and explicitness in Chinese, and form-dominance and compactness in English — that may shed light on language use.

10.7 Conclusion

Our study suggests that while the two languages English and Chinese share the same structures in their language system, they differ in how they use those structures. In communication the difference emerges, and discourse organization calls for the different choice. The study may also be seen as providing an insight into the relation between grammar and discourse: Grammar provides a basis for discourse analysis (See Chapter 11), and discourse perspectives may help to account for lexicogrammatical features, such as the use of "one" in the rheme in English and the use of more than one theme in Chinese (See also Chapters 12 - 15). In our study, the differences in the choice of the two structures shed light on typological differences between English and Chinese, and may be attributable to the difference between the two cultures.

11

Linguistic Features and Discourse Semantics*

11.1 Introduction

The topic of this chapter is "Linguistic Features and Discourse Semantics", which seems to suggest the question: How do linguistic features give expression to meanings in discourse. This would involve the whole area of Discourse Analysis, calling for a careful study of the contributions of the different components of language. I can only hope to address a fragment of the issue. My concern is with a kind of discourse meaning in literary texts that can hardly be expressed congruently or metaphorically. As the chapter will show it can be effectively expressed by the patterning of some linguistic features.

---

* 本章原载 *Grammar and Discourse — Proceedings of the International Conference on Discourse Analysis at the University of Macao* 2001 年第 75—84 页。

11.1.1 A multiple coding system

Human language is a multiple coding system, consisting of three strata; semantics, lexico-grammar and phonology. Meaning is coded as wording, that is, realized in words arranged according to grammar, while lexico-grammar is realized phonologically. The relation between semantics and lexico-grammar is one of realization. This may be referred to as the normal use of lexico-grammar to encode congruent meaning. There is another kind of meaning which is called metaphorical or transferred meaning. The meaning is metaphorical by reference to the congruent meaning. Whether congruent or metaphorical, the meaning is encoded in lexico-grammar that contains features related to the contextual features.

11.1.2 Deeper meaning

However, we also find in English discourse cases where lexico-grammatical features are used symbolically to convey larger meanings that are "deeper" than the face value of the segment of language in which these features are used. We call these meanings deeper meanings, because their lexico-grammatical realization contains no features that are directly related to the contextual features, that is, not directly associated with the configuration of situational features. As a matter of fact, these features have become signs that embody meanings of a higher order, usually involving abstraction or dissociation from the particularities of the text, like the theme of a literary text. More often than not it is the deeper meaning that constitutes the theme of a literary text or the local theme of a sub-text. "Theme" or "local theme" is used here in the sense of the general message the writer wants to get across to the reader in a text or a sub-text. As Cheng has repeatedly pointed out, it is necessary to distinguish between linguistic meaning and message. The linguistic meaning is not necessarily the message, which can only be inferred on the basis of the linguistic expression and the context of situation. This is what Hasan refers to as two levels of semiosis in all verbal art; one that is the product of the use of natural language, itself a semiotic system; and the other which is the product of the artistic system through foregrounding and repatterning of the first order meanings. Deeper meanings are encoded by the patterning or regularity of linguistic features that are not directly related to the contextual features. However, the inference has to be made by reference to the contextual configuration.

11.1.3 Three strata in verbal art

In verbal art, as Hasan points out, we need to recognize three strata: theme, symbolic articulation and verbalization. What concerns us here is the stratum of symbolic articulation, which, is where the meanings of language are turned into signs having a deeper meaning. Hasan also points out theme is the deepest level of meaning in verbal art; it is what a text is about when dissociated from the particularities of the text (1989: 97).

However, it must be pointed out that it is not the lexico-grammatical features themselves that can be used symbolically but the patterning of patterns involving the use of these features that can convey deeper meanings, or second order meanings. So by symbolic use of lexico-grammar we mean the inference of symbolic meanings from the patterning of patterns in discourse.

In this paper we shall first discuss how local themes are expressed by patterning of features and then proceed to the theme of a novel. It is hoped that this paper may help to prove the fact that in English there exist meanings of a second order, which can be inferred from the patterning of certain lexico-grammatical features. The data were taken from *The Good Earth* and *All the King's Men*.

11.2 Local Theme

11.2.1 Characterization

Let me first of all take a look at *The Good Earth* by Pearl Buck. In this book Wang Lung is the protagonist, the central character; all other characters are portrayed around him and kept in the background so as to give prominence to him as the typical peasant in the early 20th century in China. Apart from narration or the character's own discourse, one way to make him stand out is to show the difference between him and some of the other characters, for instance, between him and his son, and between him and his wife.

11.2.2 Words of different meanings

It is a fact that many English words are capable of different meanings. At discourse level this has become a resource to achieve symbolic meaning. Let's look at the following dialogue between father and son:

[1] "There is to be a war such as we have not heard of — there is to be a revolution and fighting and war such as never was, and *our land is to be free*."

[2] "Now what all this stuff is, I do not know," he said wondering. "*Our land is free already — all our good land is free. I rent to whom I will …*"

The two italicized sentences have both similarities and differences. They are similar because we have Repetition of roughly the same sentence:

In terms of thematic structure, both have "our land" as the Theme, and "is free" in the Rheme. In the grammar of experience both represent relational process involving one participant, Carrier, realized by the noun phrase "Our land" and an Attribute realized by the adjective "free". In the interpersonal structure, both are declarative, positive, with "Our land" as the Subject and "is" as the Finite.

However, in the similarity we find differences. In [1] we find a future reference realized by "is to be", while in [2] the reference is to the present realized as "is". In terms of information structure, "free" in [1] has the tonal prominence, while in [2] the prominence is on "already". Underlying the apparent differences there is a more significant difference in meaning in the use of the word "land". It is this contrast that makes the other differences possible or necessary.

The answer given by Wang Lung is irrelevant. Irrelevant, because he understands the word "land" differently. Wang Lung is an illiterate. It is possible that he does not know the word "land" can mean "country" or "motherland". However, as the word "land" is so familiar to him, and land itself so near and dear to him, that whenever he talks of land, he thinks of the land he owns and rents. So this meaning comes to him so naturally. This in fact reflects his mentality.

Here we see that the different meanings of the word used by father and son serve to bring out the difference between them. To the son "land" means "the country"; to the father "land" means "an area of ground for farming" or even more specifically "an area of ground he owns". To the son the land is to be free through war or revolution. To the father the land is already free. The son looks into the future, but the father looks at the present. The son has the nation in mind but the father puts his interests first. The difference in the understanding of the word "land" reflects the difference in their outlook. The son takes as his responsibility to join in the battle to free the country while the father keeps his eyes on the pieces of land he owns. The son sets his aim high but the father is so narrow-minded that he cannot see beyond his property. This mentality befits a member of the landed gentry. How does the author achieve the sharp contrast between these two characters?

In the context of [1], normally no one would understand "land" as "a piece of land one owns", and no one would limit the meaning of "free" to "free to rent". So what is foregrounded is the understanding or misunderstanding of the word "land" by the father. So by using the patterning of Repetition of the similar structure containing Repetition of the same word having two different meanings the writer achieves a deeper meaning, which is derived from a sign consisting of the two different first order meanings of "land", thus bringing to the notice of the reader the generation or ideological gap between the two. This helps to bring to light the local theme of the sub-text, which contributes to the theme of the novel.

11.2.3 The passive voice

Now let's look at some instances of the passive voice in the imperative mood. The usual explanation for the choice of the passive to achieve objectivity and impersonality simply does not apply. The following texts taken from *The Good Earth* by Pearl S. Buck will help us explore the meanings of the passive.

When the protagonist Wang Lung learned that the landlord Hwang was thinking of selling his land, Wang Lung decided to buy some land from him. Turning to his wife, he said "We will buy the land". "But the land — the land," she stammered. "I will buy it!" He cried in a loud voice. "I will buy it from the great house of Hwang!" "I will buy it," he repeated peevishly. Then he reaffirmed his intention, saying "I will buy Hwang's land". In what must be a very short space of time, and in writing in less than a page, Wang Lung repeated the same sentence four times. This represents the most common way of using the patterning to express a deeper meaning. The repetition of the same words and same structure becomes a sign from which a second order meaning can be derived, that is, firm determination.

After her husband repeated his intention to buy the land, O-Ian said (This structure is repeatedly used by the wife.)

[3] Let it be bought.

There are other imperative forms in English:

a) the unmarked form "Buy it",

b) the marked form "You buy it".

c) the polite form "Please buy it" and

d) the active form "Let's buy it".

Why didn't O-Ian choose one of these? Forms *a* and *b* fall into the category of command, which is something no wife should or dare do to her husband in the early 20th century in China. Form *c* is a request, which would sound too distant for O-Ian to address her husband. Form *d* would be a more likely candidate, but since "let's" is best interpreted as a wayward form of the subject "You and I" (Halliday 1994: 87), O-Ian would feel it too presumptuous to put herself on the same par with her husband. The money to buy the land was his and the land bought would be his property, for Wang Lung was the head of the family. She was not the person to buy the land, although Wang Lung used "we" the first time he expressed his intention, but in all the other cases "I" is used. He was well aware that he was going to buy the land. So the passive construction shows the status of O-Ian in the family and her subordination to her husband. She could never be mentioned as an equal to her husband, which excludes the possibility of using the active form "Let's ..." This passive form is repeatedly used. The second order meaning is inferred from the repetition of the passive construction.

11.2.4 Grammatical metaphors

Now let us turn to grammatical metaphors. As pointed out by Halliday (1994: 342), the selection of metaphor is itself a meaningful choice. Out of the contrast between the congruent and the metaphorical a deeper meaning may be derived. Let us study the following texts, also taken from *The Good Earth*. When the couple, Wang Lung and O-Ian, found themselves doing better than the landlord for whom O-Ian had worked as a slave, they were naturally happy. The description runs like this:

[4] A slow smile spread over her face and Wang Lung laughed aloud. (p.49)

When they decided to buy the land, the writer says:

[5] And the slow smile spread over her face, the smile that never lightened the dullness of her narrow black eyes.

In [4] we find two contrasts: the contrast between "laugh" and "smile", and between the congruent and the metaphorical. "Wang Lung laughed aloud" is the congruent form, a straightforward statement of fact. However, "A slow smile spread over her face" is a grammatical metaphor. Its congruent forms could be:

a) Her face exhibited a slow smile.

b) She showed a slow smile in her face.

c) She smiled a slow smile.

d) She smiled, a slow smile.

In [4] the first clause contains a relational process with "a slow smile" as Agent and "over her face" as circumstantial, and in the second clause we find a behavioural process manifesting the state of consciousness with "Wang Lung" as the Behaver. In terms of thematic structure "Wang Lung" is made the Theme in the second clause while "A slow smile" is the Theme of the first. What the message is concerned with is not O-Ian, but a slow smile. Then why is "O-Ian" not given the thematic status? This amounts to the question why the metaphorical form is used. If the congruent forms *b* to *d* were used, then "She" would be the Theme in thematic structure and Behaver in the transitivity structure, and If Form *a* were used "her face" would be the Theme and Actor. Normally this metaphorical form is used to show that the speaker wants to draw the hearer's attention to the smile rather than the person who smiled, thus achieving an effect of objectivity, which is appropriate for the description of the psychological process the person is going through. The choice is made to suit the needs of narration. However when the metaphorical form is repeated more than once one would suspect there might be some reason on the part of the person described. Is the person, O-Ian in our case, capable of smiling? Life had been so miserable that she could hardly have experienced anything that could make her smile. Long years of suffering had made her impassive. A slow smile must be a smile that is deliberate. There is nothing spontaneous about it that springs from the inner feeling of happiness. The repetition of the metaphorical form creates a second-order meaning, showing O-Ian to be impassive and submissive.

She is presented not so much as a conscious being capable of behaving (used in its grammatical sense) but as an object — her face — that the smile worked its slow way onto. That's why "the smile never lightened the dullness of her narrow black eyes". If the metaphorical form only puts her into the shade, the repetition of the form throws a side light on the effect her miserable life had had on her. Even when she smiled, or managed to smile as in [6], we find negative modifiers in the cognate object.

[6] And he laughed again at what he had thought to say, and O-Ian, seeing how merry he was, smiled her slow, painful smile. (p.152)

The second-order meaning helps to portray the character of O-Ian, which highlights Wang Lung the protagonist, thus contributing to the theme of the novel.

11.3 Theme

Theme in literature is the general meaning dissociated from the particularities of the text. Then how do we know it is the theme? This calls for an explanation. We need to look for something in the language for evidence.

11.3.1 Theme of the novel

Let's look at the novel *All the King's Men* by Robert Warren. What is the theme that can be generalized from this complicated story? Although the second-order meaning is not directly related to the context, we may find clues in the language of the story, for the context in one sense is created by the story.

We have found a conspicuously repeated use of the word "twitch" in the novel, which constitutes an identity chain running through the novel. Now let us explore the meanings of the word "twitch". The primary meaning of "twitch" as a verb is to pull with a quick, slight jerk, and as a noun it means a quick, slight jerk. Whether as a noun or as a verb it suggests a movement that is characterized by lack of conscious effort, and therefore uncontrollable.

It must be pointed out that the word is not merely repeated, although Repetition is a major device for cohesion. What is theoretically important is how it varies and how it achieves extension of meaning and how these meanings are used symbolically to bring out the theme of the novel.

"Twitch" is first of all represented as a process realized as a verb as in

[7] his head twitched. (p.5)

"Twitch" realizes a self-caused action. As a process it involves a participant, which is generally referred to as Medium, that is, an entity through which the process is actualized. In this sentence "his head" serves as Medium. It goes through the action and at the same time brings the action into existence. In this novel some other entities are also used as Medium, such as

[8] he twitched all over (p.6)

Instead of part of the body here we have the human body as the Medium, showing the whole body experiencing an uncontrollable movement. Then we find the process involving an inanimate thing as the Medium:

[9] if the earth should twitch once, as the hide of a sleeping dog twitches, the train would be jerked over ...

Here a celestial body is made the Medium as if the inanimate thing is credited with animate consciousness and made to go through a quick, short movement without conscious control. Meanwhile we find the process is also associated with part of an animal, the hide of a dog. So "twitch" as a process involves entities both animate or inanimate, human or non-human. This suggests "twitch" as a process exists in both the animate world and the inanimate world.

In the above four instances, "twitch" appears in an ergative structure. Then do we have the other structure that shows the action is passed onto another entity? Or do we have the transitive use of the verb, as in

[10] he twitched his head

Normally there is tension between [7] and [10], but there seems to be no tension between these two specific forms. The form Medium + Process is the predominant form throughout the book.

We only find very few instances where the structure involving an Agent is used (Agent-Process-Medium). One is in the sentence:

[11] She said fretfully, twitching her head as though to get the cigarette smoke out of her eyes. (p.80)

The verb is in its present participle form, serving as attending circumstance to the verbal process in order to foreground the action of saying. It is secondary to the main clause.

Another instance is:

[12] Who didn't twitch a muscle.

This is in fact an attributive clause made into an independent sentence, which, quite unusually, constitutes a separate paragraph. In a negative sentence like this the conscious effort on the part of the Agent is really of no consequence, for the action did lot materialize.

Let's look at one more instance:

[13] She ... twitched her head in the direction of the door.

Here "twitch" clearly represents a voluntary movement, meaning almost the same as "jerk", another verb the writer makes frequent use of in the book.

However, as a process "twitch" is in most cases used in Medium-Process type of structure. This can be accounted for by the inherent semantic features of the verb. It means "move suddenly and quickly or without conscious control". It is difficult to conceive that such an action can be brought to act upon some other entity. One cannot make a conscious effort to perform an action that is beyond conscious control. As a transitive verb "twitch" means "cause to move quickly and suddenly". So in the Agent-Process-Medium type of structure "twitch" loses much of its original feature as an unconscious or involuntary movement. The fact that the verb is in most cases used in Medium-Process type of structure serves to show that the writer presents it as a material process without conscious control. This is important for the development of the story.

11.3.2 Nominalization, personification and deification

Then "twitch" is represented as a "thing", as an entity. It is usually represented as a bounded thing realized as a countable noun. It can be used with the indefinite article "a":

[14] You would suddenly see a twitch in the left cheek. (p.333)

[15] he gave his head a twitch. (p.11)

It can also be used with "one" as in:

[16] Saving up one little twitch. (p.141)

As an entity realized as countable noun it has the plural form:

[17] ... the words had been taking shape from the electric twitches ...

"Twitches" can be of different kind and of different intensity. This makes it possible for it to be modified by an adjective as in [17], where "twitches" is modified by "electric". Also, in

[18] Duffy's features exhibited the slightest twitch of interest.

We find "twitch" is modified both by the superlative adjective "slightest" and the prepositional phrase "of interest" to state its intensity and kind.

Then "twitch" is further presented as an independent phenomenon, isolated from the thing that seems to be related to it.

[19] The twitch was simply an independent phenomenon, unrelated to the face or to what was behind the face or to anything in the whole tissue of phenomena which is the world we are lost in.

So "twitch" is a thing on its own that it has nothing to do with the world or anything in the world for that matter.

Then we find one more step further. If the grammar of "twitch" as a process extends its scope to include inanimate things as its Medium, then the grammar of "twitch" as a thing bestows the thing with life.

[20] It was remarkable in that face, the twitch which lived that little life all its own.

[21] What was alive was the twitch.

[22] The face knew that the twitch was the live thing.

The grammar of "twitch" keeps expanding, giving more and more meaning to the word "twitch". "Twitch" is not only presented as a live thing, it is construed as all, and interestingly, it is the twitch that can know that twitch is all, including "me".

[23] We rode across Texas to Shreveport, Louisiana, where he left me

to try for north Arkansas. I did not ask him if he had learned the truth in California. His face had learned it anyway, and wore the final wisdom under the left eye. The face knew that the **twitch** was the live thing. Was all. But, having left that otherwise unremarkable man, it occurred to me, as I reflected upon the thing which made him remarkable, that if the **twitch** was all, what was it that could know that the **twitch** was all? Did the leg of the dead frog in the laboratory know that the **twitch** was all when you put the electric current through it? Did the man's face know about the **twitch**, and how it was all? And if I was all **twitch** how did the **twitch** which was me know that the **twitch** was all? Ah, I decided, that is the mystery. That is the secret knowledge. That is what you have to go to California to have a mystic vision to find out. That the **twitch** can know that the **twitch** is all. Then, having found that out, in the mystic vision, you feel clean and free. You are at one with the **Great Twitch**. (p.334)

This passage makes us aware that twitch is omnipotent. And this is made explicit by capitalizing "Twitch" and by using the formulaic religious statement of Trinity "in the name of Father, Son ...", substituting "the Big Twitch, the Little Twitch" for "Father, Son". As it is difficult to coin a term that can replace "the Holy Ghost", it has to be stated expressly that "the Holy Ghost is Twitch, too".

[24] "Yeah", I said, "for he is born again and not of woman. I baptize thee in the name of the **Big Twitch**, the **Little Twitch**, and the Holy Ghost. Who, no doubt, is a **Twitch**, too." (p.338)

The supernatural feature or divine nature ascribed to "twitch" is made more reverent by saying what kind of attitude "we" must adopt towards it.

[25] We were bound together under the unwinking eye of Eternity and by the Holy Grace of the Great Twitch whom we must all adore. (p.417)

Further to these statements which equal "Twitch" with God, we find

[26] ... nobody had any responsibility for anything and there was no god but the Great Twitch.

11.3.3 Transitivity analysis

We have seen that twitch is construed as a process and as a thing, which progressively becomes a thing on its own, a live thing and a divine thing. Now let us take a closer look at these meanings and how they are realized linguistically in transitivity structure. Let us look at the types of process "twitch" enters into.

(A) Material process

My head	twitched		
MEDIUM	PROCESS		
He	twitched	his head	
AGENT	PROCESS	MEDIUM	
I	felt	my fingers	twitch
AGENT	PROCESS	MEDIUM	PROCESS
He	gave	his head	a twitch
AGENT	PROCESS	BENEFICIARY	GOAL

(B) Relational Process

All life	is	but the ... twitch of the nerve
IDENTIFIED	PROCESS	IDENTIFIER
Twitch	is	all
IDENTIFIED	PROCESS	IDENTIFIER
The twitch	was	an independent phenomenon
IDENTIFIED	PROCESS	IDENTIFIER
CARRIER		CLASS

You	are	at one with the Great Twitch
CARRIER	PROCESS	ATTRIBUTE/CIRCUMSTANTIAL

(C) Mental process

The twitch	can know	that twitch is all
SENSER	PROCESS	FACT

(D) Existential process

There was	no god but the Great Twitch
PROCESS	EXISTENT

From the above analysis we can see that "twitch" is presented either as process realized by a verb or as a participant realized by a noun. As a participant it can be the functional element COMPLEMENT, GOAL, IDENTIFIER, IDENTIFIED, CARRIER, SENSER or EXISTENT. The material processes are largely of the ergative pattern, showing that the process is actualized through the MEDIUM. The inherent meaning of the verb as a self-caused movement calls for the ergative pattern: "Twitch" appears in the relational process both as IDENTIFIED and IDENTIFIER. As the identifying category of relational processes is reversible so that the two elements before and after some form of "be" can be switched around. So this shows linguistically the twitch is all and all is the twitch. This clearly indicates "twitch" is the dominating factor that operates in all spheres of life. In the Mental process "twitch" is ascribed with the ability to know and therefore serves as the Senser. In the Existential process the "twitch" serves as the functional element of EXISTENT, that is, some entity in existence. So "twitch" appears is all the major processes except the verbal process. Potentially it may appear in the verbal process, for if the twitch can know it is highly likely it can also say. But what we are made aware of is that everything is under its sway. It doesn't have to pass a judgment or make a statement.

As we have seen, the word "twitch" appears in almost all the processes serving the functions of all elements in transitivity structure. This shows that twitch is present throughout the world and affects every part of life. This also suggests how the writer gives linguistic expression to what he perceives in the outside world, which is summed up as "The twitch is all", and "All is the twitch". This helps to explain all the happenings in the world and the life of all the major characters in the novel.

11.3.4 The theme arrived at

Nearly all the important observations about "twitch" are made by "I", the narrator, who is also a character in the story, as important as the protagonist, if not more important, especially in explaining the story. Near the end of the novel we have the following passage:

[27] This has been the story of Willie Stark, but it is my story, too. For I have a story. It is the story of a man who lived in the world and to him the world looked one way for a long time and then it looked another and quite different way. The change did not happen all at once. Many things happened, and that man did not know when he had any responsibility for them and when he did not. There was, in fact, a time when he came to believe that nobody had any responsibility for anything and there was no god but the Great Twitch.

As Hasan (1989: 97) points out, theme is what a text is about when dissociated from the particularities of the text. In its nature the theme of verbal art is very close to a generalization.

Here we have a generalization. Instead of Willie Stark or Jack Burton, we have "a man who ..." By generalizing the character the writer generalizes what the man believes in, that is, the explanation of everything in terms of "The Great Twitch".

This is how the writer perceives the world, gives expression to his experience of the outside world and tries to explain everything in terms of "twitch". In spite of their efforts, all the characters, Willie Stark, Adam Stanton and "I" Jack Burden all end up in their doom. Why so many people had lived and died? Why each had been the doom of the other? Why each had killed the other? Why? Life is uncontrollable as the twitch is uncontrollable. Life is so inexplicable that it can only be explicated in terms of a quick, short movement that is beyond conscious control. The writer conveys this deeper meaning, this theme, by using creatively the patterning of the patterns, that is, Repetition of the word "twitch" throughout the book, the various meanings of which have become a sign that gives the second order meaning.

11.4 Conclusion

Language has evolved to satisfy human needs, and the way it is organized is functional with respect to these needs. Every text unfolds in some context of use (Halliday 1994). It is the context that determines the text and the text reflects the context. There seem to be no limitations to what should be included in the context. Apart from processes there are relations between the processes; apart from items and relations, there are relations between the relations. What complicates the picture is that there are differences in the perception and interpretation of the outside world. This complexity of context, both in breadth and in depth, should be realized in text, and language has the resources for making meaning, congruent, metaphorical and symbolic. The symbolic use of the resources based on patterning of lexico-grammatical features may serve human needs to make deeper meanings that cannot be adequately created by congruent forms as the lexical chain of "twitch" and the imperative passive discussed above.

We have shown that deeper meanings can be derived from the patterning of lexico-grammatical features. Then how can it be derived? The answer is through inference made on the basis of the patterning, whether contrast, potential or actual, or repetition and the context in which the story is embedded. Although the patterning has no direct bearing on the contextual features, the story may provide contextual clues to the meaning of the patterning.

The patterning of lexico-grammatical features may serve as a creative way to mean, especially in literary discourse.

For detailed discussions of the novel *All the King's Men*, see chapters 17 and 19.

12

英语名词指称及其语篇功能*

12.1 指 称

12.1.1 指称链

语篇中指称(reference)涉及两个成分：指称项和被指称项。指称项的意义取决于其被指称项的意义或听话人对被指称项的理解。指称项与被指称项构成指称链(reference chain)，而指称链是一种衔接纽带(cohesive tie)，对语篇的衔接和连贯有重要意义。请看下列实例：

[1] "I can't do that," Rudolph said. *He* put his glass down.

[2] As *he* talked to Germaine, Brownwell pushed to the very periphery of his mind the subject of family.

例[1]中代词 He 回指 Rudolph，两者构成指称链，使两句粘合。例[2]中 he 预指 Brownwell，也构成指称链，使两个分句粘合。

[3] She tells me you've bought an airport in Invemere, is *it*?

---

* 本章原载《外语教学与研究》1996 年第 1 期 11—18 页。

例[1]、[2]中的代词指称名词,十分明确;例[3]中的 it 则指从句的内容,说话人要对方肯定这部分信息。指称项和被指称项构成的指称链就不那么明显。

名词也可用以指称个别词或词组,或部分话语。

[4] It soon became Mahalaleel's custom to follow Leah upstairs in the evening, and to make *his* bed at the foot of Leah's and Gidean's enormous bed. Gidean was annoyed what if the *creature* had fleas?

名词词组 the creature 回指名叫 Mahalaleel 的雄猫。

[5] "Let's talk about something else," Mitch said. "*Good idea*."

名词词组 Good idea 回指上句引号中的语句内容。

12.1.2 两种功能

名词用以指称词或词组时有两种不同的功能。试比较:

[6] John ordered a book and the book has just arrived.

第二次出现的 book 由于有 the 限定,说话人知道听话人的认知处于高度集中状态,理解时有极大的限制性,只能看作与首次出现的 book 同指一本书。所以 book 第二次出现时仅仅是词的重复,语法上由非定指转为定指,但意义没有增加。

[7] Can you tell me where to stay in Geneva? I've never been to the place.

名词词组 the place 回指 Geneva。作为泛义名词 place 虽没有给 Geneva 增加意义但却给听者或读者提供了附加信息,即 Geneva 是个 place。再看下面一句:

[8] We all kept quiet. That seemed *the best move*.

这里名词词组不回指某一个词,而是回指前句的意义。值得注意的是说话人在回指的同时对前句的内容加以概括和评论,认为"我们保持沉默是上策”。

韩礼德在讨论代词指称时曾举这样一例：

[9] It rained day and night for two weeks. The basement flooded and everything was under water. *It* spoilt all our calculations.

It是指上文的内容，指“两周昼夜下雨，地下室积水，什么都浸在水里”这一事件(event)或这一事实(fact)。韩礼德把指称部分话语的指称叫作语段指称(text reference)(Halliday & Hasan 1976：52)。本文沿用这一术语。

从例[8]看名词也可用于语段指称。韩礼德在论述词汇衔接时虽举了例，但着眼于名词的词义特点，未对名词指称语段的现象进行讨论。

12.1.3 名词语段指称

本文拟根据功能语法理论从语篇的角度对名词语段指称作一探讨。这将涉及：名词词组与其指称的语段有怎样的语义关系？两者的指称关系如何通过推理加以确定？名词词组是否也可用于回指和预指？名词语段指称在组篇中起什么作用？在语篇结构中又起怎样的作用？本文所用的语言材料取自当代文学作品，包括小说(如 *The Firm*、*Blood Test*、*Bellefleur*、*Poor Man, Rich Man*)和非虚构作品(如 *Future Shock*、*The Third Wave*)。部分材料取自美国报刊。

12.2 推　理

12.2.1 代词语段指称

名词词组用于指称语段时两者的语义关系不像代词指称名词那么一目了然，如例[1]、例[2]，甚至也不像名词指称另一名词或词组那样直截

了当。代词指称语段时就已经比较复杂。我们再来看一下例[3]:

She tells me you've bought an airport in Invemere, is *it*?

对于代词,在确定其被指称项时通常要通过两个步骤的推理过程。第一步确定被指称项。这一句中 it 指称什么成分?可以有三种假设(assumptions)。首先从句法看,it 可以指名词 airport,但是在与交谈有关的语境中,问话人在了解对方是否已购买机场之前不至于对机场有兴趣并就此提问;其次,如果 it 是指 airport,"is it?"这个问句不能成立。因其作为附加疑问句,常被视为次标准英语,意义相当于"Is that right?"与后者句中的 that 一样,it 只能指某个命题,"is it?"询问某个命题是否可以成立,不能就某一个体提问。第二个假设是,it 指前面整个陈述。说话人交代"She tells me ...",主语为第三人称,说明是第三者与说话人之间的言语活动;动词为一般现在时,说明这一信息说话时仍然可以成立。说话人对自己的经验先作肯定陈述然后又发问,要 you 对自己的话加以肯定岂不违反常理?自己不了解自己的话是否可以成立,违反了会话合作原则中的质的准则。所以第二个假设当可以排除。第三个可能有的假设是 it 指宾语从句的内容。从信息结构看,宾语从句属新信息部分,语调上 airport 重音突出(focal prominence),是说话人希望对方注意的内容所在,is it 就此提问符合语境因素和关联的要求。第二步是确定被指称项的意义。这里宾语从句的命题是"你购买机场",而 it 则指这一命题,"is it?"对这一命题提出询问。

12.2.2 名词词组的指称项

现在我们来看如何确定名词词组的被指称项。试看下面这一段话:

[10] "You know what the next step is, don't you? If Terrance keeps pushing, that idiot Lazarov will call me one day and tell me to remove him ..."
"Lazarov wouldn't order a hit on an agent."
"Oh, it would be *a foolish move* but then Lazarov is a fool. He's very anxious about the situation down here."

名词词组 a foolish move 是上句引发的,是不是指上句的内容?让我们作具体分析。Wouldn't order 以虚拟的形式说明说话人认为 Lazarov 不至于下此命令。would 表示意愿,不构成行动(move);wouldn't 又是否定的意愿,更不能用 move 回指。但 order a hit on an agent 却是一个行动,可以成为 move 的被指称项。但是从上下文和语境来看,这一假设是否符合关联的准则,是否保证语篇连贯?我们且将两个说话人分别用 A、B 表示。A 认为 Lazarov 会下令谋杀;B 认为他不会下令;A 先让步,说下令谋杀是愚蠢的,这构成了他三段论式的大前提,小前提是 Lazarov is a fool,让 B 通过逻辑推理得出结论。这个不言自明的结论是:Lzarov would order a hit on an agent,这与 A 前面的看法"... tell me to remove him"一致;fool 和上文的 idiot 也呼应。可见第三个假设可以成立,符合语言事实。这样,通过推理确定了名词词组 a foolish move 的被指称项。下面再看较为复杂的一例:

[11] "They are Canadians, aren't they?" inquired Frankie.
"He is certainly. I rather fancy she is English, but I'm not sure. She's a very pretty little thing — quite charming. Somehow or other I fancy she isn't terribly happy. It must be *a depressing life*."

首先问句中的 they 在答句中以 he 和 she 呼应,表明 they 的婚姻关系。在"He is certainly"之后,我们看到"she is English ..., she's ... quite charming ..., she isn't terribly happy";从主位进展(thematic progression)来看,这三个分句的主述位关系可以这样表示:

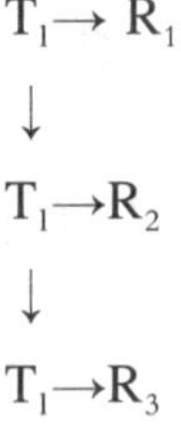

$$T_1 \rightarrow R_1$$
$$\downarrow$$
$$T_1 \rightarrow R_2$$
$$\downarrow$$
$$T_1 \rightarrow R_3$$

这说明说话人是以同一个个体作为信息的出发点。从同一词汇系统中选择某一词项作为若干小句的主位,即构成这一语段的单一展开方式(single method of development),表示说话人意欲对某一个体提供信息。述位中表示信息的词汇链体现要点(point)(Fries 1981;Martin 1992:

434）。在以 she 开始的三个小句中，第 1 句说明国籍，第 2、第 3 句的述位部分含 is charming 和 isn't happy，形成对照，这是这一语段的要点所在。对于 he，说话人只交代了国籍，未谈其他。这里，a depressing life 只能是讲 she 的 life，并以此概括语段的要点，即"虽生得娇小妩媚，但并不快乐"。这里，life 作 manner of living 解，与被指称语段的具体内容合拍。

在确定名词词组所指语段的过程中，除了分析例[3]中所进行的第一、第二步外，还得增加第三步。用于指称的名词有自己的词义，尽管往往比较空泛，但总为我们在确定被指称项时划定了范围。所以第三步就是考虑名词与其指称语段在语义上是否相符，如例[10]中的 move。第一、第二步实际上难以截然分开，而第三步也会贯穿在整个推理过程中。

12.2.3 四项准则

从语言的元功能出发，在上述推理过程中必须考虑名词词组是否与被指称语段所表示的经验相吻合，与某些语言成分所激发的图式（schema）相吻合；名词词组是否与说话人的态度和意向一致，与说话人的交际目的相符。从上面分析的三个实例看，在推理过程中需考虑格赖斯的四个准则以建立指称链，从而增进语段的黏合和连贯。

量：名词词组指称哪个段落、语句或部分语句？在语篇中什么地方起止？不应该超出这个范围，也不应该小于这个范围。

质：被指称语段所含的信息是否真实？用名词指称上下文会不会有矛盾？前后是否一致？

关联：指称项与被指称项是否关联？从关联关系（relevance relation）的角度看，可能有几个假设？哪个假设有最大的关联性？

方式：名词词组与其指称语段的语气是否一致？是肯定还是否定？指称项与被指称项在这一点上是否一致？

这四个准则中量与关联最为重要。量和关联所涉及的问题不解决就谈不上建立指称链、衔接纽带，也无助于语篇的衔接和连贯。

12.3 语义关系

名词词组及其指称语段之间的语义关系非常复杂,涉及说话人的经验和态度。同一段话,其内容甲可以用 conversation 概括,乙可以用 debate 指称,丙甚至可以用 attack 回指。名词词组既可指某一语段的语言意义,也可指这一语段的语用意义。如果是对话,可以指说话人的原意,也可以指听话人的理解或评价。

12.3.1 表示意念意义

名词词组指称一个语段时常指这一语段所表示的意思(idea),也即语言所表示的外部世界的经验或内心世界的体验,同时也可指一个事实(fact),包括事件(event)、动作(action)或情景(situation)。试看:

[12] "You'd be surprised what bargains there are to be had in second-hand cars."
"I bought one once," said Frankie, "It's a painful *subject*. Don't let's talk of it."

句中 subject 指上文有关内容:"购买旧车",说话人同时作了评论,形容词 painful 说明了说话人的态度。下面看名词词组指称有关语段所表示的事实。

[13] "... Most of the transactions were by wire transfer from four or five different banks in Caymans. It's a basic money-laundering *operation*."

此句中,a basic money-laundering operation 概括了前句所叙述的活动。

[14] "Yes, Nicholson would act. Moira's body would probably be found in some district far from Staverley ..."

The thing would appear to be an accident.

此例用 thing 概括前句所叙述的可能发生的事态。这儿不用代词 it 而用 the thing 是为了统指整个内容。有时可见用 the whole thing 回指上文。

[15] It was *a curious situation*. Quite unconscious that he was being watched, the doctor wrote steadily on.

前句中 situation 指下一句所描述的情景。这四个例句中的名词词组指称了语段所表示的意念意义(ideational meaning)。

12.3.2 传达信息

在言语活动中人们利用语言意义(linguistic meaning)传达信息(message)。在不同的语境中同样的语言意义可以传达不同的信息。名词词组有时指某一语段的信息,或言语功能,或言外之意,或言后意义。

[16] "I asked you to check on her, Mitch. I'm worried about her. If that goon is beating her, I want it stopped. If I could get out of here, I'd stop it myself."

"You will." It was a *statement*, not a question.

这里 statement 不是指 You will(get out of here)的内容,而是指说话人的言语行为。叙事人点明这一点是想说明 Mitch 有把握张罗第一个说话人出狱。

[17] "I must go. I've taken a leave of absence at school."

"For how long?" It was *a nervous question*.

同样,question 也不是指问句的内容,而是指这句话的言语功能。下面两句里名词词组点出了语句的言后意义。

[18] "I'm working on it."

"Better work hard." It was more than a *threat* and he knew it.

[19] The bartender said something to Abarks and nodded toward Mitch. He opened another Heineken and walked to Mitch's table. He did

not smile. "Are you looking for me?" It was almost a *sneer*.

例[18]中的 Better work hard 本可以是命令,但交际双方的特殊关系使这句话对听话人产生了语后效果,he knew it 足以说明这点。例[19]的问句 Are you looking for me 并没有讥笑的意思,可是结合语境,特别是交际双方的关系,这个问句有了言外之意,并对听话人产生了效果。

12.3.3 说话人的概括

以上实例中名词词组都指称说话人所表达的意义,包括语用意义。在使用名词指称语段时,说话人都得对这一语段的内容在脑子里加以处理,然后用名词表示其语义的某一个方面。不少情况下,说话人用名词表达他自己对这一语段的理解,是他提炼、概括的结果。在对话中名词词组常常表达听话人或叙事人的理解。这与说话人的本意有联系,但不尽相同。

[20] "I have never approved of this garage project. Mere folly. You must give it up."
"Can't I, Sir. I have promised. I can't let old Badger down. He is counting on me." The *discussion* proceeded ...

The discussion 不是指上面一段话的内容,而是指这段话体现的言语活动。在叙事人看这两个参加者之间进行的是 discussion,换一个人也许会用 argument。选用什么名词取决于说话人的态度。

[21] "Look here, Frankie, think a minute ... Not only must there be nothing to connect him in any way with the dead man, but he must have a proper reason for being down here ... he's the sort of person who would be quite above suspicion."
"Yes," said Frankie thoughtfully. "That's *a very good deduction*."

The deduction 是指上面一段话的推理过程。这是听话人的概括。与上面两句不同,下面两句中名词词组指听话人或叙事人对所指语段的抽象概括。

[22] "It's impossible," said the Vicar.

Bob was not hurt by *this incredulity*.

句中 this incredulity 是叙事人由上句引出的结论。名词词组指称的不仅是直接引语的内容,而且包括 said the Vicar,因为 this incredulity 是指 Vicar 而言的。

[23] "All right," said Frankie, "And once you and Badger have got him down, I'll join in and bite his ankles or something." "That's *the true womanly spirit*."

句中"the true womanly spirit"是听话人根据上段内容作的结论。名词词组回指这一内容,同时体现了听话人的看法。再看下面两句:

[24] "I agree with you. That would be inviting trouble. However, he did agree to Dr. Daleware's conducting a search of the Retreat. Promised to pay his fines and leave without a fuss if the good doctor finds nothing suspicious."

"It was *a simple solution*."

[25] During all this time he'd been traveling up and down the state, talking up the fruit with produce buyers, telling them of the wonders that would soon be blossoming in his groves.

"It must have been *an uphill battle*."

例[24]中 a simple solution 是说话人对上面一段话的总结性的评论。例[25]中说话人则用 an uphill battle 评论性地总结了前面一段所叙述的推销活动。

12.3.4 语言意义和语用意义

以上的实例[12]、[13]、[14]、[15]中,名词词组主要指称有关语段的内容,在[16]、[17]、[18]、[19]中则指称语段体现的言语行为、言外意义或言后意义;[20]、[21]中是指说话人的主观看法;[22]、[23]则是指说话人的推断;[24]、[25]是说话人对名词所指内容的总结。[12]至

[19]名词词组指称说话人的原意,[20]至[25]则是指听话人或叙事人对有关语段的理解,可称为听话人的意义。[12]至[15]指称语言意义,体现语言的意念功能;[16]至[25]名词词组指称语用意义,体现人际功能。名词用于指称时所涉及的语义面很广,这就使得名词和可以理解为各种意义的语段构成广泛的指称链,从而增进语篇的衔接。

12.4 组篇作用

第2、3节中的例句除[14]外名词词组皆用于回指。名词词组可不可以用于预指?在回指和预指时名词词组有什么内在的语法特征?在组篇中可以起什么作用?

12.4.1 预 指

名词词组可用以预指下文的一个语段。例如:

[26] It was *a very cordial event*. The four candidates for mayor came together last week to discuss the issues in their first debate since the election began.

句中 event 预指下一句的内容,引导出对事件的具体叙述。

[27] "What about 'em," asked Lord Marchington. Frankie didn't know what about them. She made a *statement*, knowing well enough that her father enjoyed contradicting. "That's a Yorkshire family, aren't they?"

句中 statement 预指引号内的话。Frankie 深知对方喜欢唱反调,虽不了解情况还是用了陈述句,但她并无把握,所以用了附加疑问句,希望 Lord

Marchington 提供情况。

[28] "Bill Clinton, calculating as he is, genuinely cares about people — he loves everyone, he is a sucker for every individual. Hillary, no. It's *an intellectual thing* — she loves the many, not the individual."

句中 an intellectual thing 预指 she loves the many, not the individual。

从以上三例可以看出名词也可用于预指,虽不及回指常见,但却有它在篇章组织中的作用。

12.4.2 语法特征

名词词组用于指称时有如下几个语法特征:

(一) 用于指称的名词在多数情况下有形容词修饰。从[12]到[27]的 16 个例句中有九句的名词词组含前置修饰语,占 56.2%。这是因为用作指称的名词常带有评价意味,即使是指称概念意义名词词组也会有形容词修饰语,如[12]。指称语段的名词常常词义空泛,评价的真正内容由形容词体现,所以这类名词词组中的修饰语常重读,而名词却不重读(Halliday & Hasan 1976: 275)。不带形容词修饰语的名词词义比较明确。上述 16 句中另 7 句的名词词组的中心词为 statement, discussion, threat, sneer, incredulity,另一个词为 thing(F. T. Wood 说 thing 是个被滥用了的词,[28]中的 thing 意义就不明确)。由此可见用于指称的名词不一定是泛义词(general words)。

(二) 用于指称的名词词组出现在主位时,一般为定指,如[14]中的 the thing,[20]中的 the discussion,而出现在述位时常为不定指,如[10]、[11]、[12]中的名词词组。[8]中有 the best move,这是因为最高级形容词要求用 the。值得注意的是名词词组有时用作辅句(minor clause),如:

[29] "Are you alone?" *Obvious question*, but he had to ask it.

在这种情况下名词词组的定指与不定指的对立不复存在,因为在正常句子中必须使用的不定冠词常常省略。

(三) 名词词组指称语段时,不论是回指还是预指,其中心词皆为单数。上面含名词词组的全部 21 个例句可以证明。这是因为用于指称语段时,名词以其代表的概念概括有关语段的内容,不可能出现复数。

12.4.3 组篇作用

英语名词词组及其指称项构成的衔接链可以在语篇结构的各个部分出现。这里我们先看它在英语的一种基本结构中的组篇功能。英语的这种基本结构含三个成分:起始(initiation)、后续(continuation)和结论(conclusion)。起始通常对事件作客观陈述,后续是对起始成分加以阐述或补充,结论则是对起始成分和后续成分所述的内容加以评说或归纳。关于这种局部语篇结构,可参阅第 10 章 10.4.3 节。试看下列语段:

[30] The corridor and all the other doors were beige. Valcrox's was scarlet and stood out like wound.
"It was *an amateur paint job*."

第一句体现起始成分,第二句为后续成分,第三句(引语部分)是结论,名词词组回指上面两句的内容,同时对油漆效果作了评价,体现说话人主观的看法。这种结构中的三个成分这里分别由一个句子体现,但也可以由数个句子体现。当起始成分已提供足够信息时,后续成分可有可无。在叙事语篇中这三个成分由叙事人的语句体现;在会话中第三成分常为听话人的评论。从[30]看,用以指称的名词出现在这一结构的末尾,用回指使语段衔接。仔细看一看上两节的实例可以发现,16 例中属于这种结构的有 10 个,即[10]、[11]、[12]、[13]、[14]、[18]、[19]、[23]、[24]、[25],占总数的 62.4%,可见指称语段的名词词组在这一结构中的组篇作用。同时也可以看出这类名词词组常有前置修饰语,这是语篇评价的需要。

指称语段的名词词组有时还会出现在后续成分中,而结论成分中则由另一名词词组作概括,使整个语段更加紧凑。

[31] It became clear that future shock is no longer a distantly potential danger, but a real sickness from which large numbers already suffer. This *psychological condition* can be described in medical and

psychiatric terms.

It is *the disease of change*.

第二句的 This psychological condition 回指第一句的内容，而第三句的 the disease of change 则对上面的内容进行了概括，一环扣一环，确保语段的衔接和连贯。

12.5 语篇功能

上节讨论了指称语段的名词词组的语法特征和在一种英语基本结构中的组篇功能。现在我们来看一看这种名词词组在整个语篇结构中的功能。

12.5.1 承上启下

先看在段落内部指称语段的名词词组能起什么作用。

[32] But as President Clinton told me in one of our conversations, "A lot of my public life has been our life. We've done it together." *This arrangement was very contingent upon his continuing success*; he said, "After I got beat (in 1980), I was concerned about it ... It was always better than I thought it would be for her."

句中 This arrangement 回指引号中 Clinton 的两句话，同时又引出下文，起到承上启下的作用。

12.5.2 段落的新信息

再看这类名词词组如何在段落之间起衔接作用。

[33] With a stroke of the pen, Gov. William Weld ended weeks of aldermanic squabbling and officially OK'd a fall date for the special mayoral election.

At about 11 a.m. on Monday, Weld signed legislation allowing the Board of Aldermen to override the City Charter and piggyback the special election on the regular state election this fall. The State Senate and House of Representatives also approved the request last week.

The action sets a preliminary election date of September 20 to narrow the number of mayoral hopefuls to two. A final run-off election is scheduled for Nov. 8, the same day as the state general election.

…

句中 The action 回指上两段,概括了两段的内容,同时引出新段落,作进一步的叙述。例[32]、[33]中的名词词组都用于回指,都用作句子的主位。功能语法区分宏观新信息(Macro-New),段落新信息(Super-New)和新信息(New)。新信息是指小句中的新信息,段落新信息是某一段落或几个段落的新信息,宏观新信息是整个语篇的新信息,用以总结语篇逐渐积累的要点,通常体现为一个句子(Martin 1992)。例[32]、[33]中的 This arrangement 和 The action 引出的两个句子概括了上文的要点,体现了段落的新信息,而这两个名词词组则成了段落新信息的一部分。

12.5.3 引出宏观主位

现在我们来看一看整个语篇的结构。名词可用于预指,为随后的语篇展开提供了方向。试看下面一例:

[34] *The whole thing could be Governor Weld's fault.*

A few weeks ago, when his son was away on vacation, Weld took over the boy's paper route for the weekend, delivering *The Boston Globe* to neighbors on Fayerweather Street in Cambridge.

The next thing you know, *the Globe* announced it will do away with paperboys and papergirls over the next four years in favor of a more mature delivery person.

句中 The whole thing 用于预指整个语篇的内容。功能语法区分宏观主位(Macro-Theme),段落主位(Super-Theme)和主位(Theme)。宏观主位确定段落主位,而段落主位则确定若干小句的主位(Martin 1992)。在这一语篇中 The whole thing 引出的句子是宏观主位,它是整个语篇的出发点,为通篇叙述提供了依托,The whole thing 就成了宏观主位的一部分。可见用于回指的名词词组的特点在于总结上文,所以可以引出段落新信息或宏观新信息;用于预指的名词词组的特点在于预示下文,所以可以引出宏观主位或段落主位。这就是用以指称语段的名词词组在更大的语篇结构里的语篇功能。

12.6 结 语

在语篇中名词词组作为指称成分可用于回指或预指,是取得语篇衔接和推进语篇的重要手段。与代词指称不同,名词词组用于指称时,它的意义不完全取决于被指称项的意义,而是由被指称项加以充实和具体化。用于指称的名词往往是泛义词,但也可以是词义明确的名词。

确定名词词组与被指称语段之间的指称关系比较复杂。这是因为名词本身已有一定的意义,而名词所指称的语段又可以有不同含义,所以必须结合语境和上下文进行推理。

语言事实说明名词词组能在语篇的不同结构层次上发挥语篇功能:在一种基本结构中名词词组常用以概括上文并加以评价;在段落中可起承上启下的作用;在语篇中回指名词短语可以成为段落新信息或宏观新信息的一部分,预指名词短语则可成为段落主位或宏观主位的一部分。

13

英语时态的语篇功能*

13.1 引　言

本章的目的在于研究英语时态的语篇功能(discourse functions),同时从这个语法范畴出发考察叙事语篇的组织。语境和语篇存在辩证的关系:语境决定语篇,语篇体现语境。交际的目的决定语篇的组织。语言中有许多组篇手段,一方面使语言与外部世界联系,另一方面又使语篇取得内在的统一。英语时态可否成为这样一种手段在组篇中起作用?请看下文。

13.1.1 话　语

话语(text)是语义单位,可以是含一个小句的句子,也可以是若干句子组成的语篇。研究语篇功能通常指研究话语信息分布和组篇的种种手段,常称为超句语法,但是也涉及将说话内容作为信息传达的手段,因而也包括小句中的信息组织。具体而言,要研究语篇组织中的连贯和黏合,

* 本章原载《外国语》1995 年第 3 期第 22—29+80 页。

控制信息流(information flow)的策略,话语如何分为若干次话语、其界限如何以及语篇信息的主次,即定景(grounding)等等。本文着眼于时态的语篇功能,主要考察叙事语篇的组篇,也将涉及定景。

13.1.2 前人的研究

对语篇中时态的功能语言学家已有一定研究,有的从语篇中上下句之间的时间关系,以法语为材料研究时态的语篇功能(Kamp et. al. 1983),有的以斯瓦希里语为材料研究语篇中的相对时态(Contini-Morava 1983),有的大体根据韩礼德的语言元功能学说,研究法语叙事文学作品中的时态功能(Fleischman 1990)。本文用英语现在时说明时态在语篇中的不同功能以及如何作为组篇机制在语篇的组织中发挥作用,特别是通篇和整节组织中的作用。

本文所用的语篇材料取自美籍华裔作家谭恩美(Amy Tan)的叙事小说 *The Joy Luck Club* 和 *The Kitchen God's Wife* 以及 *The Museum of Man*,等。

13.2 时态和时间

13.2.1 三个时间点

时态是语言的范畴,不同的语言有不同的时态系统;时间是独立于语言的概念,具有普遍性。但时态又与时间有关。在句法中英语时态用于表示句中围绕动词所表示的动作或状态的各种时间关系。语言学家们认为句子中的时间关系是由三个时间点构成的:说话时间点、参照时间点和事件时间点。

在叙事语篇中时态不仅要表示句子中的时间关系,而且要表示句子与句子、语段与语段之间的时间关系,为叙事提供时间框架,说明语境中若干事件之间的时间关系。当叙事人将外部世界的经验作为信息传达时,可按时间顺序展开也可以穿插倒叙,也就是与时间的自然顺序不一致。语篇中的参照时间点常常由上下文或语境决定,因此上述时态的基本功能在语篇中将延伸和发展以适应组篇的需要。

13.2.2 表示时间关系的其他语言手段

建立或了解时间指向或在时间轴线上所处的时间点主要依靠时态,但也可以根据词汇或其他语言特征或根据上下文经过推理了解时间关系。例如"Men were deceivers ever"。这句莎翁名言形式上是过去时,但说话人的意图是传达适用于任何时间的信息。叶斯柏森把这种用法说成是"某种文体技巧,让听话人自己作出结论:至今真实的仍然真实并将永远真实"(Jespersen 1924: 259)。但是听话人从何得出这个结论?当然可以借助他的世界知识,但非语言知识常常需要由某种语言知识激发才能在理解中起作用,而说话人在传递信息时也往往提供这种语言依据。从这句看 ever 一词可作 at all times 解,古义为 always;其次 Men 是类属指称的复数名词,所以这句话不是对过去某一时间发生的事,也不是对某个人或某些人作出说明,而是对一类人作了陈述。这样听话人便可以从主语和状语的意义结合语境推断出这是一句概括性的陈述,可适用于所有时间。理解句子的时间指向需要推理,理解语篇中若干事件之间的关系更需要推理。

13.3 英语现在时的基本语义特征

13.3.1 两种解释

叙事语篇通常追叙过去的事件,常用过去时,但在很多情况下却用现在时。这就为我们研究时态的语篇功能提供了一个很好的出发点。语法学家们常常说这种用法是为了取得戏剧性的效果，但情况并非完全如此。对于用现在时叙述过去的事件，语法学家有两种解释：其一，叙事人好似将自己移植至过去，并从那一点出发而不是从话语实际使用的语境出发来叙述发生的事件（Huddleston 1984：2）；其二，是将时间指向从叙事时间转移至说话时间（Contini-Morava 1983）。简单地说第一种看法认为说话人把立足点移至过去；第二种看法认为说话人把过去的事件拉到现在。这两种看法似乎可以解释这种用法，但不能回答以下两组问题：（1）为什么现在时可以用于叙述过去的事件？怎样解决现在时的形式和语篇中对现在意义否定之间的矛盾？（2）既然英语时态系统中有过去时，为什么要用现在时表述过去？这样使用的目的究竟是什么？

13.3.2 三个基本语义特征

要回答这些问题必须了解现在时的基本意义和语篇功能。就有无标记和时态对立而言现在时可以有三种解释：零解释、正解释和负解释。零解释体现现在时无时性的基本意义；负解释是指与 now 共时的“现在”；正解释是指过去时间，常在叙事语篇中出现（Fleischman 1990）。有的语法学家对无时性提出异议。其实无时性并非说现在时不涉及时间，而是指“无特定的时间”。例如：“The sun rises in the east”可适用于过去、现在和将来，也就是说可适用于所有时间或任何时间，因而就不指某一特定时间。现在时的这一基本特征使它有可能用于叙述过去的事实，在叙事语篇中尤其如此。这是因为叙事语篇的叙事顺序已给读者提供了时间指向，“时态已经从提供参照时间的任务中解脱出来”（Hatch 1983）。这就使用现在时表示过去成为可能。

现在时作为英语时态系统中的一个次范畴，可以看成是若干语义特征组合而成的概念，可以加以分解。从上面的分析可以看出与过去时相比，现在时具有乏时性，同时还具有事实性，即现在时可用于单纯地陈述事实。过去时所表示的动作或状态使听话人在感觉上有相当距离，而现在时所表示的动作或状态则比较贴近，比较直接，缺乏感觉上的距离（lack of perceived distance）。这是现在时的第三个语义特征（Fleischman 1990）。

英语现在时的这三个基本语义特征，即事实性、乏时性以及感觉上的乏距离性，决定了它的句法功能和语篇功能。

13.3.3 句法功能

现在时的语篇功能与其句法功能是密切联系的，先让我们简单地看一下现在时的句法功能。夸克等在现在时一节首先讨论了状态现在时和习惯现在时，说这两种现在时都与现在时间有关（Quirk et al. 1985）。例如：

Honesty is the best policy.

Water boils at 100℃.

仔细研究一下，我们可以发现这两句是适用于所有时间的陈述。说话人并不关注时间参照，而是要把这两句的命题内容作为事实陈述。英语动词总得以某种形式进入句子，而现在时是形式最为简单，与时间关系最小的时态，所以当人们着眼于表明信息的真实性时，现在时即可以为这种交际目的服务。这两句体现了现在时的表实功能，同时鉴于其陈述内容具有普遍意义，所以又具有概括功能。

夸克等提出的第三种用法是瞬时现在时。该书所给的例证全部取自口头或书面的话语（Quirk et al. 1985）。例如：

Black passes the ball to Fernandez, Fernandez shoots …

这是取自球赛的现场评论，评论员无需关注时间参照，也不用借助体（aspect）来表达这一系列动作是否完成或正在进行，重要的是他把球场的活动及时地报告给听众，这样动词就以最简单的形式——现在时服务于这一交际目的，这里起作用的仍然是现在时的表实功能，但是应该注意到这里现在时已经在语篇中发挥表实功能，如果我们把其中任何一句，比如 Fernandez shoots 从上下文中抽出来就难以了解句子的时间关系和传达的信息了。

13.3.4 语篇功能

上述句法中现在时的几种用法体现了其表实功能和概括功能，而这两个功能是源于现在时的基本语义特征：事实性和乏时性。在语篇中现在时仍具有这两个特征，因此现在时在语篇中也具有表实功能和概括功能。现在时的第三个语义特征乏感观距离性可以使语篇的一部分更为容易感受、更为贴近，因而就更为突出。这一语篇功能可称为突显功能。在叙事语篇中，当现在时用以表述过去的事件时，这三个功能都可以发挥作用，只是由于组篇的需要不同，才在不同的语篇部分分别发挥作用。

13.3.5 不同叙事人

从叙事语篇看，为了便于叙述，便于交代时间关系，作者可以让社会事件参加者中的一个做叙事人，从他的角度来叙述事件经过。比如 *The Kitchen God's Wife* 一书中作者先让"女儿"以第一人称叙事，可是到第四章便以 Here is how she told me 开头引出了转折，随后叙事人便由"母亲"承担。这样从"母亲"的 now 出发，以她说话时间作为参照时间点来使用时态：It is the same pain I have had for many years. It comes from … I think my mother gave this fault。如果仍让"女儿"叙事，那"母亲"吐露真情则应为过去，而"母亲"的不幸婚姻等等就得以此作为参照点，成为过去的过去，时态的使用就比较复杂，时间关系也难以交代清楚。所以改变叙事人实际上是实现时态语篇功能的一种手段。

13.4 现在时的表实功能

13.4.1 表实功能便于组篇

英语现在时表明句子或语段的内容是真实的，这一基本语义特征赋予现在时表实语篇功能。语篇需要体现语境中语场、语旨和语式诸因素的复杂构成。在叙事结构中常有一系列复杂行动由若干局部命题构成总命题，而每一个局部命题常包括许多事件，因此语篇的组织会涉及若干时间点和几个层面的时间。这样，要将语境体现出来就要表述有关事件的顺序和它们的时间关系。“语言在一定的语境中被说话人作为传递信息的工具以表达意义、实现意图”(Brown & Yule 1983)。时态在叙事语篇中就可以体现语境中的复杂的时间关系，而现在时的表实功能便利了语篇的组织。就拿 *The Kitchen God's Wife* 的第二章来说吧，全章记述“杜奶奶的丧礼”，参加者是死者的生前友好，包括 I、Phil、My mother 等。这一章是这样开始的：My mother left the house two hours ago with Auntie Helen so that they could decorate the funeral parlor，但下一小节开始便使用现在时，其中的描述围绕这一家四口以及其他参加者在奠堂中的举止言谈，全部用现在时：

> My cousin Frank hands us black armbands to wear …; Baobao is there to greet us as well …; “What are we supposed to do with these?” Phil whispers … My mother is dry-eyed; “Why so late,” she asks crossly …

随后转入另一语段，进入围绕另一主题的追述，以“I was fourteen, full of anger and cynicism”开始，写的是 I 在 my father 丧礼上的表现：

> I refused to go up to the casket to see my father's body …; I did not want to mourn the man in the casket …

全部用过去时，father 的丧礼在时间上在“杜奶奶丧礼”之前，“杜奶奶”的丧礼用现在时，“父亲”的丧礼即可用过去时，而“父亲”生前的事件用过去完成时。这样的信息安排有下列好处：(1) 若干具体事件的时间关系可表述清楚；(2) 不是按时间顺序叙述，允许叙事人倒叙或插叙。可见现在时用于表述过去的事件是以其表实功能服务组篇的需要，并不是为了取得戏剧性的效果。

13.4.2 为多层叙事服务

时态为叙事人的交际目的服务。小说 *The Joy Luck Club* 讲的是美籍华人俱乐部的聚会。参加者是 *I*、"安梅阿姨"、"亨利叔叔",以及未登场的my mother,叙述的目的是通过"阿姨们"之口道出 mother 的身世和隐痛。这次俱乐部活动是 I 的过去的经历,但叙事人用现在时。I 和 mother 是叙述的中心。与 I 有联系的活动过程皆用现在时;与 mother 活动、言谈有关的皆用过去时。在语篇展开中两种时态反复交替使用 29 次之多。例如:

> Where I arrive at the Hsu's house …; "Auntie, uncle," I say repeatedly …; I remember …; I can see …; I keep thinking …

另一方面有:

> Even your mother agreed …; my mother was always displeased with all her friends …; This is what my mother used to say; … your mother was the best …; my mother told it …

这里主语的连续性伴之以时态的连续性,就使 I 和 mother 成为体现主题的两条主线,两种时态的反复交替构成了多条纬线,使两个时间点上的不同事件交织在一起,从而加强语篇的统一和连贯。

13.4.3 联系不同事件的语言依据

利用现在时的表实功能组篇的第三种形式可以同一本书的第二部分"Half and Half"一章为例说明。这一章第二小节以现在时开始,交代 I 的婚姻即将破裂,已无可挽回:

> Tonight I'm watching my mother sweep, …; I watch her, sweep after sweep, waiting for the moment to tell her about Ted and me, that we're getting divorced …; I know it's hopeless — there's nothing left to save …

后以过去时叙述 I 的婚恋:

> Seventeen years ago she was chagrined when I started dating Ted …; Ted and I met in a politics of ecology class …

随后又突然讲述 I 一家到海滨度假：

> We had gone to the beach ...; So there we were, the nine of us ...; so confident as we walked along our first beach ...。

又以现在时讲述了 Bing 坠海身亡的经过，最后又回到过去时，描述 mother 如何企图从大海中救回 Bing。至此，这两件事似乎没有联系，需读者补充空缺的环节才能理解。在推理过程中读者会发现 I 婚姻的破裂和 Bing 的坠海身亡这两个事件叙事人都是用现在时叙述的，而其间的语段都用过去时。这样现在时的时态便成了读者借以联系两个事件的语言依据：之所以用现在时是因为两者都成了无可挽回的事实。现在时的表实功能使表面并无联系的话语部分获得了连贯。

以上的分析说明现在时的表实功能在语篇展开过程中起着组篇的作用，为话语设计服务，增进语段的语篇性。

13.5　现在时的突显功能

13.5.1　主位展开和及物性

现在时的乏感观距离性或直接性赋予它突显语篇功能。叙事人根据特定语境的要求在语篇中会突出某些信息，使得语篇有主有次，有轻有重。故事主线为主，附加说明为次；叙述高潮为重，一般陈述为轻。具体的体现在主位的连续性和动作的连贯性。对于这两点我们可以从主位展开和动词的及物性加以考察。当叙事人有意突出某些信息时，他的注意焦点当集中在语境中的某一参加者身上，使其成为传递信息的出发点和主位展开的轴线，因此这类语段中通常只有单一主位展开（single thematic development）。及物性传统的理解与及物动词有关，但语言学家们认为及物性是由若干因素构成的，动词带不带宾语只是决定及物性高低的因素之一。所有这些因素都与动作的有效性有关，比如动词是动态的还是静态的,是瞬间终止的还是延续不断的,是有意识的还是无意识的等等。在许多语言中这些因素的及物性的高低变化是彼此相应的。这说明及物性是语言使用中的一个中心特征。及物性的语法和语义上的显著性来自它的具有特征性的语篇功能:高及物性与前景相联系,低及物性与背景相联系(Hopper & Thompson 1980)。可见及物性的高低可以说明语段的重要程度和叙事人给予突出的程度。但是在叙事语篇中及物性高的语段通常要依靠现在时表现事件的直接性,从而突出整个语段的信息。现在时在这种情况下便发挥了突显功能。

13.5.2 及物性分析

这里我们仍以 *The Joy Luck Club* 中的一段为例,其中叙事人以"姐姐"的身份描写"弟弟"Bing 坠海身亡的片断,体现了现在时的突显功能。根据霍珀和汤普森 1980 年提出的理论,我们就及物性的七个参数对这一段作一具体分析。这七个参数是:(1) 参加者(participants),指小句中有无宾语;(2) 动态(kinesis),指动词是动态还是非动态;(3) 体貌(aspect),指动词是否表示有内在终结含义的动作;(4) 时限(punctuality),指动词是表示瞬间动作还是持续动作;(5) 意向(volitionality),指动词是表示有意向还是无意向的动作;(6) 肯定(affirmation),指动词是肯定还是否定;(7) 情状(mode),指动词所表示的动作是真实的还是虚拟的。凡是有宾语、表示动态,有内在终结含义如 eat it up,表示瞬时动作如 kick,有意向,意义肯定而真实的动词,其及物性参数都为高,反之则为低。上述一段动词过程类型分析的结果是:物质 50%,心理 40%,关系 10%。全段有两个语义链,分别以 Bing 和 I 为主项。I 作为叙事人在描述实际情景时重新经历了当时的心理活动,用作一系列小句的主位,形成单一主位展开,小句的动词皆属心理过程。而 Bing 作为叙述对象形成另一个单一主位展开,小句的动词都表示物质过程,而且表示连贯的动作。叙事人的心理活动是插在描述当中的,是向读者交代自己的心情,有关小句人际功能突出。我们可集中分析与事件有关,即与 Bing 有关的小句。从主位看,有关五个小句的主位分别是 Bing、his little body、his feet 和 he。His little body、his feet 与 Bing 是局部和整体的关系,讲的仍是 Bing;he 回指 Bing,

所以五个小句构成单一主位展开,叙事人想集中说明的是 Bing。从动词看,这五个动词中有四个是明显的动态动词,are in the air 在上下文里相当于 slip、fall 或 fall off,是坠海过程的重要一环。可见,are in the air 不可能是静止的,仍具有动态意味。动词所表示的动作是连贯发生的。修饰语 one、two、three steps、quickly、just as I think this 既说明动词不间断地发生,又说明叙事人以快速的节奏作动态描写。有关动词及物性的分析如下:

表 13-1 动词及物性表解

动词 参数	walks	is moving	are in the air	splashes	disappears
参加者	-	-	-	-	-
动态	+	+	+	+	+
体貌	+	-	+	+	+
时限	-	-	+	+	+
意向	+	+	-	-	-
肯定	+	+	+	+	+
情状	+	+	+	+	+
高及物性总计	5	4	5	5	5
高及物性百分计	68.57				

说明:+为 1,-为 0;高及物性百分比是高及物性参数值总和与参数值总和的比例。这一分析结果表明这 5 个动词的高及物性参数值是总数的 68.57%。这说明这一语段在叙事中比较突出。现在时在这叙述进入高潮的段落里便发挥了突显功能。而在这之前的段落里叙事人描述 Bing 坠海前的情景,叙述不集中于 Bing,动作也不连贯,现在时只起表实功能。

13.5.3 前景和背景

上文提到的定景指组篇中的前景和背景。语言学家们认为语篇中故事主线的成分,也就是话语中突出(salient)的成分构成前景,话语中辅佐、渲染或评议的部分为背景。语言中有许多手段可用以定景,时态是其中之一。他们认为在叙事语篇中现在时可使一部分突出,成为前景,而过去时则将次要部分成为语篇的背景。但必须指出定景有其梯阶性(scalar nature)，作为前景虽较背景重要，其中还有主有次，背景中也不乏重要信息。现在时用于前景，过去时用于背景的说法把叙事语篇组篇的复杂性简单化了。叙事中重要次要是相对的，什么部分需要突出取决于叙事的目的和意图。

这里我们需要解决的问题是：是不是在叙事语篇中所有用现在时的部分都是为了取得生动的效果。看一下第 4 节便可以知道事实并非如此。具有生动效果的语段应该是叙事人希望引起读者更多注意的语段，应是叙述节奏快的动态描写，动词所表示的动作连续发生。就动作过程而言，应该以物质过程为主。现在让我们对 *The Kitchen God's Wife* 的第二章中前约 1 000 字的语段作一定量分析。这一语段中共有 76 个小句（不包括非限定小句和引语中的小句），过程类型分析结果如下表所示：

表 13－2　分析结果统计表

过程 / 项目	物质	心理	关系	行为	言语	存在	总计
数　目	28	9	11	14	14	0	76
百分比	36.84	11.84	14.47	18.42	18.42	0	100

从这个统计看，表示物质过程的动词（如 walk、hand、put on 等）仅占总数的 36.84%，其中有些动词还是进行体（如 is walking、is standing），或被动语态（如 is blinded）；而表示心理的动词（如 feel、see）、表示言语的动词（如 whisper、say）、表示行为的动词（如 smile、watch）以及表示关系的动词（如 are、looks）等非动态的动词却占了 63.16%，因此及物性不可能很高。其次表示言语过程的动词一般却引出引语。在这一语段所含的 26 个段落中有 20 个段落含有引语，所以对话占有相当大的比重，这就不可能有快节奏的描述。再次，在这 76 个小句中共有 23 个不同的名词词组作为主语/主位，因此缺乏集中的叙述对象，也就是缺乏这一语段的统一主题。从主位展开看，叙事人并无意突出什么信息。这都说明在这个语段中叙事人使用现在时并非为了取得生动的效果。如果说高及物性与前景相联系，而叙事语篇中用现在时的部分是前景，那么在前景部分中还有进一步前景化的段落，高及物性仅与前景中的这些段落相联系。在这些段落中现在时才发挥突显功能。

13.6 现在时的概括功能

13.6.1 普遍性

现在时的乏时性使得它在语篇中可以发挥概括功能。在体现这一功能的语句或语篇里,命题内容在叙事人看来不仅是真实的,而且可适用于任何时间。试看下面这一小段:

> I also found out why I should never reveal "why" to others. A little knowledge withheld is a great advantage one should store for future use.

第一句为过去时,第二句却用现在时,原因是说话人认为这一句的内容带有普遍性,不仅过去如此,现在如此,将来也如此。句中不定代词 one 也可说明这是一般性的陈述。现在时在这里起了概括功能。

13.6.2 隐含信息

现在时所概括的信息可以是明晰的,也可以是隐含的。现在我们来看一看 *The Museum of Man*。这是一篇几乎通篇都用现在时的叙事语篇,讲述一个名叫 Smitty 的人类学家为了保存印第安文化专程访问了一个年迈的印第安老妪,打算搜集世代单传的羽饰工艺的样品,结果一无所获,空手而归。叙事人仅对途中的个别经历和景物用了过去时,其余皆用现在时。从时态上难以区分前景和背景。除故事的主线外,语篇中有七段描写传授羽饰工艺的仪式,场景和具体过程也用了现在时。这一语篇的叙事人是 Smitty 的助手。他既不像 Smitty 那样热衷于保留印第安文化,又不像那印第安老妪那样珍视自己民族的传统羽饰工艺,所以他可以客观地描述整个访问经过。Smitty 与他登程之后说了这样一句话: It has to be preserved, before it is too late ... before the culture is dead. 他觉得此话与事实不符,随即他想到在 Kenora 的经历,这是叙事人对此行的一番思索,反映了他的态度,与故事无关,所以用现在时。如果作为过去的事件陈述,用过去时,当然也是合理的。

从内容看,故事的主线应该是 Smitty 的访问,事件参加者除 Smitty 之外还有印第安老妪,故事的中心是体现印第安文化的羽饰工艺。传承过程和礼仪只能对故事起背景的作用。然而相关的七段却用了现在时。叙事人对于授艺情景和过程用现在时作了极为具体而生动的描述,这是为了说明这项工艺对于印第安人如何珍贵,如何神圣,从而解释了老妪为什么拒绝 Smitty 索取工艺样品的要求。现在时在这里起了突显功能(见 13.5.)。从定景的角度考虑,这些段落的描写只是对故事主线的烘托。这说明背景之中因叙事目的需要也会有突出的部分。

那么,故事本身为什么用现在时?是利用现在时的表实功能?组篇并没有这一要求。是利用现在时的突显功能?这 47 段中的对话很多,没有集中的主位展开,又没有动态的描写,所以也不是。我们知道一个句子有其语言形式和意义,在特定的语境中传达一定的信息,听话人通过推理从语言意义中推断出信息。同样语篇也有其意义和信息,读者通过推理获得语篇所传递的信息,但人们在推理的过程中得依靠实际的语言证据。在这一语篇中现在时便是可以借以推理的依据。以 Smitty 为代表的人们不关心印第安人的生活,却想保留印第安文化,结果遭到印第安人的拒绝。这个叙事语篇所传递的信息是:不关心印第安人就无法关心印第安文化,这个隐含的信息通过现在时的叙述加以传达,说明这一信息的普遍意义。虽然 Smitty 碰壁的经历是过去的,但语篇所传递的信息却适用于任何时间,不仅今天如此,将来也是如此。现在时在这语篇中起了概括功能。

13.7 结　语

基于其语义特征,英语现在时具有三种相互联系但又有区别的语篇功能,即表实功能、概括功能和突显功能,其中表实功能是基本的功能,概括功能和突显功能都基于表实功能。由于现在时已从提供参照时间的任务中解脱出来，其主要价值在于表明句子或语段所陈述的命题内容是真实的，因此可以用于任何时间，包括过去。叙事语篇自身的叙事顺序以及其他语言因素，如状语、类指名词词组、泛指代词等可以帮助读者了解事件的时间指向，可以避免现在时的形式和过去的内容之间表面矛盾影响理解。

从以上对英语现在时语篇功能的探讨可以看出英语时态是组篇的一种手段，用以表明语篇所体现的语境中若干事件之间的时间关系，可用于按照不同的时间层面组织语篇，便于叙事，同时增强语篇的连贯和一致；也可使表面似无联系的语段通过使用统一的时态取得语篇的连贯。英语时态的使用还可以体现信息轻重主次的分布，实现叙事目的。叙事人用现在时叙述过去的事件是组织语篇的需要。

语言的三大元功能之一意念功能是表达外部世界的经验或内心世界的体验，是用语言表达“内容”的功能。现在时的表实功能的作用在于表示句子或语段的命题内容是真实的，即便是叙事人过去经验中发生的事件也作为“现在”的实际经验加以表述，使读者了解事件的真实性。这里现在时所涉及的“内容”也体现现实的经验，可见现在时的表实功能体现了语言的意念功能。

语言的人际功能用以建立和维持人际关系，确定参加者的交际角色，同时表明说话人的角度、态度和判断。现在时的概括功能使叙事人将语段或语篇的内容作为具有普遍性的经验向读者陈述。这里除了体现叙事人和读者之间的人际关系外，还表明了叙事人对“内容”的态度。可见现在时的概括功能体现了语言的人际功能。

语言的话语功能是组成话语的功能，它使话语与语境联系，又使话语内部连贯。现在时的突显功能使语篇的一部分突出，为信息分布服务，从而起到组篇的作用。可见现在时的突显功能体现了语言的话语功能。英语现在时的语篇功能并不是任意的，而是取决于人们交际中对语言的要求，体现语言的元功能。

韩礼德认为语言的人际功能包含意念功能（Halliday 1973），话语功能有助于其他两大功能发挥作用（Halliday 1975）。可见语言的三大功能是相互联系的，在语篇中这三大功能同时为交际服务。只是在为了满足特定的交际需要时，某一元功能更为突出。同样，现在时的三项功能也是相互联系的，尽管体现不同的元功能，在语篇中却都能为组篇服务。叙事语篇需要现在时发挥这三项功能，也只有在语篇中现在时才能获得这三项功能。

14

Yes 和 No 在叙事语篇中的功能
——从认知功能视角的探索*

14.1 引　言

本章拟探讨 yes 和 no 在叙事语篇中的话语功能。概念系统中肯定和否定的对立在语言编码中一方面被语法化为归一性,另一方面被词汇化为仅含 yes 和 no 两个词的封闭词汇系统。我们拟探讨两个问题:(1) 语篇推进过程中信息在意识的作用下是如何展开的;(2) yes 和 no 为什么会出现,出现在什么地方,在语篇推进过程中起什么作用。yes 和 no 是英语中使用最为频繁的两个表示肯定和否定的词,常用于会话,所以在会话语篇中获得了特定的语义和功能。这两个词可以表示归一性,但与归一性的关系各家说法不尽相同,究竟关系如何也是需要加以考察的。我们拟首先理清 yes 和 no 的基本意义和功能,着重探讨韩礼德(Halliday 1994)、埃金斯和斯莱德(Eggins & Slade 1997)以及福西特(Fawcett 2000)的有关论述,然后探究在语篇流背后的信息流的特点和方式,主要在切夫的认知功能理论的基础上,梳理出信息流的单位、推进的障碍和展开的程

* 本章原载《外国语》2008 年第 5 期第 20—29 页。

式,最后对出现在叙事语篇 *The Armies of the Night* 中的 yes 和 no 作具体分析,如下例引文中的 no。

> Still, he made no effort to win the audience, seduce them, dominate them, bully them, amuse them, **no**, they were there for *him*, to please *him*, a sounding board for the plucked string for his poetic line, and so he endeared to them. (Mailer 1968: 44)

14.2 基本意义与功能

14.2.1 基本意义

Yes 的基本意义有二:(1) 表示肯定的应答,包括同意、断言、赞成、确认或接受,如:

— Are you ready?
— Yes, I am.

(2) 引出对否定陈述的纠正和反诘,如:

— Don't say that.
— Yes, I will.

No 的基本意义也有二:(1) 表示否定的应答,用于拒绝、否认或异议,如:

— Will you be taking the car?
— No, not today.

(2) 认可否定陈述,表示对别人否定陈述的接受或理解,如:

— Nobody seems to listen.
— No, they don't.

至于这两个词的功能,我们先来看它们与归一性的关系。在"He speaks French""He does not speak French"两句中,动词体现出来的肯定与否定构成归一性。

韩礼德是在讨论情态和归一性之后交待了 yes 和 no 这两个词(Halliday 1994: 92)。他说它们当然是归一性的表达式,但它们的功能不止一个。最重要的变数是它们是否表示言语功能。如果是,它们是语气附加语,如果不是,那它们则是接续语(continuatives),在语气结构内没有位置。他还说,归一性一般表现在限定成分内(Halliday 1994: 88),yes 和 no 不可能出现在限定成分内,因而就不属于归一性。那么 yes 和 no 又怎么可能"当然是归一性的表达式"呢?

再看埃金斯和斯莱德(Eggins & Slade 1997: 96)的观点。她们说归一性与 yes 和 no 这两个词密切相关,而这两个词我们常常错误地当成英语的归一性标记。小句的归一性总是在限定部分表示。在看待 yes 和 no 的功能上,埃金斯和斯莱德比韩礼德(Halliday 1994)似乎又退了一步,它们连归一性的表达式或标记都不是了。

福西特认为在表达肯定和否定的词中 yes 和 no 最为常用(Fawcett 2000)。他指出对"Did he attend the meeting?"这一问题,英语可以有三种回答:

> He attended the meeting. /He did not attend the meeting. (He didn't attend the meeting.)
>
> Yes./No.
>
> Yes, he did./No, he didn't./He did./He didn't. (Fawcett 2000: 153)

这就使得福西特为归一性系统建立了三个次系统。Yes/No 是其中之一。他认为理解 yes/no 的关键在于承认它们是完全的小句,尽管它们看上去并非小句(Fawcett 2000: 152)。这是因为归一性的小句常含替代或省略。只有 yes/no 的小句是含替代的小句,因为 yes/no 替代了完整的肯定或否定小句;He did/He didn't 是含省略的小句,因为被省略的成分可以复原。

虽然韩礼德认为 Yes /No 可以省略式形式出现,独立作为小句(Halliday 1994: 92)。埃金斯和斯莱德认为 yes/no 有时可以用作辅句(minor clause),但她们仍把 yes/no 排斥在归一性系统之外。只有福西特完整地提出了归一性含三个次系统的看法,解决了 yes/no 一方面是表示肯定与否定最为常用的一对词,而另一方面却与归一性无关,又不可被视为归一性标记之间的明显矛盾。这不仅从理论上解决了 yes/no 这两个词在语法系统中的地位，而且有助于分析它们在叙事语篇中的功能。

14.2.2　功　能

Yes/no 作为接续语，韩礼德指出，可以起陈述的功能，用以回答问题，认可陈述，执行命令，或接受提供（Halliday 1994：92）。埃金斯和斯莱德在研究聊天时，对 yes 的变体 yeah 进行了分析（Eggins & Slade 1997：96－98）。她们指出 yeah 是接续标记（continuity marker），表示和构建两个话轮之间的连续，或者表示对前一话轮的肯定和支持；no 则表示转折性连接或对先前否定话语的同意或反对。很明显这些功能都是基于互动的。会话是听说双方共同构建的话语，这些功能也可视为 yes/no 的话语功能，也是 yes/no 的基本功能。然而，yes 和 no 的使用并不限于对话，它们也出现在叙事语篇里。福西特（Fawcett 2000：156）在列举 yes 和 no 的功能时指出 yes 和 no 可用于独白，他的例子之一是：I like this one. Yes, it will do very well. Yes, I'll definitely take it. 这是一位妇女购物时，看到一顶帽子时的自言自语。所以这里 yes 并不用于连接两个话轮，韩礼德把 yes 这种用法解释为一个新的话步开始，如果是同一个说话人连续说话，那就是话步转向另一谈点。那么，为什么在话步开始和话步转移时需要用 yes？是什么要求 yes？yes 又发挥什么功能？这个例子虽然是口语，却与叙事的书面语中 yes/no 的用法非常相似。如果我们分析出 yes/no 在叙事语篇中的功能，就应该能回答这些问题。

14.3　信息流与意识

14.3.1　信息流

在探讨叙事语篇中 yes 和 no 的功能时，我们关注它们在什么地方出现,为什么出现,起什么作用,所表达的意义和它们在会话中表达的意义是否相同。为此,我们必须考虑 yes/no 的基本意义、基本功能和在语篇中的位置,结合语篇所提供的语境进行分析。我们关注的是叙事语篇中的 yes 和 no,也就是说不是对话里的 yes 和 no,所以不表达言语功能,因而也就不是情态附加语,而是接续语。接续语是语篇成分,与其他语篇成分,如话语标记 oh、you know 一样,都是为了满足语篇展开过程中的期待(discourse expectation)(Langcker 2001: 151),推动语篇的进展。为此我们需要了解语篇是怎样推进的。语篇进展受信息流的支配,所以,我们需要了解信息是怎样推进的。英语口语是以一系列具有旋律性的单位推进的,这个单位就是语调组。每个语调组体现一个信息单位。在无标记的情况下,信息单位与小句重合(Halliday 1994: 59)。信息是从一个信息单位向另一个信息单位推进的,这个观点与认知语言学的理论一致。认知语言学认为,在语篇展开过程中,说话人的心理空间不断被构建和改进。当前话语空间从一个注意框架向另一个注意框架推进。语音上注意框架与语调一致。语义上它们是由某一时刻脑子中充分激活的信息构成;语法上,往往与小句重合(Langcker 2001: 154)。这两种看法都说明了信息流的最基本的情况。功能语法和认知语法都关注意义,而意义是出自意识和其所处环境之间的相互影响(Halliday & Matthissen 1999: 14)。信息的传达、注意与否和关注的强弱都与意识有关,因此我们需要了解意识在语篇推进和信息流程中的作用。意识在很大程度上是由感知、行为和情感的经验构成的(Chafe 1994: 31)。切夫认为人们如何使用语言在很大程度上取决于他们在时间一点点推移过程中意识到什么——取决于他们内在注意的焦点,同时关注听话人意识中的活动(Chafe 1980: 9)。他认为思考涉及三个要素:信息、自我和意识。信息指来自三个来源的大量知识。这三个来源是对世界的感知、记忆和情感;自我指对当前活动实施中心控制的执行者;意识指为自我服务将可获取的信息加以激活,所以,意识是自我利用信息的机制(Chafe 1980: 11)。意识有四个特征:(1) 容量有限;(2) 持续时间有限;(3) 呈涌动的方式行进;(4) 具有中心焦点和边缘区域,也就是在任何时刻只有极少量的信息能够最大程度地被激活,还有其他大量信息说话人意识得到,但没有聚焦在上面(Chafe 1980: 11)。此外,意识需要有取向(orientation)才能起作用,包括意识所处环境中的时间、空间、事件、正在进行的活动和参与的人物(Chafe 1994: 30)。由于生理和认知能力的局限,意识呈一浪推一浪的形式前进。每一次意识的迸发(spurt),就出现一个意识点,语言上切夫叫意义单位(idea unit),也就是韩礼德所说的信息单位,兰艾克所说的注意框架。意义单位有三个标准:(1)语音上是一个语调单位;(2)有停顿;(3)句法上通常为一个小句。意识焦点所容纳的信息往往不能充分满足人们交流的需要。通常的信息量都要溢过信息焦点,所以就要求意识在边缘意识范围里扫描若干信息焦点,这若干信息焦点就构成超意识焦点(super-focus)或关注中心(center of interest)(Chafe 1980: 26-28),可参阅第3章3.3节,口语里通常以句末语调核心和句法结构终结为标志,体现为含几个语调单位的扩展小句或句子。例如:

The movie opened up on a this nice scene,
It was in the country,
It was oaks,
It seemed West Coast.

这是对一个场景的描述,有四个意识焦点,体现了大于意识焦点的认知单位,即关注中心。从这个例子可以看出,关注中心自身没有图式,但却可能是图式的一个部分。对场景的描述就可能是叙事结构中取向的一个部分。关注中心与心理意象有联系,在叙事中说话人把意识逐一聚焦于这意象的不同方面,最后完整地呈现场景,语音上以降调结束(Chafe 1980: 27)。

14.3.2 三种信息

切夫区分三种信息:(1)活性信息,也就是被聚焦的信息;(2)半活性信息,就是处于意识边缘区域的信息;(3)非活性信息,也就是长期记忆中的信息(Chafe 1987: 22)。他认为新信息是在会话某一时间点上新激活的信息,已知信息是在会话某时间点上已经激活的信息。他还把从半活性状态中激活的信息称为可及信息(accessible information)(Chafe

1994：72）。意识焦点是活性信息，而关注中心是半活性信息，也就是意识边缘地区的信息。它的作用在于引导意识从一个焦点向另一个焦点转移。激活通常指激活一个概念。当一个概念在语篇中已经激活，或者直接与一个已经激活的概念相联系，或者与当前语境有联系，那这个概念就是半活性信息。认知活动是一个动态过程。在某一个时间点上的半活性信息或非活性信息可以在下一个时间点上成为活性信息。激活半活性信息是激活意识边缘区域的信息，激活非活性信息是激活长期记忆中的信息，也就是回忆，所需要的认知努力要更大。一个概念如果不加以再次激活不可能长期处于活性状态；某一时间点上的活性信息在去激活化后不会立即成为非活性信息，即进入长期记忆，而是退到意识的边缘区域，在一段时间里成为半活性信息，也就是成为可及信息。关注中心在语篇中构成基本主题（basic-level topic）。主题是可以处于半活性状态的大量信息，是以某种形式相互联系地存在于说话人边缘意识中的时间、方式和参与者的组合（Chafe 1994：121）。意识往往溢过半活性意识区域，从一个基本主题往另一个基本主题行进，这样就构成超主题（supertopic）。超主题因为有总的取向而获得连贯，它支持若干基本主题，并由若干基本主题构成（Chafe 1994：138）。而基本主题是由体现意识焦点的若干次主题（subtopic）构成。关注中心、基本主题在语篇分析中未得到应有的重视，但在我们的分析中将是关键单位，而我们的分析验证了关注中心、基本主题的存在。在信息推进中，意识可以在三种方式中起作用：直接方式（immediate mode），指人们结合所处的环境表述经验；移置方式（displaced mode），即意识脱离当时当地通过记忆或想象聚焦于以往意识中衍生出来的经验；通用方式（generic mode），即意识不聚焦于特定事件或人物的情况（Chafe 2001：677）。但是在信息推进过程中关注中心的表达会受到干扰（perturbations）。干扰可能是说话人改变计划，放弃表达既定的关注中心；推迟表达关注中心；偏离关注中心之后又回到关注中心；插入另一个层面的关注中心；对已结束的关注中心添加补充，等等。意识活动方式和意识取向的改变都可以造成干扰（Chafe 1980：33）。语篇具有期待性，期待性愈强，语篇进展就愈顺利，语篇进展的势头（momentum）就愈大。在碰到干扰的情况下，语篇进展的势头减弱，就需要更大的认知努力推进语篇。

14.3.3　书面语中的功能

以上关于语篇进展和信息推进的讨论都基于口语，而我们要研究的是书面语中 yes/no 的功能，那么这些论述是否可以用于书面语？答案是肯定的。首先，口语和书面语都是语言，是适应不同情境、采用不同媒介和渠道的语言，因此同样受制于认知的局限，意识的特征也同样作用于书面语，如书面语和口语一样都受到每个信息单位只能有一个新信息的制约（Chafe 1994：108），口语中意识在停顿和说话时的活动在书面语的停顿和书写时也大同小异；不同之处在于书面语停顿时间可以较长，便于计划，所以语句比较完整。除了表现意识流的情况外，书面语的小句很少由于迟疑而拆散为几个意义单位，因此小句一般是意识焦点、意义单位、次主题，而若干小句或若干句子构成体现半活性意识的关注中心、基本主题。如：

> *What do you know of the dirt and the dark deliveries of the necessary? What do you know of the dignity hard achieved, dignity lost through innocence, and dignity lost by sacrifice for a cause one cannot name. What do you know about getting fat against your will, and turning into a clown of an arriviste baron when you would rather be an eagle or a count, or rarest of all, some natural aristocrat from these damned democratic states.* No, the only subject we share, you and I, is the species of perception which shows if we are not loyal to our unendurable and most exigent inner light, then some day we may burn. How dare you condemn me! (Mailer 1968: 41)

例中 No 之前的三个问句体现八个意识焦点。三个问题实际上是同一个问题的三个方面，或者说三个疑问句共同体现一个问题，一个言语行为。这语义上的整体性使这多个意识焦点构成一个关注中心，或基本主题。意识焦点是活性信息，如第一个 wh-问题，是因为意识聚焦于此，第二、第三个问题这时就处于意识的边缘地区，是半活性信息。说整个关注中心是半活性信息，是因为意识在这个范围内激活一个又一个焦点。此例是由并列的句子体现的基本主题。至于为什么随后跟 No，下面我们将讨论。

14.4 语篇分析

14.4.1 No 在语篇中的位置和功能

我们已经了解了 yes 和 no 的基本意义和功能，也理清了信息进程的特点、层次结构和单位，我们可以分析含 yes/no 的语篇，回答上面提出的问题：它们在什么地方出现，为什么出现，起什么作用？在诺曼·梅勒(Norman Mailer)的这本著名纪实小说中 yes 和 no 出现率相当高，据不完全统计，前 200 页中比较典型地体现叙事语篇功能的 yes 出现 47 次，no 出现 43 次。我们现选择数例加以探讨，先看 no。

[1] So Mailer went into a diatribe. "Yeah, people," he said, "watch the reporting that follows. Yeah, these reporters will kiss Lyndon Johnson's *ss, and Dean Rusk's *ss and Man Mountain McNamara's *ss, they will rush to kiss it, but will they stand up in public?" No! Because they are the silent assassins of the Republic. They alone have done more to destroy this nation than any force in it. (Mailer 1968: 51)

No 之前的四个小句体现四个意识焦点，意识从一个焦点移至另一个焦点，共同构成超意识焦点，构成一个基本主题，集中说明记者的嘴脸。No 是一个辅句，相当于"No, they will not stand up in public"，对前面的肯定问句作了否定的回应。值得注意的是梅勒在此一身三任：写作的自我、说话的自我和人物的自我。梅勒从说话自我到写作自我的转变伴随着他的意识从直接方式到移置方式的转变，所以他需要认知处理的时间。在直接方式中，即在演讲时，他提的问题可以由听众应答，但是在移置方式中，写作自我意识到他在激活记忆中的经验，他在写作，没有听众应答。语篇在进展过程中始终有某种期待，问句期待回答。所以他不得不自问自答。而 no 是最为省时省事的语言资源，而且还为梅勒提供另一个停顿，可以为他用于考虑下面激活那一个概念。这一问一答似乎和对话相似，但有一点值得注意,没有 no,随后的"because ..."就出不来,because 一般当应 why 的期待出现。但 no 是否定陈述的省略,也可以期待原因和解释。从这个意义上讲,no 不仅承接了上文,而且还引出了构成另一个基本主题的下文,提示了主题的要点(point),即讲述这番话的理由(Chafe 2001: 766),也就是 Mailer 为什么如此愤怒地谴责这帮记者。

[2] Mailer detested the thought of getting through the oncoming hours. Under the best of circumstances the nature of these heroics was too dry, too dignified, too obviously severed from bravura to make the Novelist happy (not for nothing had an eminent critic once said that Mailer was as fond of his style as an Italian tenor is fond of his vocal cords) no he liked good character when it is issued into action which was visually tumultuous rather than inspiring awe in the legal mind. (Mailer 1968: 55)

此例中引人注目的是括号。括号之前是两个句子,体现了五个意识焦点,共同构成一个超焦点或关注中心,语言上体现为一个基本主题,说明梅勒不愿卷入年轻人交回征兵卡的行动。如果我们把写作看作是作者在根据脑际的图像描述,就可以把他的意识看成是处于直接方式,那么随后作者则进入了移置方式,所述的内容已逾过了当前半活性意识的区域,构成了支线关注中心。这种偏离是叙事过程中对表达关注中心的干扰。意识活动方式改变之后要回到正题上来比之正常的叙事要困难得多,因为它离开了超主题所涉及的图式。这里意识活动方式的改变伴随了取向的改变,从梅勒的态度转到著名评论家对梅勒的评论,支线中心离正题更远,所以意识起作用的方式和取向同时改变使得回归正题就需要更大的认知努力。这也就是作者使用括号和 no 的原因。no 再次激活了否定概念,除总结括号前的关注中心外,还引出了对照性的内容。前一基本主题的否定意义由词汇和句法结构体现: detested, too, too, too ... to ...,而 no 之后的肯定态度由 liked 体现。由此可见 no 含 nevertheless 的意义。

[3] Still, he made no effort to win the audience, seduce them, dominate them, bully them, amuse them, no, they were there for *him*, to please *him*, a sounding board for the plucked string for his poetic line, and so he endeared to them. (Mailer 1968: 44)

例[3]中 no 对前一否定的基本主题作了肯定的应接。之所以要用 no,是因为这五个意识焦点要表示否定意义,但否定的范围(scope of negation)太大,意识在激活一个又一个表层肯定的焦点之后,否定的意义已难以维持,而听话人对 no effort 的记忆是否能持续到最后也是问题。关注中心的否定意义需要再次激活才能维持活性状态,由于 no 是否定小句的替代形式,可用以再次激活关注中心的否定意义。但是 no 并不是单纯地做总结回应,而是要引出对照。需要注意的是 no 之后的关注中心的取向改变,由前文的 he 转到 they,而且 him 作者用了斜体,表示特意被激活而成为对照性激活焦点,体现与前面 them 的对照。前文的中心意思是"he was not there for them", no 之后的中心意思是 they were there for *him*。这就赋予 no 以 on the contrary 的意义。

[4] What do you know of the dirt and the dark deliveries of the necessary? What do you know of the dignity hard achieved, dignity lost through innocence, and dignity lost by sacrifice for a cause one cannot name. What do you know about getting fat against your will, and turning into a clown of an arriviste baron when you would rather be an eagle or a count, or rarest of all, some natural aristocrat from these damned democratic states. No, the only subject we share, you and I, is the species of perception which shows if we are not loyal to our unendurable and most exigent inner light, then some day we may burn. How dare you condemn me! (Mailer 1968: 41)

在第 14.3.3 节已经说明 no 之前的三个问句构成了一个关注中心、一个基本主题,我们现在要探讨为什么 no 会在这个位置上出现。这三个问句都是 wh-疑问句,wh-疑问句要求提供信息,不可能用 yes/no 回答,所以 no 不是用于应答。仔细看这些疑问句我们就会发现它们仅仅在形式上是疑问句,实际上是否定句。叶斯柏森早就指出否定的陈述可以用问题的形式表达(Jespersen 1960: 24),最简单的例子是"Who cares?"虽是问句,但意义却是"No one cares"或"I don't care"。汉语也存在同样的用法:"你懂什么?"借助一定的语调,意思可以是"你什么也不懂"。这三个特殊疑问句意思就是 You know nothing。否定陈述的性质还可以从标点符号上看出,第二、第三个问句都不是以问号结束。这里语言形式和意义的错配使得语篇的期待模糊,减弱了语篇的势头。为了帮助读者了解基本主题的意义,推进语篇的展开,作者用了简便的 no 再次激活关注中心的否定意义。No 之所以出现还因为随后关注中心的取向改变,由前面的人转到事,由 you 转到 subject,这也需要付出认知努力所需的时间。No 适应了这一需要。No 随后的基本主题以问句结束,交待了前一基本主题的要点:作者为什么要问那三个问题。No 前后各有一个基本主题,共同构成超主题。

有时意识起作用的方式可以从直接方式转入通用方式。请看以下两例。

[5] On the other hand, no soldier could go into combat with the secret idea that he would not fire a gun. If nothing else, it was unfair to friends in his outfits, besides, it suggested the suicidal. No, the iron of the logic doubtless demanded that if you disapproved of the war too much to shoot Vietcong, then your draft card was for burning. (Mailer 1968: 20)

No 之前是一个基本主题,具有否定意义,语言上体现为 unfair。No 对参战而不射一枪持否定态度作了肯定,实际上是再次激活否定意义。由于随后意识取向和意识活动的方式将改变,由士兵的态度转到逻辑的要求,即由直接叙述方式转入诉诸理智的通用方式,no 总结了前一基本主题,并引出一般陈述为前一基本主题作出进一步的说明,以实现意识取向和意识活动方式的转变。语言上 no 之后语句中的不定代词 you 说明 no 之后是一般陈述,不特指任何人。

[6] Those true powers of interior decoration — greed, guilt, compassion and trust — were hardly the cornerstones of their family furnishings. No, just as money was a concept, no more, to the liberal academic, and needed no ballast of gold to be considered real, for nothing is more real to the intellectual than a concept. (Mailer 1968: 15-16)

No 之前是一个否定基本主题,语言上体现为否定副词 hardly; no 对前一基本主题的否定意义作了肯定。由于意识活动将由直接方式转入通用方式,并引出比喻性的进一步说明。此时意识不仅从直接方式转入通用方式,而且从现实世界进入了想象世界、比喻世界。这里可以看出 no 是前一句子的省略句,否则"no more, to the liberal academic"就无法理解,因为这两个短语是一个回应前句的省略小句,是"Those true powers of interior decoration — greed, guilt, compassion and trust — were no more the cornerstones of their family furnishings to the liberal academic"的省略。这可以证明 Fawcett 对 yes/no 与归一性关系的论述是符合语言事实的。No 之后是一般性陈述,可用于任何时间的 is 说明自我的意识不涉及任何特定的人和事物。

以上的实例分析说明,no 一般出现在两个关注中心的交界处。No 的出现是因为意识活动方式或意识的取向发生变化。No 为意识转向提供了认知处理所需的时间。激活 no 就是再次激活前一关注中心的否定归一性,对前一关注中心的否定意义加以肯定,实际起总结作用,随后引出对照、强调、解释或阐述,常常交待前一关注中心的要点。这是 no 作为连接语在语篇中的意义与功能。

14.4.2 Yes 在语篇中的位置和功能

下面我们来看 yes 的语义和功能。

[7] Mailer's senses are tuned to absolute pitch or sheer error — he marks a ballot for absolute pitch — he is certain there is a profound pall in the audience. Yes, they sit there, stricken, inert, in terror of what Saturday will bring, and so are unable to rise to a word the speaker is offering them. (Mailer 1968: 33)

Yes 之前是一个关注中心,说明 Mailer 强烈意识到听众中的厌倦情绪。Yes 是 there is a profound pall in the audience 的替代,再次激活肯定归一性,对基本主题作了肯定,意义接近 in actual fact 和 in point of fact,并引出进一步说明,具体描述听众如何厌倦,起了接续语的作用。Yes 的出现是因为随后关注中心的取向改变,由 Mailer 而转至听众, yes 为这一转变提供了认知处理所需时间。

［8］Lowell and Macdonald were inclined to work him rather than ostracize him. In the next minute, Dwight met his eye, gave a chilly nod, and came over to where Mailer was sitting. Yes, the fact was there, and little securities could be grounded on it: Macdonald would not escape his fondness for Mailer.（Mailer 1968: 64）

Yes 之前的关注中心说明两个人物对梅勒的态度以及可以表明对梅勒态度的行动，Yes 对此作了肯定，意义接近"indeed""in fact"，并引出肯定性的说明。同样，Yes 之后的关注重心变更了取向，由人而转到事，由 Lowell 和 Macdonald 转到 the fact。值得注意的是，yes 之前的关注中心着重说明客观事实，而其随后的关注中心则表明梅勒的主观推测，这可以从"could be""would not"看出，所以要求 yes，帮助实现这一转折。

［9］So he had no real alternative — he was not sufficiently virtuous to eschew the income tax protest, and had signed, and to his surprise had been repaid by the abrupt departure of a measurable quantity of moral congestion, a noticeable lowering of his spiritual flatulence and a reduction of his New York fever, that ferocious inflammation which New York seemed always to encourage: envy, greed, claustrophobia, excitement, bourbon, broads, action, ego, jousts, cruelty, and too-rich food in expensive hateful restaurants. Yes, signing the protest had been good for him.（Mailer 1968: 58）

Yes 之前是一个复杂的关注中心，如果四个小句体现四个意识焦点，那 by 之后的三个名词短语也可以是独立的语调单位，因而也是意识焦点，第三个名词词组最后的一个词组"New York fever"随后跟一个同位语"that ferocious inflammation"，而这个同位语为一个定语从句修饰，其中含 11 个词和词组，每个都自成一个语调组，一个意识焦点。自我的意识从 he 开始，不断从一个意识焦点到另一个意识焦点，心至言随，在不知不觉之中，从 he 转至"New York fever"，结果出现了取向的改变。自我的记忆可能已经无法保持基本主题的出发点，等到发现时，已经感到继续推进信息流程有些困难,不得不借助 yes 再次激活前一关注中心的肯定意义以总结前文,相当于 in short,并回到主题,用另一个关注中心简明扼要地提示前文。同时自我也不得不考虑读者,在一系列意识焦点之后,读者对主题的记忆也可能模糊,使用 yes 再次激活前面的信息,有利于读者提取信息。

[10] All the healthy Marines, state troopers, professional athletes, movie stars, rednecks, sensuous life-loving Mafia, cops, mill workers, city officials, nice healthy-looking, easy-grafting politicians full of the light (from marijuana?) in their eye of a life they enjoy — yes, they would be for the war in Vietnam. (Mailer 1968: 34)

Yes 之前是 11 个名词短语,每一个短语是一个意识焦点,但这么多意识焦点并未构成关注中心,因为还不能成为基本主题。主题不论是在哪一个层次,多半是一个在心理上影响我们的问题或亟待填补的缺口(Chafe 1980: 120)。这里只是一系列概念,没有要求回答什么或填补什么。也正因为如此,语篇进展受到阻碍。从语言上讲,使用这一系列名词违背了"轻主语制约"或"轻起点制约"(Chafe 1980: 85)。主语或起点只应该有很小量的信息负荷,通常为已知信息。这 11 个名词词组体现了从半活性意识中激活的概念,属于可及信息。英语容许可及信息作为出发点,但是在这一系列概念出现之后,特别是最后一个名词词组还含一个定语从句,意识活动的方式逐渐偏离,自我最初要加上什么新信息,也就是意识需要激活什么概念碰到了困难。书写中的破折号表示语篇推进遇到了阻碍和由此而产生的迟疑、犹豫,所以需要用 yes 加以总结,并以体现已知信息的人称代词 they 作为出发点,避免了头重脚轻的异常,满足了轻起点制约的要求,然后再加上新信息"for the war in Vietnam"。Yes 这里出现在一个关注中心之中,而不是在两个关注中心之间。但同样是因为语篇推进受阻。

[11] Mood was forever being sliced, cut, stamped, ground, excised, or obliterated; mood was a scent which rose from the acts and calms of nature, and totalitarianism was a deodorant to nature. Yes, and by the logic of this metaphor, the Pentagon looked like a five-sided tip on the spout of a can to be used under the arm, yes, the Pentagon was spraying the deodorant of its presence all over the fields of Virginia. (Mailer 1968: 117)

Yes之前是一个关注中心，先说明 mood 的遭遇，然后将 mood 比喻为 scent，把 totalitarianism 比喻为 deodorant。Yes 肯定这两个比喻，并将比喻转向比喻的逻辑，意识活动从直接方式转入隐语推理的通用方式。意识此刻不作用于现实环境、记忆，而是诉诸理智。既然 mood 是 scent，totalitarianism 是 deodorant，若要 deodorant 对 mood 起作用，必须要有工具。推理的过程大体是：任何喷雾剂都需要喷雾器喷射，除味剂是一种喷雾剂，所以需要喷雾器。任何政权的工具都是它统辖的机构，极权主义是一种政权形式，它的工具必定是政权机构。第一个 yes 肯定了推理的前提，并引出结论，将五角大楼比喻为喷雾器喷口上的五边形喷嘴，并通过借喻说明五角大楼是这样一个工具。在隐语等级结构中“五角大楼是喷雾器”这一隐喻是“集权主义是除味剂”这一主要隐喻的次隐语(Lakoff 1993：222)。进一步的推理是：所有的工具在使用中起作用，五角大楼是集权主义的工具，所以它要起作用，就必须使用，deodorant 也才能起作用。第二个 yes 肯定了五角大楼是个工具的推理前提，并引出结论，说明五角大楼到处在“喷洒”，在起实际作用，交代前一基本主题中提出两个明喻的理由，也就点出了基本主题的要点。从本例看 yes 不仅适应了叙事中意识活动方式改变的需要，而且有明显的承上启下的功能。

[12] After the first five seconds of the shock had passed, he realized he might be able to win — the Nazi must have taken too many easy contests, and had been too complacent in the first moment, yes, it was like wrestlers throwing themselves on each other: one knuckle of one finger a little better able to be worked on a grip could make the difference. (Mailer 1968: 142)

在向五角大楼进军中梅勒和“the Nazi”相继被捕，被押上了同一辆警车。两人怒目对视。例[12]是对梅勒此时心理活动的叙述。yes 也总结了前一关注中心，同时用比喻引出了进一步的说明。yes 的出现是因为随后意识取向发生了由人到事理的转变，更重要的是意识活动发生了由直接方式到通用方式的转变。和上例一样，意识诉诸理性思考，最后一个小句是一般陈述，未涉及具体的人。

从对这些实例的分析看，yes 一般出现在两个关注中心的交界处。Yes 的出现是因为意识活动方式或意识的取向发生变化，或因为前一关注中心信息量过大。Yes 为意识转向提供了认知处理所需的时间。激活 yes 实际是再次激活前一关注中心的肯定归一性,从而对前一关注中心的内容加以总结,同时引出进一步的阐述、解释、让步或借助隐语作进一步的说明。这是 yes 作为接续语在语篇中的意义与功能。14.2.2 提到的“I like this one. Yes, it will do very well. Yes, I'll definitely take it”这句话中之所以两次出现 yes,是因为意识的取向改变,从 I 到 it,再从 it 到 I。这也许就是话步开始和话步转移时需要 yes 的原因所在。

14.5 结　语

Yes/no 在叙事语篇中通常出现在体现关注中心的两个基本主题之间,当两个关注中心分别处于两个段落的结尾和开始时,yes/no 就出现在后一个段落的开始。

Yes/no 的出现是因为关注中心的表达受到干扰,或因为意识的取向改变或意识起作用的方式改变,或因为前一个关注中心的信息量过大,语篇提出的期待不够清楚。任何一个层次的主题没有取向就不成其为主题。取向改变意味着意识要在半活性信息中,甚至在非活性信息中激活所需的概念。意识活动方式的改变也往往需要从长期记忆中激活概念。叙事语篇的推进通常是依靠图式,借助图式成分之间的联系,意识可以比较容易地从一个意识焦点走向另一个焦点。当意识活动方式改变时,意识往往要脱离当前的图式,在长期记忆中寻找与另一个图式有联系的概念,这就给信息推进制造困难,所以需要更多的认知努力。

Yes/no 之所以在信息处理碰到困难的时候可以起作用,是因为它们各自自成一个语调单位,构成一个意识焦点,一个意义单位。在大多数情况下 yes/no 是辅句。Yes/no 是单音节词,激活之后就成为意识焦点,无须考虑从半活性信息中激活其他概念,省时省事。Yes/no 作为完全小句的省略,激活了 yes/no 就等于再次激活关注中心的活性概念。Yes/no 之后又提供一个停顿,可以提供自我考虑在半活性信息中激活什么概念,怎么用语言表达所需的认知处理的时间,所以成为信息推进碰到困难时最简便的语言资源。No 有时相当于"on the contrary""otherwise",yes 相当于"in fact""in actual fact""in point of fact""indeed",不用这些词或词组,除了个人风格的差异外,那就是因为 yes/no 比它们更为简便。

基于 yes/no 的基本语义,no 对前一关注中心的否定信息加以肯定,实际是总结,然后引出进一步的说明;yes 对前一关注中心的肯定信息加以肯定和总结,然后也引出进一步的阐述。和对话中的功能虽有联系,但在叙事语篇中 yes/no 有承上启下的功能,总结上文,引出下文。

语言上,语篇推进的困难常常是因为有较长的插入语,有一系列小句、短语、词组或冗长的排句,作者似乎已失去方向,难以为继,不得不回过头来再打量一番,借助 yes/no 加以小结,然后再继续叙述,通常直至交待基本主题的要点为止。

15

英语辅句的动因及其在语篇中的评价功能*

15.1 引　言

本章试图从认知功能的角度对语篇中辅句的动因作一探讨，并对辅句的功能作认知解释，进而从语篇语义学的角度集中讨论辅句在语篇中的评价功能。

15.1.1 各家看法

对于辅句，语言学家已有不少论述（Halliday 1994：95；Fries 1991b：8；Martin & Matthiessen 1997：71）。韩礼德把辅句定义为不表现语气（Mood）+剩余部分（Residue）的小句。辅句体现辅言语功能（minor speech function）。辅言语功能指感叹、呼唤、招呼和惊诧。马丁等持相同观点，说辅句之所以是辅句是因为不能把它们纳入主位、语气和及物性的主要系统。为了叙述的方

* 本章原载《外国语》2007 年第 1 期 26—34 页。

便,弗里斯(Charles C. Fries)在研究广告时用 sentence 而不用 clause,他的定义是:辅句是任何至少不含一个独立小句的、以标点符号标明的句子,如 Air conditioning。虽然弗里斯仍用辅句这一术语,但他的研究范围显然扩大了。

15.1.2 认知功能视角

在叙事语篇中,常常出现不含语气+剩余部分的结构,但其功能并不是感叹、呼唤、招呼和惊诧,如下面的例子:He picked up another slip of paper. *A letter*. 显然句中 *A letter* 并不体现辅言语功能,但在结构上符合 Halliday 的定义,所以我们还是称它为辅句。辅句常为后置,但也可以前置,如:*A four-day trip*. From England you cross to Belgium in just 100 minutes by hydrofoil! You are served ... 辅句既可以体现为名词词组,也可以体现为形容词词组,如:Keep staring at the pen. Web, just keep staring at the tip. You are really doing well. *Outstanding*. 本文要探讨的仅限于体现为名词词组的后置辅句。语料取自 David Baldacci 的 *Last Man Standing*(缩略为 *LMS*)和 Studs Terkel 的 *Working*(缩略为 *Wkg*)。后者是口头语篇的记录,从这里取材可以帮助我们了解辅句在口语中如何起作用。由于辅句只含一个成分,要探讨它的动因、它的功能,我们必须推理,必须了解后台(backstage)、幕后(behind the scene)的认知活动,所以我们以认知语言学的原理作为我们的理论框架。同时,我们必须探讨超越语句的意义,即从语篇意义的角度探讨辅句的功能,所以我们也同时运用功能语言学的语篇语义学的观点。

15.2 辅句的动因

15.2.1 当前语篇空间及其更新

兰艾克指出心理空间对于语篇具有重要意义(Langacker 1991b:97)。

心理空间是观念中的情景,其复杂程度不一,包含一系列成分以及成分间的关系。在语篇展开过程中,由于新的成分和关系的增加,心理空间会被提取、创造和更新。人们在说话或思考时,心理空间不断地被构建和修正。据此,他提出了当前语篇空间(Current Discourse Space,缩称 CDS)的理论。CDS 指语篇展开的某一时刻被视为听说双方共知的成分和关系构成的心理空间,是进行交际的基础。随着语篇的展开,概念结构不断根据语言表达式的语义进行修正。例如,在"If ..., then ..."的结构中,If 小句的语义对随后的概念结构提出要求,也就是说随后的概念结构根据前一小句的语义进行修正。所以语言结构可被视为以某种特定方式修正 CDS 的指令。当我们在某一时刻观察世界的时候,我们只能见到极其有限的部分,好像只能通过一个窗口观察世界,所以我们在概念化或储存记忆的时候,总有一个视窗或者叫观察框架(viewing frame),它限制了我们当前概念化的范围。心理空间的成分和关系在以我们的已有知识组合成一体之后就成了框架。在持续交际的过程中,听说双方都通过协调将注意力集中于某一个个体上。而注意的焦点也在这框架的范围之内,这就产生了注意框架(attentional frame)。注意框架在语音上与语调单位一致,语义上构成某一时刻在头脑中充分活跃的信息,在语法上往往与小句重合,但又不尽如此,有时一个注意框架包含几个小句,有时一个小句可以横跨几个框架。每一个更新当前语篇空间的指令都至少涉及两个注意框架:相当于输入框架(input CDS)的负框架(minus frame),即需要加以更新的框架,和零框架(zero frame),即更新过程创造的框架。还可以有第三个注意框架,即正框架(plus frame),这在零框架需进一步说明时才会出现(Langacker 2001: 163)。我们就根据认知语言学的当前语篇空间和注意框架的理论,探讨英语语篇中辅句的动因。现在让我们回过头来看一看上面提到的实例:

[1] He picked up another slip of paper. *A letter.* (*LMS* p.190)

这是一个包含两个小句的句子,其中一个是辅句。语音上,这个句子分成了两个语调单位,在认知上包含两个注意框架。语言单位的内容取决于前面语篇所生成的心理空间组合,因为小句所提供的信息包含在语篇心理框架之中,也就是说一个小句的意义要联系前句加以理解。因此零框架的意义要以负框架为参照点加以理解。因此,例[1]中的辅句作为图形

(figure),要以前一小句作为背景(ground)加以理解,正如弧线(arc)要以圆(circle)作为背景加以凸出一样。这样,辅句作为图形就获得了概念上的凸显(salience)。体现负框架的前一小句作为指令要求更新,因为 a slip of paper 在当前的语境中信息不足,要求零框架加以具体化,而体现零框架的辅句适应了这一需要,当前语篇空间得以更新,语篇得以进展。在语篇构建的这一阶段,零框架成为注意焦点,理由有三:(1) 与零框架重合的语调单位将语调核心置于框架内的唯一成分上;(2) 完整的名词词组将一个新的成分引进了语篇;(3) 名词词组体现了新信息,不定冠词可以说明。所以,辅句 *A letter* 得到了最大程度的凸显。现在让我们考察零框架与负框架的联系。辅句中体现零框架中成分的"a letter"可以根据一致原则用来连接负框架中的对应成分"a slip of paper"。一致原则说明:在一心理空间指称或描述一个成分的表达式可用以连接另一空间中该成分的对应成分(Fauconnier 1985)。"A slip of paper"之所以是"a letter"的对应成分是因为两者指同一事物。这样,这两个框架就连接了起来,一个成分被投射到了另一个成分上。但是,这并不意味它们具有相同的特征。A slip of paper 只是表明一个事物,而 a letter 则突出这一事物的用途,指它的功能体现。A slip of paper 可以是 a certificate、a warranty、a contract、a permit 等等。A letter 将它具体化,从而更新了 CDS。

15.2.2　零框架成分的附着点

另一个需要考虑的问题是零框架成分的附着点(point of attachment)。在例[1]中,附着点没有表达出来,也就是说是隐性的。这是因为在听说双方的脑子里可以毫不费力加以构建的成分往往被略去。但是这附着点必须从语境和背景知识中加以推断。语料说明,在辅句体现的框架中,隐性附着点通常由处于高认知状态的指称表达式体现,如 it、that、this。贡德尔等提出了六个等级的认知状态,与英语的指称表达式对应(Gundel et al. 1993):

In focus [it] > activated [that, this] > familiar [that N] > uniquely identifiable [the N] > referential [this N] > type identifiable [a N]

在例[1]中,在作者和读者头脑中出现的是 it。如上表所示,it 具有最高的认知状态。假如我们把这个隐性的附着点明晰地表示出来,并将零框架中的唯一成分与它联系起来,那么体现这一概念结构的语言结构可以是: It is a letter。但是认知语法认为,在这一语言结构中,it 作为图形被凸出,而 letter 则处于次凸显的地位。这与说话人的意图和更新当前语篇空间的需要都不符合,所以不能成为零框架的语言体现形式。现在让我们再看一例:

[2] We always saw signs of physical afflictions because of stress and strain. *Ulcers*, *headaches*. (*Wkg* p.534)

上句中包含两个小句的负框架要求更新 CDS,原因之一是"physical afflictions"所体现的成分需要进一步说明,零框架适应了这一要求,通过实例使它具体化。辅句的理解必须以前句为参照点,这就使得辅句成为图形而被凸出。零框架中的成分在负框架中有可及的对应的成分,两者都表示不良体征,通过部分与整体的关系连接了起来,两个框架以及体现两个框架的语言结构也联系了起来。零框架中的附着点听说双方无需太多的推理即可了解,也是处于高认知状态的指称表达式: they。

综上所述,辅句的出现是说话人为了给予辅句中的成分以充分的凸显,以更新 CDS,推进语篇展开。而辅句的使用有两个制约条件: (1) 这一成分在负框架中具有相当可及性的对应成分;(2) 附着点可以容易地从语境中加以推断,并由处于高认知状态的指称表达式体现。

15.3 辅句的评价功能

15.3.1 说　明

为了了解辅句在语篇中的评价功能,我们需要进一步考察体现零框架的辅句和体现负框架的前句或前一语段之间的语义关系。

[3] You have your comptroller who is highly specialized. You have your treasurer who has to know finance, ... You have manufacturing area. He has to be highly specialized in warehouse and in shipping ... You have to know marketing, the studies, the effect of advertising. *A world of specialists*. (*Wkg* p.538)

与例[1]、[2]不同,零框架中的成分不是与负框架中相应的某一个成分连接,而是依靠部分和整体的关系与多个本来隐含经过整合后明确的成分相接,两个框架因而连接起来。辅句总结了前面的叙述。不算关系从句,负框架包含了五个小句。其中虽出现了 comptroller、treasurer 专业职务名称,但语句仍以动词说明有关人员必须分别具有财务、制造、物流、营销和促销的专业知识,因此,"has to be/is highly specialized""has/have to know"各出现 2 次。而且,第 1、2 两句中的 you 和第 5 句的 you 所指不同,第 4 句的 His 指称不清,文中并无先行词。所以读者必须推理,更需要整合,数个领域需要整合,不同领域中的专业人员也需要整合,整合的过程伴以动词的名词化,"A world of specialists"便是整合的结果。负框架内容繁多,需要零框架加以总结。零框架满足了要求,更新了 CDS。再看下一例:

[4] She felt his hand wrap her neck. His hand was gloved, which surprised her until she thought of fingerprints and DNA that machines could detect off of corpses. *Her corpse*! This thought made her feel faint. (*LMS* p.440)

此例中我们可以见到从 corpses 到 her corpse,也就是从一般到个别的迁移。零框架中的成分可以与负框架的 corpses 相连接,两个框架也根据类比原则联系起来。这类比投射提示了两个输入空间(input space)(Fauconnier 2003),即含 corpses 的空间和含 my corpse 的空间。前者是使用侦查手段侦破犯罪嫌疑人的事实空间,后者是害怕不测的想象空间,两者通过 corpse 的相互投射而进入类属空间(generic space)。同时,从前一个输入空间,我们可以提取从尸体上获得指纹和 DNA,从而获得侦破犯罪嫌疑人的信息,从第二个输入空间我们可以提取一只戴手套的手掐在她的脖子上的信息,这只手之所以戴手套是为了避免留下指纹和 DNA,凶手因而可以逍遥法外。这样,经概念整合成合成空间(blended space),就生成了新生结构(emergent structure):她害怕将被杀害;凶手戴了手套,不会在她的尸体上留下指纹,所以她必死无疑。对辅句的这一理解得到正框架的支持:这一恐惧心理已经使她感到昏厥。正框架执行了辅句的指令,更新了 CDS。同样的分析也适用于下例:

[5] There were old and useless schoolbooks, journals that had nothing in them but stupid pictures by bored hands. *His bored hands*. (*LMS* p.178)

原句中 his 为斜体,这说明叙事人有意突出辅句,使 bored hands 具体化。以上五例中辅句都以不同的语义功能,对前一句或语段加以说明。

15.3.2 评 价

下面让我们看一看辅句如何对前面的句子或语段的内容进行评价。

[6] He had driven past the entrance to the Southern Belle farm ... He thought he could see a man patrolling near the entrance, but he wasn't certain of that or whether the man was armed. *An interesting place*. (*LMS* p.350)

零框架中的成分在负框架中找到了相应的成分:farm,两个框架根据一致原则相互连接。辅句对叙事人刚见到过的农场作了评述,农场之所以使他感到有兴趣是因为他见到农场有人巡逻,而此人可能持有武器,虽然他对此并无把握。Interesting place 可分隔(partitioning)(Fauconnier 1994:24)为两个心理空间,一个输入空间含 farm,另一个输入空间含 interesting place,因为同指一个农场,两个输入空间可进入类属空间。在概念整合过程中,patrolling 与我们长期记忆的知识中 farm 的意义不协调,所以整合空间生成新生概念:unusual,或 somewhat unusual。辅句的评价功能主要体现在重读的形容词 interesting 上。

[7] She was also tall and carried herself erect. *The horse rider's posture*, Web assumed. (*LMS* p.303)

辅句中的名词词组是一个概念合成的表达,具有双重意义。这合成概念意味一个空间网络，其中两个输入空间相互投射，进入"horse rider"的类属空间。这两个输入空间不是对称的：一个是指称性的指称空间；另一个是表述性的表述空间（Brandt 2003）。前者含 she，后者含"ideal horse rider"的概念，语言上有 the 体现。在整合空间就 posture 而言，the horse rider 体现的成分被投射到 she 所体现的成分上，由于 tall、erect 与我们世界知识中的理想骑手的特征对应，这样就生成了新生结构：her posture on horseback is the horse rider's posture.因此，辅句是对"她"骑马姿势的肯定评价。

[8] All she could think of was that Web was alive and her son was dead. *Some hero*.（*LMS* p.579）

这里我们也必须对辅句的信息加以分隔，同样成为两个不对称的输入空间，指称框架中含"Web as hero"；表述空间含我们世界知识中的"real hero"的概念。从指称空间我们提取"Web was alive and her son was dead"，从表述空间我们可以从我们的知识和经验中提取诸如见义勇为、视死如归、杀身成仁、舍己救人等信息。在合成空间中，当一个空间成分被投射到另一个空间成分上时，我们发现两者不匹配，孩子死了，而 Web 活着，形成了对照，所以就生成了 Web 是 no-hero 的新生概念。字面是 hero，而实际是指 no-hero，可见辅句是对 Web 的讽刺，是一种否定评价。辅句的语义因为修饰语 some 而变得更为复杂。Some 可以理解为"to a certain extent"。如果这样理解，辅句的讽刺意义就有所减弱；如果理解为 remarkable、striking，那辅句的讽刺意义就更强。同样的分析适用于下面一例。

[9] David Canfield had stared at Web with an expression that the man would never forget. It was as though the boy had put all his faith in Web, his touchstone against all the madness, and Web had let him down. *Thumps-up*.（*LMS* p.455）

Thumps-up 是表示赞许的手势，但是负框架中的"let him down"并不指望零框架有赞许的意义，相反要求零框架予以指责。含 David 的输入框架和含 Web 的输入框架一方面由于处于同一危险境地而进入类属框架，另一方面经过信息选择，David 对 Web 的急切期望与 Web 使他失望的局面形成对比，合成空间合乎逻辑地生成出 thumps-down 的信息。字面为 thumps-up，实义是 thumps-down，可见辅句是讽刺性的否定评价。

[10] Romano would make an interesting case study. I identified five major psychoses ... And he's also intelligent, sensitive, deeply emotional, incredibly independent but amazingly loyal. *Quite a smorgasboard*. (*LMS* p.408)

文中 Romano 精神状态和心理素质都极其复杂，难以加以刻画。叙事人借用瑞典语中的 smorgasboard 加以总结和评价。Smorgasboard 的意思是"a meal with a variety of dishes from a buffet"，用于事物时，指"a number of things that are combined together as a whole"。这儿源域的 smorgasboard 被投射到精神状态极其复杂的目的域 Romano 的身上(Lakoff 1993)，它们之间的对应特征是整体包含若干部分，Romano 的每一个精神因素或心理特征被比喻为一道菜或一件东西，所以这是一个隐喻性的评价。这里需要说明，这些例证是从笔者个人搜集的语料中挑选的，选择的唯一考虑是要求短小精炼，不至于占太大篇幅。只是在逐句分析之后才发现这几例的辅句都含转义评价，但情况并不总是如此。下例中的 *The ultimate cookie* 就是含直义评价的辅句。

[11] I'm writing a few million lines of code that will take cookies to a new level taking out the bad stuff and making them a lot more useful. And maybe I'll make myself a few million bucks in the process. *The ultimate cookie*. (*LMS* p.464)

辅句中的 cookie 的意思是"网络跟踪器"。辅句与前句中的成分没有联系，却与它前一句中的成分"a few million lines of code"有联系。这说明负框架跨越了句子界限包含了由数个小句组成的语段，体现为一个有结构层次的语段单位 span(Mann 1987)。辅句是对整个语段的总结(summary)，起语段新信息(hyper-new)(Martin 1992：453)的功能。从评价理论的角度看，"a few million lines""new level taking out the bad stuff""a lot more useful"都是积极评价，这一系列积极评价词语构成了这一语段的评价"韵律"(prosody)(Martin & Rose 2003：51)。而获得凸显的辅句使这评价韵律达到顶点。辅句不仅总结前文，而且作了极高的评价。

Ultimate 的意思是 most important and powerful,说明软件是终极成果,是极品。例[11]整个语段的目的是为了说服听话人,辅句在实现这一语篇目的中起了积极的作用,结果 Web 被说服了。这正是作为零框架的辅句对随后的正框架的语篇期待(discourse expectations)(Langacker 2001:151)。请看:

[11a] The admiration was clear on Web's features. "Okay, you convinced me you know computers." (*LMS* p.464)

从上面的实例分析可以看出,第[1]至[5]例中,辅句对前句或句段作了各种说明;第[6]至[11]中,辅句对前句或句段作了不同的评价。下面我们就辅句的评价意义和评价维度作一探讨。

15.4 评价维度

15.4.1 身份转变

在前五例中,辅句分别以具体说明(specification)([1])、举例说明(exemplification)([2])、从个别到一般的总结(generalization)([3])和从一般到个别的个别化(particularization)([4]、[5])说明前句或句段的内容。体现零框架的辅句中的成分在前句或前语段体现的负框架中可以找到具有可及性的相应成分;零框架与负框架借助一致原则、类推原则和个别与一般的关系联系了起来,从而更新了 CDS。值得注意的是,叙事人在表述辅句内容的时候总会改变角色,从记录者转变为解释者,从客观介绍,到主观解释。*A letter*、*ulcers and headaches*、*a world of specialists*、*her corpse*、*his bored hands* 都是叙事人就前句内容向读者进行解释。从例[6]至[11],辅句对前句或句段进行评价,叙事人经历另一种角色转变,从解释者转为评价者,或对人的行为作判断(judgement),如[7]至[10],或对事物作鉴别(appreciation)如[6]、[11]。不难发现作为评价性的辅句往往具有隐喻性,具体地说,有委婉语([6])、类比([7])、反说([8]、[9])、隐喻([10])。这是因为叙事人有意避免唐突和直白的否定评价。由于辅句具有隐含意义,在构建辅句意义的时候,我们必须利用概念合成,通过输入空间成分的相互投射,进入类属空间,再将心理空间与世界知识联系起来,检验合成空间的结构是否与长期记忆相符,从而得到新生结构,即辅句的意义。

15.4.2 人际功能

无论是作为解释还是评价,辅句都体现了语篇的人际功能,体现了语篇的对话性。那么叙事人对辅句的内容可有什么态度?或者说在哪些评价维度上表明了态度?

莱姆克指出,我们不仅针对实际或潜在的受话人通过语言确定我们的取向,而且我们还对我们语篇的概念或命题内容采取某种态度(Lemke 1998)。不论我们对于世界想说些什么,我们在同一话语中还告诉别人在多大程度上我们相信我们所说的内容是可能的、可取的、重要的、容许的、意外的、严肃的或可理解的。这样,就对命题或提议作了不同维度的评价。莱姆克归纳了七种评价维度,即有理性(warrantability)、经常性(usuality)、规范性(normativity)、可取性(desirability)、重要性(importance)、严肃性(seriousness)和可理解性(comprehensibility)。前四种与韩礼德的概率(probability)、频率(usuality)、义务(obligation)、意愿(inclination)对应,不同之处在于韩礼德包括概率和频率的情态着眼于人际功能,而莱姆克则认为即使是主要体现概念功能的语句也有说话人的某种态度,情态只是表达评价维度的一种方式,有理性和经常性包括韩礼德的人际语法隐喻和其他评价词语(evaluator),如在一定的语句里 show 体现有理性,与概念意义重合的 riches 体现可取性,excesses 体现否定可取性。重要性等三种评价维度是较为次要的。

辅句不体现语气+剩余成分结构,即非命题也非提议,无法作语气分析。就辅句单独而言,也无法进行评价意义的分析。但是辅句不是孤立的,不在语篇里就不成其为句。福柯涅指出,单句并不是作为自给自足和承载意义的形式加以研究,而是作为整个语义构建过程中的步骤加以探讨(Fauconnier 1994：14)。本文对辅句的探讨就基于这一理念。上面第二节的分析说明辅句与前句是密切联系的。既然联系前句可以确定辅句的意义和功能,那我们就可对体现零框架的辅句中的成分与体现负框架的前句中相应成分的联系,以及由此获得的辅句的解释和评价意义进行分析。这是因为解释和评价是一种隐含的命题(implied proposition),叙事人在作解释和评价的时候,会就解释和评价的内容是否需要、可能、恰当、可取等等有某种态度。在语篇中,评价维度往往由词、词组、小句结构加以体现,如今辅句缺乏体现评价维度的词语,但是由于辅句与前句确立了联系,前句中说明相应成分的词语可以参考。

15.4.3 解释的维度分析

那么在辅句中,叙事人在什么维度上表达其态度意义呢？现以例[1]为例说明。前句有"A slip of paper",辅句中有"a letter",后者对前者作具体说明,即 specialize,将两个成分根据说明与被说明的关系联系起来,我们就得到了["A slip of paper" is specialized as "a letter"]的命题及其语言表达,对此我们可以进行分析。这虽然是通过推理获得的语用意义或隐含命题,但从其中却可以分析出叙事人的态度。既然"a slip of paper"意义过于笼统,负框架要求零框架对当前语篇空间予以更新,那么,用 a letter 加以具体说明就是必要的。用弗朗西斯的测试框架" It is (Degree) [Attribute：evaluative] that [proposition/proposal]"(Francis 1995)加以检验,可以看出规范性是这一解释命题的评价维度：It is *necessary* that "a slip of paper" should be specialized as "a letter"。或者 It is *necessary* for "a slip of paper" to be specialized as "a letter"或"A slip of paper" should be specialized as "a letter"。*necessary*, *should* 都属于规范性维度的评价词语。

同样,对于例[2],我们可以说：It is *necessary* that "physical afflictions" should be exemplified with "ulcers and headaches"。莱姆克指出不同评价维度是可以重叠的。这儿如果我们深究这个解释命题的意义,那我们可以发现 physical afflictions 可以是 ulcers、headaches,也可以是其他症状,如 constipation、insomnia。这样,就出现了这些症状的可能性。

用上面的框架检验：It is probable/likely that physical afflictions are ulcers, headaches. 或者 Physical afflictions can be ulcers, headaches. 辅句中 ulcers、headaches 之间没有 and，说明后面还可能举其他病症为例。*probable/likely*、*can* 是有理性的评价词语。这样看，例[2]同时又是在有理性的维度上对解释内容表示态度。

例[3]的情况比较复杂，要求我们先将动词词组名词化为 specialists，再整合部门，得出 specialists in various departments，辅句的成分与此联系，对此加以总结。前文五个小句，不便于记忆，因而也不利于语篇展开，所以要求负框架对这内容加以归纳。所以就有了 It is necessary to wrap up the whole situation as "a world of specialists"。与[1]、[2]一样，评价维度是规范性。前面提到过，这一例中的解释含有评价意义：a world of 并不是前文的内容，而是叙事人主观的评价。这样一看，除规范性的维度外，评价还涉及可取与否，即 It is desirable to wrap up the whole situation as "a world of specialists"。这是在可取性维度上对解释命题的评价。

第[4]、[5]例中，辅句成分是对相应成分作个别对一般的说明，与例[1]相仿，解释的意义是 It is necessary to say "her corpse"/his hand。还可以有另一种解读：叙事人在用了 corpses、hands 之后，发现自己没有说明白，于是赶紧更改，就像在老派英国作家习惯用的 I must hasten to add 之类的插入语之后加上了 I must be more precise and say："her corpse"/"his bored hand"。这一解读也要求将 corpses/bored hands 改为 her corpse/his bored hand。这样，还是在规范性的维度上评价命题意义。辅句用作解释时，评价维度的顺序是：规范性、可取性、有理性，其中规范性是主要的维度。

15.4.4 评价的维度分析

我们再来看辅句作评价时的评价维度。例[6]中的辅句 An interesting place 对前句的 farm 作评价。上面说过，interesting 暗含 unusual，因为叙事人见到 a man patrolling near the entrance。叙事人据此作出评价：I think the farm is an interesting/unusual place. I think 是人际语法隐喻，这句相当于 The farm is probably an interesting/unusual place。*I think*、*probably* 是

有理性评价词语,因此叙事人是在有理性维度上作评价。评价维度具有归一性,unusual 是否定的经常性维度。Unusual 引发"It is unusual that there should be a man patrolling on a farm"。因此,例[6]还在否定经常性的维度上评价辅句的隐含命题。

例[7]中,评价命题的意义是:叙事人借人物之口说明"I assumed that her posture on horseback could be compared to the horse rider's posture"。前文的 tall、erect 可以作为这一比较的语言依据。*I assumed*、*could* 是有理性评价词语,因此,例[7]的评价维度也是有理性。但是 could 也可以理解为提出建议(Sinclair 1990: 232),那样评价的维度就是可取性,我们可以说:It is desirable to compare her posture on horseback to the horse rider's.

例[8]的辅句 some hero 说明前句的人物 Web。意义是:I thought he was a hero/no hero 或 He was probably a hero/no hero 或 He might be a hero/no hero。用检验框架检验有理性:It was probable that he was a hero,或否定有理性:It was doubtful if he was a hero.

例[9]表示反语的辅句也可以这样分析,都是在有理性/否定有理性的维度上对辅句评价的内容加以评价。例[10]的辅句是隐喻,更是说话人的认知活动的结果。其意义是:I think Romano can be compared to a smorgasboard,评价维度是有理性。同样的分析也适用于[11]。辅句用作评价时,评价维度往往是有理性,在转义的情况下,如反语,否定有理性与有理性重叠。但是和[7]一样,随后五句我们也可以用 could:He could be a hero/We could give him a thumps-up/Romano could be a smorgasboard. 这样命题就成了提议,评价的维度则是可取性。

对辅句隐含命题分析可以在翻译时得到应用和检验。比如[1]至[5]的辅句隐含命题主要是在规范性维度上进行评价,所以这几句的意思里含"当"(It is necessary to say ...):如[4]的辅句可译为"当是她的尸体";[5]的辅句则为"当是他那闲得无聊的手"。[6]至[11]的辅句的隐含命题主要是在有理性维度上表示态度,所以几句的意义含"可"(It is probable to say ...):[6]的辅句可译为"可算得上职业骑手的姿势";[7]的辅句为"可谓英雄"。当然同时体现其他维度的辅句,意义就可以不同,如[2]可以译为"如溃疡、头痛"。

15.5 结 语

使用辅句的动因是为了给它以最大程度的凸显,以便它说明前文,有时为后语作准备。从语篇的角度看,辅句是谋篇的需要。这是它的语篇功能。

辅句对前句相应成分具有说明和评价的功能。这是辅句的人际功能。结合前句的有关成分和辅句对前句的功能,我们可以对辅句的隐含命题作评价维度的分析,从而可以了解叙事人对命题可能具有的态度。当辅句作说明时,叙事人主要在规范性评价维度上表示态度,说明需要;当辅句作评价时,叙事人主要在有理性维度上表示态度,说明可能。我们的分析说明辅句是一个评价手段,一种评价资源。

辅句是一种特殊结构,例如辅句"A letter"不能为"It is a letter"所替代。这是因为:(1)"It is a letter"中的 letter 不能像辅句"A letter"那样被最大限度地突出;(2) It is a letter 只能是叙述的继续,主要体现概念功能,不可能像辅句 A letter 那样,随叙事人角色改变,起解释的作用,主要体现人际功能;(3) 与此有联系的是,辅句是评价手段,而 It is a letter 则不是;(4) 辅句可以通过与前句联系在隐含命题中体现某种评价维度,表示态度意义,而 It is a letter 一般不体现评价意义。所以,有些语法学家(如 Quirk et al. 1985)把辅句看成是省略句,值得商榷。

第四部分

语 篇 与 认 知

Part Four

DISCOURSE AND COGNITION

16

概念隐喻与语篇

——对体现概念隐喻的语篇的多维分析*

16.1 引 言

16.1.1 隐喻及其语言体现

雷考夫指出,概念隐喻是我们对世界加以概念化的一个主要的、必不可少、习以为常的方法(Lakoff 1993: 204)。概念隐喻指概念系统中跨领域的投射,是用一种迥然不同领域的经验理解另一领域的经验。要表达抽象概念和复杂事物,人们通常使用表达具体经验时所使用的语言和概念。一旦我们离开具体经验的话题,开始谈论抽象概念和情感时,我们总是采用隐喻理解(Lakoff 1993: 205)。隐喻的中心是思维,可以在语言组织的各个层次上体现,可以体现为单词、词组、句子,也可以体现为语篇(Koller 2003)。体现为语篇时,可以是小说,见第17、19章,或散文,见第18章,或短篇小说,见第20章,也可以是诗歌。本章拟根据隐喻理论、功能语法和评价理论对体现概念隐喻的两则诗歌语篇作一探讨,试图回答

* 本章原载《外语教学与研究》2008年第3期83—92页。

以下两个相互联系的问题：根据什么说一则语篇体现了隐喻？语篇体现的隐喻又有哪些特征？我们先从认知的角度对体现概念隐喻的语篇作隐喻分析，然后再对语篇作语言分析，以验证隐喻分析的结果，揭示概念隐喻的本质属性。

16.1.2 语料——两首诗

我们采用的语料是朱熹的一首古诗和美国诗人狄金森（Emily Dickinson）的一首英诗：

观 书 有 感

半亩方塘一鉴开，
天光云影共徘徊。
问渠那得清如许？
为有源头活水来。

［宋］朱 熹

He Ate and Drank the Precious Words

He ate and drank the precious Words —
His Spirit grew robust —
He knew no more that he was poor,
Nor that his frame was Dust —

He danced the dingy Days
And this Bequest of Wings
Was but a Book — What Liberty
A loosened spirit brings —

（Emily Dickinson）

16.1.3 体 现

对于“体现”需略加说明。首先我们要区分隐喻和隐喻表达式。隐喻是概念系统中跨领域的投射,隐喻表达式(metaphorical expression)则指语言表达式:一个词、短语或句子,也就是跨领域投射的表层体现(surface realization)。这里"体现"是指以词汇语法表达意义。但是,并不是以语法词汇对应地体现意义,语言表达式是从概念隐语衍生出来的,概念隐喻为理解这词句提供推理的前提和基础。譬如,"We are at a crossroad"是隐喻表达式,它从"Love Is A Journey"的概念隐喻衍生出来,后者为前者提供推理的基础。其次,语篇体现概念隐喻与词、短语或句子体现概念隐喻完全不同。兰艾克说,"认知语法把意义和概念化在其最广泛的意义上等同起来"(Langacker 1991b:278),因此概念隐喻是语义层的范畴。语篇是语义单位,当然也属语义层。当概念隐喻体现为语篇时,并不是用词汇语法表现语义的体现,而是语篇对概念隐喻的实例化(instantiation),也就是在语义系统中由语篇将概念隐喻具体化。韩礼德和马蒂森指出,"实例化指在总的语义系统中从语义潜势到一特定语篇实例的转移"(Halliday & Matthiessen 1999:14)。概念隐喻是以具体经验理解抽象经验的方法,是经验语义系统中的一种语义潜势,如"Life Is A Journey"这一概念隐喻是诠释 life 的一种语义资源。它不是命题,只是概念隐喻的名称(Lakoff 1993:207),在被实例化之前,它没有进入语境,所以是语义潜势,可以加以具体化。为了叙述的方便,我们仍沿用"体现",意指"以实例体现"。

16.2 隐喻分析

16.2.1 隐喻背景

隐喻可以理解为从源域到目的域的投射。在"Life Is A Twitch"的概念隐喻中,twitch 是源域,life 是目的域。叙事人用人们可以直觉到的无法控制的抽搐说明世事无常,人生难料。上面两首诗体现了两个概念隐喻,朱诗的隐喻是读书是池塘映景;狄诗的概念隐喻则是"Reading a Book Is Eating and Drinking"(读书是饮食)。值得注意的是并非任何认知域都可以投射到任何另一个认知域上。投射要遵循一个原则,这个原则被雷考夫通俗地称为隐喻背景(metaphorical scenario)(Lakoff 1993:206)。它为隐喻提供理据,是投射得以成立的推理基础。朱诗的隐喻背景是:读者的心境被视为反映景色的池塘,这池塘犹如刚刚打开的镜子,一尘不染,清澈见底,映出天光和云影。书被视为宝库,提供知识和智慧。读者读书全神贯注,心静神定,因而可以汲取知识和智慧,从而增进读者的才智和德行。扼要地说:池塘水清映景,读书心定有得。狄诗的隐喻背景是:Food provides nourishment. Nourishment is necessary for one's life, growth and health. One eats to get nourishment so that one lives and works well. A book is a treasure house, which provides knowledge and wisdom. Knowledge and wisdom are necessary for one's intellectual and spiritual life. One reads to learn knowledge and obtain wisdom so that one's intellectual horizon is broadened and one's spiritual life enriched. 扼要地说:饮食维持生命,读书涵养精神。隐喻背景提示了作者借助隐喻进行形象推理(imaginative reasoning)的路径,说明投射具备了隐喻理据,概念隐喻可以成立。那么,语篇究竟怎样体现概念隐喻呢?下面进行具体分析。

16.2.2 目的域

隐喻是源域向目的域的投射,所以体现隐喻的语篇必须交待两个认知域。朱诗共四行,前两行为境句,写景;后两行为意句,在写景的基础上传意。这是隐喻的源域,诗人描写静中有动的景色,但在诗中并没有暗示他以此要说明什么。标题"观书有感"作了交待:朱熹以观景的具体经验诠释抽象的读书要旨。读书就是目的域。没有目的域就不存在源域向目的域的投射,就不成其为隐喻,也谈不上对隐喻的体现。本文讨论的这首狄诗在第一句就交待了目的域——读书,这也是用首行作为标题的原因。语篇的首行往往是语篇的宏观主位(见16.3.3)。与其他语篇一样,隐喻语篇的标题往往表达语篇的宏观结构,说明语篇的主旨,其组篇功能也源于此。总之,语篇体现隐喻就要交待目的域。

16.2.3 本体对应

隐喻基于源域和目的域的对应,而且是一系列概念的对应。雷考夫指出,投射是一套本体对应,通过将一个认知域的知识投射到另一个认知域上,从而上升为认识上的对应(Lakoff 1993: 207)。恒定原则(Invariance Principle)说明:隐喻投射保持源域的认知本体,也就是形象图式结构(image-schema structure),并以某种方式与目的域的内在结构相一致(同上: 215)。形象图式结构并非是人们需要时在脑海里唤起的具体图画,而是基于身体经验,在更为概括、抽象层次上构成概念体系的结构。比如我们使用方位隐喻时,我们依靠形象图式(Brown 2003: 3)。上下左右已不是具体图画,而是抽象了的概念。这正说明概念隐喻是一种概念上的概括。以我们的材料说明,朱诗中的"池塘映景"作为源域是一个抽象化了的形象图式,"池塘"不必是具体的"半亩方塘",但在与"读书"对应时,池塘的本体特征必须保持,如池塘有水,能够反映景物等。至于如何与"读书"对应,要看作者侧重什么,赋予"读书"怎样的内在结构;也要看读者在想到"读书"时,对"池塘映景"有怎样的情绪、感情和认识。

在朱诗中我们看到以下对应:

表 16-1 源域目的域对应表

源 域	目的域
池塘映景	读书
池塘	心境
天光	启迪人的智慧
云影	现象和常识
徘徊	反复出现
(水)清	(心)定
源头活水	勤读而得的新知识
来	得

狄诗中的隐喻对应:

eating and drinking	reading
food	precious Words
Dust	a miserable condition
danced	being ecstatic
Bequest of Wings	a Book
Liberty	ecstasy
loosened spirit	liberated person

这说明两则体现隐喻的语篇中确实存在一组概念对应。但是,这两组对应的内容有明显的不同:朱诗目的域中的概念都表示读者的心态或书的内容;狄诗目的域的概念皆是指人或人的精神状态。这说明两位诗人对读书这一复杂过程的侧重点不同,因而赋予目的域以不同的内在结构。朱诗重读书的心态,狄诗重读书的效用,所以源域的认知本体特征以上述方式与各自目的域的内在结构相一致。

我们还可以看到有些在源域中用于常规意义的词语在目的域中就不一定如此。比如狄诗中的"the bequest of wings",在常规意义中 wing 并不用于指书,但在目的域中由于"Reading is Eating and Drinking"的投射,它获得了延伸意义。概念隐喻将用于对"饮食"进行推理的知识用于对"读书"进行推理,将"饮食"的效用应用于"读书",同样,将 wings 的效用应用于 a book,这就赋予了 wings 以延伸意义或隐喻意义。隐喻往往带有心理形象(mental image)。如 wings 就是一个心理形象,我们对这一心理形象的部分知识是 wings 是飞行器官,可以使生物或物器飞翔。这就帮助我们理解 wing 用于 book 时可能有的延伸意义。再如在"池塘映景"中,"池塘"是一个心理形象,我们对它的部分知识是:池塘水清映景,池塘水浊则不能映景。概念隐喻"读书是池塘映景"把关于这一心理形象的知识用于"读书",以说明读书时心境的重要。

16.2.4 投射范围

既然语篇体现隐喻,那我们有理由指望隐喻贯穿整个语篇,在语篇的每个部分都有体现。在朱诗中源域和目的域的概念对应贯彻始终。

从内容和形式看,语篇用池塘映景表现了读书的整个过程:"一鉴开"暗示开卷、"天光、云影"表示阅读内容,第三行提问提示求解,第四行的解答说明得益。开卷、阅读、求解和得益构成了读书的全部过程,所以在语篇的每个部分隐喻都有体现。狄诗的情况有所不同。它以概念隐喻开头,作为全诗的出发点。但是它不关注读书的过程,而是关注读书对于读者的效果,所以第一节的其余三行皆描述读书在 He 身上产生的奇效,是读书的延伸。第二节中主要的隐语是"Wings are a Book",其余三行则是读书带来的精神愉悦,也是诗人想象中读书过程的延伸。关键是第二节的隐喻与第一节的隐喻有怎样的联系。语篇中出现的这两个隐喻并不是相互割裂的,而是以等级层次结构加以组织的,其中低层次投射继承高层次投射的结构,雷考夫把这种层次结构叫做继承层次结构(Inheritance hierarchies)(Lakoff 1993: 222)。从下面的隐喻推理中,我们可以看出两个隐喻的关系: Reading is Eating and Drinking. Food provides nourishment/Reading provides knowledge and wisdom. Nourishment keeps one alive and healthy/Knowledge and wisdom make one knowledgeable and wise, which makes one free from earthly cares and worries and therefore happy. When one is happy one is in high spirits and therefore is seen on the wing of freedom. So it is a Book that gives wings to the reader. 可见,"Wings are a Book"这一隐喻在等级层次结构中从属于"Reading is Eating and Drinking"这个主要隐喻,是它的衍生隐喻,用以说明读书的效果。所以读书是饮食这一隐喻支配了整个语篇。从另一个角度看,整个语篇体现了概念隐喻。

16.2.5 中心思想

概念对应使我们能用一个概念理解另一概念的某个方面,但同时又要求我们将该概念的其他方面掩盖起来。这说明隐喻总是要根据说明目的域某一方面的需要凸出源域概念的某一方面。在我们讨论的两个隐喻中,目的域都是读书,但读书看似简单,却是一个复杂的智力活动,涉及读者的目的、读书的心态、书的选择和读书的方法;还涉及书的内容、可能产生的效果,以及作者的直接目的,是传授知识、晓人以理或者是进行劝说,其信仰体系、哲学观和世界观如何,等等,有关读书的隐喻只能借助源域凸出其中一个方面。究竟诗人要凸出哪个方面要看诗人具有怎样的态度、观点和信念。我们先来看朱熹(1130—1200)。他是宋代的哲学家和教育家。他继承二程思想,又独立发挥,形成了自己的体系,后人称为程朱理学。他提出"格物致知"说,认为应该从考察客观事物求得认识。他提出"居敬穷理",居敬是指心的专一,不受外物的牵累,穷理是指穷尽万物的道理,所以既是修身,也是治学的方法和原则。关于读书,他主张"为学之道,莫先于穷理,穷理之要,必在读书"。所以读书有正心和求知双重目的。据此,我们可以看出朱熹借助池塘映景说明读书必须心定。而以源头活水说明若要心定,必须持之以恒、勤读精思。所以朱熹在隐喻中所凸出的是读书正心、穷理的哲学要旨。再看狄金森(1830—1886)。表面上她的一生可谓平淡,生命的最后 25 年她过着离群索居、与世隔绝的生活。她从未结婚,但先后与几名男子由于学识志趣相投建立了较为密切的友谊。她留给后人 1 775 首诗,其在世时只发表了六七首。她生活简单,但却生活在沉思和遐想中。近来她被视为具有哲理性的悲剧性诗人(Gottesman 1979: 2350)。这可以从她的编号为 1755 的诗中看出:

> To make a prairie it takes a clover and a bee/One clover and a bee/And reverie/The reverie alone will do/if bees are few.

凭借幻想即使没有蜜蜂和红花草丛也可以让广袤的草原出现。这说明想象对于诗人的重要。更为明显的是她的编号为 632 的另一首诗:

> The Brain is wider than the Sky —/For — put them side by side —/The one the other will contain/With ease — and you — beside —//The mind is deeper than the sea —/For — hold them — Blue to Blue —/The one the other will absorb —/As Sponges — Buckets — do —/

在她看来心比天大、比海深,可见她对精神世界的专注。由此可以看出狄金森在读书是饮食的隐喻中要突出的是读书的效用,指出读书可以使人从人世间的烦恼中解脱出来,获得精神升华,从而获得近代以来西方哲学宣扬的自由。所以两首诗各有其中心思想。

16.2.6 隐喻体系

16.2.2 节中,系列对应中的每一个对应实际上是一个跨领域的次投射,每一个次投射就是一个次隐喻,所以在语篇体现隐喻时会有一系列的次隐喻,它们围绕隐喻所要传达的中心思想构成一个隐喻体系,共同为体现隐喻、传达隐喻的中心思想服务。比如,朱诗的"池塘如镜",是为了凸出池塘必须清澈才能映景的理念;狄诗中的 Wings are a Book 凸出书或读书的神奇效果,读者如生翅膀,可以展翅翱翔,享受自由。可见,语篇体现概念隐喻需要一个隐喻体系来实现。我们已经看到虽然两则语篇体现了各自的概念隐喻,但两者的隐喻程度并不相同。这就要求我们区分隐喻和非隐喻的概念。这是一个复杂问题,但是从分析的需要出发,我们可以认定,本义就是直义,隐喻意义就是间接意义。前者无须通过隐喻理解(Lakoff 1993: 205),后者的理解要依靠隐喻。我们可以以搭配的选择限制(selective restrictions)为基础判断两者的区分。比如,"He ate and drank the precious Words"中 the precious words 不能与 ate and drank 搭配,这种对搭配限制的违背说明 precious words 是用于隐喻意义,意思是搭配所要求的 food。同样,我们也可以根据 the precious words 的搭配要求,借助隐喻把 ate and drank 理解为 read。有时隐喻概念和非隐喻概念界限模糊。例如朱诗中九个实词: 半亩方田、鉴开、天光、云影、徘徊、清、源头、活水、来,其中"徘徊"与"来"似乎是本意概念,但就局部而言,这两个动词一般用于人,因此就将"天光"和"云影"拟人化了;就总体的隐喻而言,可以理解为读书内容的"反复出现"和阅读所"得"。狄诗中的 spirit 因为与 robust 搭配,可以看成是指人,因此也可看成用于隐喻意义。狄诗与朱诗就实例化而言,不同之处在于: 朱诗是全盘隐喻化,诗中没有出现任何与目的域有关的概念,只字未提读书;而狄诗提到了 Words 和 Book,这说明此诗的隐喻焦点以本义框架为背景,作为隐喻概念形成过程的切入点,语言象征化先于概念象征化。但是,两首诗都体现了概念隐喻。

16.2.7 隐喻推理

概念隐喻使我们将对一个概念进行推理的程式应用到另一个概念

上。这种推理是基于经验的推理。在以饮食理解读书的对应中,因果关系(causation)这一基本概念域在起作用。在人们对世界概念化的过程中,有三个基本结构,因果关系是其中之一,其余两个是时间和空间。我们来具体看看狄诗:推理的内容在隐喻背景中已经说明,即以饮食维持生命,促进健康的经验对读书进行推理,得出拓宽视野、获得自由的结论。现在我们要在概念层面上分析这一推理。贯穿这一推理始终的是变化(change)。变化表现了起因和结果之间的联系,但变化要求某种力量起作用或存在某种先期必要条件。变化也可以概念化为从一个状态到另一个状态的转移。雷考夫和约翰逊认为因果关系必定涉及作用力(agent)和承受者(patient),作用力是能量之源,承受者是能量的目标(Lakoff & Johnson 1980: 70-71)。在狄诗中,作用力是理解为食物的书,承受者是"他"。作用力对承受者所产生的结果是精神方面的,但却显而易见。雷考夫还说因果关系可以视为"接受"(taking)或"给予"(giving),在"他"身上的变化可以视为"拥有"(possession):"他"有了财富和健康,"他"添了翅膀,"他"获得了自由(Lakoff 1993: 225)。这是变化的结果,是读书使得"他"从先前的穷愁潦倒转变到了如今的心旷神怡。再看朱诗:从推理梗概中我们可以看出,将池塘水清才能映景的推理应用于读书,得出心定方能有得的结论。水清如镜是先期必要条件,映出天光云影是结果。同样,心定是条件,获取知识是结果。再进一步,活水是必要条件,水清是结果,同样勤读是必要条件,心定是结果。由此可知,因果关系在朱诗中也是主要的基本概念结构,与狄诗的不同之处在于狄诗的因是一种能量之源,而朱诗的因是一种必要的状态。

16.2.8 隐喻连贯

一个隐喻,如果在展开过程中推理成立,自然就获得连贯。这两首诗所体现的隐喻在因果关系上非常明确,连贯当然不成问题。但是这两个隐喻是创新隐喻(novel metaphor)。雷考夫和约翰逊指出,创新隐喻不是用于构建我们日常概念体系的一部分,而是对于事物的一种新颖的思维方式(Lakoff & Johnson 1980: 53)。而日常隐喻体系对于理解创新隐喻起中心作用。我们需要依靠常规隐喻才能明白创新隐喻的意义。这说明常规隐喻对概念隐喻的连贯至关重要。现在我们就从概念隐喻所涉及的常规隐喻是否前后一致考察隐喻连贯,以狄诗中的概念隐喻为例说明。"Precious Words Are Food"这一隐喻是建立在"Ideas Are Food"的本体隐喻之上,而这个本体隐喻又是建立在"Ideas Are Objects, the Mind Is a Container"的本体隐喻之上,这样便在 Words 和 Food 之间建立了相似性,所以,Words 和 Food 一样可以吞食、消化并提供营养。英语中有弗朗西斯·培根的名言:Some books are to be tasted, others to be swallowed, and some few to be chewed and digested。汉语中有"囫囵吞枣""贪多嚼不烂",虽然侧重点不同,但都是读书是饮食这一概念隐喻的隐喻表达式,都是建立在与读书有关的若干本体隐喻的基础之上。同样,"His spirit grew robust"和"a loosened spirit brings liberty"所隐含的隐喻是建立在"The Spirit Is an Entity"和"The Spirit Is a Person"的本体隐喻基础之上。"This bequest of wings was but a book"所隐含的隐喻是建立在"The Book Is an Entity, A Book Is A Vehicle"的本体隐喻基础之上。由于这些本体隐喻是我们日常概念体系的一部分,我们已习以为常,所以可以保证我们对创新隐喻的理解,成为隐喻连贯的基础。再来看常规隐喻中的方位隐喻。除了首行之外,诗的第一节所渲染的概念意义是 health,当属"Health Is Up"(Lakoff 1993: 15),第二诗节的第一行凸出"Happy Is Up"。其余三行含 wings、liberty。Wings 提示展翅高飞,其乐无穷,所以概念意义也是 Happy Is Up。Liberty 意思是"power or right to decide for oneself what to do, how to live",因而"he has full control of his personal affairs",这就进入了雷考夫所说的"Having Control Is Up"的概念范畴。可见,贯穿狄诗概念隐喻的是 Up 的方位隐喻意义。这与本诗隐喻的中心思想完全一致:uplifting effect of reading books,因而也就促进了隐喻的连贯。可以说概念隐喻的内在逻辑合理性是隐喻连贯的保证,本体隐喻作为理解概念隐喻的依据,是隐喻连贯的基础,方位隐喻的一致则是隐喻连贯的支撑,在概念上使连贯充实。

从以上八个方面所作的隐喻分析,我们看到概念隐喻在语篇中具备怎样的特征。下面我们主要考察隐语推理、隐喻连贯、中心思想以及作者利用隐喻的目的在语篇中的体现。

16.3 语篇分析

16.3.1 语　境

当我们在语言的层面上考察语篇的时候，我们把话语看成是多功能的建构，所以我们要考察与三大元功能对应的三个语义基础（base），即概念基础、互动基础和语篇基础（Halliday & Matthiessen 1999：11）。但是语义是受语境制约的，所以不能不考虑语篇的语境。语篇是在一定语境中发挥功能的语言。隐喻作为语义潜势，它的实例化也首先要求语篇为它提供语境。根据语篇和语境的辩证关系，语境构建语篇；同样，语篇也构建语境（Halliday & Hasan 1985：47）。我们可以作双向推导：从语境推导出语篇，也可以从语篇推导出语境（Halliday & Hasan 1985：36）。就书面语篇而言，总是语篇提供内在的语境。以朱诗为例，这四句诗作为语篇为读者提供了语境，但这首先是本义的语境，但是当目的域明确之后，目的域便为理解语篇提供了隐喻视角，提供了对语篇作隐喻理解的框架，这就使得语篇获得一层隐喻意义。从这隐喻意义中就可以推导出隐喻语篇的语境。既然隐喻是利用源域的经验理解目的域的经验，那么隐喻语境应该是通过对直义语境的理解，借助读者的经验与知识，通过概念整合从隐喻意义中推导出来。韩礼德和马蒂森指出，语篇和语境是一起加以理解的（Halliday & Matthiessen 1999：354）。语境又是基于语篇通过推理构成、存在于语篇之中的，因此，直义和隐喻意义、直义语境和隐喻语境是同时理解的。这样隐喻就被置于一定的语境之中，因而也就被具体化为一则语篇。

16.3.2 及物性

概念基础是我们解释世界经验的资源，既体现我们对经验的一致性（congruent）解释，也体现隐喻性解释（Halliday & Matthissen 1999：365）。我们的世界充满各种过程，所以我们首先看概念基础中的及物性——关于过程的语法。

先看朱诗：第一个小句中含关系过程，原诗中体现为零形式的系动词，将“半亩方塘”与“鉴”联系了起来。就内在的延伸含义（implicative）而言，“塘”指“水”，“鉴”即“镜”，意指“清”，所以是将“水”与“清”联系了起来，赋予“水”以“清”的特征。前小句的语言结构可被视为以某种特定的方式修正当前语篇空间的指令。后小句为更新过程的结果，回应前句的指令。这为小句之间过程的扩展作了认知上的说明。朱诗的第一个小句作为输入框架，要求说明关系过程所表明的状态引起了什么，作为更新当前语篇空间的结果，第二个小句适应了这个要求，说明第一个小句的状态导致了物质过程，而且关系过程凸出的特征恰恰是物质过程所表示的动作的前提。水不明如镜，就不能映景；心不定读书就难有得。第三个小句与第一小句意义相同，以疑问句形式出现，问句要求解答，解答对第一句所表明的状态作进一步的说明。所以第四小句的动作为第三句的状态的特征提供了最终解释。池清是因为源头活水；心定是因为持之以恒的勤读。可见物质过程表明关系过程的结果，而关系过程又为物质过程所解释。过程推进的模式是关系过程+物质过程，说明先期状态引起的结果，这在语言层面上验证了上一节的隐喻推理。

再看狄诗。第一小句含物质过程，由 ate and drank 体现，“动作者”是 He，“目标”却是 the precious Words。我们的世界知识告诉我们 precious Words 是不能饮食的。这里直义和隐喻意义，直义语境和隐喻语境都不仅可以，而且必须同时理解与诠释。第一小句作为输入框架要求第二小句对其动作作出说明，第二小句满足了这一要求，用 grew 体现的关系过程，将 robust 这一特征赋予了载体 His Spirit，表明动作产生了变化。第三、第四行含一个小句复合体，主句含心理过程，由 knew 体现，“体验者”是 he，而他所体验的“现象”却是以 was 体现的两个从句中的关系过程，说明“载体”所处的状态。假如第二小句说明动作产生的精神变化，那随后的小句则说明饮食/读书前后的心理变化、生活变化和健康变化。总体上看，第一诗节中过程推进的模式是物质过程+关系过程，说明动作带来的结果。第一诗节要求第二诗节更新当前语篇空间，而第二诗节用进一步阐述推进语篇。第一小句含物质过程，体现为 danced，但实际上诗人以动作表示“动作者”的快乐心情。“He danced the dingy Days”应理解为“He danced on the dingy Days”。作为及物动词，dance 随后可以跟某种音乐或

"婴儿"之类的词,如 dance waltz 或 dance a baby,无论从逻辑上还是从词义色彩(通常说:优美的音乐、可爱的宝宝)上,也就是无论是用于直义还是隐喻意义,dance 都不能与 dingy Days 搭配。更重要的是,如果是及物动词,dance 只对"目标"产生影响,对"动作者"不产生任何影响,但是作为不及物动词,那 dance 就是作格动词,he 是使动作得以实现的"中介",是直接参与全过程的参加者,dance 就可用以表示"动作者"的快乐心境,与语境相符。介词 on 的省略是英诗抑扬格的要求。所以这个小句暗含 He was ecstatic 的关系过程(见 16.4.1)。第二小句含关系过程,实际上这里有语法隐喻,bequest 暗含 bequeath,小句的意思是"He was given wings by the Book",所以隐含物质过程,是对第一小句的解释。第二小句的 book 与第一节第一小句的 precious words 呼应,都是指读书;而第二节的第一小句实际是对第一小节后三行的小结,说明读书的成效。第二节的第三小句含物质过程,在更高的境界上说明读书的奇效。总体来看,第二节在隐喻意义上仍然是以物质过程说明关系过程所表现的状态,表示前因后果。

16.3.3 宏观主位和宏观新信息

宏观主位预示语篇将如何展开,宏观新信息则提炼语篇积累的新信息。宏观主位通常是语篇的首句,即所谓的主题句;宏观新信息通常处于语篇末尾。朱诗的第一句是语篇的宏观主位,预示了语篇将沿着"池塘水清如镜"展开。我们从这宏观主位可以了解到语篇描述景物,但题目提供的目的域让我们在"读书"的框架里理解这一宏观主位,"池塘水"只能理解为读书人的"心境","清如镜"也只能理解为"明"或"定"。这就使我们知道语篇将围绕这一宏观主位展开。最后一句是宏观新信息,是整个语篇新信息的总结,交待"塘水"为何"清","心"为何"定"。此句是意句,"意句难制"是因为意句传达诗人的主旨:"活水"当指"通过读书源源不断地吸收新知识",而"源头"暗示"本性"。朱熹认为性即理,也就是性本善。但是由于气的问题,即"其气质之禀或不能齐",所以不能保持本性。读书就是为了发现心中之"理",即恢复本性。

狄诗的宏观主位是非常清楚的,我们着重看宏观新信息: What

Liberty/A loosened spirit brings. 作为感叹句的主位 What Liberty 本已凸出。但它是有标记的主位,原本是述位中的新信息却提到句首作为主位,而且它又是信息焦点所在,是有标记的新信息。作为新信息,它总结了语篇的要点。Liberty 意思是 the state of being free,说明读书可以使人摆脱烦恼,获得自由。有两点值得注意。第一,这是本诗唯一使用现在时的小句: brings,从过去时变成了现在时。第二,"他"在新信息中消失了。Bring 这个动词有两种句子结构,我们可以说: Spring brings flowers 或 Spring brings us flowers。狄诗表示新信息的小句用了前者,不含受益者 him。而且 loosened spirit 用了不定冠词 a,自然就不指 he 的 loosened spirit。如果说 him 的省略是抑扬格的需要,那格律就解释不了不定冠词 a 了。一般现在时通常表明在所有时间都适用的状态或动作。主人公的 he 消失说明读书的效用不限于这个别人。这就使语篇的中心思想发生了从个别到一般的变化,宏观新信息在总结通篇新信息的基础上把结论普遍化了。这正是诗人要传达给读者的信息。诗以破折号结束,让读者去品味言犹未尽的蕴涵。

16.4 评价分析

我们现在来探讨互动基础。马丁和怀特指出,在语篇语义学的层面上有三个系统共同表达人际意义,它们是评价(appraisal)、商榷(negotiation)和参与(involvement)(Martin & White 2005: 33)。评价关系到几方面的评价——即语篇中所商榷的各种态度、有关情感的强度以及表明价值和争取读者的各种方式(*ibid.*: 33)。马丁的评价系统中把评价资源分为三个方面: 态度、介入和分级。这个系统特别重视态度中的情感、判定和鉴别。另外两个系统,即商榷和参与都对评价作积极的补充。汤普森指出: 评价是人际意义的一个核心部分,任何对语篇的人际意义的分析都必须考虑评价(Thompson 2000: 65)。从语篇实际使用的评价资源出发,我们集中讨论态度、介入和评价维度。

16.4.1 态 度

态度包括情感的流露、对人的判定和对物的鉴别。朱诗中作者用了"鉴"、"清"和"活",表明对池塘的水的鉴别。这三个词实际表示了同一个特征,那就是"清澈"。马丁和罗斯指出,这种对评价资源韵律式的选择构成作者所持的姿态(stance),即作者对"方塘"和读者心境所持的态度(Martin & Rose 2003: 53)。在"天光"中,"天"并不赋予"光"以任何特征,只是作分类说明,即不同于阳光、月光、灯光等等。但是令人感到奇怪的是为什么这塘水不倒映塘边的花草树木,而映"天光"?按照朱熹天人合一的观点,人的本性来自天理,天理即人性。恢复本性就是保存心中的天理。这里朱熹的"天"之"光",实际是指启迪本性的"理",是助人明理的智慧。假如这个分析合理,那"天"就表示了作者的态度,也就成了评价资源。狄诗中表示态度的评价资源有: precious 对 Words 作鉴别, robust 对 His Spirit 作判定,都是肯定评价;poor 对 he 作判定,dust 对 his frame 作判定,都是否定评价,但分别与否定评价语 no more 和 nor 联系,就成了肯定评价。评价理论认为情感可以是即时的升腾和持续的性情。前者可以用动词,如 He wept 表示;后者用形容词,如 He was sad 表示。狄诗中的 danced 作为过程是对 he 的情感评价,说明 he 快乐。本诗唯一的负面评价语是 dingy,对 Days 作鉴别。上节最后两个小句说明了 he 内在的前后变化,dingy 的评价与 danced 所表现的情绪形成了外部的对照,进一步说明读书带来的快乐: 即使天日阴暗,he 仍快乐起舞。再看 this Bequest of Wings,虽然这个比喻并不对任何词语作评价,只是表示概念意义而已,但是 bequest 总是和贵重的家产相联系,而 Wing 提示展翅高飞,自由翱翔,所以这一比喻性短语不仅回指上句,而且把读书的效用提到更高的境界。But a book 中的 but 属于评价系统中的分级,用以限制,同时又凸出 a book。评价语 What,用以判定 Liberty。

出现在感叹句中,what 比任何评价语都更具积极评价意义,作为有标记主位 What Liberty 不仅引进了新的参加者,而且表示话语进入了一个新阶段(Martin & Rose 2003: 178)。loosened 是对 spirit 的判定,由 robust 到 loosened 的变化使精神完全获得了解放,自然带来 Liberty。最后一句总结了读书的奇效,使之高度升华。从叙述 he 的内在变化到外部对比,从飞翔到进入自由天地，都表现诗人对读书效果的态度。

16.4.2 介　入

介入关注表示语篇和作者声音来源的语言资源，考察人际意义和概念意义商榷的方式。我们将根据伏罗希洛夫(Valentin Voloshinov)的观点，把书面语篇看成是某种意识的对话，它作出回应，肯定点什么，指望得到可能的应答和反诘，希期得到支持，等等(Martin & White 2005：93)。朱诗描写景物，没有人物，唯一没有出场的人物是诗人自己。他期望说服读者接受他早成体系的理学思想。但除了他以外还有其他声音。如果我们对“天光”的分析合理的话，那这里蕴含了朱熹之前董仲舒等哲人的声音。同时，诗人也预期读者会提出疑问。在景句之后，他便问“问渠那得清如许?”这可能是诗人自问自答，以进一步阐明塘清的缘由，但更可能是作者感到读者对此有疑问，不如自己主动提出，这叫“言之在先”(counterexpectancy)的语篇策略。所以这个问题代表读者的声音。读者向作者索取更为深入的解释，而诗人提供了信息。这一问一答使得语篇的对话性明显了，朱熹把自己放在一个深谙哲理的学者的立场上，希望读者在治学和修身方面接受他的主张。狄诗中有许多声音，我们先来看一看 He。这个代词没有先行词，语篇没有交代 He 是谁。在英语中，为了表示一致，缩略的体现原则是：对某人越是熟悉，说话就越不用一清二楚(Martin & White 2005：30)。He 作为人称代词处于很高的认知地位。诗人用 he 说明她对他很了解。当诗人说“He knew ...”，就等于说 I know he knew，“他”的感受，就是她的感受。他是谁根本不重要，从最后一句可以看出 he 只不过是诗人借以传达她对读书感受的一个中介。虽是讲 he 的感受，但实际是诗人的声音。狄诗三、四行中含两个否定小句。这 no more 和 nor 的否定引出了与作者声音对立的潜在声音：He used to be poor 和 His frame was dust。正是这两个声音的对立才产生了饮食/读书前后的变化。再看第二节第一行：He danced the dingy Days. 这是一个异乎寻常的状况，读者可能会问怎么会如此。诗人料到了这一点，所以随后作了解答与解释：And this Bequest of Wings/was but a Book. And 在语篇层次上既是意念标记，又是互动标记。这里 And 不仅连接两个命题，而且引出解释。这个解释功能得到 this 的加强。This 回指上句,把上句称作 Bequest of Wings。为什么把上句表达的意思说成 Bequest of Wings? 只有两个可能。第一,这是一个部分投射(scare quote),即别人说过的话。假如是这样,那就引进了别人的声音。第二,操英语的读者都认可或习惯这种用法。假如是这样,那作者就引进了大众的声音。如果读者不能用这比喻理解前一句,那交际就会出现问题。我们看到作者利用多种声音,和读者商榷语篇的意义,以争取读者的认可。

16.4.3 评价维度

莱姆克指出,不论我们对于世界说些什么,我们在同一话语中还会告诉别人在多大程度上我们相信我们所说的话是可能的、可取的、重要的、容许的、意外的、严肃的或可理解的(Lemeke 1998)。他认为即使主要体现概念意义的语句也有说话人的某种态度。实际上朱诗中的"鉴",狄诗中的 bequest、wing 都有诗人的态度,都有评价意义。朱诗中贯穿了逻辑推理,池清映景,心静读书有得;活水池清,勤读心方能定。池清、心静、活水、勤读分别是映景、有得、池清、心定的条件。诗人突出了池清、心定的必要性,所以语篇的评价维度是有理性(warrantability)。在狄诗中,诗人边描述,边惊叹,在她看来读书之妙,妙不可言。所以她所传达的态度是对读书效果的惊叹。用弗朗西斯的测试框架"It is ... that"加以检测"It is wonderful that a loosened spirit brings liberty by reading a book"。所以狄诗的评价维度是可取性(desirability)。可见评价维度与语篇的目的完全吻合,体现了隐喻的中心思想。

16.5 结　语

我们的分析说明,隐喻可以为语篇所体现,而体现隐喻的语篇必须具备若干特征。但是必须指出并不是先有概念隐喻,然后再用语篇加以体现,隐喻必定有语言体现,所以两者是不可分割的。在分析过程中我们发现两首诗存在许多不同之处:如朱诗作为语篇体现为语言行为——劝导,而狄诗体现为叙事;朱诗借景发挥,狄诗借人传意;朱诗重理性,狄氏重感受;朱诗含蓄,狄诗明了,等等。他们语义取向不同,修辞语气不同。归根结蒂是他们的意识形态不同,文化不同。这当属于社会符号层面上的探讨,这里且不议了。

17

概念隐喻和语篇连贯*

17.1 引 言

17.1.1 研究目的

及物性是人们对客观世界经验的表述。人类活动的经验在语言中反映为由动词体现的 6 个过程。现以小说《国王的人马》(*All the King's Men*)为例。此书 1946 年出版,次年获普利策奖,作者罗伯特·佩恩·沃伦(Robert Penn Warren,1905—1989)1986 年获美国桂冠诗人称号。在这本小说中,twitch 作为动词出现在及物性几乎所有的过程之中,作为名词则用于及物性的各种"参加者"的功能,参阅第 11 章 11.3.4 节。为什么以语言代表的意象可用于叙事人所体验到的经验?这就要求我们从语言领域进入认知领域对此进行探讨。

* 原载《外语教学与研究》2006 年第 2 期第 91—100 页。

17.1.2 认知语法和语篇分析

首先,语篇分析旨在说明一则语篇如何表达它的意义。认知语法研究语言和语言使用,解释语言如何使经验概念化并加以诠释,并在广义上将概念化与意义等同起来(Langacker 1991b: 278)。其二,语篇分析研究实际使用的语言。有效的语篇分析必须与语言体系或描写语言体系的某种语法相联系。认知语法着眼于语义,在语言描写上只有两个层次:语义层和语音层。词汇和语法形成一个象征成分的连续体。我们通常称为句法的层面已融入语义结构,并为语义结构所表达。语义结构由相关的认知域表现。兰艾克用侧面/基体(profile/base)等基本认知域加以描写。这说明以词或句的形式出现的意象可以用来解释事件,也说明认知语法致力于解释语言是如何表达意义的。可见认知语法是功能的,适用于语篇分析。其三,认知语法为语篇分析提供了路子。认知语法的基本主张是:语言单位是从语言使用事件中抽象出来的。每一个使用事件是全面的概念化过程,包括对基底(ground)和当前话语空间(Current Discourse Space)的理解。基底由言语事件、说话双方以及他们之间的互动和直接环境构成;当前话语空间指一心理空间,它包含在话语展开中某一时刻,被视为说话人和听话人交流基础的共知成分和关系。语法结构可被视为修正当前话语空间的指令,话语的一系列视框(viewing frame)中,每一个都是对当前话语空间的更新升级(Langacker 2001)。这为语篇不断推进提供了认知基础。其四,语篇作为元功能的复合构建体,具有三个维度,即语言使用、信仰传递(认知)和社会情境中的互动,因此语篇可以从语言、认知和社会的不同视角加以分析,见第1章。鉴于隐喻在思维和语言中的重要性和普遍性,在对语篇进行认知分析的时候就不能不将隐喻作为一个重要的中心部分来考察,特别是当一个长篇叙事语篇中出现中心隐喻的时候,分析中就更加应该突出对隐喻的分析,舍此难以理解语篇如何取得连贯以及语篇如何传递主要信息。这正是我们分析《国王的人马》(Warren 1974)面临的状况。

17.1.3 关于隐喻的基本认识

主要有这么几点:(1)隐喻的中心(locus)不是语言,而是思维。隐喻不是修辞格,而是思维方式。它是使经验概念化并加以诠释的工具(Lakoff 1993: 204,209)。(2) 隐喻的实质在于借助一类事物理解和体验另一类事物(Lakoff & Johnson 1980: 5)。(3) 隐喻是一种映射,即从源域向目的域的映射。两个领域的具体特征具有系统的本体对应(Lakoff 1993: 207)。(4) 隐喻有常规隐喻和原创隐喻之分。本文考察的是原创隐喻。(5) 隐喻可以在语言组织的各个层次上体现,可以体现为单词、词组、句子,也可以体现为语篇(Koller 2003)。这最后一点往往为人们忽视。

17.2 社会经验和理性思考

《国王的人马》是围绕"Life Is A Twitch"这一概念隐喻展开的。因此我们需要考察语篇是如何陈述作为隐喻基础的作者/叙事人(以下皆用"叙事人"表示)的经验和体验以及在这复杂纷繁的现实面前是如何进行理性思考的,另一方面叙事人又如何逐步形成这一概念隐喻,用以表现和解释各式各样的社会经验,解释人生。

17.2.1 社会经验

我们先看叙事人是如何根据叙事结构陈述现实经验。故事发生的时间: 20 世纪 30—40 年代;地点: 美国南方;人物: 主人公 Willie Stark,出生于美国南方农村,自学成才,热衷于从政。最初有意为大众服务,初次竞选失败,后凭借对农村民众的承诺和出众的口才,赢得选举胜利,当上了州长。另一个主角是 Jack Burden,专攻历史,曾任记者,工作敬业,为人坦诚,被 Willie 招入麾下,辅佐他操理州务。在语篇中,他一身二任,既是一个角色,又是叙事人,其重要性不亚于 Willie。Sadie 是 Willie 竞选的组织者,后成为 Willie 的秘书和情妇。Willie 上任后便醉心于权力,日益腐败，不惜用讹诈推行自己的政策，谋取私利。在语篇展开过程中，另有几个人物出现。他们是 Adam Standon，Jack 小时候的朋友，一个技术精湛的外科医生、理想主义者；Anne Standon，Adam 的妹妹，未婚淑女，曾是 Jack 青梅竹马的情侣；Judge Irwin，颇负盛名的法官，人们心目中的仁人君子。Willie 为了要议会撤销对他的弹劾，利用 Jack 查出 Irwin 过去的污点，进行讹诈，迫使他就范。叙事从此节奏加速，悲剧也以此开始。Judge Irwin 拒不屈从，自杀身亡。由于 Jack 的缘故，Adam 成了以 Willie Stark 名字命名的一所医院的院长，而 Anne 暗中取代了 Sadie，成了 Willie 的情妇。由于 Sadie 精心策划，Adam 接到一则电话，得知妹妹 Anne 与 Willie 有染，气愤之极，决心杀死 Willie。在他进入州议会大厦之后，枪杀了 Willie，而他自己也被击毙。叙事人兼用直接叙述和人物自白的手法，陈述他所体验和经历的这些社会经验。

17.2.2 理性思考

复杂的社会现实促使叙事人思考，要求他作出解释。在讲述经验的过程中，叙事人对理性思考也有陈述，内容涉及人、人与人之间的关系、事业、爱情、善与恶、是与非、罪与悔等哲学与伦理问题，内容繁多，这里只能择其要点，稍加归纳，提出问题，以示叙事人如何思考。首先，叙事人思考了人是什么这一根本问题？他作了这样的解答：

> … the human being is a very complicated contraption and that they are not good or bad, but are good and bad and the good comes out of bad and the bad out of good, … (p.248)
> （人是一种非常复杂的玩意儿，非好非坏，既好又坏，坏中出好，好中出坏……）

对人的一生，从生到死，叙事人通过 Willie 之口表达了这样的观点：

> Man is conceived in sin and born in corruption and he passth from the stink of the didie to the stench of the shroud. There is always something. (p.191)
> （人在罪恶中成胎，在堕落中出生，从出生的污浊走向裹尸布的恶臭。

总会有点什么污点。)

善与恶的关系如何,又怎样加以区分?叙事人这样说:

Goodness. Yeah, just plain, simple goodness. Well, you can't inherit that from anybody. You got to make it, ... And you got to make it out of badness. And you know why? Because there isn't anything else to make it out of. (p.257)

(善,平常而简单的善,你不能从任何人那里继承到善,你必须造善,必须用恶造善,你知道为什么?因为舍此无以造善。)

在复杂的现实变动中,是关注过程还是结果?对过程与结果叙事人又怎么认识?

Process as process is neither morally good, nor morally bad. We may judge results but not process. The morally bad agent may perform the deed which is good. The morally good agent may perform the deed which is bad. Maybe a man has to sell his soul to get the power to do good. (p.393 - 394)

(过程自身在道德上无所谓善与恶,必须看结果,而不是过程。道德上恶的力量可能行善,道德上善的力量可能作恶。也许一个人要出卖灵魂取得权力去行善。)

这是叙事人从经验中获得的认识,他称之为"中性道德史观"。对某一现象的解释是否有正有误?叙事人认为:

But those aren't reasons ... But the trouble is, they are half right and half wrong, and in the end that's what paralyses you. (p.403)

(那些不成其为理由,麻烦在于它们半是半非,结果使得人们莫衷一是。)

那么,什么是"对",是"正"?且看叙事人让 Willie 是怎么说的。

And right is a lid you put on something and some of the things under the lid look just like some of the things not under the lid. (p.258)

(正确是一个贴在某些事物上的标签,贴有标签的有些事物和不贴标签的并无二致。)

德行与罪恶能否区分？叙事人对两者的关系如此说明：

A man's virtue may be but the defect of his desire, as his crime may be but a function of his virtue. (p.437)

(一个人的德行可能仅仅是他欲望的缺陷，正如他的罪过也可能是他德行的功能而已。)

在叙事人看来，爱情又是什么？叙事人在词汇层次上说明了他对爱的理解：

The word love is a word for the mysterious itch. (p.309)

("爱情"这个词是一个表示神秘发痒的词。)

从这些例子(有些观点下面会提到)已不难看出叙事人在陈述经历和体验时所关注的焦点，他如何就这些问题进行思考，并试图作出解答。

17.3 概念隐语的形成

人们的思维具有想象性。隐喻的作用在于将理性思考和想象结合起来。人们一旦离开了具体的实际应验，开始谈论抽象概念和感情，隐喻理解就成了常规(Lakoff 1993: 205)。以上介绍的叙事人的经验是借助 twitch 这一意象加以概念化并加以诠释的。这实际上是概念隐喻形成的过程。

17.3.1 语言象征化

隐喻是一种影射，所以必然涉及两个领域。然而，属于认知领域的隐语必然有其语言体现。为此，我们区别隐喻和隐喻表达式(metaphorical expression)。语篇中的 twitch 单独不能构成隐喻，只是隐喻表达式。隐喻焦点往往以直义框架(literal frame)为背景,因此在语篇中,概念隐喻常常先以语言象征出现。词汇形态和句法结构构成一个象征单位的连续体。语法和词汇一样为概念内容提供结构和象征,所以具有象征性和意象性。作为语言单位的词,如 twitch 或句子如 His head twitched,都是意象(imagery),体现对复杂情景的解释。twitch 作为意象,它表明这个词在人脑中形成的情景,以及这一情景形成的具体方式。作为象征单位,它的形式约定俗成地代表一定的意义。在这一语篇中叙事人一开始就引出 twitch 这一意象,目的是让读者在头脑中产生包含这个形象的心理空间。例如:

[1] He twitched all over. (p.6)

[2] His head twitched. (p.5)

[3] I could see the jaw muscles twitch. (p.42)

语义有语义结构,由其约定俗成的义项构成。兰艾克指出,为描述语义单位的语境被称作领域(domain)(Langacker 1987a: 147)。领域必然是认知性的。认知域指描写某一语义结构时涉及的概念领域,可以是知觉、或概念,也可以是极其复杂的认知系统(沈家煊 1994)。语义结构通常使人联想到多种认知域,而某一突显个体的方方面面的特征就由这些认知域表现(Langacker 1987b)。要了解 twitch 的语义和语义结构,必须考察 twitch 所涉及的认知域。意义基于知识,根据我们的世界知识,我们知道 twitch 的语义结构所涉及的认知域有过程,说明 twitch 是一个动作;时间,说明动作发生迅急、短促;方式(manner),说明动作的突然和痉挛性;控制,说明动作无法控制;最后是主体(host),说明 twitch 通常发生在有生命体上。这从上面三例可以看出。

Twitch 在上面三例中都用于本义,本义指直义,而喻义则指间接意义。但在这两种意义中间很难划出明确的分界线。例如:

[4] And Sugar-Boy's head would twitch, the way it always did. (p.3)

人们有理由相信 Sugar-Boy 习惯性地受某种外界影响而恼火,twitch 可以看成"恼火"的象征,这样 twitch 就用于其隐喻意义。再如:

[5] If the earth should twitch ... (p.76)

Twitch 与无生命的地球相联系。这可以有两种解释:说话人用

twitch 理解和解释 quake(地震)或者将 earth 拟人化,总之都经过语义延伸,使 twitch 隐喻化。一个意象的意义取决于侧面/基体、射体/界标、图形/背景这些基本认知域中两个对立面如何结合,取决于意象的那一部分突出。[2]"His head twitched"是一个意象。按认知语法对一般不及物小句的分析,his head 是射体、图形和侧面。但是,例[2]是一种特殊的句型。当不及物主语与及物宾语相匹配时,动词就表现了双向性(ergative)的型式。兰艾克用 A(Autonomous)/D(Dependent)层次性(A/D layering)说明不及物小句单独为 A,及物小句为((D)A)(Langacker 1991b: 387)。A(不及物小句)可以独立,描写一个相当特定的主位过程,通常为主位提供实质性的信息:只有某些个体能够 crack、tear、snap、lock、melt、ignite。这说明在双向结构中,动词不仅表明过程,而且充实主位的概念内容,因而在这意象中具有重要意义,在高一级语法层次上突出。同样,

[6] She twitched her head.

在这个句子中,从射体/边界的关系分析,She 先使 twitched 的抽象射体具体化,然后 her head 使 She twitched 的标界具体化。按认知语法对一般及物小句的分析,主语相当于图形,宾语相当于基体,动词表示图形与基体之间的关系(Ungerer & Schimid 1996: 172)。可是例[6]属于((D)A)结构,其中 She twitched 为 A,可以独立,在这一层次上是图形、侧面,her head 为 D,是意象结构的基底和背景,必须依附于 A。此外 her head 虽是能量链的终结点,但它和 She 是部分与整体的关系,动作最终还是归结到 She,只是说明具体部位而已。

外部世界的事物(things)比之关系和过程更容易为人们感知,很自然,认知语法对作为意象的句子结构进行分析时,给表示个体的名词以中心地位,动词只是表示过程,起联系名词的作用,但是认知语法也承认,由于视角、方向或立场不同,突显的情况可以不同,动词可以在更高的语法组织层次上为全句提供侧面(Langacker 1991b: 387)。由于 twitch 的语义特点及其所在的双向句型,加之叙事人的注意,twitch 在句子层面上有相当程度的突显。

在语篇层次上,twitch 的突显表现在其出现频率上。*All the King's Men* 共 378 页,每页平均 568 个词,全书共 248 784 个词,据我们仔细统计,twitch 在全书共出现 52 次,出现频率为 1/4 784。作为比较,我们在

BNC 语料库中随机提取了 3 674 个文档，利用 Oxford Wordsmith 的 Wordlist 获得这些文件的总词数为 4 734 697，尔后用 Concord 获得这些文件中 twitch 出现次数为 39。这样就获得了 twitch 出现的频率为 1/121 402.24。我们又在 BNCIndexier 中选择了 Prose(Novel)这个语类，从 BNC 中调入 10 个这类文档。Wordlist 告诉我们这些文档总词数为 398 565，从 Concord 对这些文件的运作中得知，在这近 40 万个词中，twitch 仅出现 1 次。可以看出，这叙事语篇中 twitch 的出现率是一般语篇的 25.3 倍，是同类小说语篇的 83.8 倍。这验证了我们对 twitch 在这语篇中颇为突出的印象。值得着重指出的是 twitch 重复 52 次，形成一个贯穿全书的词汇链，在隐喻化过程中，它就是隐喻链，对语篇的衔接与连贯起了有效的作用。不仅如此，在概念隐喻形成的时候，twitch 密集出现，形成了隐喻丛，集中阐明这一原创性隐喻的两个认知域之间产生怎样的映射。

17.3.2 Twitch 的隐喻化过度

上面我们把 twitch 作为语言象征作了考察，但至此，twitch 尚未进入隐喻化的阶段。概念化涉及概念加工。这可以在概念化过程中以不同的形式在不同的阶段出现。在这一语篇中名词化是 twitch 由语言象征到概念象征的第一步。

[7] He gave his head a twitch.

[8] Twitch was simply an independent phenomenon ...

例[7]中 twitch 是动词的名词化。名词化涉及概念具体化。在名词化中，潜在的关系的哪个方面被挑选出来加以具体化和突出？这儿 twitch 属于兰艾克的第二类名词化，即名词化只表示动词突出的单次性(single episode)过程(Langacker 1991b：23)，例[7]中的不定冠词可以说明。这对语篇中的概念隐喻具有意义。twitch 的名词化是隐喻化的需要，因为名词化是感知上由过程到个体的变化，而 twitch 所映射的目的域是认知上的个体。认知语法认为，任何动词都可以名词化，而且并不会引起其概念内容发生实质性变化(Ungerer & Schimid 1996：25)，不同之处在于动词将过程的若干状态逐一加以突出，而相应的名词则将这些状态从总体上作为事物加以突出(Langacker 1987a: 247)。所以,上面对动词 twitch 认知域的分析也适用其相应的名词。功能语法把名词隐喻化视为语法隐喻,即将一种语法形式隐喻为另一种语法形式。马丁指出:语法隐喻涉及名词化,而名词化是现代英语中语法隐喻的主导语义沿流(Martin 1992: 406)。鉴于名词从根本上说是经验语法的产物,这就使得一切意义向经验意义倾斜。这说明名词更有利于经验概念化和对经验作出诠释。名词在概念上是自足的,我们可以对其所指加以概念化而毋庸考虑它高一级过程中的参加者(Langacker 1991b: 25)。而且,名词词组在语篇中常常指特定的事物,因此提供量(quantity)的标记,并产生其语义基础(grounding),指明与言语事件及其参加者如何联系(Langacker 1991b: 53)。这就使得名词更容易为听话人或读者所体验。由于名词和动词在语义结构上的差异,在语言发展过程中,名词习得比动词早,神经语言学也证明名词比动词更容易在记忆中保留,所以更宜于作为心理接点(mental contact)。在句子层面上,例[7]这一语法结构所象征的语义结构中,名词 twitch 比相应的动词更为突出。在例[8]中,twitch 成了图形,其余部分为它的背景,就更为突出了。这种突显也有利于概念隐喻的形成。所以在这一语篇中 twitch 的名词化可以视为从语言象征化到隐喻化的过渡。

17.3.3 Twitch 的拟人化、神化

语篇展开的过程中,引进新的成分和关系可以引发、创造和修改心理空间。当前话语空间不断改变,新的细节不断增加,其他的则渐渐从意识中消失。与当前话语空间有关的一个重要概念是心理接点,它指在概念化主体当前的心理状态下,一个被挑选出来加以特别关注的个体(Langacker 1991b: 91)。下例中的"independent phenomenon"就是这样一个心理接点。

[9] The twitch was simply an independent phenomenon, unrelated to the face or what was behind the face or to anything in the whole tissue of phenomena which is the world we are lost in.

Twitch 被名词化之后,就被喻为一个独立的现象,一个与人、人体以及我

们所处世界无关的现象。在例[9]中,被突出的是 twitch,是图形,是注意焦点。从 *the* twitch、*the* face、*the* whole tissue、*the* world 中的定冠词可以看出,尽管前两个成分是回指语篇已提到的个体,后两个是从与心理空间有联系的长期知识中提取的,但都是叙事人和读者共知的成分,应该属于当前话语空间。但是 independent phenomenon 却是一个心理接点。把这一新成分引进视框,当前话语空间随之更新。叙事人希望读者接受他的认识,而读者根据话语期待(discourse expectation)会按叙事人的认识来解读语篇,当前话语空间得到更新,语篇随之推进。

如果说在 twitch 作为语言象征时,多少是作为外部刺激的条件反射的话,如例[4],到此,twitch 已被视为独立的现象。这里叙事人是以独立的个体比喻 twitch,产生了 **THE TWITCH IS AN INDEPENDENT ENTITY** 的概念隐喻。在此基础上,叙事人又赋予 twitch 超乎它辖域或基体的特征:

[10] The twitch lived that little life of its own. (pp.313 - 314)

[11] What was alive was the twitch. (p.314)

[12] The twitch was the live thing. (p.314)

Twitch 不仅是个体,而且还被赋予了生命,成了活生生的个体。摩尔根说,隐喻总违背"选择限制",使隐喻成为一种语义偏离(Morgan 1993: 125)。在 twitch 隐喻化的过程中,又有了进一步的语义偏离。新的心理接点进入了视框,进一步拓展了当前话语空间。再看:

[13] The twitch was all. (p.314)

[14] The twitch can know that twitch was all. (p.314)

至此,对 twitch 的拟人化已经完成。例[10]至[12]从内涵上充实了 twitch 的概念内容,例[13]、[14]则从外延上扩大了它的概念意义。Twitch 不仅是独立的个体,而且有生命,有认知能力。现在可以概括出的概念隐喻是: **THE TWITCH IS A KNOWING BEING**。对 twitch 隐喻化的结果到目前为止是两个原创隐喻,是将 an independent entity 和 knowing being 分别映射到 twitch 上产生的对应。隐喻不是命题(Lakoff 1993: 207),不存在是否符合真值条件的问题。心理空间组合可以联结两个空间的成分,但并不暗示它们有共同的特性或特征。原创隐喻是叙事人主观解释世界的结果,是有意识有目的的创造。原创隐喻所涉及的两个认知域的差距愈大,推理所需的耗力也愈大,张力就愈大,收到的效果也就愈大;另一方面,这也会给读者理解造成一定的困难,因此叙事人需作相对明晰的说明,如例[18]。细心的读者一定会注意到[10]到[14]都出自同一页。其实在这一页上 twitch 密集出现 13 次,占全书出现总次数的 1/3,形成了隐喻丛,旨在对 twitch 隐喻化结果作较全面的交待。那么为什么要将 twitch 拟人化?雷考夫指出(Lakoff 1993: 232),当一个事件(如 death)通过某种作用力的运作(如 reaping)才能理解时,那个作用力就会被拟人化(如 reaper)。作物被收割后不复存在,所以死亡就出现了。叙事人将 twitch 拟人化是为了赋予它"使然结构"(causation structure),说明它不仅是一切,而且还能左右一切,借以说明目的域的概念。这个概念隐喻形成的认知基础又是如何?一方面叙事人扩大 twitch 的辖域,从 he、his head、the jaw muscles 到 what was alive、the live thing,最后到 all,说明 twitch 的认知覆盖面无所不包;而另一方面,在 twitch 所引发的诸多认知域中,突出并拓展 control 这一领域。twitch 既不受人的控制,被视为独立现象或个体,在此基础上又被赋予生命和认知能力。拟人化也就此完成。事实上,当 twitch 成了 all,并且知道它是一切的时候,twitch 已被赋予了超人的特征。这就为 twitch 的神化作了准备。于是叙事人引出新的心理接点,改变当前话语空间,将 twitch 神化:

[15] Then, having found that out, in the mystic vision, you feel clean and free. You are at one with the Great Twitch. (p.314)

句中 having found that out 指叙事人发现一个奥秘,那就是 twitch is all,此后他茅塞顿开。既然 twitch 无所不是,无所不知,那 twitch 不就神了吗?作者按照英语书写规范,像 God 一样,将 twitch 大写,并以大写开头的 Great 加以修饰,这样就将 twitch 在一定程度上神化了。更为明显的是:

[16] I baptize you in the name of the Big Twitch, the Small Twitch and the Holy Ghost, who, no doubt, is a Twitch, too. (p.319)

这明显模仿基督教施行洗礼时的习语:I baptize you in the name of the Father, and of the Son and the Holy Ghost (Matthew 28: 19),叙事人用 Big Twitch 和 Small Twitch 分别替代 the Father 和 the Son,并把 Holy

Ghost 与 Twitch 等同起来,这样就产生了 **THE TWITCH IS THE ALMIGHTY GOD** 的概念隐喻。对 twitch 的隐喻化也已完成。但这并不是叙事人的最终目的。他需要用隐喻化了的 twitch 来诠释他所经历和观察到的人生。隐喻化后的 twitch 指 all,当指世界上的一切,包括人,请看:

[17] And if I was all twitch how did the twitch which was me know that the twitch was all? (p.314)

I was all twitch 不等于 I was a/the twitch,但 the twitch (which) was me 却说明在叙事人的认知中 twitch 也指人。这样 twitch 既指物又指人,所以它指世界的一切,也指人生的一切。叙事人从他的经验中已经体验到:A career is a twitch, love is a twitch, moral standards are a twitch. 因此,他作了这样的概括:

[18] ... all life is but the dark heave of blood and twitch of the nerve. (p.311)

这样叙事人就把 life 和 twitch 对应了起来,twitch 不仅能左右一切,而且一切都是 twitch,人生就是 twitch,新的心理接点更新了当前话语空间,从而就产生了语篇的中心概念隐喻:**LIFE IS A TWITCH**。

17.4 跨领域映射

17.4.1 跨领域的对应

隐喻是由源域向目的域的映射,目的在于利用一个非常不同领域的经验理解另一个领域的经验。但两个领域应该具有相同的整体事件形态。Life 与 twitch 在事件形态上的共同点是:它们都被视为持续存在的个体。映射结构严谨,具有本体的对应。雷考夫据此提出了恒定原则(Lakoff 1993: 215):隐喻性映射保持源域的认知本体(即意想图式结构),以某种方式与目的域的内在结构一致。可见隐喻是将源域固有的本体特征映射到目的域的内在特征上,目的域的这些特征是叙事人对经验的体验和诠释。在 LIFE IS A TWITCH 这一隐喻中, LIFE 是概括性的,指人的一般的生存状态,不限于某个个人的人生,而 TWITCH 则指单次性过程。隐喻所体现的对应可以列表如下:

表 17-1 源域目的域对应表

TWITCH 源域		LIFE 目的域
Motion/Movement(运动,急速运动)	→	Motion/Movement(运动,沿生活历程的运动)
Unintended(无目的)	→	Inexplicable(无法解释)
Spasmodic(痉挛性)	→	Unpredictable(难以预料)
Uncontrollable(无法控制)	→	Uncertain(变化多端)

Twitch 作为动词意思是"to make a sudden spasmodic motion"的过程,作为名词意思是"a sudden uncontrollable movement"的个体。上面四点正是 twitch 的本体特征。Life 的意思是"the general or universal condition of human existence"。这儿指从语篇人物的经验中概括出来的 life。从上面的讨论中,我们可以看出无论哪一个人物的生活都具有与源域这些本体特征相对应的特征。叙事人依靠以图式为基础的知识系统(schema-based knowledge)中"人"的图式中心特征"有个人意志的","上帝图式"核心语义特征"无所不在,无所不能",来解释人生为什么竟是如此:无所不知、无所不是的 twitch 左右人生。

雷考夫指出:跨领域的映射并不完全是对称的,而是局部的(Lakoff 1993:245)。隐喻在突出某一特征的同时,淡化和掩盖了其他特征(Lakoff & Johnson 1980:163)。所以隐喻的标准之一是:只利用某些特征的部分结构(Lakoff & Johnson 1980:84)。比如 John is a fox 这个隐喻只突出了 fox 狡猾这一特征,却掩盖了 fox 野生、犬科、尾巴蓬松等特征。LIFE IS A TWITCH 这一隐喻突出了 twitch 的偶然性,同时忽略了 twitch

的生理性、急速性等等特征。当代隐喻理论认为,可以将一个领域的推理模式应用于另一个领域(Lakoff 1993：205)。从 twitch 的知识结构出发,我们可以推断 twitch 具有偶然性。把这个推理模式应用于目的域,即可应用 twitch 的偶然性说明 life 的不可知性。

17.4.2 隐喻的经验基础

雷考夫指出：隐喻大多是基于我们经验中的对应(Lakoff 1993：245)。当代隐喻理论强调隐喻的经验基础,雷考夫和约翰逊还说：离开经验基础我们根本不可能理解隐喻,也无法充分表现隐喻(Lakoff & Johnson 1980：19)。Twitch 与 life 的对应是建立在叙事人的经验之上的。概念隐喻是在常规隐喻的基础上建立起来的,所以要了解隐喻的经验基础,就需要考察与 life 有关的常规隐喻。根据雷考夫用事件隐喻所作的分析,有目的的人生是长期的有目标的旅程(Lakoff 1993：223)。人生的行动的总和是一条道路。人生的困难就是行动的阻碍,等等。根据叙事人的叙述,语篇中的人物似乎都有人生目标：Willie Stark 胸怀政治抱负,意欲造福于民,Judge Irwin 刚正不阿,公正执法,Adam Stanton 崇尚医德,精于医道,在人生道路上他们似乎各有追求,走上了从政、行医、执法的不同的道路,但在旅程中都遇上了意想不到的阻碍,最终都没有什么好的结果。Willie 虽踌躇满志,却醉心于权力,忘却了竞选初衷,腐化堕落,最后死于非命;Irwin 虽刚正不阿,却难免沾染政坛的污浊,最后在威逼之下,饮弹自尽;Adam 虽精于医道,却忍受不了 Willie 与妹妹有染的耻辱,结果也未得善终,他们都由于人生道路上意想不到的障碍而没有达到他们各自的人生目标。从这些人物看,人生所呈现的共同特点是难以预料、变化多端、无法解释。这正是与 twitch 特征相对应的 life 的特征。叙事人的亲身经历为隐喻提供了更为直接的经验基础。Jack 虽热恋 Anne,独善其身,坚持操守,绝不越雷池一步,却将 Anne 推进了 Willie 的怀抱。他敬业尽职,工作认真,却秉承 Willie 的指令,查找 Irwin 历史上的污点,以供 Willie 作为把柄进行讹诈。Jack 经过曲折的调查,甚至找到了失去联系多年的父亲,从而找到了当事人,抓住了 Judge Irwin 曾经受贿并迫使 Mortimer 自杀的证据,回来后当面向他交底,亮出罪证。结果 Irwin 拒不屈服 Willie 的压力,在 Jack 离开后即开枪自尽。后来 Jack 从他悲痛欲绝的母亲口中得知，Irwin 原来是他的生父。Jack 的行为致使爱人失去贞操，生父失去生命。对于 Anne 的失足，他说："这是他难以面对的可怕事实，因为它使我失去了我以往不知不觉遵循的原则"（p.311）。对于 Irwin 以及 Adam 和 Willie 的死，他说："我似乎被卷入了一个我不明白其意义的可怕阴谋"（p.417）。这些刻骨铭心的切身经历使他感到无所适从，难断是非。他失去了做人的原则，他觉得身不由己，彷徨、焦虑、茫然、无助。因此，他用 twitch 解释这些经验：I was all twitch. Twitch was me. 人生为什么会如此？被喻为人生道路上的障碍是怎么产生的？Jack、Willie、Irwin、Adam 的经验表明世界充满偶然，人生没有什么目的可言，也不存在什么是非、正误、善恶。芸芸众生，沧桑变迁，无一不在 twitch 的操纵和控制之下。一切都由神化了的 twitch 支配。17.1.2 提到的那些模棱两可、似是而非的理性思考正是叙事人基于自己的经验用 twitch 对现实的解读。

17.5 语篇的连贯

17.5.1 语篇展开和隐喻化

在《国王的人马》中，语篇结构、语篇进展以及隐喻化的过程是一致的，这保证了语篇的连贯。请看下表：

表 17－2 语篇展开和隐喻化过程对照表

语篇结构	语篇展开 （经验陈述）	隐喻化过程
取向	人物、时间、地点	引出隐喻表达式 twitch（隐喻链开始）
进展	关于 Willie，Jack 等人物的故事展开	引出语法隐喻
评价	理性思考	twitch 隐喻化：拟人化，神化

（续表）

语篇结构	语篇展开 （经验陈述）	隐喻化过程
结局	问题解答	
结尾	故事结局，人物下场	概念隐喻形成（隐喻丛）

从这个表可以看出，这一叙事语篇是在叙事结构的框架内展开的，而语篇的展开也和隐喻化的过程并行不悖、相辅相成：隐喻需要语篇展开过程中显示的经验作为基础，而语篇需要借助隐喻化过程中 twitch 的形象进行经验陈述和理性思考。这两者的结合构成叙事人的隐喻思维过程，语篇只是这思维过程的语言体现。在经验的联想和隐喻形象所激发的图式结构知识相互作用下，语篇便在宏观上取得连贯。

17.5.2 语篇主题

从上表我们还可以看出，经验陈述和隐喻化是贯穿整个语篇的，这就使得 LIFE IS A TWITCH 成为统驭语篇的中心隐喻，是语篇的主题，因而是使语篇连贯的主要因素。主人公 Willie Stark 和 Jack Burden 的经历迥然不同，但叙事人说：Willie Stark 的故事和 Jack Burden 的故事在一个意义上是一个故事（p.157）。他们在一点上却是共同的：Willie 对政治权力的追求和 Jack 对道德完善的追求皆以失败告终。他们的人生都受 twitch 的支配。隐喻可以在语言各个层次上体现，可体现为语篇。既然源域是在语篇中通过隐喻化最后被映射到目的域上，而目的域又是在语篇展开过程中从大量经验中引出的一种人生观，那整个语篇不就体现了这一概念隐喻？Twitch 对 life 的映射不是一蹴而就的，需要整个语篇来完成。当前话语空间是在隐喻形成的过程中逐步更新、拓展的。整个语篇体现一个概念隐喻，因而必然是连贯的。

17.5.3 “离题”的插曲

这本叙事小说里有一段插曲，叙事人明言：这插曲与 Willie Stark 的故事没有任何直接联系,但与 Jack Burden 的故事有很大的关系(p.157),然而 Jack 并没有在插曲中出现,那关系何来? Jack 在一次调查中发现 Cass 与其朋友 Duncan 的妻子 Annabella 有染,Duncan 发现之后即饮弹自尽。在 Duncan 自杀之后,由于在对待奴隶问题上的冲突,Cass 与 Annabella 劳燕分飞。叙事人用了很大的篇幅描述 Cass 与 Annabella 的私情交往,有的评论家认为这是此书的败笔。其实,这也是为隐喻提供经验基础。请看叙事人的交代:

[19] So, I observed, my nobility (or whatever it was) had had in my world as dire a consequence as Cass Mastern's sin in his. (p.297)
(所以,我注意到,我的高尚(或随便叫什么)在我的世界里与 Cass Mastern 的罪孽在他的世界里具有几乎相同的悲惨后果。)

不是吗? 由于 Jack 洁身自好,以"超我"(superego)战胜了"本我"(id),结果使 Anne 沦为 Willie 的情妇,因此造成 Adam 和 Willie 的死亡,而 Cass 的罪孽导致了 Duncan 自杀。一个道德高尚,一个道德沦丧,但结果一样。可见这一插曲并不离题,而是叙事人精心设计,借以说明人世无常,善恶难分这一主题,所以还是在概念隐喻的统驭之下,因而无损于语篇连贯。

17.5.4 哲学思想

这叙事语篇之所以连贯的根本原因,在于中心隐喻体现了一种哲学思想。许多评论家都认为,《国王的人马》是一本政治小说;其实,其中的政治事件只是一个载体,借以探讨人生哲学。语篇关注的是人、人生。存在主义是一种人本主义哲学,是以人为对象的哲学,不过这个"人"是指意识到自我的个人(刘放桐 1984: 29),我仅仅是我意识到的自我存在(Lavine 1984: 330),是个人的精神存在。所谓精神存在是指人的非理性的情感意志。存在主义认为人是由情感意志支配的,意志就是欲望,而欲望就意味着痛苦。拉文指出:存在主义认为痛苦是人的潜在的、全面渗透和无所不在的存在状况(Lavine 1984: 330)。语篇所呈现的正是这样一幅暗淡的图景:所有的人都在焦虑中挣扎,在痛苦中生存。语篇最后有这样的说明:

[20] They were doomed but they lived in the agony of will. (p.436)
(他们被毁了,但他们生活在情感意志的痛苦之中。)

叙事人的朋友死了,但他们曾有情感意志,而这情感意志给他们带来痛苦。存在主义认为宇宙没有意义,人生也没有意义,语篇中的那些模棱两可、似是而非的理性思考只能反映一种茫然,这也是体现了存在主义的观点:现实是无法最终理解的(Perry 1990: 533)。请看这观点在语篇的体现:

[21] ... his friends had been doomed, he saw that though doomed they had nothing to do with any doom under the godhead of the Great Twitch. (p.436)
(他的朋友被毁了,他看到虽然他们被毁了,但与这天底下的任何劫难无关。)

他们死了,但他们的毁灭并不是由于某种劫难。他们的毁灭没有理由,无法解释。叙事人还通过 Willie 之口,阐述了这一存在主义的观点:

[22] "You don't know why you work for me. But I know," he said, and laughed.
"Why?" I asked.
"Boy," he said, "You work for me because I'm the way I am and you are the way you are ..."
"That's a hell of a fine explanation."
"It's not an explanation," he said, and laughed again. "There ain't any explanations. Not of anything."

我是我的存在,你是你的存在,这当然不成为 Jack 为 Willie 工作的理由。实际上 Willie 提不出理由,对什么都作不了解释。我最后的虚无是死亡,所以人们总是生活在死亡随时临头的恐惧之中。语篇中出现 5 次非正常死亡正是为了说明存在的虚无。隐喻也体现了存在主义的荒诞观点:我是我的存在,但我的存在是荒诞的(Lavine 1984: 331)。对一般人来说,用 twitch 说明人生是荒诞的。其实,叙事人正是用隐喻的荒诞说明人生的荒诞。事实上 Jack 也不相信。最后他说:

[23] ... he did not believe in the Great Twitch any more. He did not

believe it because he had seen too many people live and die. ... the ways of their living had nothing to do with the Great Twitch. (p.436)

他不再相信 Twitch，是因为他见到很多人的生生死死，因为他们的生活方式与 Twitch 无关。既然世界和人生是无法解释的，当然 twitch 也不能作为一种解释。人生是盲目、偶然发生的过程，人生永远是悲剧。这正是语篇通过概念隐喻要传达的哲学思想。这实际上是一种神秘主义的不可知论。

17.6 结 语

语篇是在叙事结构的框架中展开的，一方面展现人生，从而提供认知经验和社会语境，另一方面通过不断更新当前话语空间，对 twitch 加以隐喻化，最终形成概念隐喻，所以整个语篇体现这两个领域的映射，体现认知隐喻，而隐喻体现了存在主义的世界观。这确保了语篇连贯。经验是隐喻的基础，但这经验不是客观实际的反映，而是叙事人主观体验的经验，隐喻化的过程体现叙事人对经验的主观诠释。这主观性为艺术创作提供了广阔空间。小说成功的基础就在于此。

语篇分析的任务在于说明语篇如何表达它实际表达的意义，关注的是语义。在讨论概念隐喻的时候，我们是在认知层面上考察语篇中源域对目的域的映射。然而，认知语言学在广泛的意义上把概念化和语义等同起来，而杰肯道夫(Ray Jackendoff)把语义结构看成是概念结构的一部分，即由语言体现的那个部分(Halliday & Matthiessen 1999：425)，由于我们的讨论始终建立在语言之上，所以是在讨论语义，讨论语篇如何表达意义，也就是从认知的角度进行语篇分析。实际上，我们的分析过程就是隐喻识别(metaphor identification)的过程，而概念隐喻只有在语篇分析的过程中才能逐步识别。

语篇是多功能的构建体。既然整个语篇体现一个概念隐喻,那这个隐喻就应具有语言的三大元功能。概念隐喻是用以使经验概念化并加以诠释的工具,因此它自然具有语言的经验功能或意念功能。隐喻同时向读者表示了叙事人的态度,将 life 喻为 twitch 就是一种评价,所以它也具有人际功能。从我们的讨论可以看出,语篇是围绕隐喻化展开的,隐喻实际上是组篇的一种有效的手段,因此它也具有语篇功能。这是语篇可以体现隐喻的功能基础。

18

概念隐喻及其语篇体现

——对体现概念隐喻的语篇的多维分析*

18.1 引　言

18.1.1 体现隐喻的语篇

雷考夫指出,概念隐喻是我们对世界加以概念化的一个主要的、不可缺少的司空见惯、习以为常的方法(Lakoff 1993: 204)。隐喻指概念系统中跨领域的投射,指用一种非常不同领域的经验理解另一领域的经验。例如用 journey 理解 life,就产生了 Life Is A Journey,或 Life As A Journey。Life-As-A Journey 是这一隐喻的名称,隐喻本身则指将有关 journey 的知识投射到 life 的知识上,从而产生一套表明认知对应的本体对应。这种对应使我们能将对 journey 的推理程式应用于对 life 的推理。隐喻的中心是思维,而不是语言。隐喻可以在语言组织的各个层次上体现,可以体现为单词、词组、句子,也可以体现为语篇(Koller 2003)。本章拟根据隐喻理论、功能语法和评价理论对体现概念隐喻的语篇作一探讨。我们面临的问题是:

* 本章原载《外语与外语教学》2006 年第 10 期第 17—21 页。

语篇如何体现隐喻？根据什么说一则语篇体现了隐喻？我们拟就这一串问题结合具体语篇进行探讨，首先从认知的角度对体现概念隐喻的语篇作隐喻分析，然后在语言层次上对语篇作进一步分析，以验证隐喻分析的结果。

18.1.2 语 料

我们采用的语料是杨绛的一篇谈读书的散文（以下称杨文）。现抄录如下：

杨绛妙说读书

我觉得读书好比串门儿——隐身的串门儿。要参见钦佩的老师或拜谒有名的学者，不必事前打招呼求见，也不怕搅扰主人。翻开书页就闯进大门，翻过几页就升堂入室；而且可以经常去，时刻去，如果不得要领还可以不辞而别，或者另找高明，和他对质。不问我们要拜见的主人住在国内国外，不问他属于现代古代，不问他什么专业，不问他讲正经大道理或聊天说笑，却可以挨近前去听个足够。我们可以恭恭敬敬旁听孔门弟子追述夫子遗言，也不妨淘气地笑问言必称“亦曰仁义而已矣”的孟夫子，他如果生在我们同一时代，会不会是一位马列主义老先生呀？我们可以在苏格拉底临刑前守在他身旁，听他和一位朋友谈话，也可以对斯多葛派伊匹悌忒斯的《金玉良言》思考怀疑。反正话不投机或言不入耳，不妨抽身退场，甚至砰一下推上大门——就是说，啪地合上书面——谁也不会嗔怪。“书的世界却真的‘天涯若比邻’。佛说‘三千大千世界’，可算大极了。书的境地呢，‘现在界’还加上‘过去界’，也带上‘未来界’，实在是包罗万象，贯通三界。而我们却可以足不出户，在这里随意阅历，随时拜师求教。”（《报刊文摘》2005 年 10 月 14 日）“谁说读书人目光短浅，不通人情，不关心世事呢！这里可得到丰富的经历，可以识各时各地、多种多样的人。经常在书里‘串门儿’，至少也可以脱去几分愚昧，多长几个心眼儿吧？”（《北京日报》2005 年 10 月 10 日）

18.1.3 英 译

为了便于对语篇进行分析我们将杨文译成英文：

A Witty Talk on Reading Books by Yang Jiang

I think that reading books can be compared to paying informal visits — "invisible visits". If you want to call on an esteemed teacher or pay a visit to a renowned scholar, you don't have to notify him in advance, nor should you fear that you might disturb him. Open the book and you push the door open, and enter his hall after you turn over a few pages; you may drop in as often as you want and come by anytime. If you fail to see what he is driving at, you may leave without having to say good-bye, and turn to other wise man and confront him with your own viewpoint. No matter where he lives, in China or abroad, whether he belongs to ancient times or the contemporary age, or what field he is specialized in, or whether he is giving a formal lecture, or a rambling talk, you may sit close to him and enjoy it to the full. We may sit in on lectures on Confucius doctrine by his disciples, or we may mischievously ask Mencius, who never speaks without saying "it all comes down to benevolence and righteousness", if he were our contemporary, could he be an old gentleman upholding Marxism? We may also approach Socrates and listen to his talk with a friend of his before his execution; we may also ponder over or take objection to some of the views in *Discourses* by Epictetus, an exponent of Stoicism. Anyway, hearing a word out of place, or a remark that is not pleasing to the ear, you may as well retreat, even shutting the door with a bang — closing the book with a thump — no one would feel offended.

18.2 词句的体现和语篇体现

18.2.1 体 现

首先我们要区分隐喻和隐喻表达式。隐喻是概念系统中跨领域的投射,隐喻表达式(metaphorical expression)则指语言表达式:一个词、短语或句子,也就是跨领域投射的表层体现(surface realization)。这里"体现"是指以具体实例体现隐喻。如雷考夫的一例"We're stuck"(Lakoff 1993:207)。这个表达式唤起了关于旅行的知识和用旅行的知识理解爱情的隐喻,即 The Love-As-Journey Mapping。这一投射意味着若干跨领域对应,如:The lovers correspond to travelers. The love relationship corresponds to the vehicle. "We're stuck"意味着在爱情的旅程中受阻,碰到了困难,所以是 The Love-as-Journey 隐喻的表层体现,而自身并不是隐喻。概念隐喻和隐喻表达式的区别在于概念隐喻总涉及两个领域,如源域 journey,目的域 love,而隐喻表达式则不需要;更为重要的是:隐喻是概念层面上的概括(generalization),而隐喻表达式则是语言层面上的个别(individual)语言表达式。"隐喻是一种概括"有两层意思:(1)概念隐喻是从经验中概括出来,用以使经验概念化并加以诠释。比如在 *All the King's Men* 一书中叙事人用自己和其他人物的经验说明:Love is a twitch, friendship is a twitch, virtue is a twitch, a career is a twitch. 从这许多经验中,叙事人和读者概括出 Life Is A Twitch 的概念隐喻。(2)概念隐喻所涉及的投射都处于上义(superordinate)层次,这是因为上义范畴涵盖许多基本概念,可以最大程度地将源域概念结构投射到目的域(Lakoff 1993:211)。我们说"Love Relationship Is A Vehicle",但不说"Love Relationship Is A Car/Boat/Train/Plane",就是这个缘故。上面 Life Is A Twitch 中目的域 life 涵盖了 love、friendship、virtue、career,这使源域的概念结构也最大限度地运用于目的域。这一例还说明隐喻是有层次结构(hierachical)的,Love Is A Twitch 也是一种概括,是下一个层次的隐喻,对上一个层次来说,它只是次投射(submapping)。

18.2.2 不同的体现

其次,我们要区分不同的"体现"。概念隐喻体现为语篇与体现为词、短语或句子完全不同。兰艾克说认知语法把意义和概念化在其最广泛的意义上等同起来,因此概念隐喻是语义层的范畴(Langacker 1991b:278)。语篇是语义单位,当然也属语义层。当概念隐喻体现为语篇时,并不是用词汇语法表现语义的体现,而是语篇对概念隐喻的实例化(instantiation),也就是在语义系统中由语篇将概念隐喻具体化。韩礼德和马蒂森(1999:14)指出,实例化指在总的语义系统中从语义潜势到一特定语篇实例的迁移。马丁和怀特简明扼要地指出,"体现是抽象的级阶"(Martin & White 2005:23),实例化是概括的级阶。概念隐喻是以一种经验理解另一种经验的方法,是经验语义系统中的一种语义潜势,如 Life Is A Journey 这一概念隐喻是诠释 life 的一种语义资源。在被体现或实例化之前,它没有具体的语境,所以是语义潜势,可以加以实例化(为了汉语叙述的方便,我们在无需强调实例化的情况下仍沿用"体现",意指"以实例体现")。

那么,语篇在哪些方面使概念隐喻实例化呢?从理论上讲,应该包括以下六个方面:(1)语篇和语境是辩证统一的,语篇总是适应一定的语境而形成,没有语境就不存在语篇。将隐喻实例化首先就得将概念隐喻置于一定的语境之中。(2)既然隐喻是跨领域投射,那语篇就必须交代两个领域——源域与目的域,特别是目的域。(3)投射涉及一系列本体对应,将概念隐喻实例化,语篇必须阐明这两个领域间的一整套对应。每一组对应实际是一种次投射,可能在下一层次上构成隐喻。(4)概念隐喻为了说明目的域的特征总是凸出源域概念的某一方面,同时掩盖该概念的其他方面(Lakoff & Johnson 1980:10),这就形成了隐喻的中心思想。实例化概念隐喻的语篇基于隐喻的这一特征应该显示出隐喻的中心思想。(5)概念隐喻使对源域知识的推理程式应用于目的域的推理。这应该贯穿整个语篇,否则隐喻的源域就不能说明目的域。(6)创新隐喻总是建立在日常隐喻的基础之上,实例化隐喻的语篇应该提示是哪些常规隐喻为理解创新隐喻提供了基础。我们对以实例体现隐喻的语篇当从这几个方面加以分析。

18.3 隐喻分析

隐喻的实质在于以另一事物理解和体验某一事物(Lakoff & Johnson

1980：5)。杨文体现了读书是串门儿这一概念隐喻。隐喻基于目的域——源域的对应。串门儿是源域，那么，语篇是如何交代目的域的呢？

18.3.1　目的域

在体现隐喻的语篇里，目的域都必须由语篇以某种方式提供。杨文兼用题目《杨绛妙说读书》和首句“我觉得读书好比串门儿——隐身的串门儿”交代目的域。此外，杨文中有书名《金玉良言》：“也可以对斯多葛派伊匹悌忒斯的《金玉良言》思考怀疑”，这是目的域的成分，有提示目的域的功能。目的域的重要性从朱熹的一首诗可以看出：《千家诗》中诗的题目是《泛舟》：

昨夜江边春水生，
艨艟巨舰一毛轻。
向来枉费推动力，
此日中流自在行。

Ship-Sailing

Last night the spring water came and overbrimmed the river,
Large ships floating on the river looked as light as feathers.
Before the spring came, efforts were made in vain to move the ships.
Which are having a smooth and easy sailing in the stream.

诗的内容说明春水上涨以后行船就十分自在，似乎别无他意。在另一些著作中，如《宋诗鉴赏辞典》，此诗是《读书有感二首》中的第二首，同样也是以读书为题，以水上行舟比喻读书。《泛舟》只说明了诗所描写的情景，没有点出诗人意欲说明的目的，也就是说只有源域，没有目的域，读者只能就事论事理解。没有目的域就不存在源域向目的域的投射，就不成其为隐喻。点题的作用在于向读者提供有关的心理空间以及结合读者的经验和知识形成的概念框架。没有这一框架，读者无法框定诗中描述的事物，也无法了解诗人的目的所在。但是，我们了解到朱熹是用春水行舟说明读书，我们就可以把“春水生”放在读书的框架里加以理解，知道“春水生”之前可能是冰封，比喻读书的日积月累，“春水生”意指掌握了要领而豁然开朗，在这之后读书是如何轻松与自在：“艨艟巨舰”在读书的框架里可以理解为读书吃力，举步维艰；"一毛轻"则是在开窍之后的轻松自得，优哉游哉。此例可以说明，语篇不同于其他隐喻表达式，它需要交代目的域。当然，如果读者根据自己的知识和经验能为理解源域提供一个框架，那也绝非不可能。不同读者对同一首无题诗可以有不同理解，原因即在此。

18.3.2 本体对应

根据当代隐喻理论，隐喻是源域向目的域的投射，两者之间有相互的对应。然而这种隐喻性投射必须保持源域的认知本体，以某种方式与目的域一致（Lakoff 1980：215）。杨文中以"串门儿"喻读书，这一投射产生了一系列对应：

表 18-1　源域目的域对应表

源域（串门）	目的域（读书）
闯进大门	翻开书页
升堂入室	翻过几页
抽身退场、推上大门	把书合上
拜访的经过	读书的过程
作者	作品

这里的借喻包括用"钦佩的老师""有名的学者""主人""高明""孔门弟子""孟夫子""苏格拉底"指代他们的著作。可见语篇中确实存在两个认知域之间的一套本体对应。语篇是不是体现概念隐喻，还要看概念隐喻是否贯穿整个语篇。杨文中，从"升堂入室"到"砰一下推上大门"，用串门的全过程比喻了读书的整个过程，而且贯穿了语篇。那么杨文究竟通过隐喻传达什么信息？

18.3.3 中心思想

杨文所体现的概念隐喻是读书是串门儿，但这隐喻究竟凸出串门的哪个方面,又着重说明读书的哪个方面呢?这里我们必须交待杨文的出处。杨文刊于2005年10月14日的《报刊文摘》。该报说明此文摘自10月10日《北京日报》,作者是罗银胜,题目是《"读书种子"杨绛轶事》。此文中有一长段,开头是:钱钟书逝世后,杨绛一如既往,杜门谢客,潜心读书。她的闭门读书不是消极避世,不通人情世故,而是"追求精神享受"。接下去就以"她说"直接引用了杨绛关于读书的妙语。就是这一段被摘刊于《报刊文摘》,并另加了题目。不论在《北京日报》,还是在《报刊文摘》,这段话都是放在引号里的,所以我们可以认定这是杨绛的原话。此外,这段话可以构成一个独立的语篇,而这个语篇体现了概念隐喻,所以可以作为我们分析的语料。交待了杨文的出处,实际上我们也就了解了作者的读书观。把读书喻为串门,而且是隐身的串门,就会令读者感到读书的轻松自在。杨绛读书是为了追求精神享受,她用隐喻谈论读书也是为了凸出读书是精神享受这个侧面。

18.3.4 隐喻推理(metaphorical reasoning)

杨文的隐喻推理比较明显:拜访作者毋庸事先通知,拜访何人可以随心所欲,拜访时间自行安排,何时退场主随客便。概念隐喻使得读者可以用造访过程这些环节的自由对读书加以推导,可以理解为读什么书,怎么读,什么时候读,什么时候改读其他书,什么时候结束都完全由读者自己决定。贯穿源域和目的域的推理模式是 p 或者 q,即可以随心所欲地选择。作者给读者以充分的选择自由,以便他们享受读书之乐。

18.3.5 隐喻连贯(metaphorical coherence)

雷考夫指出:日常的隐喻系统对于理解诗学隐语具有中心作用(Lakoff 1993: 203)。人们需要常规隐喻的知识来理解绝大多数诗学隐喻(同上: 205)。杨文中的概念隐喻是诗学隐喻或创新隐喻(novel metaphor)。创新隐喻不用于构成我们日常概念系统的一部分,而是作为对事物的一种新颖的思考方式(Lakoff & Johnson 1980: 53)。但理解这些隐喻离不开我们借以思考和行事的常规隐喻。杨文的概念隐喻是：读书是“串门儿”。这个隐喻是建立在两个常规隐喻上的。一个是读书如行路。这在英汉两种语言里都有表现。英语中有诸如“**go/plod through** the book”“**halfway** through the book”“I cannot find **the place** where the name was mentioned”等；汉语中有诸如“读到什么**地方**忘掉了”，生词成了“拦**路**虎”，“寸**步**难**行**”。行路有目的，那就是达到某个地点，读书也有目的，那是达到某种知识境界。行路有困难，读书也有障碍。行路有同路人，读书有同学。两者之间有明显的隐喻相似性。以作者代作品是我们很熟悉的借喻，但这个借喻的后面却是**作品是作者**的常规隐喻。这是杨文中作为概念隐喻基础的另一个常规隐喻。作品即作者，那很自然地把阅读作品看成是向作者请教。串门得行路，不过杨文中的行路是跨越时空，贯穿三界的行路，所以可以向古今中外的作者们拜谒求教。杨文中的“不必”“也不怕”“不问”……“不问”“可以”“也不妨”“可以”“也可以”，清楚地传达了读书的自由与轻松，读者完全掌握主动权，可以去享受读书的乐趣。在概念领域里，这与“Control Is Up，Happy Is Up”的方位隐喻一致（Lakoff & Johnson 1980：15）。

可见，源域——串门——在语篇中通过隐喻化逐步被投射到目的域上，而目的域——读书——又在语篇展开过程中从经验中根据对源域的推理逐步引出一种人生观和价值观，所以整个语篇就体现了这一概念隐喻。隐喻总是凸出源域的一个方面，当这被凸出的方面被投射到目的域上，就形成了语篇的中心思想，隐喻所涉及的认知对应以及作为创新隐喻基础的常规隐喻都服务于这中心思想。现在让我们在语言层面上检验这些分析结果。

18.4 语篇分析

在我们由概念层面转到语言层面的时候，首先要解决的问题是语境。语篇对概念隐喻实例化首先是将隐喻置于一定的语境之中。韩礼德和韩茹凯指出语篇和语境的关系是辩证关系，语境创造语篇，语篇也同样创造语境(Halliday & Hasan 1985: 47)。意义就产生于这两者的摩擦之中。杨文有两层意义:本义和隐喻意义。本义可以根据语境加以理解,而隐喻的定义表明理解目的域的意义要依靠源域,源域与本义相联系,因此隐喻意义的理解要靠本义,也就是说要结合读者的知识与经验通过本义的中介经过推理从语境中获得。语篇和语境是一起加以理解的(Matthissen & Halliday 1999: 354),而且概念基底(ideation base)既体现对经验的一致性诠释也同时体现对经验的隐喻性诠释(*ibid.*: 565),因此语篇的本义和隐喻意义可以同时加以理解。下面我们仅从验证隐喻分析结果的需要作部分语言分析。

18.4.1 进展方式(Method of development)

语篇的进展与主位和述位的概念密切相关。若干小句主位的程式构成语篇的进展方式。若干小句新信息的程式构成要点(point)(Martin & Rose 2003: 184)。要了解语篇如何展开,就必须考察进展方式和要点。杨文中小句的主位除了第二个小句中的"读书"和最后一句的"谁"以外,都是人称代词。人称代词的分布在英译文中是:I 出现 1 次,you 出现 12 次,he 出现 6 次,we 出现 4 次。you 大部分出现在语篇的开始部分,随后是 he,we 出现在语篇的后部分。这表明作者杨绛(I)与潜在的读者(you)谈访问/阅读某个作者(he),这正是语篇所要说明的。作者在语篇的后部分以 we 代替了 I 和 you,把读者放在与自己平等的地位上,拉近了与读者的距离。如果我们比较一下汉英两种语言人称代词的使用,我们会发现英语用 you 的地方,汉语常用零代词,使得动词成为主位。汉语的"要"作为情态动词至少有两种意义:"表示要做某事的意志"和"应该"。杨文中的"要"用于第一个意义。在"我们"和"他"的运用上与英语的 we,he 相同。

18.4.2 要点(Point)

杨文若干小句的 New 构成了两个基调(motif),一个是由串门(informal visit)、打招呼(notify)、也不怕(nor ... fear)、闯进大门(push the door open)、进入大门(enter the hall)、听个足够(enjoy it to the full)、问(ask)、听(listen)、抽身退场(retreat),提示作为源域串门的过程和目的域读书的过程;另一个基调是由一组包含两可的词语,说明在访问/读书的每一个环节读者享有的选择,包括"钦佩的老师"(esteemed teacher)/"有名的学者"(renowned scholar)、"国内"(in China)/"国外"(abroad)、"现代"(contemporary age)/"古代"(ancient times)、"正经大道理"(formal lecture)/"聊天说笑"(rambling talk)、"夫子遗言"(lectures on Confucius doctrine)/"伊匹梯忒斯的《金玉良言》"(Discourse by Epictetus)。文中连续用连接词"不问"、"或"、"也"、"而且"也足以证明这种选择的自由。这两个基调共同表明读者在串门/读书的过程中享受的自在和惬意。

18.4.3 宏观主位和宏观新信息(Macro Theme and Macro New)

从上面的分析可以看出在语篇展开的过程中,信息是如何流动的。马丁和罗斯基于派克和韩礼德的观点,提出了与信息流程有关的语篇的周期性(periodicity)。语篇的节奏有几层,好似小浪推大浪,大浪推巨浪。他把小句的主位和新信息称为小浪,语段的段主位和段新信息(Hypertheme and Hypernew)为大浪,宏观主位和宏观新信息为巨浪。杨文只有一段,所以我们可以直接考察宏观主位和宏观新信息。宏观主位通常位于篇首,使读者预见语篇将如何展开;宏观新信息位于篇末,对累积的新信息进行提炼。杨文的宏观主位是"我觉得读书好比串门",点出了语篇所涉及的两个领域,"好比"从语言上提示了两者的对应,并将"串门"投射到"读书"上,说明语篇的内容就是这一隐喻,或者说这一概念隐喻在这里将被语篇化。宏观新信息是我们足不出户,却可以跨越时空"在这里随意阅历,随时拜师求教"。在《北京日报》原文的末尾,杨绛进一步点出读书的意义,她说:"这里可得到丰富的经历,可以识各时各地、多种多样的人。经常在书里'串门儿',至少也可以脱去几分愚昧,多长几个心眼儿吧?"这实际上是《北京日报》一文的宏观新信息。是更大的信息巨浪带来的总结性的新信息。

即使对语篇的这部分分析也可以验证隐喻分析的结果,语篇体现了概念隐喻的中心思想以及用串门比喻读书所要说明的要点。但是杨绛为什么用这个隐喻？她在语篇中表示了什么态度？她又如何传达她的信念，说服读者？这是我们要在评价分析中解决的问题。

18.5 评价分析

评价理论用于对语篇进行评价，包括语篇如何通过商榷表达各种态度、情感的强度，价值源于何处，如何表达以及如何与读者取得一致。马丁和罗斯提出的评价系统由介入、态度和分级三个子系统构成（Martin & Rose 2003）。下面我们着重分析杨文如何利用态度资源和介入资源。

18.5.1 态　度

态度资源可以表示态度，具体地说就是表达情感，对人的评定和对事物的鉴别。在杨文中，态度评价词语并不太多。在说到作家时，杨绛用了肯定性评价词语："钦佩的""有名的""高明的"；区分时代时，用了"现代""古代"的鉴别词语；谈及讲课内容和方式时，用了"正经大道理""聊天说笑"；在叙述访问者/读者的态度时，用了"恭恭敬敬地""淘气地"。从对作家的评价词语中我们可以看出杨绛对作家们的敬重。但其余的评价词语都构成对照，只衬托出读者享有的选择，加强了语篇中"可能性"的情态意义。

18.5.2 介　入

介入是理解语篇对话性的资源。书面的言语活动好似在进行大规模的对话，它对某事做出回应，预料可能产生的反应和反对意见，寻求支持，等等（Voloshinov 1995：139；转自 Martin & White 2005：93）。杨文表现了作者与读者的对话。杨绛针对预计读者可能提出的问题逐一解答。马丁把这种情况叫做 counter-expectancy,可以译为“抢先陈述”,也就是预计读者会发问、反诘,但不等他们开口就先作陈述。这是语篇多声现象(hectergloss)的表现之一。杨绛预计读者会提怎样的问题呢？根据作者所述当有：怎样参见名师？是否要事先约谈？怎样登门求教？拜访的时间和次数怎样得当？应该访问怎样的作家？应该怎样听名家授课？听得不中意该怎么办？怎样结束拜访？看了杨文的人都会感到这篇散文很有针对性。那针对性从何而来？实际上作者的陈述是针对读者可能提出的问题。从这个意义上讲,作者一直在与读者对话。对话就涉及两种声音：读者的声音和作者的声音。

语篇的多种声音来自情态(modaliy)、投射(projection)和转折(concession)。杨文集中使用了情态。归一性(polarity)是对肯定和否定的选择。否定隐含两种声音,即否定的声音和与之相反的另一种声音。杨文中有“不必”“不怕”“不妨”,这三个否定的声音是杨绛的声音,但同时隐含了相反的声音:“不必”表示事理上或情理上不需要,潜在的声音是“应该事先打招呼”;“不怕打搅”的潜在声音是“怕打搅作者”;“不妨”表示可以这样做,没有什么妨碍,但相反的声音是“你不该抽身退场”。这相反的声音都是读者的声音,是他们可能产生的顾虑。在肯定与否定之间是表示不同程度可能性和经常性的语义空间,这就是情态起作用的地方。杨文以人际语法隐喻“我觉得”(I think)开头,表示“可能”(subjective：I think = objective：probably)。这就使得杨绛的话语留有余地,虽然她竭力想说服读者,但是她给其他声音留出了空间。在原文中“可以”出现 6 次,“不妨”出现 2 次,其他情态词有“要”“不必”。在英译文中 may 一共出现 7 次,还不包括暗含的 may,如 You may leave without having to say good-bye and (may) turn to other wise man and (may) confront him with your own viewpoint 中的 may。“不问”相当于“不论”,是连词,表示条件不同而结果一样。“不论”……“不论”的连续使用暗示了读者中的不同声音。事实上,读者的志趣不同,目的不一,有的喜欢古典的,有的喜欢现代的,有的喜欢本土作品,有的喜爱外国名著,杨绛一一予以考虑,且用 may 说明个人可自由选择。May 的反复使用,并与一连串的“不问”……“不问”相结合,加之作者虽通晓古今,学贯中西却以平等的态度对待读者,这就足以说服各类读者：读书享有充分的自由,可以根据自己的爱好选择,从而取得读者的认可与赞同,因而形成一个志同道合的喜爱读书的群体。这样,她不仅与读者分享读书的乐趣,而且鼓励读者在读书中追求精神享受。这正是概念隐喻所要凸出的中心思想。语篇辅以投射,如用“言必称‘亦曰仁义而已矣’的孟夫子”描述孟子,“佛说‘三千大千世界’”和局部引用(scare quote)“天涯若比邻”形容读者可跨越时空,尽情享受读书的乐趣。可见这多种声音都是为语篇目的服务。

18.5.3 评价维度

所有的话语都持某种姿态或态度(Martin & White 2005: 92)。不论我们说什么,我们在同一话语中还告诉别人在多大程度上我们相信我们所说的内容是可能的、可取的、重要的等等(Lemke 1998)。这样,就对命题或提议作了不同维度的评价。杨文英译文的第一句“I think reading books can be compared to paying informal visits”中 I think 和 can 都表示可能性,相当于“It is possible that reading books be compared to paying informal visits”(Francis 1995)。因此,作者对语篇内容的有理性(warrantability)维度上作了评价。但是,作者告诉读者什么都可以读,怎么读都可以,那读者肯定可以在读书中获得乐趣。用英文说就是 It is certain that the reader will find pleasure in reading。Certain 是高值情态词,但它仍然是一种判断,不及 They find pleasure 肯定,所以 certain 仍属有理性的维度。这意味杨绛是以建议的口吻跟读者促膝谈心。

以上的分析说明作者杨绛以串门的随便与轻松说明读书的乐趣。隐喻的中心思想在语篇中得到了表现;或者说语篇是以概念隐喻构成的,隐喻的中心思想就是语篇的中心思想。

18.6 结 语

我们的分析是从概念隐喻出发的,其实隐喻已化为语篇,语篇成了隐喻。从语篇的角度出发,不难看出隐喻对于使经验概念化并加以诠释,协商语篇意义,表明作者态度,与读者取得一致以及推进语篇的进展和语篇的构成都起着积极的作用。

读书的乐趣似乎无关宏旨,其实十分重要。古人云:知之者不如好之者,好之者不如乐之者(《论语·雍也》)。当代著名的教学理论专家斯蒂芬·克拉申(Stephen Krashen)在 20 世纪 90 年代提出了阅读的乐趣假说(The pleasure hypothesis)(Alatis 1994:399)。这些都足以说明隐喻和语篇凸出读书的乐趣既有经验基础,也有理论依据。

19

Multiple Blending in *All the King's Men*[*]

19.1 Introduction

This chapter is an attempt to look into the narrative novel *All the King's Men* from a cognitive perspective with special reference to metaphor and blending.

19.1.1 *Twitch* in transitivity

As has been shown in chapters 2 and 17, the word *twitch* as a verb appears only in the material processes, but as a noun it appears in nearly all the processes and serves various functions in the transitivity structure in the book. Look at the sentences in which *twitch* occurs:

---

* 本章原载《文体学研究论丛》2010 年第一辑第 139—158 页。

Table 19 - 1 Processes in which *twitch* can appear

Material process:

My head twitched. (Process)

He twitched his head. (Process)

He gave his head a twitch. (Goal)

Relational process:

All life is but the twitch of the nerve, (Identifier)

Twitch is all. (Identified)

The twitch was an *independent phenomenon*, (Identified/Carrier)

Mental Process:

The twitch can *know that twitch is all.* (Senser)

Existential process:

There was no God but the Great Twitch. (Existent)

The grammatical system of transitivity embodies the experiential function of language, serving as a way of representing patterns of experience, and enabling human beings to build a mental picture of the reality and make sense of what goes on around them and inside them, the extensive use of the word points to the fact that a twitch is presented as an action or a kind of force affecting all spheres of human experience. However, what role does the word play? If it is used figuratively and its concept is to be made the source domain, then what is the concept that the concept of "twitch" is to be mapped onto? This amounts to asking what metaphor is employed to structure and construe the perceived experiences of the characters? As models of mapping do not by themselves explain the relevant data (Fauconnier & Turner 1998a), how does conceptual integration or blending account for the mapping and provide inference that links our analysis and interpretation and gives the general meaning of the novel? This is what this paper is concerned with.

19.1.2 Metaphor and blending

Metaphor is a set of correspondences between two concepts in two different knowledge domains. As such metaphor serves as a device to comprehend one concept in terms of another. Here the concept to be comprehended may refer to a simple event, process or entity, but it may refer to a host of complex phenomena. It serves to conceptualize and construe experience. In literary discourse metaphors are more often than not deliberate, which makes it possible for the writers to create correspondences so that they can represent the world as they see it. This gives rise to deliberate conceptual metaphor, which is sometimes made explicit in order to help the reader to set up the mapping between two domains so that the writer/speaker may get across the intended message, the theme. Metaphor is one of the phenomena that give rise to blends (Fauconnier & Turner 1996: 116) and blending is a further development in cognitive science research. According to Fauconnier, blending is a basic mental capacity that leads to new meaning, global insight, and conceptual compression useful for memory and manipulation of otherwise diffuse ranges of meaning. It is a process of conceptual mapping and integration that results in meaning construction.

19.1.3 Two strands of discourse running parallel

A close reading of the book reveals the fact that the writer conceptualizes and construes life experiences in terms of a twitch and the whole book is found to embody a conceptual integration of the two normally unrelated spaces or a mapping across the two domains: the twitch — the source domain and life — the target domain. This conceptual metaphor is made explicit on page 311 in the book to help the reader to identify it, where the narrator says, "... all life is but the dark heave of blood and the twitch of the nerve". Accordingly there are two strands of discourse running through the book, one about the source domain, the twitch, and the other about the target domain, the life experiences of the protagonist, the narrator and other characters. They are interwoven, and their figure and ground transposition occurs when one or the other is placed in focus. The encompassing metaphor forms and the multiple blending develops as the text unfolds. Look at the general correspondence between the metaphorical development of the source domain concept and the narrative structure of the novel:

Table 19 - 2 Correspondence between the progression of discourse and development of *twitch*

Discourse Structure	Life Experiences Narrated	Development of *Twitch*
Orientation	Characters, time, place introduced	*Twitch* introduced initiating metaphor chain
Complicated actions unfolding	Stories of Willie and Jack	Grammatical metaphor
Evaluation	Reasoning on moral values	Personification
Resolution	Questions answered	Deification
Coda	Deaths and failures	Metaphorical cluster Mapping completed

19.1.4 A brief storyline

All the King's Men, the classical novel by Penn Warren (1974), which won the Pulitzer Prize, is the story of the rise and fall of Willie Stark, a Southern backcountry, self-educated man, infatuated with power and dreams of public services, after initial setback manages to progress to the state governorship. Once in power, Willie strives to carry out his campaign promises concerning reform and justice for the poor and disadvantaged, but he becomes increasingly drunk with power, soon rifle with corruption, and his administration operates on political favors and blackmail to force through his desires. He attracts into his employ Jack Burton, a newspaperman and a "student of history" in search for truth, who is the narrator of the story; Sadie Burke, a campaign organizer, an intense and intrepid secretary, who became Willie's mistress. There are some other characters. Jack's childhood friends Adam Stanton, an idealist surgeon, and his sister Anne, Jack's first love, an unmarried patrician, and Judge Irwin, the surrogate father of Jack's youth and a man of widely acknowledged rectitude. Willie's political corruption leads to an impeachment from the opposition party. In his effort to revoke the impeachment he tries to blackmail Judge Irwin. When Willie asks Jack to dig some information on Judge Irwin, the story is set in motion and the stage is set for tragedies. Willie's moral corruption leads to an affair with Anne Stanton, who eventually replaces Sadie as his mistress. Jack's conscientious work enables him to get evidence that Irwin took a bribe, but the judge refuses to submit to Willie and commits suicide. From his grief-stricken mother Jack learns that Irwin turns out to be his father. Adam, after receiving news of Anne's affair with Willie by an anonymous call instigated by Sadie, gets into the Capitol, and in shooting Willie, is killed himself. Jack winds up in losing his love and in a sense killing his own father.

With this plot in mind, we shall look at the metaphoric expression *twitch* first to see how it is developed, metaphorically so as to be capable of conceptualizing and construing the life experiences of the characters.

19.2 Linguistic Symbolization

Metaphorical focus usually stands against the background of literal frame, so linguistic symbolization goes before conceptual symbolization as a kind of entry in the process of conceptualization. Grammar, like lexicon, provides for the structuring and symbolization of conceptual content, and is thus symbolic or imagic in character. When we use a particular word or construction, we select a particular image to structure the conceived situation for communicative purposes.

19.2.1 High frequency of occurrence

Twitch is a word that is marked as least frequently used in *Collins*

Cobuild English Dictionary, but it occurs fairly frequently, there being 6 occurrences in the first 20 pages of the book. The frequency of occurrences of the word is found to be 52 in the entire book of 248, 784 words, so the average is 1/4784, while in the ten Prose (Novel) files we randomly take from the BNC Indexier totaling 398, 565 words *twitch* occurs only once. So the frequency of occurrences is 83.8 times higher in this book than in the ten Novel files. This gives it obvious prominence. This invariably attracts the attention of the reader, which facilitates the identification of the metaphor. What is more, the word occurs in the description of the protagonist and some other major characters. Now let us look at some more of the instances in which *twitch* occurs:

[1] He twitched all over ... (p.6)
[2] His head twitched ... (p.5)
[3] I could see the jaw muscles twitch ... (p.42)
[4] The hide of a sleeping dog twitches ... (p.76)
[5] If the earth should twitch ... (p.76)

According to cognitive grammar, linguistic units, whether words or sentences are images, which represent the construals of the complex situation. Their semantic value reflects not only the content of conceived situations but also how the situations are structured and construed. As cognitive grammar equates meaning with conceptualization, the task of semantics is to describe and explain conceptual structures, and since conceptual structures reside in cognitive processing, the ultimate task of linguistic semantics is to characterize the cognitive processing that constitutes mental experience. Cognitive grammar claims that semantic structures, which, are called predications, are characterized relative to cognitive domains, where a domain can be any sort of conceptualization: a perceptual experience, a concept, a conceptual complexity, an elaborate knowledge system, etc. This is because certain conceptions presuppose others for their realization. For instance, "before" presupposes time domain for its characterization. By the same token, to characterize "hallway" space domain is presupposed.

19.2.2 Domains evoked by *twitch*

It follows then that the word *twitch* and the sentences containing it are images used to structure and construe the events or situations. To look into the meaning of these predications it is necessary to examine the domains the word *twitch* evokes and how it acquires its salience in the structure in terms of the facets of the image. As meaning is grounded in knowledge, we know from our linguistic knowledge and cultural knowledge that the domains invoked by *twitch* as linguistic convention are **process**, which indicates that it is a motion or action, **time**, which shows it happens all of a sudden, spasmodically or involuntarily, **control** which shows the movement is out of control, and finally **animacy**, which tells us that *twitch* is associated with animate beings, whether humans or animals, as shown in [1] to [4]. These domains are made clear in the context in which *twitch* occurs. Let's look at a full sentence:

[6] And Sugar-Boy's head would twitch, the way it always did when the words were piling up inside of him and couldn't get out and then he'd start. (p.3)

Sugar-Boy is the Boss's chauffeur. What he is experiencing is a kind of convulsion, a kind of reflex to the unpleasant condition when he finds it difficult to get out certain words. The language serves to conceptualize and symbolize the situation in which Sugar-Boy's head (*part of the man*) responded (*action*) spasmodically (*sudden and uncontrollable*) to the stimulus, the difficulty of speaking he is experiencing. The domains invoked are made quite clear. It may be pointed out that a twitch here is depicted as a conditional reflex, but as we go along we shall see a twitch is no longer represented as a response to a stimulus.

19.2.3 *Twitch* as a biopolar symbolic unit

It should be noted that a symbolic unit is said to be bipolar, consisting of a semantic unit defining one pole and a phonological pole defining the other (Langacker 1991b: 287). As a symbolic unit *twitch* has two sides to it. Apart from its semantic symbolism, it also provides sound symbolism. In *twitch* the initial consonant cluster *tw* and the final consonant *ch* suggest a kind of motion or action that is brief, trivial, insignificant and even transient as can be seen in the pronunciation of words like *tweak*, *twiddle*, *twinge*, *twinkle* for *tw*, and of words like *catch*, *switch*, *snatch*, *blotch*, *scratch* for *ch*. And the short vowel [i] in between "serves very often to indicate what is small, slight or weak" (Jespersen 1960: 557). It is not accidental that all the words listed above beginning with tw are followed by [i]. The correspondence between conceptualization and vocalization makes *twitch* a good imagery to portray the life experiences presented in the novel.

19.2.4 *Twitch* used in literal and metaphorical meaning

In the above examples *twitch* appears to be used in its literal meaning. Literal meaning is direct meaning and metaphorical meaning is indirect meaning. On a closer examination we find it difficult to draw a clear-cut line between literal meaning and metaphorical meaning. In Item [6] it is reasonable to think that *twitch* may be a sign of the irritation the man experiences. If this is the case, then we have an instance of metaphor, for the feeling of irritation is construed in terms of the motion of a *twitch*, which involves a correspondence between the two domains and the meaning is indirect. Item [5] is also a case in point. One of the relevant domains of the image of *twitch* is that the host on which a *twitch* occurs is animate, whether a human or animal, but here the spasmodic motion is ascribed to a celestial body, the earth, which is inanimate. There can be two explanations that can justify such a composition: either the earth is metaphorically used, that is, personified, or *twitch* is metaphorically used by semantic extension that conflicts with conventional expectations. In lexical semantics, apart from relevant domains an image may invoke, cognitive grammar is also concerned with levels of abstraction in relation to the senses of a word. Some senses are schematic relative to others, which instantiate or elaborate the schemas. Others are related by relationship of semantic extension (which implies some conflict in specification). Item [5] is an example and this gives the writer the license to create new metaphors. Cognitive grammar also looks at the degree of cognitive salience or degree of specification.

19.2.5 The level of specificity

Now take a brief look at how the word as an image gets its salience in terms of *base/profile*, *figure/background*, and *trajectory/landmark*. In [2], His head twitched ... The **profile** of his head corresponds to the schematic **trajectory** of *twitched*, and the former serves to elaborate this substructure, or we may simply say his head serves as the *base* specifying *twitched*, which is the **profile**. If we look at the first element in the first three examples above, we find *he*, *his head* and *the jaw muscles*, which progressively narrow down the predication and constitute **the level of specificity** or **the scope of predication**, which is the same as its **base**. This is how the semantic facets of the image of a twitch conceptualize specific situations as the narrator sees them.

19.2.6 Two features to note

But we shall concentrate on the word *twitch* itself here. Two points need to be made with respect to its linguistic features displayed in the discourse.

First, as a verb *twitch* is mostly used intransitively, or ergatively. This means that the Actor is the Medium through which the process is actualized. There is no other participant affected by the process. Even when it is used as a transitive verb, the Actor remains the Medium, but only part of it is affected by the process, as *her head* in

[7] She twitched her head. (p.75)

Although there seems to be a volitional element involved, the fact remains that the twitch does not affect any external entity. This shows the verb is low on transitivity scale and in most cases does not need any element to make its action complete. Another point is that the word *twitch* occurs mostly without any modification, as a verb without any adjunct, as a noun without any modifier. The absence of grammatical modification makes the word *twitch* emerge as stark and undifferentiated. These syntactic features suggest that there is something **self-contained** about the concept of "a twitch", which informs the roles the word *twitch* will play on its own as a single image in the cognitive process.

19.3 Metaphorical Symbolization

Now we'll look at *twitch* as a metaphorical symbol used to structure and construe the general social events the narrator observes or participates in and to answer the questions that come up in the process of his social life. The book appears to be a political novel, but it is a serious probe into such fundamental problems as the essence or value of life including experiences related to love, family and career, and also to the ethical dichotomy between good and bad, virtue and sin, sin and penitence, and right and wrong. The political scene serves as a vehicle for the reasoning. The focus in the story seems to be on Willie Stark, but the main emphasis is also on Jack Burden, the narrator, and his search for truth. We'll see how the writer conceives and construes all this in terms of a twitch.

19.3.1 Personification

Conceptualization involves concept processing, which could happen in different stages and in different forms. In this book we first find nominalization, which later leads to personification and deification in the discourse. Now let us first of all look at nominalization:

[8] He gave his head a twitch. (p.8)

Here *twitch* is used as a noun. Functional grammar explains the nominalization of a verb as grammatical metaphor, which is called for by a concept of the world as consisting only of relations between things. In cognitive grammar nominalization involves a change in the perception from a process to an entity, thus freeing it from the mover or trajectory, therefore freeing it from the constraints of tense, person and mood, and thus making it more general. On the other hand, as an entity it can be bounded (a twitch or twitches), and becomes more concrete and tangible and therefore more accessible to comprehension. In the process of nominalization the likely volition on the part of the agent that appears in the transitive use of the verb diminishes or even disappears altogether. However, it retains much of its verbal meaning, therefore invokes the same domains, which makes semantic extension possible. This prepares for the personification, which takes several steps. The first step is to isolate a twitch from anything human, animate or even inanimate:

[9] The twitch was simply an independent phenomenon, unrelated to the face or what was behind the face or to anything in the whole tissue of phenomena which is the world we are lost in. (p.313)

So the twitch has become an independent phenomenon. It cannot be a conditional reflex to a stimulus. The conceptual metaphor thus built up can be represented as THE TWITCH IS AN INDEPENDENT ENTITY. As the second step the twitch is raised to the status of a living being.

[10] The twitch lived that little life all its own. (p.313)

[11] What was alive was the twitch. (p.314)

[12] The twitch was the live thing. (p.314)

A further step in the conceptualization is to ascribe the ability of knowing to the twitch:

[13] The twitch was all. (p.314)

[14] The twitch can know that the twitch is all. (p.314)

Now the conceptual metaphor has become THE TWITCH IS A KNOWING BEING.

It is worthy of note that the conceptual metaphor is elaborate, which is the result of the subjective construal of the world on the part of the writer. Unlike everyday conceptual metaphors, which we use without being conscious of using them as metaphors, it is created consciously. In everyday life we talk about things that way because we conceive them that way. In literary discourse, the writer talks that way because he conceives things that way and he wants the reader to comprehend things that way.

19.3.2 Deification

However, personification is only part of the metaphorical process. To construe the events the narrator experiences, personification is still not powerful enough. This gives rise to the deification of the twitch. In fact [13] already suggests this direction. After the statement we find

[15] Then, having found that out, in the mystic vision, you feel clean and free.

You are at one with the **Great Twitch**. (p.314)

What is found out is the secret knowledge that the twitch is all. Following the convention of capitalizing the word "God" and the pronoun "He", the writer uses the capital letter T and modifies it with "Great", thus putting the twitch on a par with God. This is seen even more clearly in

[16] I baptize you in the name of the Big Twitch, the Small Twitch and the Holy Ghost, who, no doubt, is a Twitch, too. (p.319)

This is modeled on the formulaic statement used in the Christian rite of baptism; I baptize you in the name of the Father, and of the Son and the Holy Ghost (Matthew, 28: 19) by replacing "the Father", "the Son" with "the Big Twitch" and "Small Twitch", and stating that the Holy Ghost is a Twitch, too, the writer equates the Twitch with God, thus creating the conceptual metaphor THE TWITCH IS THE ALMIGHTY GOD, giving it not just full control of the sudden, uncontrollable movement but the omnipotence over everything. This is exactly what the writer needs for his explanation of the real world.

19.3.3 Multiple blending

Then how is this metaphorical process possible? How do we arrive at the conceptual metaphors? The answer lies in our basic cognitive faculty, which is conceptual integration or blending. The twitch and a person or God represent two input mental spaces, which reflect salient aspects of each of them: they are viewed as entities, which are independent, and to varying degrees they are beyond control of external agents. These are the salient features that form the "generic space" that connects the two input spaces, which projects selectively into a fourth space — the blended space, in which through composition a relation is set up between the counterparts. While "twitch" and "person" remain separate, some of the features are fused, thus giving the emergent structure: the partial match between the two concepts the twitch and a person makes it feasible to comprehend the former in terms of the latter, thus producing the metaphor The Twitch Is A Person. Specifically, the metaphor is created by extending the scope of predication or the base of the concept of "a twitch" from *he*, *his head*, *the jaw muscles*, *to an independent phenomenon*, *what was alive*, *the live thing* and finally *all*, which means that the metaphor covers everything. And also, more importantly, it is created by narrowing down the domains the metaphor invokes and extending one of them to such an extent as to suit the needs of conceptualization. As shown in example [9], out of the four relevant domains, process, time, control and animacy, it is the domain of control that is picked out and extended. The twitch is beyond control of a person or any part of a person, which is understood as being independent of anybody. This is ascribed to the fact that the twitch has the control of itself and therefore it has its independence and it is an independent phenomenon. By one more step in the extension, the twitch is given life and made into a living being, and thus personified. By further extension the twitch as a living being is given the attribute of knowing, which is the aspect of a person that is picked out by the personification here. A similar analysis may apply to the deification. So it is through multiple blending that the personification and deification of the twitch is effected.

19.3.4 Dynamic image schema

This metaphorical process raises the issue whether it runs counter to Lakoff's (1993: 215) Invariance Principle, which states that metaphorical mappings preserves the cognitive typology (this is, the image-schema) of the source domain, since the twitch represents the source domain in the general metaphor in the book. Simpson (2004: 40) holds that image schema is susceptible to ongoing modification as more new information comes in. Importantly, ICMs (Idealized Cognitive Model) are subject to modification in the course of an individual subject's experience and development.

Stockwell holds that image-schematic structure-mappings are interanimating rather than unidirectional (as cited in Simpson 2004: 216). To my mind Lakoff's (1993: 207) principle applies to what Stockwell refers to as central features of a mental representation, for the mapping is a set of ontological correspondences that characterize epistemic correspondence by mapping knowledge about one domain onto knowledge about the other. In our case the hypothesis applies to the basic domains or features of the twitch, but it is also subject to change in tandem with the accumulation of new experiences in the mind of the writer or narrator. We need to be aware of the fact that the correspondence between the two domains in a metaphor is created by the mapping. People can hardly relate a twitch to a person or God, nor will they relate life to a twitch. As the inherent structure of the target domain is enriched or altered, the image-schematic structure of the source domain has to be enriched and altered accordingly. We must not lose sight of the fact that we use metaphor as an effective means to facilitate the understanding of the target domain. If this primary goal holds, the source domain needs to be subject to change. Besides, image-schematic structures are dynamic, although the prototypical features are preserved. Besides, Lakoff (1980: 13) says clearly that metaphorical concept can be extended beyond the range of ordinary literal ways of thinking and talking into the range of what is called figurative, poetic, colorful, or fanciful thought and language. Furthermore, as we shall see, the extension is used more in elaboration in the blended space than in the mapping between the two input spaces.

19.4 Life Experience Structured and Construed

Now, we'll look at the other strand of discourse, the development of the events that constitute the experiences of the protagonist, the narrator and other characters. It should be noted that the metaphorical development of the twitch is interwoven with the presentation of life experiences of the characters. When the metaphorical process is presented, the life experiences of the characters fade into the background, while the characters' life experiences are described, the image-schema of the twitch is kept in the background.

19.4.1 Experiential basis of the metaphor

The experiential function of language serves to construe some processes in ongoing human experience both around us and inside us. This means that experiential function serves to give expression to both our outer experiences of the external world and inner experiences of consciousness. Therefore for the life experiences of the characters I shall limit myself to two aspects. As the saying goes, all is well that ends well. The ending points to what kind of life the characters live. I shall first look at how they end up in life and then how they reason about life, especially how they look at moral or ethical principles that reflect their general outlook on life.

Let us first look at how the characters end up. For brevity's sake let's limit ourselves to the four main characters. Willie Stark, the protagonist, is killed because of his corruption and an affair with Anne Stanton. Jack Burton, the narrator, a man of principle, in a way kills Judge Irwin, who turns out to be his father and loses his love because of his nobility. Adam Stanton, a well respected doctor, is killed in the act of shooting Willie Stark to avenge his sister. Judge Irwin, a judge of acknowledged rectitude, commits suicide because he refuses to submit to Willie Stark's blackmail. Our cognitive faculty of blending tells us that what is common in these life stories is tragic death or total failure. To the narrator as well as to the reader life as perceived in the text world is **uncertain**, **unpredictable and inexplicable**.

19.4.2 Outlook on life and moral values

Man's social being determines his consciousness. Such vicissitudes shape their outlook on life and their value system. Now let us look at how they reason about man, good and bad, right and wrong, virtue and sin, etc. How does the writer conceptualize man in the first place? In the words of Willie Stark:

[17] Man is conceived in sin and born in corruption and he passth from the stink of didie to the stench of the shroud. There is always something. (p.191)

This seems to say man is born bad. However, Jack Burden exclaims from the point of view of a student of history:

[18] "The human being is a very complicated contraption and they are not good or bad but are good and bad and the good comes out of bad and the bad out of good, and the devil takes the hindmost." (p.248)

So, the distinction between good and bad is blurred. Then what about human relationship? Listen to the dialog between Willie Stark and Jack Burden:

[19] "Boy", he said, "you work for me because I'm the way I am and you're the way you are. It's an arrangement founded on the nature of things." — "That's a hell of a fine explanation." — "It's not an explanation," he said and laughed again. "There ain't any explanations. Not of anything. All you can do is point at the nature of things." (p.192)

Why there cannot be an explanation of anything? What is meant by "the nature of things"? The answer comes near the end of the novel when the writer construes human relationships in terms of the twitch.

[20] We are bound together ... by the Holy Grace of the Great Twitch

whom we must all adore. (p.417)

To learn more about their view on the distinction between good and bad, we may do well to listen to the dialog between Willie Stark and Judge Erwin.

[21] "Goodness. Yeah, just plain, simple goodness. Doc. If you want it. And you got to make it out of badness." "You know why? Because there isn't anything to make it out of." — "If, as you say, there is only the bad to start with, and the good must be made from the bad, then how do you know what the good is? How do you even recognize the good?" — "You just make it up as you go along." (p.257)

Here good and bad are nominalized as things and goodness can only be made out of badness. So ultimately there is nothing that is good. From a high historical point of view, the narrator gives the following statement concerning process and results in the judgment of good and bad:

[22] Process as process is neither morally good nor morally had. We may judge results but not process. The morally bad agent may perform the deed which is good. The morally good agent may perform the deed which is had. Maybe a man has to sell his soul to get the power to do good." (p.393 - 394)

Here results are isolated from process or end from means, thus confusing good and bad. Related to good and bad is right and wrong. The writer makes this even clearer:

[23] It is just that those people who say that to you — or don't say it — aren't right and they aren't wrong ... But the trouble is, they are half right and half wrong, and in the end that is what paralyze you. (p.403)

[24] And right is a lid you put on something and some of the things under the lid look just like some of the things not under the lid, and there never was any notion of what was right ... (p.258)

In the process of reasoning the writer sees no notion of right or wrong. Half right and half wrong practically means neither right nor wrong, and right is seen as a lid and what is under it and what is not under it makes little difference so right is a mere label and the distinction between right and wrong is blurred and obliterated. Related to these concepts are virtue and crime. The narrator says:

[25] ... a man's virtue may be but the defect of his desire, as his crime may be but a function of his virtue. (p.437)

[26] So, I observed, my nobility (or whatever it was) had had in my world a dire consequence as Cass Mastem's sin in his. (p.297)

Here we see both virtue and crime, and nobility and sin are thrown together There is no telling which is which. In addition, one cannot talk about man, human relationship and the moral principles of their conduct without mentioning love. In the text world not a single person has experienced true love. Neither Jack Burden nor Anne Stanton, his childhood sweetheart; neither Willie Stark nor his wife; neither Jack's mother nor her husband, who left her, nor Judge Irwin, who took her away from her man. The experience of all this leads the writer to construe the complicated emotional issue in terms of the itch:

[27] ... the word *love* was a word for the mysterious itch. (p.309)

It is apparent that the word *itch* is used because it rhymes with *twitch* and similar in sound symbolization. To relate these observations with the actual lives of Billie and Jack we need to examine what they say at their critical moments. On his death bed Willie, looking back on his life, says to Jack:

[28] It might have been all different. Jack, you got to believe that. (p.436)

As to Jack, his moral integrity keeps him within the bounds of his norm of behavior, for instance in his relationship with Anne, who later becomes Willie's mistress. Jack feels guilty, saying,

[29] ... somehow by an obscure and necessary logic I had handed her over to *him*. (p.311)

With regard to his lather's death, he says,

[30] Judge Irwin had killed Mortimer L. Littlepaugh. But Mortimer had killed Judge Irwin in the end. Or had it been Mortimer? Perhaps I had done it. (p.353)

He also states,

[31] "It wasn't simply that I again saw myself as party to that conspiracy ... It was more than that. It was as though I were caught in a more monstrous conspiracy whose meaning I could not fathom." (p.417)

19.4.3 Patternings suggesting uncertainty

Apart from the content of these utterances which shows what kind of life they live that gives rise to such views, we find patternings of striking syntatic features, which are formed mainly through repetition. First of all, we find most of the transitivity processes in the examples in this section are relational processes. In fact, all of them contain at least one relational process except [28] and [29]. In relational clauses a relation is being set up between the two entities either in identifying mood or attributive mood. The extensive use of the relational process by the writer suggests his intention to identify or define those concepts discussed or to ascribe certain attributes to them. But he does not get anywhere. This is shown, by another patterning, which is concerned with polarity, that is, the choice between positive and negative. In the discussion of good and bad, right and wrong, we find both positive and negative used in the same clause, as shown in examples [18], [22], [23], [24], accompanied by the use of *neither ... nor* and lexical items of opposing meanings. This mixed use of both positive and negative is indicative of contradiction in logic and suggestive of ambivalence in conception, which is uncertainty. This uncertainty is reinforced by a third patterning, which is made up of quite a number of modal verbs, which show how possible is the statement in which a modal verb occurs, such as *may*, which is low in the scale of probability, in [22], [25]; *might*, which is even lower, in [27], and modal adjuncts as *maybe* in [22], *somehow* in [28] and *perhaps* in [29]. The use of these low-possibility modal words also points to the uncertainty on the part of the writer or narrator. A fourth patterning we find in the important remarks by Billie and Jack is the use of the subjunctive mood as in [27] and [30], which is in full agreement with the meanings the other patternings suggest. We find other examples of this patterning such as *If it were absolutely either way, you wouldn't have to think about it* ... (p.403) *If we should ever break the conspiracy of silence we might have to face the fact of that other conspiracy* ... (p.406) The subjunctive mood suggests the hypothetical condition showing the attitude of the writer/narrator that what is stated is least likely to happen, especially those suppositions that are contrary to the fact. Near the end of the book when the narrator is confused, puzzled and paralysed in the face of the experiences we do find cases of negative polarity, but it should be noted that they occur only in mental processes, such as *I couldn't fathom* in [29], and *Perhaps he could not tell his greatness from ungreatness* (p.427). These are the patternings we find out of our analysis of the language Billie and Jack use in talking about their ideas on moral issues. In the light of Hasan's two levels of semiosis in all verbal art, patternings in the text constitute signs that embody meanings of a higher order, usually involving abstraction or dissociation from the particularities of the text. They provide a basis for us to infer the higher-order meanings by reference to the context in which these utterances are made. The context here refers to the life experiences of the main characters. In these patternings we see the gradual change from uncertainty to negation. The meanings that can be arrived at through inference are meanings that are shared by these patternings, that is, life is **uncertain**, **unpredictable and inexplicable**.

19.5 Conceptual Mapping and Blending

These meanings reflect the frustration and bewilderment of the characters, which is construed in terms of the twitch by the narrator, who says

[32] The Twitch was all. (p.314)

As the two elements before and after *was* are reversible, hence all was the twitch. In the course of the narration the narrator has put the twitch through the metaphorical process and given expression to his own life experiences and those of others, he has thus completed the conceptual mapping between the two domains and exclaims,

[33] I had discovered the dream. That dream was the dream that all life is but the dark heave of blood and **the twitch** of the nerve. (p.417)

The mapping may be represented as the following:

Table 19 - 3 Conceptual mapping between the twitch and life

Twitch	life
Source Domain	Target Domain
1. Motion	Passage through time
2. Spasmodic	Uncertain, Vicissitudinous
3. Uncontrollable	Unpredictable
4. Unintended	Inexplicable

The ontological features of the target domain are inherent in the basic domains evoked by the image-schema of the twitch, and the features of the target domain are derived from the life experiences of the characters and their viewpoints on moral values. The partial cross-mapping that takes shape in the progress of the narrative discourse gives rise to conceptual integration and in fact constitutes one aspect of conceptual integration (Fauconnier & Turner 1998b). It should be noted at this point that the product of blending can become the input to a new operation of blending (Fauconnier & Turner

2002: 279). The twitch, which is the product of prior blending, becomes an input in the general conceptual integration network, thus forming multiple blending in the book. The two domains correspond to two input mental spaces, which reflect the salient features of each of them as stated in the above figure. The **first input space** is the twitch space. The **second input space** is life space, life as conceptualized and construed by the writer on the basis of actual experiences. They may be viewed as entities and share a more schematic feature of being a motion or movement (a twitch: a sudden uncontrollable movement; life: motion through time), which makes up the **generic** space that links them and provides ground for the **blended** space. There is a fourth space, a blended space in the space network that receives selective input projection from the two input spaces, projection on the one hand of uncontrollable, spasmodic movement from the twitch input space and on the other uncertain, unpredictable passage through time involving tragic deaths and total failures on the part of the characters from the life input space. The blend through composition sets up a relation between the twitch and life that does not exist in the input spaces. While the counterparts of life and the twitch remain separate, some of their features are fused in the blend. Completion as a cognitive process recruits a familiar background scenario where life is uncertain, unpredictable and inexplicable as is often experienced or perceived in reality. As some of the salient features of the counterparts are fused in the blend it is reasonable to imagine assigning the features of the twitch to life. Emergent Structure ensues from imaginative mental simulation of this dismal situation and we are able to grasp instantly the effects of the mapping. The resulting effects are projected back to the input space of life, where they yield an inference: life is as unpredictable as a twitch is uncontrollable, or life is the twitch. The organizing frame in the blend is the extension of the life frame, the kind of life lived by the characters that fall under the sway of an unknown or supernatural force that is symbolized as the twitch. Life, which is the God-like twitch, is the agent that moves the characters around blindly and wilfully, thus bringing them to their tragic ends. It is necessary to point out that the meaning suggested by the metaphor

The Twitch Is God is used here in the elaboration of the emergent structure in the blend instead of in the mapping so the ontological features of the twitch are preserved. It is obvious that whether for metaphor or for blending what is crucial is inference. The theory of metaphor leaves much of the reasoning to the language user, but blending provides a schematic way of constructing meaning on the basis of inference from the shared features with reference to available background and contextual structures. The space network may be represented as follows:

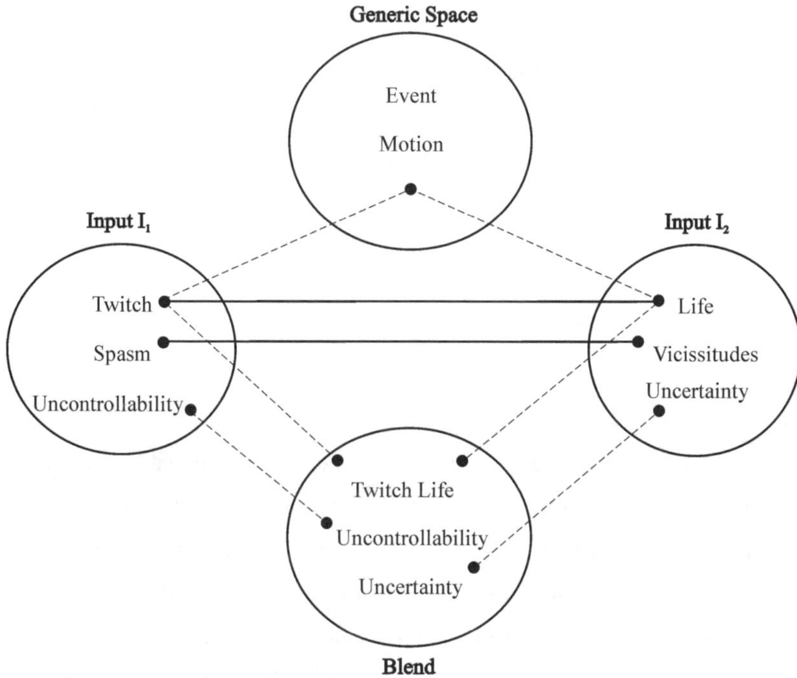

Figure 19 – 1 The Space Network in Blending

19.6 Conclusion

1) It is multiple blending that, on the one hand, effects the

personification and deification of the twitch that gives it all the power to dominate as a supernatural force, and, on the other, integrates what is shared in the lives of the characters with respect to love, family and career. The emergent construal in the general blending gives the thematic meaning of the book: life is as unpredictable as a twitch is uncontrollable, or further generalized as **Life Is A Twitch**. This indicates that the prominence of the word *twitch* contributes to the total meaning of the book, so its use is motivated, and the foregrounding makes the style of the novel. This accounts for the impact the book has on us.

2) It is worth noting that the conceptual integration not only gives an in-depth representation of the experiences of the characters (experiential meaning) but also brings out their helplessness (interpersonal meaning showing the attitude on the part of the writer) and also constitutes a unifying factor around which the text unfolds, thus giving structure to the whole text (textual meaning).

3) As a matter of fact the twitch still cannot adequately explain the life experiences described in the book, for the narrator "woke up one morning to discover that he did not believe in the Great Twitch any more. He did not believe in it because he had seen too many people live and die. He has seen Lucy Stark and Sugar-boy ... live and the ways of their living had nothing to do with the Great Twitch". So what the narrative discourse intends to get across to the reader is the existentialist view that life is full of anxiety and uncertainty and that life has no meaning at all. As Lavine (1984: 330 – 331) points out, according to existentialism, anguish is the underlying, all-pervasive, universal condition of human existence. I am my own existence, but the existence is absurd. To exist as a human being is inexplicable and absurd. Doesn't the writer present to us such a bleak picture of life?

20

The Interplay Between Implicit Conceptual Metaphor and Discourse Flow in Somerset Maugham's *Rain* *

20.1 Introduction

20.1.1 Cognitive-functional approach

This chapter looks into the implicit conceptual metaphor realized by the short story *Rain* by Somerset Maugham. It is part of my project on how discourse realizes conceptual metaphor. *Rain* is taken up for two reasons: one, as a short story it represents a different sub-genre from those of the works I have already studied (See chapters 16, 17, 18 and 19); two, it realizes a metaphor with the target domain implied, or in the terminology of Steen and others (2010: 15), an implicit metaphor, while the previous

* 本章原载《外国语》2016 年第 1 期第 1—18 页,个别地方已有改动。

analyses discuss the realization of metaphors that are mappings between more or less explicitly expressed domains. The works studied all fall into the general genre of literature, which, as a form of verbal art, involves the use of language and, as Clark (1996: 3) points out, language use embodies both individual and social processes. The individual process calls for a cognitive analysis of how a speaker or writer conceptualizes and construes experience, whereas the social process of language use calls for an analysis of the social functions of the language used. This makes it necessary to adopt a cognitive-functional approach to the study of the realization of metaphor in discourse.

20.1.2 The story

The short story *Rain* was based on direct observations. Maugham wrote when he commented on the source of the story, "I was travelling from Honolulu to Pago Pago, and hoping they might at some time be of service I jotted down as usual my impression of such of my fellow-passengers as attracted my attention" (Beecroft 1957: ix). He talked to Davidson and his wife on the ship and jotted down his impressions of the missionary, his wife and the prostitute Thompson. With the missionary and the prostitute in mind he might have drawn on the novel *Thais* by Anatole France that has origins in the Middle East in the 7th century, telling a story of an austere monk who sets out to convert a famous courtesan and ends by going mad with desire for her. So the story *Rain* was thus created, and is now considered an almost archetypal tale of an encounter between a harlot and a priest. Reviewers hold that *Rain* charts the moral disintegration of a missionary Fred Davidson attempting to convert the Pacific island prostitute Sadie Thompson (*Wikipedia*), but there is no explicit description of how Davidson morally disintegrates, and if Davidson and Thompson are the protagonists, as this statement suggests, why so little is said of the real relationship between the two while so much space is devoted to the description of the rain? How is the central meaning expressed or implied in the discourse? These are the issues this paper will look into.

20.1.3 Research question

As the title shows that the paper involves both metaphor and discourse, my research question is by necessity two-fold: while my concern is with how the discourse provides the basis for the realization of the metaphor, attention is also paid to seeing how the metaphor guides, structures and unifies the discourse. Thus it follows that this is a discourse analysis as well as metaphor analysis (Steen 1999a: 59), which naturally involves the identification of metaphor in the light of some procedure, for instance, the procedure put forward in Pragglejaz Group (2007) and Steen et al. (2010) where it is applicable, although it is lexical unit-based. Lakoff (1993: 241) points out that it is common for the plot of a novel to be a realization of a metaphor, where we are likely to come across what is called indirect conceptualization expressed directly (Steen et al. 2010: 57), which makes it difficult to identify not only the frame or the source domain, but also the metaphor referent or the target domain. In addition, the metaphor realized by this discourse falls into what Steen calls the implicit contextual metaphor, which is characterized by the fact that no mention is made of the metaphor referent in the text and it has to be inferred from the context (Steen 1999b: 88, 90). In talking about the identification of metaphor referent, Steen (ibid.: 90) admits that it can become problematic, as in some literary discourse. This narrative discourse is a case in point. What complicates the issue here is that not only the target domain is left implicit, the metaphorical meaning of the word "rain" has also to be inferred from the discourse. In the identification of the metaphor in this short story it is necessary to start with what looks like the metaphor focus, but what is really crucial is to make inferences on the basis of the discourse from which to derive the other element that the metaphor focus applies to in order to construct the implied comparison of the two concepts and ultimately to set up the correspondences between the two domains in the mapping.

20.2 The Word "Rain" Foregrounded: Why and How?

20.2.1 High frequency of occurrence

The word "rain" is used as what appears to be the source domain probably because in Maugham's (1915) view *the rain fell alike upon the just and the unjust*, which seems to be derived from the biblical saying that *God will send sun shine or rain on the just and the unjust* and, therefore, suggests something general, common and natural about the rain, which lends itself to the intended meaning of the metaphor in the discourse. No one who has read the short story *Rain* (Maugham 1944) can fail to be struck by the unusual frequency of occurrence of the word "rain". The following results serve to confirm the impression.

The word "rain" occurs 41 times in the short story, and, what is more unusual, as many as 38 cases of them are used as nouns or pronouns standing for it and only 3 occurrences take the form of a verb. This is because a noun profiles an entity while a verb profiles a relation and the writer needs an entity for his cross-domain mapping. When used as a noun the noun phrase "the rain" occurs 38 times in the narrative discourse, which is only 13200 words long, whereas the same noun phrase has a frequency of occurrence of 1574 in NBC, which has 100 million words. Converted into occurrences per thousand words, the figures are as follows:

Rain	2.878	1000 words
NBC	1.574	1000 words,

which means the word "rain" occurs almost twice as frequently in the discourse as in NBC. This serves to bring out the unusualness of the frequency of "the rain" in the discourse.

20.2.2 Theme position

The word "rain" is used mainly as the Theme of a clause. For example,

[1] The rain began to fall in torrents. (p.311)

[2] The rain showed no sign of stopping. (p.312)

[3] The rain poured down without ceasing. (p.312)

[4] The rain was falling again. (p.320)

As the word repeats itself in the Theme position in a series of clauses, it constitutes Theme continuity, which helps the metaphorical chain to carry forward the discourse.

20.2.3 Less usual structure

Closely related to the use of the word "rain" as a noun and used in initial position of clauses, as a verb it enters into a less usual structure showing the atmospheric condition. In English when rain falls people usually use an impersonal construction saying "it's raining". It is more usual to say,

"It was raining" than

"The rain fell", or

"The rain was falling."

The following search results from BNC show that "the rain" is used in a less common structure in

It was raining. (119 occurrences)

The rain fell. (18 occurrences)

The rain was falling. (4 occurrences)

Mention must be made of the fact that when the word "rain" is used as a verb it is used either in negative or hypothetical structure (Quirk 1985: 1012) in the discourse.

it was not raining (p.316)

For once it was not raining. (p.339)

If only it would stop raining for a single day. (p.350)

This is because it would be impossible to say:

"The rain was not falling". or

"The rain would stop".

For both negative and hypothetical constructions with "rain" as the subject the BNC results are "No solutions found for the query". This shows that the writer makes a point of using the noun wherever he can. It is only when language convention does not allow such constructions that he switches to the verb.

20.2.4 Foregrounded qualitatively and quantitatively

All this points to the fact that the word "rain" is foregrounded in the discourse in the sense that it is given motivated prominence (Halliday 1973: 104). The foregrounding is both qualitative, that is, deviation from language convention (incongruity), as is shown in the use of less common construction, and quantitative, that is, deviance from expected frequency (deflection), as the unusual frequency of occurrence shows (Leech & Short 1981: 48). However, it remains to be seen how the prominence relates to the total meaning of the discourse. The title of the short story is *RAIN*, but rain is not what the story is about. The story is about the protagonist Mr. Davison who got stranded with his wife on a Pacific island because of an outbreak of measles on their voyage to nearby islands where they had been working. They had to stay with two fellow passengers, Dr. Macphail and his wife, at a hotel, where a Miss Thompson happened to stay in a room downstairs. Soon they found her to be a prostitute, who attracted many sailors, and caused a lot of noise singing and dancing to a gramophone. Davison felt indignant and decided to stop it. Being a missionary he thought it his duty to save her soul, praying for her and spending much of his time with her. Meanwhile, using his influence in Washington he made the Governor decide to send her to San Francisco where she was to be put in penitentiary while she herself implored Davidson to let her go back to Sydney to turn over a new leaf. But the missionary refused, yet promised to come on board with her the next day. Then at dawn on the very day of her departure the body of Davidson was found on the seashore. He committed suicide.

So even this rapid sketch serves to show that the story centers around the protagonist Davidson. It is about what happened to him in his effort to save the soul of a woman during his short stay on an island. Then why is the rain made to stand out so prominent as if it were the topic? The only possible answer is that the rain is used symbolically to offer a frame in terms of which the reader is expected to understand the story, or Mr. Davidson. Rain is a natural phenomenon, while the protagonist is a human being. How can one understand the man in terms of the rain? Here let us presume that the conceptual tool metonymy comes in. While the rain may stand for nature, the man may stand for human nature, for whatever Davidson did was dictated by human nature. In this way it is possible to assume a correspondence between the two. In terms of conceptual metaphor the rain or what the rain stands for is made the source domain, but what after all is the target domain?

20.3 Metaphorical Chain and How It Carries Forward the Discourse

20.3.1 The two domains in the metaphor

As the target domain is still unclear, it is reasonable to start with what looks like the source domain. "The rain" is used literally in its basic meaning of "water that falls in drops from clouds in sky" (*Macmillan Dictionary*), but when the word is intended to refer to something inherent in the protagonist in the short story, it is used metaphorically. In the identification of the metaphor "rain" may be assumed to be a metaphor focus, which is termed the source domain in the theory of metaphor. What does make a focus into a focus is the fact that it expresses a concept which is to be related to another concept to which it cannot be applied in a literal fashion (Steen 1999a: 62). Steen (1999a: 60) also points out that when the expression is identified as metaphorical, it is the focus of the metaphor we are dealing with, and this is only one part of the complete metaphor. It has to be followed by the step to identify the metaphor referent or the target domain. For the metaphor to be realized by the discourse it is necessary for the focus expression to run through the discourse. As has been mentioned, there are 41 occurrences of the expression that form a metaphoric chain, which, together with Theme continuity, moves the discourse through the narrative structure. Besides, there is a metaphorical cluster in the middle of the discourse, which serves to define and highlight the kind of rain the writer construes through language as the source domain in terms of which the target domain is to be understood.

20.3.2 Stages of development in the narrative structure

As this is a narrative discourse, I shall look at its stages of development in the light of Labov's theory of narrative structure (Labov & Waletzky 1967).

For **Orientation**, there is a preliminary introduction of four characters in the story, Mr. and Mrs. Davidson, who were missionaries, and Mr. Macphail, who was a medical doctor and his wife Mrs. Macphail, mostly through dialogues between them that took place on a ship sailing to an island named Pago Pago in the Pacific, showing their social positions and attitudes.

But the story did not really take place until they reached the harbor when *Heavy grey clouds came floating over the mouth of the harbor. A few drops began to fall ... and the rain began to fall in torrents* (p.311), which ushers in the protagonist Mr. Davidson, who, being silent, rather sullen, reserved and morose, gave you the feeling of suppressed fire.

Complicating Actions consists of 11 phases, each of which is initiated or accompanied by the occurrence of "the rain":

First, Davidson said "*As soon as the rain lets up we should go ...*" In spite of that *The rain showed no sign of stopping. The rain poured down without ceasing* (p.312). *The rain will beat in on it* [*luggage*] *all the time* (p.313). This persistence of the rain brings in Miss Thompson, who to Mrs. Davidson *looked fast and was not good style at all. She was twenty-seven perhaps, plump, and in a coarse fashion pretty* (p.314).

Second, *It was not raining. The sky was still grey and the clouds hung low* (p. 316). This let-up creates an interval for providing background information about Davidson's work, which consisted in making sins out of what natives thought were natural things, showing he was seized with a religious fanaticism.

Third, at the end of the long passage came quite unexpectedly the sentence *The rain was falling again* (p. 320). This brings in an important event in the development of the discourse. They heard the sound of a gramophone, harsh and loud, wheezing out a syncopated tune. They heard the sound of dancing.

Fourth, *Davidson said*, "*... in the wet season you can't afford to pay any attention to the rain*" (p.323). The steady rain came with the sound of a gramophone mixed with men's voices that floated up. Miss Thompson was giving a party. Davidson found out that she was out of Iwelei, a Red Light district in Honolulu. He cried indignantly, "*I'm not going to allow it. I'm going to stop it.*" (p.326) Although Dr. Macphail thought it rash to go in just now, he went down to Miss Thompson's room, only to be thrown out. A glass of bear had been thrown over him.

Fifth, *They got in just before the rain began to fall again* (p.328). *Mr.*

Davidson sat, morose and silent, refusing to eat more than a mouthful, stared at the slanting rain (p. 328). As the rain began to fall again, Davidson wanted to see Miss Thompson again. He told a native maid to "*ask Miss Thompson when it would be convenient for me to see her*" (p.329). "*What do you want to see her for?*" (p.329) his wife asked. "*It's my duty to save her*" (p.329), he replied. When the native girl came back with a positive response, he got up and without a word went out of the room. They heard him go down and they heard Miss Thompson's defiant "Come in" when he knocked at the door. He remained with her for an hour.

Sixth, *Dr. Macphail watched the rain* (p. 330). This is where the metaphorical cluster occurs with 12 occurrences of "the rain" and its pronoun "it" in a passage of 112 words when the story reaches the climax as the protagonist had met the woman. Davidson came back, saying, "*I have given her every chance. I have exhorted her to repent. She is an evil woman.*" (p.330)

Seventh, *Dr. Macphail looked at the falling rain. He said*, "*Well, I don't suppose it's any good waiting for it to clear up.*" (p. 332) But suddenly the gramophone began to play, yet without anyone in her room to sing. It played to cheat her loneliness. Thompson became arrogant, but the arrogant expression had soon changed. There was a hunted look in her face. Davidson was found mysteriously at work. He told Horn, "*if at any time she wanted him she only had to send and he'd come.*" (p.333)

Eighth, *Macphail said*, "*... the rain ... that's enough to make anyone jumpy.*" *He continued irritably*, "*Doesn't it ever stop in this confounded place?*" Mr. Davidson saw the governor every day. Thompson soon learned that Davidson, using his influence in Washington, made the governor decide to send her back to US to be punished. She came up to see Davidson, spluttering with rage and cursed him.

Ninth, *For once it was not raining* (p. 339). The doctor said to the missionary, "*I think one does better to mind one's own business.*" (p.339) To this Davidson replied, "*Her presence is a peril here.*" "*I'm trying to do my duty.*" (p.339) The doctor took advantage of the rain stopping to go out.

He went at the request of Thompson to see the governor in his attempt to ask him to stretch a point and let Thompson stay there until the next boat came in from San Francisco to Sydney, but he failed. The governor daren't go against the missionaries.

Tenth, *Outside, the pitiless rain fell, fell steadily, with a fierce malignity that was all too human* (p.345). Then Miss Thompson came to see Davidson again, this time a broken and frightened woman. She implored him not to send her back to San Francisco and told him she was to be put in a penitentiary for three years. At this point Dr. Macphail asked the missionary to give her another chance. "*I'm going to give her the finest chance she's ever had. If she repents let her accept the punishment*," (p.344) the missionary insisted. The doctor thought him very harsh and tyrannical.

Eleventh, *Meanwhile the rain fell with a cruel persistence. You felt that the heavens must at last be empty of water, but still it poured down straight, with a maddening iteration, on the iron roof.* "*If it would stop raining for a single day it wouldn't be so bad*," Dr. Macphail exclaimed (p.350). The cruel rain is thus used to wrap up the story. Thompson sent for Davidson. She said to him, "*I have been a bad woman. I want to repent.*" Davidson said, "*Thank God! He has heard our prayers.*" and then turned to Macphail and Horn, saying, "*Leave me alone with her.*" (p.346) During the next three days the missionary spent almost all his time with her. Thompson was to leave next morning. Davidson had meant to go on board with her himself. Early next morning Dr. Macphail was awakened and brought to the beach and saw, lying half in the water and half out, the body of Davidson with his throat cut from ear to ear and his right hand holding a razor with which the deed was done.

20.3.3 The functions of the metaphorical chain

There are 12 phases in the first two stages of the narration, each forming a basic-level topic or super-topic (Chafe 1994), and flagged by the occurrence of "the rain". It must have become clear that the metaphorical chain of "the rain" runs parallel to the development of the discourse, moving it forward from one phase to another so as to help the reader see the sequences of meaning that realize the social activity. "The rain" ushers in Davidson, witnesses the revelation of Thompson's identity, initiates Davidson's first two visits to her and her two visits to him, and finally the cruel persistence of the rain echoes Davidson's cruel insistence on her deportation back to San Francisco for punishment before he took his own life. When it was not raining, two episodes, which are not on the main story line, are narrated: Davidson's religious fanaticism as shown in his previous work and Dr. Macphail's visit to the Governor in his vain attempt to save Thompson from being deported (*ii*, *ix*). This shows that the metaphorical chain performs cohesive, structuring and symbolic functions in the discourse. While the metaphorical chain gives prominence to the rain, the discourse centers around Davidson and Thompson and their interactions to provide the experiential basis for the emergence of the target domain, or the entire metaphor. It should also be noted that the rain and the protagonist are placed side by side, and the repetition of the one in company of the other gives the impression that the rain is intended to be symbolic of the protagonist, and makes him the metaphor referent, and prompts the reader to construct a comparison of some sort between the two as a further step in the identification of the metaphor. However, even if we accept the assumption that the two concepts have undergone a semantic change through metonymy so that there is a conceptual basis for the comparison, then the question remains: what kind of human attribute can be comparable to an attribute of the rain. To identify the metaphor is to identify the two specific concepts that are brought into comparison for the purpose of explanation. This requires both linguistic analysis and conceptual analysis of the discourse.

20.4 Linguistic Analysis of the Structures in Which "the Rain" Appears

20.4.1 Three strata of meaning in verbal art

Meaning is realized by lexico-grammar and more general meaning in discourse is derived from lexico-grammatical patternings, which are formed mainly by contrast or parallel structures. Hasan (1989: 96–98) suggests that we need to recognize three strata in verbal art, which are Theme, Symbolic Articulation and Verbalization. Verbalization refers to the point of primary contact with the work ... We can begin to know a piece of work if we know the language. The stratum of symbolic articulation is where the meanings of language are turned into signs having a deeper meaning. Foregrounding and patterning of patterns play an important role in ascribing the second order meaning to the work. The stratum of Theme is the deepest level of meaning in verbal art; it is what a text is about when dissociated from the particularities of the text. It must be pointed out the three levels of meaning can only be arrived at through inference.

20.4.2 Patterning analyzed for the second order meaning

Part of the second order meaning of this discourse can be derived from the following patterning of sentences in which "the rain" appears:

[5] The rain began to **fall** in torrents. (p.311)

[6] The rain **poured** down without ceasing. (p.312)

[7] The rain **was falling** again. (p.320)

[8] ... the rain **stopped** ... (p.334)

[9] ... the rain **will beat** in on it all the time. (p.313)

[10] ... the rain **swept** in from the opening of the harbor in sheets. (p.315)

[11] The rain did not **pour**, it **flowed**. (p.330)

[12] It **rattled** on the roof with a steady persistence. (p.330)

This SV structure repeats itself again and again, forming a conspicuous patterning in the discourse. To obtain the meaning of the patterning it is necessary to look at the transitivity of the structure, for phenomena of the real world are represented as linguistic structure and reality is made up of processes. It is clear that this structure embodies a Material Process, which consists of a process of doing with a particular participant, an obligatory actor and optionally also a goal, which is missing in the structure here. As the verbs *fall*, *pour*, *stop*, *beat*, *sweep*, *flow and rattle* are all verbs of doing, realizing the Material Process (Halliday 1985a: 109 – 112). The Actor is realized by "the rain", which performed all these actions, the goings-on perceived when the story took place. It should be noted that "the rain" and the verb that follows it form an ergative relationship. In this ergative structure, the Actor is the key figure through the medium of which the process is actualized and without which there would be no such process. Halliday (1985a: 163) calls this element Medium. As all the verbs in Examples [5] to [12] designate an action with some degree of force and the force that comes with the action is realized through the obligatory element Medium, it is natural to see the force as one of the attributes of "the rain". The patterning, therefore, serves to foreground the structure and suggests the second order meaning of force of the rain, which is reinforced by the Circumstantial elements such as *in torrents*, *without ceasing*, *in sheets*, *with a steady persistence that was maddening*, *with a fierce malignity that was all too human*, *with a cruel persistence* and *with a maddening iteration*.

20.4.3 Another patterning analyzed

There is a second patterning, which is made up of a series of clauses representing Behavioral Process, which is a process of consciousness represented as a form of behavior (Halliday 1985a: 139).

[16] You can't afford to **pay any attention to** the rain. (p.323)

[17] Davidson **stared at** the slanting rain. (p.328)

[18] Dr. Macphail **watched** the rain. (p.330)

[19] Dr. Macphail **looked at** the falling rain. (p.322)

The meaning of the Behavioral process is that the Behaver, which is usually some conscious being, is behaving (Halliday 1985: 139). The important fact is that the behavior does not affect the object that indicates the Range. When you stare at something you don't affect it. In clauses [17] to [19] *Davidson* and *Dr. Macphail* function as Behaver and in [16] the indefinite pronoun *you* performs the function. This suggests that people in general cannot do anything about the rain. In the face of the rain people are helpless. It is the powerful force of the rain that renders people powerless.

So far the two strains of deeper ideational meaning of the discourse are revealed and how they are enabled to function in the creation of text are discussed. Next comes the interpersonal meaning, which will be taken up with special reference to Evaluation as an element of narrative structure, and also in the light of appraisal in Appraisal Theory (Martin & Rose 2003; Martin & White 2005).

20.5 Metaphorical Cluster and Evaluation: Conceptual Analysis

20.5.1 Relational processes analyzed

The metaphorical cluster turns out to be an evaluation focus on the rain, specifying what kind of rain it is that the author has in mind when he is mapping it onto something related to the protagonist. It should be noted that the cluster occurs after Davidson saw Miss Thompson for a second time, which brings the story to a climax. Read the following:

> *Macphail watched the rain. It was beginning to get on his nerves. It was not like our soft English rain that drops gently on the earth; it was unmerciful, and somehow terrible; you felt in it the malignancy of the primitive power of nature. It did not pour, it flowed. It was like a deluge from heaven, and it rattled on the roof of corrugated iron with a steady persistence that was maddening. It seemed to have a fury of its own. And sometimes you felt you must scream if it did not stop, and then suddenly you felt powerless, as though your bone had suddenly become soft; and you were miserable and hopeless.* (*p*.330)

There are altogether 12 occurrences of "the rain" and its pronoun "it" in 15 clauses, 9 out of which construe Relational Process (Halliday 1985a: 119 - 137), either intensive or possessive. In this type of process an attribute is ascribed to the carrier as in *it was unmerciful*, *It seemed to have a fury of its own*, the attribute *unmerciful* is ascribed to *it* and so is the attribute *a fury of its own*. In both clauses *it* refers back to the rain. The following attributes are ascribed to the rain: *irritating* (get on one's nerves), *not like the soft English rain*, *unmerciful*, *sometimes terrible*, *like a deluge* in intensive process, and in possessive process the attributes *malignancy of primitive power of nature* (you felt in it = you felt it had), *and a fury of its own* are ascribed to it. In two clauses the attributes *powerless*, *miserable and hopeless* are ascribed to an indefinite "you", which refers to people in general. So the metaphorical cluster serves as an evaluative focus showing it is the incessant, unmerciful and cruel kind of rain that the author conceives, and it is powerless and hopeless kind of mental state people found themselves in when they faced the rain. From the evaluations made on "the rain", there appears to be an increasing intensity of force and cruelty, which makes "the rain" more symbolic of something about the protagonist. As all the words and phrases give undesirable and negative meanings, they resonate with each other from one moment to another as the discourse unfolds. They form a pattern and the pattern of choices forms a prosody of attitude running through the passage. This pattern constructs the stance of the appraiser (Martin & Rose 2003: 51), which is the narrator. This is the attitude he wants to negotiate in the discourse with the reader.

20.5.2 Cognitive analysis

Now it is necessary to take a step further and look at some of the expressions related to the rain in the discourse from a cognitive perspective: *unmerciful*, *and somehow terrible*, *pitiless*, *with a fierce malignity that was all too human*, *with a cruel persistence* and *with a maddening iteration*, in which the adjectives "unmerciful", "terrible", "pitiless" and "cruel" indicate some undesirable human attributes, and "malignity" means "deep-rooted ill will" (*The Oxford Advanced Learner's Dictionary*) and can only be used of humans. The word "maddening" may apply to human actions and remarks, but also to human beings and their attitudes. So these expressions that are normally used of human beings are now being used of the rain as if the rain were a person, thus implying the cognitive process of personification, as the phrase *all too human* clearly indicates. The nonhuman rain is seen as human. This allows us to comprehend the experience with the rain in terms of human motivation, characteristic and activities. The underlying metaphor appears to be The Rain Is A Person. But, as Lakoff & Johnson (1980: 34) point out, each case of personification picks out different aspects of a person or ways of looking at a person, the rain is not seen as an ordinary person but as a person who acts willfully and makes people powerless, as can be inferred from the discourse, and who is *unmerciful*, *cruel* and *pitiless* as these words indicate. Such a person is a despot. So the image metaphor underlying the personification is The Rain Is A Despot, which gives "the rain" additional metaphoricity and brings to light what attribute of "the rain" the narrator keeps in view when he relates it to some attribute of the person Davidson. This is how the writer conceptualizes the experience with the rain so that it serves as the source domain in the dominant metaphor in the discourse. The personification of the rain makes an intermediate link bridging the conceptual gap between "the rain" and the protagonist, thus making the comparison more readily acceptable.

20.5.3 Evaluation focus on the protagonist analyzed

There is another evaluation focus, this time on the protagonist. He is introduced as part of the Orientation in the narrative structure in a passage which includes the following:

> *Mr. Davidson was a silent, rather sullen man, and you felt that his affability was a duty that he imposed upon himself Christianly; he was by nature reserved and even morose. His appearance was singular, …; he had so cadaverous an air that it surprised you to notice how full and sensual were his lips … His dark eyes, set deep in sockets, were large and tragic; and his hands with their big, long fingers, were finely shaped; they gave him a look of great strength. But the most striking thing about him was the feeling he gave you of suppressed fire. It was impressive and vaguely troubling. He was not a man with whom any intimacy was possible.* (*p*.311)

There are 15 clauses, 12 out of which construe Relational Process, 4 identifying, 6 attributive and 2 possessive processes. In the identifying processes Davidson is identified as *a silent*, *rather sullen man*, and *not a man with whom any intimacy was possible*. Besides, there are also such expressions *his affability was a duty*, and *the most striking thing about him was the feeling of suppressed fire*. The attributes he was ascribed to in attributive processes are *reserved and even morose*, *singular*, *full and sensual*, *large and tragic*, *finely shaped*, *impressive and vaguely troubling*.

In possessive processes, there are the following attributes: *so cadaverous an air*, *a look of great strength* (they gave him = he had). As Relational Process is a process of being, this passage gives a description of what kind of man Davidson was. However, unlike the evaluation focus on the rain where the attributes fall into the same semantic field, with specifications showing varying degree of force, the attributes ascribed to the protagonist in this evaluation focus can be grouped into two classes; real evaluations such as *He was a silent*, *sullen man*, and attributes subdued by vague sensory impressions as can be inferred from *You felt*, ... *gave him a look of* ..., *gave the feeling*, *had an air*, which indicate that there was something about the protagonist which the author finds difficult to lay his finger on or he knows what is was, but would deliberately hold the reader in suspense until the story gradually sheds light on it. Nevertheless, in the light of the evaluations in the focus it is clear that there were two sides to the character Davidson as clearly shown in the sentence *his affability was a duty that he imposed upon himself Christianly*. Affability is a fine trait of human nature, but for Davidson it was turned into a self-imposed duty because of his religious belief. The duality of the man's self is apparent: natural self and religious self. He was sullen and morose, but he had suppressed fire. *Fire* when used of human beings means feelings of great warmth and intensity. It means fervor, ardor or passion. Although he was sullen he was capable of passion. Suppressed as the passion was, it lurked there alive. In him there are both fire and something that suppressed the fire. The contrast, or rather, the conflict, is also seen in *he had so cadaverous an air that it surprised you to notice how full and sensual were his lips*. While *full and sensual lips* suggests vigor of life, *cadaverous* suggests nothing other than death, which gives a premonition of the tragic ending.

20.5.4 "Fire" used to structure the perception of desire

As the word "fire" occurs several times (p.311, 317, 320, 346) in the portrayal of the protagonist, now a careful study of the word from a cognitive perspective is in order. As the word "fire" is used of the male protagonist Davidson, it must be used figuratively or metaphorically, meaning fervent or passionate emotion or enthusiasm, or burning passion. In the above analysis about the dual character of Davidson, "fire" is said to mean passion. Freud saw "fire" as an aspect of libido (sex drive) representing forbidden passions (*Dictionary of Symbolism*). Then, is passion the right assumption that is consistent with the context? A look into two instances of the use of "fire" will provide an answer. The word first occurs in "suppressed fire" as the striking characteristic of Davidson, and it occurs again in "inhuman fire" in the description of what Davidson looked like on the morning after he had met Thompson alone very late the night before. "Suppress" means "hold in check with difficulty", or "keep hidden" (*Cambridge Dictionary of American English*). When the fire was held in check and prevented from finding an outlet, Davidson is described as being *silent*, *sullen*, *reserved and even morose*. But when the word occurs in "inhuman fire" in the sentence *He was paler than ever*, *tired*, *but his eyes shone with an inhuman fire* (p. 346), he took on a different appearance. "Inhuman" means "not like anything that a human being normally does or has" (*Macmillan Dictionary*). So "inhuman fire" must be a fire that is unusual to the perception of human beings, and the subsequent observation *Davidson's eye shone with ecstasy* (p.347) sheds light on the meaning of the phrase. There appeared to be a drastic change in Davidson's mood: *It looked as though he were filled with an overwhelming joy* (p.346). One would wonder what was it that brought about this change.

So something must have taken place that inflamed his passion, thus freeing him from the self-imposed repression and tipped him towards the sensual in the balance between his two selves. The contrast confirms that the word "fire" refers to passion, for this interpretation fits in well with the context for the two stretches of discourse. He was sullen when his passion was held in check, but he was ecstatic when his passion was gratified. "Suppressed fire" is intended to mean suppressed passion; "inhuman fire" is intended to mean unusual burning passion. "Fire" is employed to structure the perception of desire and mapped onto it to form the underlying metaphor: Desire Is Fire, which is again an intermediate link and serves to foreground desire, making it the central concept that is to be understood in terms of the force of rain in the dominant metaphor. Now we are in a position to conclude that in the story the rain stands for the natural force of the rain, where the metonymy of the general for the specific is at work, and Davidson embodies desire, an inherent human nature, where the metonymy of the whole for the part is brought into play. This serves to bring out the exact conceptual basis of comparison, or the scenario of the metaphor.

20.6 Resolution and Recontextualization

20.6.1 Surprise ending

Resolution serves as the conclusion of the story. So far, the inner conflict in Davidson does not seem to come to any dramatic confrontation. Thompson wanted to repent and Davidson thought that God had heard his prayers. This gives the impression that he succeeded in his attempt to save her soul. But much to the surprise of the reader Davidson was found dead on the seashore. He committed suicide on the very dawn of the day Thompson was scheduled to leave. So the Resolution takes the form of his death. As text unfolds in context, one cannot understand a text without taking the context into consideration. In the context of the story, according to Halliday and Hasan (1989: 12), the Field of discourse, which is concerned with the nature of social activity, is that a preacher appeared to be trying to save the soul of a woman. The Tenor of discourse, which refers to who is taking part and what kind of relationship obtains between the participants, appeared to be the relationship between the missionary Mr. Davidson and the sinner Miss Thompson, with the former having control over the latter. The Mode of discourse refers to what part language is playing. Language here is constitutive, mainly written language interspersed with some dialogue in writing. Obviously there is something incongruous about the ending of the story. It is simply incompatible with the context just described. What is wrong? The tragic ending forces one to look back and try to re-contextualize the story mainly by looking into the Tenor of discourse so that the story can achieve its coherence. On the relevance-theoretic approach, the context for comprehension is no longer seen as fixed in advance of the utterance, but is constructed as part of the comprehension process (Wilson 2001: 9). As text and context are dialectically related, and the text creates the context as much as the context creates the text (Halliday & Hasan 1989: 47), text or discourse is capable of different interpretations, depending on different contexts in which it occurs. This explains how the reader can hold more than one context at once while concentrating on one context in particular (Simpson 2004: 91). It must be noted that in the context of discourse two separate levels of interpersonal relationship are involved, one between the participants, Davidson and Thompson; the other between the writer/narrator and the reader. Literary works are dialogic by nature, which suggests the relationship between the writer and the reader with the former conveying messages to the latter and negotiating the meaning of the messages with him. It concerns the way the writer presents the messages and guides the reader to comprehend the discourse so that he will be aligned with the writer's point of view with regard to the activity and the participants. Specifically he packages the messages in a way that enables the reader to infer them as he intends, for instance, by providing contextual cues.

20.6.2 Recontextualization

A close reading of the text reveals a number of contextual cues that may point to a different direction in finding an alternative context. In narratives the experiential focus is on something remarkably out of the ordinary. Expectancies about how an activity will unfold are countered, with ensuing events departing from the norm in some significant way (Martin 1992: 565). The cues may take the form of events that run counter to expectations and also a series of linguistic expressions that may trigger a different context. The contextual cues are found in how Davidson was behaving in relation to Thompson. They give rise to quite a number of counter-expectancies, which raise important questions. Why should Davidson go to Miss Thompson's room when Dr. Macphail said to him *it was rather rash to go in just then*? (p.326) If this was out of his sense of duty to stop the party, then why should he want to see her again after he had just been thrown out of her room? Even his wife asked him, "*What do you want to see her for?*" (p.329) Then after his wife asked him to tell Horn to turn her out, and he himself said, "*her presence is a peril here*" (p.339), why should he insist that Horn let Thompson have a room there? Why should he want to be left alone with her when she said she wanted to repent? Because she wanted to make a confession, which is usually done privately as a religious ritual? Then what caused Horn to utter "*Gee whiz*" (p.346), which is more often used as a negative exclamation? Why should Davidson spend almost all his time with Thompson during the next three days? Most important, the final event runs diametrically counter to the reader's expectations, for Davidson took his life when Thompson was to depart as he had expected. And, what is more astonishing, as a missionary Davidson should know well that in Christian doctrine suicide is a sin, for the one who commits suicide cannot repent and be forgiven. Then what led him to take this fatal step? All the counter-expectancies point to the fact there must be some kind of relationship that is different from the schema the reader has in mind, for his suicide gives the lie to all his religious pretences and disrupts the schema of a missionary trying to save a sinner's soul. Then what kind of relationship obtains between Davidson and Thompson that may throw some light on his death? The answer is found first in the drastic change of Davidson's mood that took place after he met with Thompson alone.

There is another evaluation focus on the man, which presents a sharp contrast with the meaning of the first focus on him. Apart from the expressions mentioned in the discussion of "fire", this focus has the following: It looked as though he were *filled with an overwhelming joy* (p.346). The doctor remarked, "you look *as pleased as Punch*." (p.347) Davidson's *restlessness was intolerable even to himself* (p.348). But he was *buoyed up by a wonderful exhilaration* (p.348). How come his meeting with Thompson could bring him such joy? An attachment must have been formed and an intimacy must have ensued between them. And this must be an exceptional kind of intimacy, for Davidson was *not a man with whom any intimacy was possible* (p.311).

Even more revealing are what he said and thought in relation to Thompson.

First, Davidson used Thompson's first name "Sadie" (p.346) when he asked Macphail to go down and see her. This name had not appeared before in the narration, the reader would have no clue who it was until one page down where the writer used her full name "Sadie Thompson". It may be common for people to be on first-name terms nowadays, but in the story all the characters used Mr., Dr. and Mrs. when they talked to or about each other except Mrs. Davidson, who used his first name when she called her husband, as in "*What's the matter, Fred?*" (p.324) Mrs Macphail called her husband Alec when she asked him not to joke about religion (p.306). First name was used only between wife and husband in the story world, so Davidson's use of "Sadie" suggests familiarity.

Second, *Davidson had been dreaming about the mountains of Nebraska* (p.348), which Dr. Macphail remembered how it struck him that they were like women's breasts. To Freud dreams are fundamentally about wish-fulfillment and those wishes are the results of repressed or frustrated sexual desires. The instigation of a dream is often to be found in the events of the day preceding the dream, which he called "the day residue" (Google search). Davidson had such dreams after he met Thompson alone. It stands to reason to say that the dreams suggest sensuality on the part of Davidson.

Third, Davidson said to Macphail explicitly, "*I love her as I love my wife and my sister*". (p.348) Even taken at face value the remark shows that to Davidson Thompson's presence was no long a peril and her existence no longer a scandal as he had said earlier, but she was someone he put on a par with his wife and his sister emotionally. It would be too brazen for him to proclaim openly, "I love her" without the manner adjunct, which is used only to make the remark less obtrusive. However, by saying so he showed he was tied to her by affection.

Fourth, Davidson said, "*I'm not worthy to touch the hem of her garment.*" (p.348) This is an allusion to an event in the Bible, which says that a woman wanted to be healed for her bleeding. When Jesus appeared in a crowd, she pressed in to touch the hem of His garment and immediately her bleeding stopped. Here Davidson made himself a patient, or a sinner and Thompson the savior. This shows not only had the relationship between him and her changed but the roles they each played in the relationship had also been reversed. Thompson had control over Davidson. The remark shows he was infatuated with her.

From the analysis of these contextual cues it is possible to infer that the relationship between Davidson and Thompson was no longer one between a missionary and a sinner, but an intimate relationship between a man and a woman. This change of Tenor results in a different contextual configuration or schema that can account for the counter expectancies listed above. What made Davidson behave the way he did was not so much his religious fanaticism as his inner urge, his passion, or his desire, which proves to be an irresistible force. Between his two selves now the sensual self prevailed. However, his religious self was still at work. He never wavered in his determination to send Thompson back to San Francisco to be punished, for *he's obstinate, and when he's made up his mind, nothing can move him* (p. 318). So his internal conflict between the religious and the natural, or between the spiritual and the sensual came to a crisis that drove him irretrievably to desperation. The conflict led to his suicide. Or his passion led to his destruction, for his passion brought the conflict to a point where he took his life as a way of escape. In the final analysis, however, it can be said that it was his religious fanaticism, which made his sensual-self irreconcilable to his religious-self that results in his suicide.

20.7 The Conceptual Metaphor and the Coda

20.7.1 A set of correspondences between the domains

The recontexualization confirms the identification of the metaphor referent as well as the metaphor focus. With the despot-like rain identified as the source domain and the fire-like desire in the protagonist as the target domain, the metaphor begins to surface. The implicit metaphor in the discourse is a mapping between the source domain of rain and the target domain of desire. It is true that conceptual metaphor is a cross-domain mapping in the conceptual system and that the mapping is a set of correspondences between the domains, but it must be further noted that a conceptual metaphor is a mapping that is a generalization in which the two concepts are ontologically correspondent and the mapping is at the superordinate level. Lakoff (1993: 211) points out that it is the superordiante category Vehicle, not the basic-level category Car that is in the general mapping in the Love-Is-A-Journey metaphor. Rain is a superordinate category for it includes all kinds of rain, such as cruel rain, torrential rain, light rain, spring rain and British rain. But Davidson as a particular man is a basic category, so is the desire he possessed. It is necessary to search the discourse for a more general concept. It is clear that desire is not limited to Davidson but inherent in all men. In fact Maugham has this in mind and provides stretches of discourse testifying to this point. Apart from his account of people of various nationalities and trades were driven by desire to the red light district in Honolulu, the very last sentence of the short story also confirms the point: *He understood* (p. 355), which means Macphail understood why Thompson condemned all men as pigs after she learned of Davidson's suicide, for Macphail realized why Davidson ended up in suicide, and that as a man he himself was not infallible. Davidson is picked to stand for the class of men. Again metonymy is at work: the specific for the general. Desire inheres in all men alike. Now it is time to work out the set of correspondences that characterizes the metaphor. In the light of the discussion in the previous sections the features of the two concepts are brought out as defined with reference to their relevant domains evoked by their image-schemas and also from the narrator's depiction of the rain and the protagonist as he construes the reality. The Desire-As-Rain mapping is found to be characterized by the following correspondences:

The rain corresponds to desire.

The force of nature corresponds to the force of human nature.

The primitive power of nature corresponds to the power of human inner urge.

The cruelty of the rain corresponds to the sadness of desire.

The irresistibility of the rain to the people corresponds to the irresistibility of desire to men.

The powerlessness of the people in face of the rain corresponds to the powerlessness of men against desire.

20.7.2 The emergence of the metaphor

As rain is an element of nature, so desire is an element of human nature. Both of them are natural, and therefore normal, even necessary for world ecology and human reproduction, for "nature" may mean a creative and controlling force in the universe, or an inner force or sum of such forces in an individual (*Merriam-Webster Online Dictionary*). This is clearly in evidence in the Chinese saying "If it is going to rain or your mother wants to remarry, there is no way to stop them." People will say, "Let nature take its course." Other features of the domains are derived from the specific concepts described in the discourse. Normally rain is not seen as cruel, but the narrator perceives the rain as cruel as he depicts the rain that fell incessantly and maliciously in torrents. And passion can be intolerable, but the narrator sees it as sad when he describes how desire drove men to a red light district: *They were silent and as it were oppressed. Desire is sad* (p. 325). It may be mentioned that Maugham observes in another short story ***Red***: "passion has always in it a shade of sadness (Beecroft 1957: 183)". The way the rain affects the people is comparable to the way desire harasses men, making them powerless just as the rain making people powerless. Thus the conceptual metaphor **Desire Is Rain** takes form. The ontological correspondences between rain and desire can be summarized as in the following chart:

Table 20 - 1 Correspondences in the Mapping

Source Domain	Target Domain
Rain	Desire
Nature	Human nature
Force	Force
Primitive power	Inner urge
Cruelty	Sadness
Irresistibility	Irresistibility
Making people powerless	Making men powerless
Asserting itself under appropriate natural circumstances	Manifesting itself under appropriate social conditions

The set of correspondences permits us to reason about desire using the knowledge we use to reason about rain. Heavy and prolonged rain can be destructive causing floods and deaths. To map the scenario about rain onto the desire scenario, one finds that desire can also be destructive if not properly restrained and may cause disaster such as death as is the case in the short story. The above discussion has centered round how discourse realizes metaphor, which, in turn, structures and unifies the discourse, therefore it naturally subsumes the identification of the metaphor, which has been done through the steps of identifying the metaphorical focus or the source domain and the metaphor referent or the target domain, constructing the comparison between the two concepts, and sorting out the set of ontological correspondences between the two domains, which is what a conceptual metaphor is, although such steps as suggested by Steen (1999a) are not marked.

20.7.3 Coda

After the Resolution comes the Coda, which is conflated with the final evaluation made by Miss Thompson after she learned the news of Davidson's death. It takes the form of an abusive exclamation. No one could describe the scorn of her expression, or her contemptuous hatred she put in it: *You men, You filthy pigs! You are all the same, all of you. Pigs! Pigs.* (p.355) Coda is an optional element in narrative structure, but the Coda in the structure of this narrative serves to confirm what we have inferred from the linguistic and conceptual analyses and also helps to lift the target concept to a superordinate level.

20.8 Conclusion

Now our research question has been answered. The above discussion shows how the discourse means what it does as it realizes the metaphor, and how the metaphor takes shape and plays its role in packaging and conveying the message of the discourse, which is what discourse analysis and conceptual analysis are all about. Discourse and metaphor interact in the discourse flow: the metaphor, as a cross-domain mapping in the conceptual system, is realized by the discourse, which is a unit of language in context; the discourse, on the other hand, as a semantic unit (Halliday 1975: 123) is shaped by the use of the metaphor as a way of conceptualization, or a way of meaning, for cognitive grammar equates meaning with conceptualization (Langacker 1991a: 278). In the interpretation of discourse the reader's intellect always plays an important part, and linguistic fact-based inference, which underlies all the analyses, is indispensable.

In the chart, of all the ontological correspondences between the two concepts, what stands out most prominent is: desire is as irresistible to men as rain is irresistible to people, or, men are powerless against desire as the people are powerless in the face of the rain. In more general terms the inevitable in nature or human nature must be accepted, or simply the inevitable must be accepted. This is the Theme of the story, which is a generalization when dissociated from the particularities of the text.

Lakoff (1993: 205) points out that as soon as one gets away from concrete physical experience and starts talking about abstractions or emotions, metaphorical understanding is the norm. That is why metaphor is used when the narrator talks about desire in this discourse. Then why Maugham makes the target domain implicit? The answer is that he wants to achieve dramatic effect. The writer's intention is made more obvious by the conspicuous absence of any conversation between Davidson and Thompson when they were together alone as he tried to convert her or to seduce her and take advantage of her, nor any account of the process of his suicide, let alone his state of mind before he did it. For this Maugham made it clear in his notes that his experience as a dramatist taught him to leave out everything that did not service the dramatic value of his story (Beecroft 1957: x). However, it then calls for a lot more of inferencing on the part of the reader to arrive at the interpretation of optimal relevance. As inference requires more cognitive effort, implicitness therefore produces greater effect. This is in fact made a cognitive stylistic device that makes the story stylistically unique and contributes to the impact of the short story.

When the reader finishes reading the short story, one last question may arise: why is it possible for Maugham to tell the story with the essential part — the moral disintegration of a missionary — omitted, yet still can tell the tale and get the message across? The answer is: we live by metaphor and this is especially true of writers when they present our life. Here metonymy plays its role using the result to stand for the action or process that produces the result, just as in the utterance: "He came out of the casino a millionaire", the result shows he had gambled and won a lot of money, although the process is not expressed. Davidson's death tells us what he must have gone through in that particular context of situation. It is interesting to note, however, what is omitted by Maugham is likely to be in focus in contemporary literature.

参考书目

Arthur, C., et al. 1997. Cognition. In T. A. van Dijk (Ed.), *Discourse as Structure and Process* (pp.293 – 319). London: SAGE.

Arthur, C., Graesser, A. C., Gernsbadier, M. A., & Goldman, S. R. 1997. Cognition. In T. A. van Dijk (Ed.), *Discourse as Structure and Process* (pp.373 – 405). London: SAGE.

Beecroft, J. (Ed.) 1957. *The Best Short Stories of W. Sommerset Maugham*. New York: Modern Library.

Brandt, L. 2003. Humorous use of metaphor in everyday speech: A mental space analysis. Paper presented at the 8th International Cognitive Linguistic Conference.

Brown, G., & Yule, G. 1983. *Discourse Analysis*. Cambridge: CUP.

Brown, T. 2003. *Making Truth: Metaphor in Science*. Urbana & Chicago: The University of Illinois Press.

Buck, P. S. 1964. *The Good Earth*. Washington Square Press: New York.

Cao, X. 1982. *A Dream of Red Mansions*. Beijing: People's Literature Press.

Chafe, W. 1974. Language and consciousness. *Language*, *50*, 111 – 133.

Chafe, W. 1976. Givenness, contrastiveness, definiteness, subjects, topics and point of view. In C. Li (Ed.), *Subject and Topic* (pp.25 – 55). New York: Academic Press.

Chafe, W. 1979. The flow of thought and the flow of language. In T. Givon (Ed.),

Syntax and Semantics 12 (pp.159 – 210). New York Academic Press.

Chafe, W. 1980. The deployment of consciousness in the production of a narrative. In W. Chafe (Ed.), *The Pear Stories* (pp.9 – 48). Norwood: Ablex.

Chafe, W. 1987. Cognitive constraints on information flow. In R. Tomlin (Ed.), *Coherence and Grounding in Discourse* (pp. 21 – 51) (Typological Studies in Language 11). Amsterdam: John Benjamins.

Chafe, W. 1994. *Discourse, Consciousness and Time: The flow and displacement of conscious experience in speaking and writing*. Chicago: University of Chicago Press.

Chafe, W. 1996a. How consciousness shapes language? *Pragmatics and Cognition*, *4*, 35 – 54.

Chafe, W. 1996b. Comments on Jackendoff, Nuyts, and Allwood. *Pragmatics and Cognition*, *4*, 181 – 196.

Chafe, W. 1996c. Consciousness and language. In J. Verschueren, J. Ostman, J. Blommaert, & C. Bulcaen (Eds.), *Handbook of Pragmatics* (pp. 1 – 14). Amsterdam: Benjamins.

Chafe, W. 2001. The analysis of discourse flow. In D. Schiffrin, D. Tannen, & H. Hamilton (Eds.). *The Handbook of Discourse Analysis* (pp.673 – 687). Oxford: Blackwell.

Chafe, W. 2007. Language and consciousness. In P. Zelazo, M. Moscovitch, & E. Thompson (Eds.), *The Cambridge Handbook of Consciousness* (pp.355 – 374). Cambridge: CUP.

Cheng. Y. 1991. The interpretation of linguistic signs and the role of inference. CUHK Papers in *Linguistics*, *3*, 125 – 151.

Chomsky, N. 1957. *Syntactic Structures*. The Hague: Mouton.

Clark, H. H. 1996. *Using Language*. Cambridge: CUP.

Comrie, B. 1985. *Tense*. Cambridge: CUP.

Contini-Morava, E. 1983. Relative tense in discourse: the interference of time orientation in Swahili. In F. Kelein-Audren (Ed.), *Discourse Perspectives on Syntax* (pp.3 – 21). New York: Academic Press.

Coulthard, M., & Montgomery, M. (Eds.) 1981. *Studies in Discourse Analysis*. London/Boston/Henley: Routledge & Kegan Paul.

Dancygier, B. 2005. Blending and narrative viewpoint: Jonathan Raban's travel through mental spaces. *Language and Literature*, *14*(2): 99 – 127.

Dancygier, B. 2006. What can blending do for you? *Language and Literature*,

15(1), 6 - 15.

Dooley, R. A. 2007. Explorations on discourse topicality. *SIL Electronic Working Papers 10.*

Eggins, S., & Slade, D. 1997. *Analyzing Casual Conversation.* London: Wellington House.

Fauconnier, G. 1985. *Mental Space.* Cambridge: MIT Press.

Fauconnier, G. 1994. *Mental Spaces: Aspects of Meaning Construction in Natural Languages.* Cambridge: CUP.

Fauconnier, G. 2003. Conceptual Integration. *Journal of Foreign Languages*, *2*, 1 - 7.

Fauconnier, G., & Turner, M. 1996. Blending as a central process of grammar. In A. Goldberg (Ed.), *Conceptual Structure, Discourse, and Language* (pp.113 - 130). Standford, CA: CSLI Publication.

Fauconnier, G., & Turner, M. 1998a. Conceptual Integration Networks. *Cognitive Science*, *22*(2), 138 - 187.

Fauconnier, G., & Turner, M. 1998b. Principles of conceptual integration. In J. P. Koening (Ed.), *Discourse and Cognition: Bridging the Gap* (pp. 269 - 293). Standford, GA: CSLI Publication.

Fauconnier, G., & Turner, M. 2002. *The Way We Think: Conceptual blending and the mind's hidden complexities.* New York: Basic Books.

Fawcett, R. A. 2000. *Theory of Syntax for Systemic Functional Linguistics.* Amsterdam/Philadelphia: John Benjamins.

Firbas, J. 1992. *Functional Sentence Perspective in Written and Spoken Communication.* Cambridge: CUP.

Firbas, J. 2007. *Functional Sentence Perspective in Written and Spoken Communication.* Beijing: World Publishing House.

Fleischman, S. 1990. *Tense and Narrativity.* Austin: University of Taxes Press.

Francis, G. 1989. Thematic selection and distribution in written discourse. *Word*, *40*, 1 - 2.

Francis, G. 1995. Corpus-driven grammar and its relevance to the learning of English in a cross-cultural situation. In A. Pakir (Ed.) *English In Education: Multicultural Perspective.* Singapore: Unipress.

Freud, S. 1900. *The Interpretation of Dreams.* Online ebook version.

Friedman, L. B., & Sulby, E. 1986. Cohesive harmony analysis: issues of text pragmatics and macro-structure. *Research in Literacy: Merging Perspective*

Yearbook of the 36th National Reading Conference.

Fries, C. 1952. *The Structure of English.* New York: Harcourt, Brace and Company.

Fries, P. 1981. On the status of theme in English: arguments from discourse. *Forum Linguisticum*, *6*(1): 1-38.

Fries, P. 1982. On Repetition and interpretation. *Forum Linguisticum*, 7(1): 50-64.

Fries, P. 1991a. Signal of cohesion in English. Handout.

Fries, P. 1991b. The structuring of information in written English text. In M. A. K. Halliday, & F. C. C. Peng (Eds.), *Current Research in Functional Grammar, Discourse, and Computational Linguistics with a Foundation in Systemic Theory.* Special Issue of *Language Sciences*, *14*(4), 1-28.

Fries, P. H. 1993. Information flow in written advertising. In J. E. Alatis (Ed.), *Language, Communication, and Social Meaning* (pp.336-352). Washington, D. C.: Georgetown University Press.

Gee, J. P. 2000. *An Introduction to Discourse Analysis: Theory and method.* Beijing: Foreign Language Teaching and Research Press.

Gleason, H. A., Jr. 1965. *Linguistics and English Grammar.* New York: Holt, Rinehart and Winston.

Glucksberg, S. & Danks, J. H. 1975. *Experimental Psycholinguistics.* London & New York: Psychology Press, Tyler & Francis Group.

Goodman, K., Smith, E. B., Meredith, R., & Goodman, Y. M. 1986. *Language and Thinking in School.* New York: Richard C. Owen Publishers.

Grice, H. P. 1967. Logic and conversation. In P. Cole, and J. L. Morgan (Eds.), *Syntax and Semantics III: Speech Acts* (pp.41-58). New York: Academic Press.

Gumperz, J. 1982. *Discourse Strategies.* Cambridge: CUP.

Gundel, J. K., Hedberg, N., & Zacharski, R. 1993. Cognitive status and the form of referring expressions in discourse. *Language*, *69*, 274-307.

Gülich, E., & Quasthoff, U. M. 1985. Narrative analysis. In van Dijk (Ed.) *Handbook of Discourse Analysis 2* (pp.169-197). New York: Academic Press.

Halliday, M. A. K. 1963. The tones of English. In J. Webster (Ed.), *Studies in English Language* (pp.237-263). London: Continuum.

Halliday, M. A. K. 1967a. Notes on transitivity and theme in English (Part 1). *Journal of Linguistics*, *3*(1), 37-81.

Halliday, M. A. K. 1967b. Notes on transitivity and theme in English (Part 2). *Journal of Linguistics*, *3*(2), 199-244.

Halliday, M. A. K. 1968. Notes on transitivity and theme in English (Part 3). *Journal of Linguistics*, 4(2), 179–215.

Halliday, M. A. K. 1970. Language structure and language function. In J. Lyons (Ed.), *New Horizons in Linguistics* (pp.140–165). Baltimore: Penguin.

Halliday, M. A. K. 1973. *Explorations in the Functions of Language*. New York: Elsevier North-Holland.

Halliday, M. A. K. 1975. *Learning How to Mean — Explorations in the Development of Language*. London: Edward Arnold.

Halliday, M. A. K. 1985a. *An Introduction to Functional Grammar*. London: Edward Arnold.

Halliday, M. A. K. 1985b. *Spoken and Written Language*. Victoria: Deaken University Press.

Halliday, M. A. K. 1985c. English intonation a resource for discourse. In J. Webster (Ed.), *Studies in English Language* (pp.287–292). London: Continuum.

Halliday, M. A. K. 1994. *An Introduction to Functional Grammar* (2nd ed.). London: Edward Arnold.

Halliday, M. A. K., & Hasan, R. 1976. *Cohesion in English*. London: Longman.

Halliday, M. A. K., & Hasan, R. 1985/1989. *Language, Context and Text: Aspects of language in a social-semiotic perspective*. Oxford: OUP.

Halliday, M. A. K., & Matthissen, C. M. 1999. *Construing Experience Through Meaning: A language-based approach to cognition*. London and New York: Continuum.

Halliday, M. A. K., & Matthissen, C. M. 2004. *An Introduction to Functional Grammar* (3rd ed.). London: Edward Arnold.

Hasan, R. 1984. The nursery tale as a genre. *Nottingham Linguistic Circular* (Volume 13).

Hasan, R. 1987. *Linguistics, Language and Verbal Art*. Victoria: Deaken University Press.

Hasan, R. 1989. *Linguistics, Language, and Verbal Art*. Oxford: OUP.

Hatch, E. M. 1983. *Psycholinguistics: A Second Language Perspective*. Rowley, MA: Newbury House.

Hemingway, E. 1954. Soldier's home. In R. P. Warren, & A. Erskine (Eds.), *Short Story Masterpieces*. New York: Dell Publishing Co.

Herndon, J. 1970. *A Survey of Modern Grammars*. New York: Holt, Rinehart and

Winston.

Hoey, M. 1991a. *Patterns of Lexis in Text*. Oxford: OUP.

Hoey, M. 1991b. Some properties of spoken discourse. In R. Bowers, & C. Brumfit (Eds), *Applied Linguistics and English Language Teaching* (pp.64 - 85). London and Basingstock: Macmillan Publishers, Ltd.

Hopper, P. J., & Thompson, S. A. 1980. Transitivity in grammar and discourse. *Language*, *56*(2), 251 - 299.

Huddleston, R. (1984). *Introduction to English Grammar*. Cambridge: CUP.

Jespersen, O. 1924. *The Philosophy of Grammar*. London: George Allen & Unwin Ltd.

Jespersen, O. 1925. *Mankind, Nation and Individual*. Oslo: Aschehong.

Jespersen, O. 1933a. *Essentials of English Grammar*. London: George Allen & Unwin Ltd.

Jespersen. O. 1933b. *Analytic Syntax*. London: George Allen & Unwin Ltd.

Jespersen, O. 1937. *Analytic Syntax*. Chicago: University of Chicago Press.

Jespersen, O. 1942. *A Modern English Grammar* (Part VI). Copenhagen: Ejnar Munkgaard.

Jespersen, O. 1960. *Selected Writings of Otto Jespersen*. London; George Allen & Unwin Ltd.

Kamp, H. R., ChristianKamp, H., & Rohrer, C. 1983. Tense in texts. In R. Bauerle, C. Schwarze, & A. von Stechow (Eds.), *Meaning, Use and Interpretation of Language* (pp.250 - 269). Berlin: de Gruyter.

Koller, V. 2003. Metaphor Clusters, Metaphor Chains: Analyzing the Multifunctionality of Metaphor in Text. *Metaphorik de*, *5*, 115 - 134.

Krashen, S. 1994. The pleasure hypothesis. In J. E. Alatis (Ed.) *Georgetown Round Table on Languages and Linguistics* (pp. 299 - 322). Washington: Georgetown University Press.

Labov, W., & Waletzsky, J. 1967. Narrative analysis: oral versions of personal experience. In J. Helm (Ed.), *Essays on the Verbal and Visual Arts: Proceedings of 1996 Annual Spring Meeting of the American Ethnography Society* (pp.12 - 44). Seattle: University of Washington Press.

Labov, W. 1972. The transformation of experience in narrative syntax. In *Language in the Inner City* (pp.354 - 398). Philadelphia: University of Pennsylvania Press.

Lakoff, G. 1993. The contemporary theory of metaphor. In A. Ortony (Ed.),

Metaphor and Thought (2nd ed.) (pp.202 – 251). Cambridge: CUP.

Lakoff, G. 2005, Cognitive linguistics: what it means and where it is going. *Journal of Foreign Languages*, *1*, 2 – 22.

Lakoff, G., & Johnson, M. 1980. *Metaphor We Live By*. Chicago: The University of Chicago Press.

Lambrecht, K. 1994. *Information Structure and Sentence Form*. Cambridge: CUP.

Langacker, R. W. 1987a. *Foundations of Cognitive Grammar*, *Vol. I*. Stanford: Stanford University Press.

Langacker, R. W. 1987b. Nouns and verbs. *Language*, *63*(1), 53 – 94.

Langacker, R. W. 1991a. Cognitive grammar. In F. G. Droste, & J. E. Joseph (Eds.) *Linguistic Theory and Grammatical Description* (pp.275 – 306). Amsterdam: John Benjamins.

Langacker, R. W. 1991b. *Foundations of Cognitive Grammar. Vol. II*. Stanford: Stanford University Press.

Langacker, R. W. 2001. Discourse in cognitive grammar. *Cognitive Linguistics*, *12*(2), 143 – 188.

Langacker, R. W. 2004, Metonymy in grammar, *Journal of Foreign Languages*, *6*, 2 – 24.

Lavine, T. Z. 1984. *From Socrates to Sartre: The Philosophical Quest*. New York: Bantam Books.

Leech, G. N., & Short, M. H. 1981. *Style in Fiction: A linguistic introduction to English fictional prose*. London: Pearson Longman.

Lemke, J. L. 1995. Intertextuality and text semantics. In M. Gregory, & P.H. Fries (Eds), *Discourse in Society: Systemic functional perspectives* (pp. 85 – 114). Norwood (N.J.): Ablex Publishing.

Lemke, J. L. 1998. Resources for attitudinal meaning: evaluative orientations in text semantics. *Functions of Language*, *5*(1), 33 – 56.

Li, C. N., & Thompson, S. A. 1981. *Mandarin Chinese: A functional reference grammar*. Berkeley and Los Angeles: University of California Press.

Longacre, R. E.1981. A spectrum and profile approach to discourse analysis. *Text and Talk*, *1*(4), 337 – 359.

Longacre, R. E. 1989. Two hypotheses regarding text generation and analysis. *Discourse Processed*, *12*, 413 – 460.

Mailer, N. 1968. *The Armies of the Night*. New York: New American Library.

Malinowski, B. 1923. *The Problem of Meaning in Primitive Languages*. Supplement I to C. K. Ogden, & I. A. Richards (Eds.). *The Meaning of Meaning* (pp.296 – 336). New York: Harcourt Brace & World.

Mann, W., & Thompson, S. A. 1987. Rhetorical structure theory: a theory of text organization. In L. Polanyi (Ed), *The Structure of Discourse*. Norwood NJ: Ablex Publishing Corporation.

Martin, J. R. 1992. *English Text: System and structure*. Philadelphia/Amsterdam: John Benjamins.

Martin, J. R., Matthiessen, C.M.I.M., & Painter, C. 1997. *Working with Functional Grammar*. London: Arnold.

Martin, J. R., & Rose, D. 2003. *Working with Discourse: Meaning beyond the Clause*. London and New York: Continuum.

Martin, J. R., & White, P. R. R. 2005. *The Language of Evaluation: Appraisal in English*. Palgrave: Macmillan.

Matthiessen, C. M. I. M., & Thompson, S. A. 1988. The structure of discourse and subordination. In J. Haiman and S. A. Thompson (Eds.), *Clause Combining in Grammar and Discourse* (pp.175 – 329). Amsterdam: Benjamings.

Maugham, S. 1915. *Of Human Bondage*. New York: George H. Doran Company.

Maugham, S. 1990. The Luncheon. In B. Wegmann, & M. P. Knezevic (Eds.), *MOSAIC I: A reading skills book*. New York: McGrow-Hill Publishing Company.

Maugham, S. 1944. Rain. In Weidman, J. (Ed.), *Somerset Maugham Pocket Book* (pp.305 – 355). New York: Pocket Books.

Morgan, J. L. 1993. Observations on the pragmatics of metaphor. In A. Ortony (Ed.) *Metaphor and Thought* (2nd ed.), Cambridge: CUP.

Ochs, E. 1997. Narrative. In van Dijk, T. A. (Ed.) *Discourse as Structure and Process*. London: SAGE.

O'Neill, W. L. 1980. *Coming Apart*. New York: Quadrangle/The New York Book Co. Inc.

Perry, M. 1990. *Western Civilization*. Boston: Houghton Mifflin Company.

Pragglejaz Group. 2007. MIP: A method for identifying metaphorically used words in discourse. *Metaphor and Symbol*, *22*(1), 1 – 39.

Quirk, R., et al. 1972. *A Grammar of Contemporary English*. London: Longman.

Quirk, R., et al. 1985. *A Comprehensive Grammar of the English Language*. London/New York: Longman.

Radden, G., & R. Dirven. 2007. *Cognitive Grammar*. Amsterdam: John Benjamins.

Ren, S. 1994. Culture, discourse and choice of structure. In J. E. Alatis (Ed.), *Educational Linguistics, Cross-cultural Communication, and Global Interdependence* (Georgetown University Round Table on Language and Linguistics, 1994) (pp.150 - 172). Washington, D. C.: Georgetown University Press.

Ren, S. 2001. Linguistic features and discourse semantics. In S. Ren, et al. (Eds.) *Grammar and Discourse* (pp.75 - 84). Macao: University of Macao Publication Center.

Ren, S. 2010. Multiple Blending in *All the King's Men*. In D. Yu (Ed.), *Selected Papers on Stylistics I* (pp. 139 - 158). Shanghai: Shanghai Foreign Language Education Press.

Renkema, J. 1993. *Discourse Studies: An introductory textbook*. Amsterdam: Benjamins.

Schiffrin, D. 1994. *Approaches to Discourse*. Oxford: Blackwell.

Shaw, I. 1969. *Rich Man, Poor Man*. New York: Dell.

Sheldon, S. 1982. *The Master of the Game*. New York: Warner.

Simpson, P. 2004. *Stylistics: A resource book for students*. London and New York: Routledge.

Sinclair, J. (Ed.) 1990. *Collins Cobuild English Grammar*. London and Glasgow: Collins.

Sperber, D., & Wilson, D. 1986. *Relevance: Communication and cognition*. Oxford: Basil Blackwell Ltd.

Sperber, D., & Wilson, D. 1987. Précis of relevance: communication and cognition. *Behavioral and Brain Science*, *10*, 697 - 710.

Steen, G. J. 1999a. From linguistic to conceptual metaphor in five steps. In R. W. Gibbs, Jr., & G. J. Steen (Eds.), *Metaphor in Cognitive Linguistics* (pp.57 - 77). Armsterdam: John Benjamins.

Steen, G. J. 1999b. Metaphor and discourse: towards a linguistic checklist for metaphor analysis. In L. Cameron, & G. Low (Eds.) *Researching and Applying Metaphor* (pp.81 - 104). Cambridge: CUP.

Stockwell, P. 2002. *Cognitive Poetics: An introduction*. London & New York: Routledge Taylor & Francis Group.

Stubbs, M. 1983. *Discourse Analysis*. Chicago: The University of Chicago Press.

Tan, A. 1989. *The Joy Luck Club*. New York: Ivy.

Thompson, G. 2000. *Introducing Functional Grammar*. Beijing: Foreign Language and Research Press.

Thompson, S., & Mann, W. 1987. Rhetorical structure theory: a framework for the analysis of texts. *Pragmatics*, *1*, 79 - 105.

Threadgold, T. 1986. Language, semiotics, ideology. In T. Threadgold, et al. (Eds.) *Language, Semiotics, Ideology* (pp.15 - 60). Sydney: Pathfinder Press.

Turkel, S. 1975. *Working Source of Data*. New York: Avon Books.

Ungerer, F., & Schmid, H. 1996. *An Introduction to Cognitive Linguistics*. London & New York: Longman.

Van Dijk, T. A. 1977. *Text and Context*. London & New York: Longman.

Van Dijk, T. A. 1997. Study of discourse. In T. A. van Dijk (Ed.), *Discourse as Structure and Process* (pp.1 - 34). London: Sage Publications Ltd.

Warren, R. P. 1946. *All the King's Men*. New York: Harcourt, Brace and Company.

Warren, R. P. 1974. *All the King's Men*. New York & London: Harcourt Brace & Company.

Wilson, D. 2001. Introduction. In Z. He, & R. Ran (Eds.), *Pragmatics & Cognition: Relevance Theory* (pp.1 - 16). Beijing: Foreign Language Teaching and Research Press.

Wilson, D. 2003. Relevance and understanding. In Zh. He (Ed.) *Selected Readings for Pragmatics* (pp.435 - 466). Shanghai: Shanghai Foreign Language Education Press.

Wood, F.T. 1981. *Current English Usage*. London: Macmillan.

Yang, M. 1958. *Song of Youth*. Beijing: The Writers Publishing House.

Yang, S. 1978. *Selected Essays by Yang Shuo*. Beijing: People's Literature Press.

Ziff, P. 1960. *Semantic Analysis*. Ithaca and London: Cornell University Press.

谌馨荪[Chen, X.]. 1997. The New World. 大学英语·快速阅读. 上海:上海外语教育出版社.

程雨民[Cheng, Y.]. 1989; 2004(修订版). 英语语体学. 上海:上海外语教育出版社.

程雨民[Cheng, Y.]. 1990. 词汇意义、逻辑推理和语用学. 现代外语(2): 1 - 7.

程雨民[Cheng, Y.]. 1997. 语言系统及其运作. 上海:上海外语教育出版社.

胡壮麟[Hu, Z.]. 2004. 理论文体学. 北京:北京大学出版社.

胡壮麟[Hu, Z.]. 2004. 认知隐喻学. 北京：北京大学出版社.

李战子[Li, Z.]. 2000. 语言的人际元功能新探. 北京：军事谊文出版社.

刘方桐[Liu, F.]. 1984. 现代西方人本主义哲学思潮的来龙去脉. 复旦学报(社会科学版)编辑部编. 现代西方哲学思潮评介. 上海：复旦大学出版社.

任绍曾[Ren, S.]. 1991. The Texture of Norman Mailer's *The Armies of the Night*. 杭州大学外语系学术委员会编. 外语论丛(pp.1–34). 杭州：杭州大学出版社.

任绍曾[Ren, S.]. 1992. 语境在叙事语篇中的体现. 外国语(2)：15–20.

任绍曾[Ren, S.]. 1993. The narrative structure of *The Armies of the Night*. 朱永生主编. 语言·语篇·语境. 北京：清华大学出版社.

任绍曾[Ren, S.]. 2000. 语篇中语言型式化的意义. 外语教学与研究(2)：110–116.

任绍曾[Ren, S.]. 2003. 语篇的多维分析. 外国语(3)：35–42.

任绍曾[Ren, S.]. 2006a. 概念隐喻和语篇连贯. 外语教学与研究(2)：91–100.

任绍曾[Ren, S.]. 2006b. 概念隐喻及其语篇体现. 外语与外语教学(10)：17–21.

任绍曾[Ren, S.]. 2008. 概念隐喻与语篇. 外语教学与研究(2)：83–92.

申丹[Shen, d.]. 2005. 关于西方文体学新发展的思考. 外语教学与研究(3)：56–64.

沈家煊[Shen, J.]. 1994. R. W. Langacker 的"认知语法". 国外语言学(1)：12–20.

束定芳[Shu, D.]. 2000. 隐喻学研究. 上海：上海外语教育出版社.

王振华[Wang, Z.]. 2001. 评价系统及其运作. 外国语(6)：13–20.

卫真道[Webster, J. J.]. 2002. 篇章语言学. 徐赳赳译. 北京：中国社会科学出版社.

熊学亮[Xiong, X.]. 1999. 认知语用学概论. 上海：上海外语教育出版社.

徐崇温[Xu, C.]. 1984. 评萨特的"存在主义的马克思主义". 复旦学报(社会科学版)编辑部编. 现代西方哲学思潮评介. 上海：复旦大学出版社.

杨永林[Yang, Y.]. 2002. 英语论文写作研究. 北京：中央广播电视大学出版社.

殷企平[Yin, Q.]. 2001. 英国小说批评史. 上海：上海外语教育出版社.

张德禄[Zhang, D.]. 2005. 语言的功能与文体. 北京：高等教育出版社.

附　录

各章中英文摘要

1

语篇的多维分析

摘　要：语篇作为多功能的构建体具有三个维度，即语言使用、信念的传递（认知）和社会情景中的互动。本章从语言、社会和认知三个角度对语篇的多维分析作了探讨。对语篇作语言分析必须基于语法的基本结构，但鉴于隐喻在反映现实中的普遍性和重要性，对隐喻的分析当是对语篇进行语言分析不可忽视的部分。同时，除分析经验意义的语言体现外，还应对语篇的社会意义和主题的语言体现进行分析。把语篇作为社会互动加以分析当然要分析体现人际意义的语气结构，但是作为社会实践，语篇必须结合社会结构加以分析，才能显示其社会意义。从评价系统出发的分析是必要的补充。信念传递是一个认知过程。要了解体现信念的主题，需要推理，而推理的语言基础是型式化，推理的依据是从认知语境中提取的知识。语篇的这三个维度是相互联系、相互影响的，在语篇分析中都必须加以考虑。
关键词：语篇；多维；分析

Multi-dimensional Analysis of Discourse

Abstract: Discourse as a metafunctional construct is characterized by its three dimensions, that is, language use, the communication of beliefs (cognition), and interaction in social situations. This chapter aims to look into the multi-dimensional analysis of discourse from linguistic, social and cognitive perspectives. The linguistic analysis of a discourse has to be based on the basic structures of grammar, but owing to their universality and importance in reflecting reality, metaphors should be taken into account as an integral part of the analysis. Furthermore, not only the linguistic realization of experiential meaning of the discourse, but also the linguistic features of its social meaning and theme should be made the object of study. Discourse as social interaction has to be analyzed in terms of mood structure, but as social practice it has to be studied in relation to social structure so that its social meaning can be brought out. An additional analysis in the light of Appraisal System is an indispensable supplement. The communication of beliefs involves a cognitive process. To understand the theme as the belief to be conveyed in the discourse, inference is called for, and inference has to be made on the basis of linguistic patternings and knowledge accessed from cognitive context. These three dimensions, which interact and influence each other in creating discourse, should all be taken into consideration in discourse analysis.

Key words: discourse; multi-dimensional; analysis

2

叙事语篇的多层次语义结构

摘　要：在话语分析领域中已经有几种有影响的语篇结构理论，如拉博夫的叙事结构理论，韩礼德和韩茹凯的语类结构潜势理论。这些理论勾勒的语篇结构只含若干成分或阶段，仅对语篇作线形描述。但是叙事语篇不仅讲述故事，而且作为社会实践具有社会意义以及体现语篇意图的主题。这说明叙事语篇具有三个层次的语义结构。本章试图从功能理论出发，通过对三则叙事语篇的分析，验证叙事语篇的这三个语义层次，说明这三个意义层次如何体现整体语境中不同层次，如何与语境配置中的三个因素相对应,又如何为词汇语法特征所体现。

关键词: 叙事语篇;多层次;语义结构

Multi-level Semantic Structure in Narrative

Abstract: There have been several models setting out the structure of a genre, which consists of a series of linearly sequenced elements or stages, for instance, narrative structure (Labov 1972), and generic structure potentials (Halliday & Hasan 1985). However, a narrative does not merely tell a story. As social practice, it has its social significance and, with its intentionality, offers an explanation or gives a moral. This suggests that a narrative has three levels of meaning. This chapter is an attempt to bring out the multi-level semantic structure in the light of functional theory by analyzing a short text, a short story and a novel. The findings in the analyses show how the first two levels of meaning are determined by the physical context, and how the deep meaning is constrained by the cognitive context. The chapter also shows how the three levels of meaning center round the three contextual factors, and how they are realized by different features in lexico-grammar.

Key words: narrative; multi-level; semantic structure

3

关注中心和基本主题

——试析小句与段落之间的语篇单位

摘　要: 在话语分析中话语究竟如何推进当是一个根本性问题。韩礼德指出英语话语是作为一系列不间断的具有旋律特征的单位推进的。对于话语进展,切夫有另外一种看法,其出发点是意识在语言和语言使用中的作用。他把韩礼德的信息单位称之为体现意识焦点的意义单位(idea unit)。意识有若干特征,主要的是意识有焦点;此外,意识焦点总是处于边缘意识的包围之中,活性焦点周围的半活性信息为焦点提供语境。但是单个意识焦点所包含的信息常常不足以充分地满足人们的需要。通常的情况是,足以满足说话人需要的信息量要溢过单个意识焦点的有限容量。这就需要允许几个焦点扫描这一信息,构成切夫所说的关注中心(center of interest),也就是语篇层次上的基本主题。意识焦点是活性信息,而关注中心是半活性信息,也就是意识边缘地区的信息。它的作用在于引导意识从一个焦点向另一个焦点转移。切夫说主题是可以处于半活性状态的大量信息的组合。基本主题构成介于小句和段落之间的语篇单位。在实践中基本主题并不难识别,基本主题之间往往有话语标记或附加语标识,当意识取向或意识起作用的方式改变时,就会出现新的基本主题。

关键词: 意识;焦点;关注中心;基本主题

Center of Attention and Basic Topic

Abstract: To the question how discourse proceeds we find an answer in Halliday (1994) where it is stated that English speech progresses as an unbroken succession of melodic units called tone groups and each tone group realizes one unit of information. There is an alternative way of looking at the development of discourse, which starts with the role consciousness plays in language and language use. What Halliday calls an information unit Chafe refers to as a focus of consciousness or an idea unit. One of the properties of consciousness is that it has a central focus and a periphery. It is often the case that what can be embraced within a single focus is often too little to adequately serve the needs of the human organism. It is necessary to allow several focuses to scan available information so a number of focuses of consciousness may make up a super-focus which constitutes a center of interest or basic-level topic. While a focus of consciousness is constrained by human cognitive capacity, a center of interest is not. A basic-level topic ends where the speaker decides the topic has been adequately covered for whatever purpose he may have in mind. The scope of a basic-level topic constitutes an intermediate discourse unit between a clause and a paragraph. Basic-level topics are not difficult to identify in practice. The boundaries between them are often marked with discourse markers or adjuncts and a new center of interest occurs where there is a shift of consciousness in orientation of mode.

Key words: consciousness; focus; center of attention; basic-level topic

4

信息单位与信息状态

——试析语言信息的二分说与三分说

摘　要：话语究竟是如何推进的？韩礼德的回答是英语话语推进呈现为不间断的系列旋律单位，每个旋律单位称作一个语调组，而每个语调组体现一个信息单位，由已知信息和新信息构成。切夫把韩礼德的语调组叫做意识焦点。意识的特点之一是它具有焦点中心和边缘区域。切夫认为不考虑意识就无法理解已知信息和新信息的区别。他根据概念的激活状态把信息作三项划分，即已知信息、可及信息和新信息。本章试图探讨两种信息划分的依据、异同，并提出使两者相容的思路。

关键词：功能；信息单位；意识；信息状态

Information Unit and Information Status

——A Tentative Inquiry into the Binary Division and Three-way Breakdown of Information

Abstract: To the question how discourse proceeds, Halliday's reply is that English speech progresses as an unbroken succession of melodic units called tone groups and each tone group realizes one unit of information, which consists of given information and new information. What Halliday calls an information unit Chafe refers to as a focus of consciousness. According to Chafe it is impossible to understand the distinction between given and new information without taking consciousness into consideration. On the basis of activation cost of concepts Chafe comes up with a three-way breakdown into given, accessible and new information in place of the binary distinction of given and new. This chapter looks into the justifications of the two types of division of information, brings out their differences and suggests a way to reconcile the three-way breakdown with the binary distinction.

Key words: function; information unit; consciousness; information status

5

语境在叙事语篇中的语言体现

摘　要：语篇和语境是辩证地相互联系。语境决定语篇，语篇体现语境。本章详细分析了《夜幕下的大军》一段样文的语言特征，旨在说明叙事小说如何在语境的三大要素，即语场、语旨和语式上体现语境，如何具体地在语言使用的渠道和媒介上体现语境。

关键词：语言体现；语境；叙事语篇

Linguistic Realization of Context in Narrative Discourse

Abstract: Text and context are dialectically related. It is the context that determines the text, and the text reversedly gives linguistic expression to the context. This chapter aims to bring to light how a narrative discourse realizes the context in which it unfolds in terms of Field, Tenor and Mode of discourse, and more specifically in terms of Media and Vehicle in the use of language by analyzing the linguistic features of a sample passage taken from the novel *The Armies of the Night*.

Key words: linguistic realization; context, narrative discourse

6

《夜幕下的大军》的组篇

摘　要：本章从功能语言学的视角出发研究梅勒所著小说《夜幕下的大军》的组篇。组篇基于黏合，所以本文对段落、章节之间，最后对小说的两卷之间的黏合纽带进行了详细的探讨。结果说明指称和重复是段落间的主要黏合手段,而且也是章节之间使用较多的黏合手段。段落之间的黏合纽带往往出现在某段的首句和上段末句之间,这是对个人经验叙事的语篇特征。两卷副标题所含黏合纽带足以说明这两个部分语义上是黏合的。要研究黏合,必须要重视贯穿全书的语义链。我们找出了12条主要语义链并对其相互作用进行了研究,从而获得了四个宏观主题。这四个主题构成小说的整体主题,并揭示了全书的组篇。

关键词: 组篇;黏合;黏合纽带;黏合链;互动;宏观主题

The Texture of *The Armies of the Night*

Abstract: This chapter looks from a functional perspective into the texture of the novel *The Armies of the Night* by Norman Mailer. Texture is based on cohesion. The paper examines in detail the cohesive ties between paragraphs, those between chapters and ultimately between the two books of the novel. The results show that reference and repetition are the two major cohesive devices by which paragraphs are linked together, and are also more favored cohesive devices between chapters. The cohesive tie often found between the first sentence of a certain paragraph and the last of the previous one might be a characteristic feature of long narration of personal experience. The cohesive tie contained in the subtitles of the two books alone clearly indicates that they are semantically related. To study the cohesion of a full-length novel, it is necessary to identify the semantic chains that run through the text. Twelve major semantic chains are identified and their interactions explored, out of which four macro-propositions are found and then reworded after the investigation of cohesive chains of propositions. They constitute the global proposition of the novel, thus bringing to light the texture of the novel.

Key words: texture; cohesion; cohesive tie; cohesive chain; interaction; macro-proposition

7

《夜幕下的大军》的结构

摘　要：本章是上一章的续篇。上一章讨论叙事小说《夜幕下的大军》的组篇，本章讨论该小说的结构。对组篇的讨论揭示了四个宏观命题或主题。这四个主题为语篇提供了构成不同层次的几个成分。简而言之，它们是：主人公 Mailer 作为人物，向五角大楼进军作为事件，不同政见构成的政治图景，以及前景难以预料的美国这一国家。关于 Mailer 的第一层次贯穿本书第一卷，但在小说开篇第一段就得到充分的语言体现，而 Mailer 又作为叙事载体，贯穿全书的抗议事件作为第二层次获得了详细报道。第三层次语言上集中表现为五花八门的派别、组织、政治运动的名称以及他们各自的政见，加上年龄和性别的差异，呈现了当时纷繁复杂的美国政治图景。该书的最后一段借助隐喻总结了叙事人向读者传递的信息——美国的前景难以预料，这便是语篇的第四个层次。可见，这本叙事小说具有多层次的结构。

关键词：结构；叙事小说；主题；成分；层次

The Narrative Structure of *The Armies of the Night*

Abstract: This is a sequel to Chapter 6, the texture of the novel *The Armies of the Night* by Mailer, which reveals the four macro-propositions or themes of the book. Here the concern is with the structure of the novel. The four themes provide the elements it takes to form the various levels of the structure. They are: Mailer the protagonist as a character, March on the Pentagon as a political event, the difference of viewpoints among participating social groups as constituting the political scene, and finally the uncertainty the United States, the country faces for its future. The first level about the character finds concentrated linguistic expression in the very first paragraph, and then the participant is made a narrative vehicle for the account of the event throughout the book, which makes up the second level. The third level about the political scene is, among other things, linguistically expressed by a variety of names of groups, organizations and political movements, each with its own views on political affairs, and complicated by the difference in sex and age. The last passage of the book sums up the message the narrator wants to get across to the reader about the uncertainty of the country by means of a metaphor, which represents the fourth level. All this shows that this narrative discourse is hierarchically structured.

Key words: structure; narrative novel; theme; element; level

8

词汇语境线索与语篇理解

摘　要：语篇理解需依靠语境。理解书面语篇必须依靠从语篇推导出来的认知语境。本文集中讨论单句书面语篇如何依靠词汇语境线索激活心理图式，经过推理，理解语篇。语言研究中，结构主义利用语法形式作为标志研究语法结构，社会语言学利用语音、语调和语篇程式等语篇特征作为语境线索了解说话人意图、态度等人际意义。唯独词汇未加利用。言语交际首先建立在语言基础之上。理解语篇的信息内容离不开词汇；当字面理解受阻时，则需要词汇语境线索。词汇语境线索可以解决歧义、表面搭配不当、词义空泛、词的临时组合和新词的意义等问题，也有助于翻译和外语教学。

关键词：词汇；语境线索；语篇；理解

Lexical Contextualization Cues and Discourse Comprehension

Abstract: Context is indispensable for the understanding of texts. To understand a written text we rely on the cognitive context inferred from the text. This paper deals with texts realized by single sentences, the comprehension of which relies on lexical contextualization cues for the psychological schemata they trigger as the frame for inference. In linguistics, structuralists use grammatical devices as formal markers to study syntactic

structure while psycholinguists employ intonation, stress and some discourse features as contextualization cues to get at such interpersonal meaning as intention and attitude on the part of the speaker. However, speech communication is primarily based on language. It is impossible to understand the message content of a discourse without understanding the words, and in cases where the direct message is hard to arrive at, lexical contextualization cues are indispensable. Words as contextualization cues may solve problems in comprehension arising from ambiguity, seemingly improper collocation, words of too general meanings, nonce word combinations and new words.
Key words: lexical; contextualization cue; text; comprehension

9

语篇中语言型式化的意义

——探索语篇主题的一种途径

摘　要：叙事语篇，特别是短篇小说（如毛姆的《午宴》），往往有三层含义：本义、社会意义和主题。主题是从语篇的具体特征中分离出来的，就其性质而言它近乎一种概括。因此对主题的理解必定经过推理，而推理又必须依靠语境和世界知识，但也必须建立在语言证据的基础之上。语篇中的型式化是语篇表达深层意义的手段。型式化有主次之分。主要型式化是语篇的前景化部分，与语篇的整体意义有关，因此通过查寻和分析语篇的若干型式化及其对比，可以为了解主题而进行的推理提供可信的语言依据。
关键词：语篇；语言型式化；主题

The Significance of Patternings in Discourse

——A Way to Find the Theme of Discourse

Abstract: There are three levels of meaning in narrative discourse, especially in narrative novel, such as *The Luncheon* by Maugham, which are the literal meaning, social meaning and theme. Theme is what the discourse is about when dissociated from the particularities of the discourse, which is a

kind of a generalization in nature, so theme can only be arrived at through inference. And inference has to be made in relation to context and the world knowledge of the reader, and it has also to be made on the basis of linguistic evidence. Patternings in discourse constitute an effective way to make deeper meaning, and the main patternings are oriented to the foregrounding of discourse, therefore related to the total meaning of discourse. So by finding, analyzing and comparing the main patternings in discourse we can get linguistic evidence on the basis of which theme can be arrived at.
Key words: discourse; linguistic patterning; theme

10

语篇和结构选择

摘　要：本章从功能视角出发考察语法与语篇的关系，集中研究英汉语篇在选择两种语法基本结构的差异。叶斯柏森区分两种连接首品词（如名词）和次品词（如形容词）的方式，并称这两种结构为连系式和组合式。语篇是语义单位，其语义由词汇语法体现，但是，语篇对选用语法结构具有决定作用。英美人常说“I have a flat tire”，而在相同的语境里中国人则说“我车胎瘪了”。英语常选组合式，汉语则爱用连系式。语料显示，英语有多种便于使用组合式的结构资源，而汉语具有不少宜于使用连系式的结构资源。两种语言在使用这两种结构上的区别是由于这两种语言的类型区别：英语是主语突出的语言，而汉语是主位突出的语言，也可以有理由说，英语是句子导向语言，而汉语是语篇导向语言。这两种语言在选择不同结构上的区别最终或许是由于文化的影响。
关键词：语篇；语法结构；选择；连系式；组合式；类型差异

Discourse and Choice of Structure

Abstract: This chapter aims to study the relationship between grammar and discourse from a functional perspective by looking into the difference between English and Chinese in the choice of two basic grammatical structures in discourse. Jespersen distinguishes two ways of combining a primary (for instance, a noun) and a secondary (for instance, an adjective). The resulting structures are called junction ("a red rose") and nexus ("The rose is red"). Both are found in the two languages, but where English favors a nexus Chinese shows a marked inclination for a junction. In English people usually say "I have got a flat tire", while Chinese speakers will say "*wo chetai biele*" in the same context. A discourse is a semantic unit with its meaning realized lexical-grammatically. However, discourse plays a decisive role in the choice of grammatical structures. There are quite a number of structural resources in English that facilitate the use of junction whereas Chinese is rich in structural resources that contribute to the use of nexus. Linguistic data show that the preference of one of the structures is determined by how the language packages the messages in discourse, or simply determined by discourse. The study sheds light on the fact that the difference in the choice of the structures is attributable to the typological difference between the two languages: English is a subject-prominent language while Chinese is a theme-prominent language, or it may be sensible to say that English is a sentence-oriented language and Chinese a discourse-oriented language. The difference may be ultimately ascribed to the impact of culture on the two languages.

Key words: discourse; grammatical structure; choice; junction; nexus; typological difference

11

语言特征和语篇意义

摘　要：语言特征可用以表达语篇的深层意义，具体地说，是语言特征的型式化赋予语篇以深层意义。本章从功能语言学的视角探讨《大地》和《国王的人马》两本小说中的某些语言特征。一词多义可以成为表示父子之间见解差异的手段。被动式和语法隐喻的使用可以表明家庭主妇的顺从和从属地位。这些都有助于揭示《大地》中次语篇的局部主题。在《国王的人马》中 twitch 一词多次反复使用。它作为动词被用于几乎所有及物性过程,作为名词被拟人化、神化,从而成为至高无上、主宰一切的上帝。作者用 twitch 解释小说人物的爱情、家庭和事业的悲剧性的结局。这就为小说提供了主题。
关键词: 语言特征;推理;语篇语义

Linguistic Features and Discourse Semantics

Abstract: In English discourse lexical-grammatical features can be used to make deeper meaning. It is the patterning of linguistic patterns involving the use of these features that can be used symbolically to convey deeper meaning, either the local theme of a sub-text or the theme of a full-length novel. This paper looks into linguistic features taken from the two novels *The Great Earth* by P. S. Buck and *All the King's Men* by H. P. Warren from a functional approach. English words capable of different meanings can be turned into a device to show the difference in mentality between father and son, and the repeated use of the passive construction and the use of grammatical metaphor may give the impression of the woman's submission and subordination to her husband. This contributes to the local theme of the sub-text. The repeated use of *twitch* turns out to be an outstanding feature in the novel *All the King's Men*. As a noun it is used in all transitivity processes, and as a noun it is first personified and the deified so that it becomes omnipotent. The writer comes up with "All is twitch" and "Twitch is all" and explains all the life experiences of the characters in terms of twitch, which is the theme of the novel.
Key words: linguistic feature; inference; discourse semantics

12

英语名词指称及其语篇功能

摘　要: 英语名词词组可以在语篇中作为指称项回指或预指一个语段,构成指称链,成为组篇的一个重要手段。确定名词词组的指称语段必须通过推理。名词词组与其指称语段之间的语义关系十分复杂。名词词组用于指称语段时可以在语篇的不同结构层次上发挥语篇功能：在一种基本结构中名词词组常用以概括上文并加以评价;在段落中可起承上启下的作用;在语篇中回指名词短语可以成为段落新信息或宏观新信息的一部分,预指名词短语则可成为段落主位或宏观主位的一部分。
关键词： 英语;名词词组;语段指称;语篇功能

Reference of the Nominal Phrase in English and Its Discourse Function

Abstract: When a phoric element is realized as a nominal group it may presume as its referent an identifiable portion of a text. The text reference of nominal groups is an important resource for the texture and structure of discourse. As a portion of text may admit of different meanings and the nominal group can only refer to one of the semantic aspects of the presumed passage, it is necessary to make inference to identify the passage as referent and the aspect of meaning referred to.
Key words: English; noun phrase; textual reference; discourse function

13

英语时态的语篇功能

摘　要： 本章从功能的视角出发探讨英语一般现在时的语篇功能。英语一般现在时具有三个语义特征,即事实性、乏时性以及感觉上的乏距离性。这三个特征赋予现在时三个语篇功能,即表实功能、概括功能和突显功能,而这三个功能是现在时在语篇使用中语言的三个元功能的具体体现。
关键词： 现在时;语篇;功能;元功能

The Discourse Functions of Tense in English

Abstract: The chapter shows that out of the features of the present tense,

factuality, a temporality and lack of perceived distance are derived three functions that contribute to the organization of discourse. They are factual, generalizing and highlighting functions, which, in the final analysis, are the manifestation of the three metafunctions of language.
Key words: present tense; discourse; function; mata-function

14

Yes 和 No 在叙事语篇中的功能

——从认知功能视角的探索

摘　要：本章从认知功能的视角探讨 yes 和 no 在叙事语篇中的功能及其动因。英语的信息是以语调组为单位推进的。在切夫的理论中，一个语调组就是一个意识焦点，若干意识焦点构成一个关注中心，语言上体现为基本主题。在探讨中，我们始终关注 yes 和 no 的基本语义、在对话中的基本功能以及它们在书面语篇中所处的位置。对实例的分析表明作为接续语的 yes 和 no 一般出现在两个关注中心的交界处，当信息流、语篇推进受到干扰，需更大认知努力时，yes 和 no 可以起无可替代的作用。
关键词：yes/no；关注中心；叙事语篇；语篇功能

The Discourse Function of *Yes* and *No* in Narration

——A Cognitive-Functional Approach

Abstract: This chapter aims to look into the textual function of *yes* and *no* and find out the motivation for their employment in written narrative from a cognitive-functional approach. English speech progresses in tone groups. In cognitive terms a tone group is seen as realizing a focus of consciousness and a number of such focuses may make up a super-focus, which constitutes a center of interest or a basic-level topic. In identifying the textual function of the two words we keep in view their basic meaning as indicators of polarity, their basic functions in spoken interaction and their location in written discourse. Our data show that *yes* and *no* typically occur at the boundary of two centers of interest, used irreplaceably when some perturbation occurs so that more cognitive effort is called for to further the flow of information and the flow of discourse.

Key words: yes /no; center of attention; narrative discourse; textual function

15

英语辅句的动因及其在语篇中的评价功能

摘　要:本章从认知语言学和语篇语义学的角度探讨英语语篇中辅句的动因及其评价功能。根据当前语篇空间和注意框架的理论,辅句可视为体现零框架,适应负框架更新当前语篇空间的需要,并获得最大程度的凸显。这是辅句产生的动因,但有两个制约因素。语料分析显示:辅句对前句或句段作说明或评价。在这过程中,叙事人从记录者的角色转变为解释者和评价者。结合语篇可以对辅句提供的说明和解释进行评价维度的分析。辅句作解释时,评价维度的顺序是规范性、可取性、有理性,其中规范性是主要维度。辅句用作评价时,评价维度是有理性,在转义的情况下,如反语,否定有理性与有理性重叠,也可以是可取性。这一切都说明辅句是语篇的一个评价手段,一种评价资源。

关键词:英语;辅句;动因;语篇;评价功能

The Motivation and Evaluative Functions of Minor Clauses in English Discourse

Abstract: This chapter aims to study the motivation and evaluative functions of minor clauses in English text in the light of cognitive linguistics and discourse semantics. A minor clause can be understood as the realization of a zero-frame, which meets the expectation of the minus-frame to update the Current Discourse Space and thus achieves maximal salience. This is what motivates the use of minor clauses in discourse. Our analysis shows that minor clauses serve to elaborate or evaluate the preceding clause or chunk of discourse as the narrator changes his role from recorder to explainer or evaluator. As a minor clause is closely related to the preceding clause with its element mapping onto its counterpart, it is feasible to study the evaluative dimensions of the elaboration and evaluation that minor clauses provide as implied proposition. When a minor clause provides elaboration, the evaluative dimensions are normativity, desirability, and warrantability with normativity as the main dimension. When a minor clause serves as evaluation, the dimension is warrantability, and in case of metaphoric use of words, negative warrantability conflates with warrantibility, with the possible alternative of desirability. All this testifies to the fact that minor clauses constitute an evaluative resource in discourse.

Key words: English; minor clauses; motivation; discourse; evaluative function

16

概念隐喻与语篇

——对体现概念隐喻的语篇的多维分析

摘　要：隐喻可以体现在不同的语言层次上，如一个词、短语、小句或语篇。体现为语篇时，可以是小说或散文，也可以是诗歌。本文分析两首体现隐喻的诗，即朱熹的《观书有感》和艾米莉·狄金森的“He Ate and Drunk Precious Words”，拟回答这样两个相互联系问题：根据什么说一则语篇体现了隐喻？语篇体现的隐喻有哪些特征？本章对此进行隐喻分析、语篇分析和评价分析，以考察语言分析结果是否与隐喻分析的结果一致，从而揭示概念隐喻的本质特征。

关键词：概念隐喻；体现；语篇；分析

Conceptual Metaphor and Discourse

Abstract: Metaphor can be realized at various levels of linguistic organization, a word, phrase, clause or sentence, and discourse as well.

When realized in discourse, the discourse may take the form of a novel or an essay. It may also take the form of a poem such as "Reflections on Reading" by Zhu Xi and "He Ate and Drunk Precious Words" by Emily Dickinson, which are the concern of this chapter. It aims to address the question of what characterizes a discourse as the realization of a conceptual metaphor by a multi-level analysis consisting of a metaphor analysis, a text analysis and an appraisal analysis. The linguistic analysis is made in order to see whether the results are compatible with and in support of those found in metaphor analysis and how text realizes a metaphor.

Key words: conceptual metaphor; realization; discourse; analysis

17

概念隐喻和语篇连贯

摘　要:本章从认知的角度,根据雷考夫和兰艾克的理论,分析了罗伯特·佩恩·沃伦的叙事语篇《国王的人马》。语篇在叙事结构的框架内展开,一方面陈述人物经验,为隐喻提供经验基础;另一方面,通过对 twitch 的隐喻化完成对经验的概念化和诠释,结果是跨领域的概念映射——概念隐喻。隐喻是统驭语篇的因素,保证了语篇的连贯,而语篇则体现了概念隐喻。

关键词:概念隐喻;认知语法;语篇连贯

Conceptual Metaphor and Discourse Coherence

Abstract: This chapter is an analysis of the narrative discourse *All the King's Men* from a cognitive approach, centering round a conceptual metaphor, using theories advanced by Lakoff and Langacker. The text is found to unfold within the frame work of narrative structure, presenting the life of the characters, thus providing the experiential basis for the metaphor, and, meanwhile, proceeding with the conceptualization and construal of the experience by means of the metaphorization of the metaphoric expression

twitch! The result is a conceptual mapping across the domains — a conceptual metaphor: Life Is A Twitch. The metaphor serves as the unifying factor in the text, which ensures the coherence of the discourse, and the text, in its turn, represents the realization of the metaphor.
Key words: conceptual metaphor; cognitive grammar; discourse coherence

18

概念隐喻及其语篇体现

——对体现概念隐喻的语篇的多维分析

摘　要：概念隐喻可体现为词、短语或句子。隐喻也可体现为语篇。本文拟就一则体现隐喻的语篇（即杨绛《妙说读书》）进行多维分析。语言表达式体现隐喻，语篇则使隐喻实例化，两者不同。我们根据雷考夫提出的当代隐喻理论进行隐喻分析，根据韩礼德的功能语法理论进行语篇分析，根据马丁提出的评价理论进行评价分析。我们在概念层面上从目的域、本体对应、投射范围、中心思想、隐喻体系、概念推理和隐喻连贯等方面考察语篇；然后，再在语言层面上从主位进展、要点、宏观主位、宏观新信息等方面进行分析，并就态度、介入和评价维度作评价分析以验证隐喻分析的结果，从而了解语篇如何体现隐喻，隐喻又如何推动语篇的构成。
关键词：概念隐喻；语篇；体现；分析

Conceptual Metaphor and Its Realization in Discourse

Abstract: Metaphor may be realized at various levels of linguistic organization, a word, phrase, clause or sentence. It may also be realized as discourse. A distinction is made between the realization of metaphor by linguistic expressions and the instantiation of metaphor as a text. What we are going to undertake is a multi-level analysis of an essay "A Witty Talk on Reading Books" by Yang Jiang, consisting of a metaphor analysis made in the light of the contemporary theory of metaphor advanced by Lakoff, a text analysis within the framework of Hallidayan grammar and an appraisal analysis using the theory of appraisal system initiated by Martin. Metaphor analysis will be made in terms of target domain, ontological correspondences, coverage of the mapping, central idea, metaphor system, metaphorical reasoning and metaphorical coherence. Text analysis is concerned with method of development, point, and Macrotheme and Macronew. The appraisal analysis is discussed under such headings as attitude, engagement and evaluative dimensions. The linguistic analysis is made in order to see if the results are compatible with and in support of those found in metaphor analysis and how the text realizes the metaphor and how the text is structured by means of the conceptual metaphor.

Key words: conceptual metaphor; discourse; realization; analysis

19

《国王的人马》的多层次概念合成

摘　要：本章从认知功能视角对美国叙事小说《国王的人马》进行分析。初步的研读发现 twitch 这个词被应用于几乎所有及物性的过程，这说明 twitch 作为一种活动或一种力量存在于小说人物生活的所有方面。其出现率与 10 个 BNC 近 40 万字的小说文档相比较，高出 83.8 倍，这就使这个词在语篇中异常突出。仔细研读之后，不难发现作者是利用 twitch 对现实生活进行概念化并加以识解，而全书体现了两个通常互不关联的空间的集合，或者说两个互不关联的领域的投射。一方面是多层整合集合了书中人物共同的爱情、家庭以及以悲剧性的死亡或彻底失败而告终的事业；另一方面则拟人化和神化 twitch，使之成为超自然的主宰一切的力量。空间网络中的混合空间从上述两个空间接受输入投射，并产出新生空间，从而提供本书的主题意义：生命不可解，诚如 twitch 不可控，或简言之，生命乃 twitch。这说明含 twitch 的型式对于构成语篇整体意义的重要性，而前景化为小说文体提供了基础。

关键词：认知视角；投射；概念整合；twitch；生活

Multiple Blending in *All the King's Men*

Abstract: This chapter presents an analysis of the narrative novel *All the King's Men* from a cognitive-functional approach. A preliminary study shows that the word *twitch* is found in nearly all the processes of transitivity in the text, which suggests that a twitch seen as an action or as a kind of force pervades all the spheres of the lives of the characters in the novel. The frequency of occurrences of the word is found to be 83.8 times higher in this book than in the ten Novel files taken from BNC Indexier, totaling 398,565 words. This gives it obvious prominence. A close reading of the book reveals the fact that the writer conceptualizes and construes life experiences in terms of a twitch and the whole book is found to embody a conceptual integration of the two normally unrelated spaces or a mapping across the two domains; the twitch — the source domain and life — the target domain. It is multiple blending that, on the one hand, integrates what is shared in the lives of the characters with respect to love, family and career that end up in tragic deaths or total failures, and, on the other, effects the personification and deification of the twitch that gives it all the power to dominate as a supernatural force. The blended space in the space network receives input projection from the two spaces and develops the emergent space that gives the thematic meaning of the book: life is as inexplicable as a twitch is uncontrollable, or simply Life Is a Twitch. This indicates that the prominence of the patterning with the word *twitch* contributes to the total meaning of the narrative discourse, so it is motivated, and the foregrounding creates the stylistic fabric of the novel.

Key words: cognitive approach; mapping; conceptual integration; twitch; life

20

毛姆《雨》中概念隐喻与语篇进展的相互作用

摘　要：本章从认知功能的视角出发探讨毛姆的短篇小说《雨》中的隐性

概念隐喻。Rain 这个词在该篇小说中出现频率异乎寻常地高,而且用于较少使用的结构之中,显然是已被加以前景化了。然而,rain 并不是这一作品的主题,主题是主人公传教士 Davidson 以及他和一个名叫 Thompson 的妇女之间的关系。可以设想 rain 被象征性地用作源域,那么目的域是指什么?叙事以主人公自杀结尾。这就要求读者对叙事内容重新加以语境化,从而使语篇连贯。语言分析和认知分析产生了 Desire Is Rain 的隐喻,同时显示语篇体现了隐喻,而隐喻引导了语篇的形成。隐喻之所以是隐性的,是为了能让作品取得最大的文体效果。

关键词: Rain;概念隐喻;语篇;语言分析;认知分析

The Interplay Between Implicit Conceptual Metaphor and Discourse Flow in Somerset Maugham's *Rain*

Abstract: This chapter looks into the implicit conceptual metaphor in the short story *Rain* by Somerset Maugham from a cognitive-functional perspective. The word "rain", with its unusual frequency of occurrence and used in a less common clause structure in the discourse, is obviously foregrounded. But rain is not what the story is about; it is about the protagonist, a missionary, Davidson by name and his relationship with a woman named Thompson. Rain is used symbolically as the source domain, but where is the target domain? The recurrence of "the rain", which forms a metaphoric chain, moves the narrative through its entire structure, beginning with Orientation, through 11 phases in Complication Actions until it reaches Resolution, which takes the form of Davidson's suicide. The ending comes as a surprise to the reader and forces him to look back and re-contextualize the story on the basis of a series of counter-expectancies and linguistic expressions so that he finds the relationship between Davidson and Thompson was not one between a preacher and a sinner, but one between a man and a woman. Linguistic analysis and cognitive analysis bring to light the fact that what made Davidson behave the way he did was not only his religious fanaticism but, more decisively, also his inner urge or desire, which turns out to be the target domain. The fascinating role metaphor and metonymy play in the unfolding of discourse makes it possible to establish the cross-domain mapping of knowledge about rain onto knowledge about desire, so the dominant conceptual metaphor, Desire Is Rain, finally takes shape. This is how the discourse realizes the conceptual metaphor. As the metaphor is implicit, it takes a lot of inferencing to see how the discourse realizes it as it unfolds, and how the metaphor shapes the meaning of the discourse as it gradually emerges. The target domain is implied in order to make the story stylistically unique and heighten the cognitive impact of the short story.

Key words: *Rain*; conceptual metaphor; discourse; linguistic analysis; conceptual analysis

后　记

经过努力，散落在四处的文稿终于结集成册。欣慰之余，回顾整个过程，我万分感激我的几位年轻同事。她们工作繁忙，但倾力相助。她们不辞辛劳，将下载和扫描的数百页原始文稿逐一进行认真仔细的校对、互校、订正，从无到有，从粗到细，从细到精，仅准备工作便历时半年有余，最终形成清稿，为编写论文集打下了良好的基础；随后，她们又对文稿的行文、体例、图表、参考书目等反反复复作了六次校对。没有她们的鼎力支持，这本论文集不可能问世。她们是绍兴文理学院的裘燕萍、袁秀风、钟莉莉和杨坚定教授以及嘉兴学院的张菊芬教授。在此谨向她们致以最诚挚的谢意。必须说明的是，我校对了全稿，特别是完成最后第4、5、6、7四稿的定稿，因而，书稿中如果出现失当和错误，当由我个人负责。

笔者

2017年10月